Java 2
Network Protocols
Black Book

Al Williams

President and CEO
Roland Elgey

Publisher
Steve Sayre

Associate Publisher
Katherine Hartlove

Acquisitions Editor
Jawahara Saidullah

Product Marketing Manager
Tracy Rooney

Project Editor
Kelly Messer

Technical Reviewer
Andrew Indovina

Production Coordinator
Peggy Cantrell

Cover Designer
Laura Wellander

Layout Designer
April E. Nielsen

CD-ROM Developer
Chris Nusbaum

Java 2 Network Protocols Black Book

Copyright © 2001 The Coriolis Group, LLC. All rights reserved.

This book may not be duplicated in any way without the express written consent of the publisher, except in the form of brief excerpts or quotations for the purposes of review. The information contained herein is for the personal use of the reader and may not be incorporated in any commercial programs, other books, databases, or any kind of software without written consent of the publisher. Making copies of this book or any portion for any purpose other than your own is a violation of United States copyright laws.

Limits of Liability and Disclaimer of Warranty

The author and publisher of this book have used their best efforts in preparing the book and the programs contained in it. These efforts include the development, research, and testing of the theories and programs to determine their effectiveness. The author and publisher make no warranty of any kind, expressed or implied, with regard to these programs or the documentation contained in this book.

The author and publisher shall not be liable in the event of incidental or consequential damages in connection with, or arising out of, the furnishing, performance, or use of the programs, associated instructions, and/or claims of productivity gains.

Trademarks

Trademarked names appear throughout this book. Rather than list the names and entities that own the trademarks or insert a trademark symbol with each mention of the trademarked name, the publisher states that it is using the names for editorial purposes only and to the benefit of the trademark owner, with no intention of infringing upon that trademark.

The Coriolis Group, LLC
14455 N. Hayden Road
Suite 220
Scottsdale, Arizona 85260

(480) 483-0192
FAX (480) 483-0193
www.coriolis.com

Library of Congress Cataloging-in-Publication Data
Williams, Al, 1963-
    Java 2 network protocols black book / by Al Williams.
       p. cm.
    Includes index.
    ISBN 1-58880-147-0
    1. Internet. 2. Computer network protocols. 3. Java (Computer
program language) I. Title.
TK5105.875.I57 W553 2001
005.2'762--dc21
                2001042415

TK5105.875
I57W553
2001

Printed in the United States of America
10 9 8 7 6 5 4 3 2 1

CORIOLIS

The Coriolis Group, LLC • 14455 North Hayden Road, Suite 220 • Scottsdale, Arizona 85260

A Note from Coriolis

Coriolis Technology Press was founded to create a very elite group of books: the ones you keep closest to your machine. In the real world, you have to choose the books you rely on every day *very* carefully, and we understand that.

To win a place for our books on that coveted shelf beside your PC, we guarantee several important qualities in every book we publish. These qualities are:

- *Technical accuracy*—It's no good if it doesn't work. Every Coriolis Technology Press book is reviewed by technical experts in the topic field, and is sent through several editing and proofreading passes in order to create the piece of work you now hold in your hands.

- *Innovative editorial design*—We've put years of research and refinement into the ways we present information in our books. Our books' editorial approach is uniquely designed to reflect the way people learn new technologies and search for solutions to technology problems.

- *Practical focus*—We put only pertinent information into our books and avoid any fluff. Every fact included between these two covers must serve the mission of the book as a whole.

- *Accessibility*—The information in a book is worthless unless you can find it quickly when you need it. We put a lot of effort into our indexes, and heavily cross-reference our chapters, to make it easy for you to move right to the information you need.

Here at The Coriolis Group we have been publishing and packaging books, technical journals, and training materials since 1989. We have put a lot of thought into our books; please write to us at **ctp@coriolis.com** and let us know what you think. We hope that you're happy with the book in your hands, and that in the future, when you reach for software development and networking information, you'll turn to one of our books first.

Coriolis Technology Press
The Coriolis Group
14455 N. Hayden Road, Suite 220
Scottsdale, Arizona
85260

Email: ctp@coriolis.com
Phone: (480) 483-0192
Toll free: (800) 410-0192

Look for these related books from The Coriolis Group:

Java 2 Black Book
By Steven Holzner

Java 2 Exam Cram, 2nd Edition
By Bill Brogden

Java 2 Exam Prep, 2nd Edition
By Bill Brogden

Also published by Coriolis Technology Press:

Open Source Development with CVS, 2nd Edition
By Karl Fogel and Moshe Bar

Designing Visual Basic.NET Applications
By David Vitter

HTML Black Book
By Steven Holzner

Perl Black Book, 2nd Edition
By Steven Holzner

PHP Black Book
By Peter Moulding

XML Black Book, 2nd Edition
By Natanya Pitts

Windows 2000 TCP/IP Black Book
By Ian McLean

For Amber Rowen, who loves books more than I do.
And, always for Pat.
—Al Williams

❧

About the Author

Al Williams is a long-time programmer who started out on a Univac 1106. Since then, he has been a Unix coder, an MS-DOS programmer, a Windows developer, and today finds himself writing mostly in Java. Al is the Java and development columnist for *Web Techniques* magazine and has written columns for several other magazines, including *Dr. Dobb's Sourcebook* and *Visual Developer*. When Al isn't writing or consulting, he teaches classes on computer programming around the United States. In his sparse spare time, he enjoys amateur radio, a hobby he's pursued for the last 24 years. He lives near Houston, Texas, with his wife and a variable number of children, dogs, and cats.

Acknowledgments

An old African proverb says, "It takes a village to raise a child." I'm not sure if I agree with that or not, but I do know that it takes a whopping number of people to produce a book. Like the tip of an iceberg, you only see the author. However, there are editors, production staff, compositors, indexers, and technical editors that all contribute to the final product. This book would not be in your hands without them, and they have my gratitude for a job well done. There are too many to list everyone, but thanks to Kelly, Hilary, Andrew, Cheryl, Peggy, Chris, Kevin, and Jawahara.

In addition to the Coriolis staff, Mana Tominaga (a colleague from *Web Techniques* magazine) was invaluable for her assistance with the CD-ROM contents. Speaking of *Web Techniques*, some of the programs in this book originally appeared in my "Java@Work" columns (at least, in some form), and my thanks to Amit Asaravala, our Editor in Chief, for his support.

Finally, I couldn't write anything without the understanding and help that I get from my family. This is especially true for this book because we had some trying times during its production. However, I can honestly say that Madison, the dachshund, and Sassy, the pomeranian, didn't help much. And Lacey, my son's cat, was of no help at all.

—*Al Williams*

Contents at a Glance

Table of Contents

Chapter 11
Protocol Handlers 339

Chapter 14
XML 439

Introduction

My first exposure to a large-scale network like the Internet was probably DIA-LOG. This was a service (founded by Roger Summit and eventually bought by Lockheed) that allowed you to connect to different databases for a fee. Back in the early 80s, access fees depended on the database, but ran about $100 an hour. Later, the company I worked for needed to receive Telex messages. After looking at how expensive it was to set up for Telex, we discovered that we could sign up for EasyLink through CompuServe (or their rival The Source) for somewhere around $30 a month (that didn't count the per minute connect charges, but it was still cheaper than Telex).

Of course, I had to experiment with CompuServe. Not only did I have to pay by the minute, but it was also a long distance call on top of that! No unlimited surfing in those days. Of course, there wasn't that much content. Remember, this wasn't the Internet—just the CompuServe network. Internet access through CompuServe was still years away.

CompuServe offered "forums" where you could post messages about a variety of topics. They also hooked into other services of the day like EasyLink and Saabre (for making airline reservations). I think they may have offered realtime chat, as well, but with a total cost of two or three dollars a minute, I didn't check it out. CompuServe also let you download files. Of course, with a 1200-baud modem, you probably didn't want to download much. It was cheaper to dial into a local bulletin board system to download what you wanted.

How different things are today. The bulletin board computers are all but gone (or just converted to Web servers). There are more people on the Net today than ever before, and many of them have broadband access that exceeds a megabit per second. You can find a bewildering array of products, information, and services on the Web. From humble beginnings, the network has changed the very world in which we live.

The true test of a mature technology is when it completely disappears. If you are technology-minded, this might not be apparent at first, because you probably have a good idea about how many things around you work. Try an experiment. Ask a few nontechnical people to explain how electricity gets to their house, or how a long distance phone calls gets connected. Chances are you won't get very good answers.

Computers are rapidly disappearing as well. Twenty years ago, the average computer user could tell you how many cycles each instruction required and the details of every chip used in their computer. Today, most users are lucky to know what type of CPU it has and what clock speed the manufacturer claims for it.

Networking has disappeared, in a large part due to the overwhelming growth of the Internet. If you've only been involved in the Internet lately, it is hard to realize just how fast the growth has accelerated. Consider this: You could argue that the Internet started when a machine from UCLA and a machine from SRI connected at 50Kbps in October 1969. True, the network didn't look much like the Internet we know today—TCP/IP was eight or nine years in the future. Still, the Internet can directly trace back to the old ARPANet. By 1982, there were 200 hosts on the network. It would be 1984, before that number reached 1,000. That's 1,000 computers in 15 years. Three years later, in 1987, the number reached 10,000. By 1992, just five more years—there were more than one million computers on the Internet. The last I heard, there were more than 16 million computers on the Internet, and in 2000, someone registered the ten millionth domain name.

Not long ago, networking was a mysterious black art that only a few programmers had to worry about. Today, it is a rare program that doesn't have some network interaction. Even if your program has no functions on the network, you still may want to allow network installs or automatic upgrades.

Luckily, the Java language has powerful network capabilities—if you know how to use them. Some network operations in Java are so simple that they disappear—much like making a long distance phone call is invisible. However, other networking chores require careful use to avoid compatibility problems or security issues.

Although it is true that most of us only have a fuzzy notion of how our electricity, water, and phone services work, it is also true that somewhere there are professionals that do know the details. Without them, these basic services would not function (and then you notice them). The Internet is the same way. Behind the scenes, a loose-knit group of standards organizations and individuals (like the late Jon Postel) more or less control the Internet's technology. Just the politics and history of how the Internet got to where it is today is interesting enough. But to the practitioner, it is even more interesting that this giant network works well enough to connect people around the world every day.

What's in This Book?

This book covers network programming at a variety of levels using Java. Not only does it cover high-level techniques like protocol handlers, but it also shows you how to develop programs that use low-level socket objects to handle a variety of protocols including the following:

- Telnet
- FTP and TFTP
- SMTP
- POP3
- NNTP
- HTTP
- HTTPS

In addition, you'll find information about simpler protocols and multicasting. However, network communications is only part of the story. Formatting and interpreting data is just as important. You'll find entire chapters covering how to interpret HTML and XML data. You'll also find information about formatting mail messages and other data types throughout the book.

Is This Book for Me?

If you've programmed in Java, it's a good bet you've at least tried some network programming. However, opening a socket is only part of the story. Not only do you need to establish communications with another computer, but you also have to know what to say (and how to say it) once you do connect.

This book will show you how to use Java to build clients and servers for a variety of common protocols. You will learn how to work with sockets, of course. But once you make that connection—to an FTP server, a Web browser, or an email server—you'll know what to say and how to say it.

Another Internet phenomenon is that programmers don't have to work in a vacuum any more. The Internet makes a wide variety of example programs and free libraries available—many of them in Java. This can be a tremendous timesaver because you can leverage someone else's code to build your programs.

This book is geared to provide fast results. Each chapter covers a protocol or family of protocols. The In Depth section provides a detailed look into the protocol, operation, and the implementation details. The Immediate Solutions section provides capsule solutions to specific questions you might have as you develop your own code. In addition, both sections will point out freely-available software you can find on the Internet that can help with the job.

If you want to leverage your knowledge of Java to write custom network software, or you just want to know more about how network protocols work, then this book is for you. Armed with the information in this book, you'll be able to write Java programs that transfer files, send email, and handle Web pages with ease.

What Should I Already Know?

You should be relatively familiar with simple Java programming. If you haven't worked with sockets (or, you haven't worked with all the different types of sockets), you'll find Chapter 2 useful. In addition, that chapter will cover other Java techniques you might not be familiar with, that are often required for network programming.

How much Java do you need to know? You'd be surprised at how little Java you really need to write many types of network programs. Obviously, you need to understand the class system and the difference between static and nonstatic members. You should have a good handle on the basic language structure (**if**, **for**, and **similar statements**, for example).

Java treats network sockets as just another source of input and output, so understanding the **java.io** library is important. However, if you haven't used this library, you'll find what you need to know in Chapter 2.

Text and Graphics

As much as possible, I've avoided using graphical user interfaces in this book. There are a few places—for example, displaying HTML—where a windowed interface makes sense, and in those places you'll see code that uses the Swing library.

However, a large number of network programs don't really need a graphical user interface. A console program is simpler to understand and is all that is necessary. Besides, the emphasis is to develop objects that work with the various protocols. If you have a reusable object, you can apply it to any program—graphical, or otherwise.

Some of the examples that use the reusable classes are Java Server Pages (JSPs). If you want to read news on the Web, or operate a finger gateway, JSPs combined with network-aware classes can do the job.

Why Java?

For years, the traditional language for developing network programs has been C or C++. There are many examples of C language network programs, and most networking textbooks assume C.

In addition, the Unix socket library is the model for many other socket libraries, including Microsoft's WinSock library. With so much example code already around for C, why switch to Java?

There are two answers to that question. First, Java's library is deliberately made to help you write network-aware programs. It succeeds both because it is object-oriented, and because the designers had this goal in mind from the start.

The other reason Java is an interesting network language is because—at least in theory—you can write Java code on one type of computer and run it on another type of computer. Consider applets (the little programs that run inside Web browsers). A Web surfer might be using any computer (a Mac, Unix, Windows, or even something stranger). Other systems (like ActiveX) require you to have a separate program for each type of machine. A Java applet will run unchanged on any machine that can support Java.

Of course, applets didn't become as widely accepted as many people thought they would. But the principle is still valid. Imagine a networked multiprocessor system where computers send programs to other computers to execute. Even if the computers are of disparate types, the same Java programs will execute on them all.

What Do I Need?

To work through the example programs in this book, you'll need some way to compile Java programs. I built the programs in this book with the standard Java SDK version 1.4, although most should also work with version 1.3. Like Java, the programs are operating system neutral.

Of course, you may prefer to use a compiler that isn't command-line oriented. If that's the case, there are several alternatives that may work with your operating system:

- *CodeWarrior*—**www.metrowerks.com/desktop/java/**
- *Forte*—**www.sun.com/forte/ffj/overview.html**
- *FreeBuilder*—**nisoft.orbitel.bg/freebuilder/**
- *Jbuilder*—**www.borland.com/jbuilder/**
- *JCreator*—**www.jcreator.com/**
- *Jipe*—**e-i-s.co.uk/jipe/**
- *RealJ*—**www.freejava.co.uk/**

If you insist on doing everything on the Web, you can compile your code online at **www.chami.com/webide/**, but I haven't tried it!

Of course, to get the most from the programs in this book, you need a network. Two or three computers on a network will do, or an Internet connection is even better. In a few cases, you might want to have your own server so you aren't experimenting with someone else's servers.

In addition, some of the chapters use additional libraries from Sun, or open source libraries and tools. The chapters will tell you how to obtain the tools you need. A few of the chapters include JSP code. To run that code you'll need access to a JSP container. Luckily, there are many free ones available including Tomcat (**http://jakarta.apache.org/**) and the developer's edition of JRun (**www.allaire.com/products/jrun/index.cfm**). In most cases, the JSP portion of the code is optional—you'll still be able to test the classes without using JSPs.

Because many of the programs use the command line, you may find the Windows command prompt limiting (especially under Windows 98 where there is no scrolling buffer in command windows). If you are familiar with Unix or Linux, you might prefer to download the free Cygwin package at **http://sources.redhat.com/cygwin**. This package provides a complete Unix-like environment for Windows. From the user's perspective, you get a bash shell and all the tools you expect from Unix. From the developer's point of view, you get all the Unix system calls in a DLL. For Java programming, that isn't very interesting, but the user's environment alone is worth the free download.

Get Started!

Your next step depends on your exact needs. Some of the later chapters depend somewhat on material from earlier chapters. Therefore, you may want to read the chapters in sequence. However, if you are in a hurry, you can pick and choose which protocols you want to examine and go directly to the appropriate chapters.

If you are planning on skipping around, you should probably at least skim Chapter 1. Also, you might want to glance at Chapter 2 and make sure you understand all the Java techniques discussed in that chapter. If you find something that isn't familiar, you should read that section before tackling the later chapters.

Like all Black Books, this book features detailed chapters including immediate solutions to give you a quick summary of the topics. If you're in a big hurry, you might consider starting with the immediate solutions and referring to the main part of the chapter only as necessary.

Each chapter contains code listings to illustrate topics. The complete listings are included on the accompanying CD-ROM for your convenience.

I welcome your feedback on this book. You can email The Coriolis Group at **ctp@coriolis.com**. Regardless of the path you choose, you won't learn much reading the Introduction! Pick a topic and get started.

Chapter 1

Internet Basics

In Depth

I'm old enough to remember when making an international telephone call was a big deal. You had to get an operator to help you. Not only that, the operator would probably take your number and call you back once the call was set up.

Once the operator connected you, you'd have a poor-quality line full of noise and echoes. The real agony, however, came with the bill. Today, international calls are simple to make. The global phone network is one of those modern marvels that people don't even notice. However, no matter how easy it is to make a call, there is still one fundamental problem: language. Calling China won't help if you don't share a language with the person on the other end. Even on a domestic call, you probably can't directly talk to a fax machine or modem unless you are even geekier than I am.

The Internet is like a phone network of its own. The underlying network infrastructure allows any two computers to make a connection. However, connecting an IBM mainframe to a PalmPilot requires more than just a connection. The two computers have to agree on the topic of conversation and the format of the data.

Computers agree to communicate through a variety of protocols. Some of these are very familiar to you. For example, HTTP (Hypertext Transport Protocol) is the protocol that allows Web browsers to fetch Web pages. At a deeper level, low-level protocols govern the flow of raw data over the vast Internet.

What about Java?

Java is especially important to Internet protocols. Why? Because—at least in theory—the same program can run on different types of computers. If you are connecting a PC to a Unix workstation, it makes things simpler if they both are running the exact same program.

Java's "write once, run anywhere" philosophy is ideal for Internet programming. In addition, the standard Java libraries have many very useful classes that take the pain out of traditional network programming.

With the Java libraries, making a connection with a server is as simple as asking for a new **Socket** object. You'll need to know the server's address (like a phone number) and a port number (an extension). Building a server to listen for requests is just as easy.

As important as Java is to the Internet process, protocols are not Java-specific. So for the rest of this chapter, don't worry about Java. You'll read more about Java's relationship with networking in Chapter 2.

Protocol Soup

An incredible number of protocols are in common use on the Internet. Many of them are for special purposes, and you'll probably never use them. Of the common protocols, many build on each other, which makes life easier.

For example, consider Telnet. You've probably used a Telnet program to log in to a remote computer. You can identify three things as Telnet when you do this. First, you are using a Telnet client on your computer. The computer you log in to has to have a Telnet server (or a daemon in Unix parlance). Finally, the client and server communicate with the Telnet protocol.

So, the Telnet client uses the Telnet protocol to communicate to the Telnet server. That doesn't seem very surprising. However, email clients use essentially the same Telnet connection to talk to Simple Mail Transfer Protocol (SMTP) servers. In fact, you can use a Telnet program to manually talk to an SMTP server. Mail messages have a distinct way of representing data, and Web servers use the same format. What's more, Web servers also use a Telnet-like connection.

So while it may seem daunting to learn so many protocols, the truth is that many of the higher-level protocols build on the lower-level protocols, which makes the learning curve less steep than it appears. You can often recycle some of what you know about simpler protocols when developing code for more sophisticated ones.

Another thing that can make your life simpler is the wide array of source code available on the Web to allow Java programs to work with different protocols. Many open source packages and examples for any protocol you can imagine exist on the Web. Java has some built-in support for adding custom protocol handlers. Also, Java's object-oriented approach makes it a natural for creating reusable building blocks to handle Internet protocols.

Of particular interest is the **NetComponents** package from the Jakarta Project (**http://jakarta.apache.org**). The Jakarta Project is the Java arm of the group that produces the popular Apache Web server. **NetComponents** (originally written by David Savarese) contains classes for the common protocols you'll encounter on the Web.

Jakarta is a good place to find many useful Java classes, not all of which are Internet related. Another interesting project is the Giant Java Tree (**www.gjt.org**). In addition, you'll find plenty of code elsewhere online and in this book.

Internet Addressing

If you think of the Internet as a phone network, you need to know how to call different computers. There are actually several ways you can specify the exact program you want to use. Suppose you call your bank on the phone. You need to know the bank's main number, of course. When you call, you'll probably get an automated system, and you'll have to punch in the extension of the department you want, for example, the loan department. Of course, the loan department's phones probably roll over so that they can handle many callers at one time.

The same situation exists with computers on the Internet. Each computer on the network has an IP (Internet Protocol) address that looks like 4 decimal numbers between 0 and 255, separated by periods (for example, 192.16.32.182). Each number is known as an *octet* because it represents 8 bits. This IP address corresponds to the bank's main number.

Of course, one computer might provide many services, including email, Web documents, file transfers, and other services. You need what amounts to an extension. This is known as a port number. Port numbers 1023 and below are reserved for well-known services. For example, Web servers usually use port 80. That way, any interested Web browser can connect to the server and request port 80 to fetch Web pages. You'll find a list of common port numbers later in the "Immediate Solutions" section.

Just as the loan department has multiple lines on the same extension, a server can respond to multiple requests on the same port. That way, many Web browsers can access the server at once. Of course, just as a small company might have a single phone line, a server can elect to handle only one request at a time. The choice is up to the author of the server.

How do computers get IP addresses? That depends. At some level, a central authority—the Internet Corporation for Assigned Names and Numbers or ICANN—assigns organizations blocks of IP addresses. For most people, however, their computer's IP address is assigned by their Internet provider or a network administrator. For client machines, it is common to use Dynamic Host Configuration Protocol (DHCP) to automatically assign IP addresses from a pool of available addresses. This isn't a good idea for a server, however, because clients may depend on the server being at the same address all the time.

The numbers of an IP address actually have some meaning and aren't just arbitrary. The numbers are categorized into three major categories. Each category uses a different number of bits to specify the network number. Everyone who has the same network number is on the same network. Requests to other networks must be routed off the network.

1. Internet Basics

Very few people will ever use a class A address because there are only 126 of them. In a class A address, the first octet specifies the network number—that is, everyone with the same first octet is on the same local network. That leaves 3 octets for individual addresses, which means each class A network can accommodate over 16 million computers. Class B addresses use two octets for their network number. This allows each network to have over 64,000 distinct addresses. Finally, class C addresses use 3 octets for the network number, which leaves only 254 IP addresses per network (some addresses are reserved for broadcast purposes).

A newer scheme, Classless Interdomain Routing or CIDR, uses a varying number of bits to specify the network number. You'll hear talk of "/24 addressing," for example, which means use the first three octets for the network address (same as class C).

ICANN reserves several blocks of addresses for local testing. These are good IP addresses to use for your own private debugging network, for example. The class A addresses that begin with 10, the class B addresses from 172.16 to 172.31, and the class C addresses that begin with 192.168 are all reserved for private networks. These computers should not directly connect to the Internet, and if they do, routers and other Internet hardware will ignore them.

TIP: *Another special block of addresses begins with 127. These addresses are used to refer to your local machine (usually 127.0.0.1). You can always use this address to connect to your local machine regardless of its actual IP address. Many computers will recognize the special name localhost and use this address for that hostname.*

DNS: The Internet Phonebook

It is hard to remember long phone numbers, and it is at least as hard to memorize IP addresses like 192.48.12.101. To prevent confusion, the Internet supports a hierarchical system of servers known as Domain Name Servers (DNS).

When you ask for a server, such as **www.coriolis.com**, your computer queries a local database, usually called a *hosts file* or *hosts database*. Some computers don't even have this database, and it is typically quite small anyway. If the name appears in the database, your computer uses the associated IP address to find the server. Most likely, your computer will then check with a DNS server provided by your company or your ISP (Internet service provider). If the DNS server can't find the name, it asks its parent DNS server. This continues until one of the servers knows the IP address, or the DNS server is one of a handful of root servers (that is, a server that has no parent). Eventually, your DNS server will return the IP address—or an error—to your computer.

DNS is like a phonebook—it usually only provides the main number, not the extension (port number) that you need. In addition, only computers that appear in the DNS system have usable names. For example, if you dial into an Internet provider, such as AOL or MSN, your IP address is randomly picked from a pool (DHCP). Although your computer may have a name, DNS won't know about it, and therefore others can't access your computer by name; however, they can access your computer if they know your current IP address.

Addresses like 127.0.0.1 (the loopback address) won't show up in the DNS system. However, many local IP databases will have an entry for this special address (typically localhost). Your local machine may even act as your primary DNS server. Windows 2000, for example, provides a DNS service that caches entries you look up. This speeds up multiple connections to the same host. Because the local DNS server queries your normal DNS server for any hosts it doesn't recognize, this is largely transparent to the user and programmer.

URLs, URIs, URNs

Anyone who has browsed the Web has used a Uniform Resource Locator (URL). However, there might be a few fine points that aren't apparent from everyday use.

Here is a typical URL with a few parts you might not be familiar with:

http://aaw:startrek@www.coriolis.com/jbb/go.jsp?v1=100&v2=doctor

Consider each portion of the URL:

- **http://**—This is the protocol identifier. In this case, the protocol is HTTP, which is typical for a Web page. A secure Web page will use **https://**, while an FTP address would use **ftp://**.

- **aaw**—This is the user ID used to log in to the resource. Of course, many URLs don't require a login, so this is optional.

- **startrek**—If you provide a user ID, you might want to also include a password. Of course, the password isn't encrypted. You can leave the password blank which will cause the browser to either use a password you've told it to remember or prompt you for a password.

- **@**—If you provide a username (or a username and a password), you'll use the @ character to mark the start of the host name. If you don't supply a username, you'll omit the @ character.

- **www.coriolis.com**—The hostname directs the browser to the machine. This address could be an IP address, or—as in this case—a DNS name.

- **/jbb/go.jsp**—Within the IP address is a path to the document you are requesting. Many servers will provide a default document if you don't specify one (or if you only specify a path name).

- **?v1=100&v2=doctor**—This portion of the URL, which is optional, is the query string. This is one way that a client can send data to a server. For example, some Internet forms use the query string to submit their data to the server.

The protocol identifier selects a port that the client will use to connect to the server. The hostname identifies the server. The client sends the other information to the server and doesn't really have much interest in its contents.

Here's another URL:

http://www.al-williams.com/glossary.htm#solder

The *octothorpe* (the # character) stops the document name and begins the hash string. For a Web page, this indicates an anchor that the browser locates after loading the document.

URLs are easier to deal with than raw addresses and data. However, the biggest advantage that URLs provide is a protocol-independent way for clients to deal with Internet resources. For example, if you enter **telnet://www.coriolis.com** into your Web browser, the browser will realize it doesn't know how to communicate using Telnet; therefore, it starts an external Telnet program to do the job.

You'll occasionally hear the acronyms URN (Universal Resource Name) and URI (Universal Resource Identifier). You can usually think of these as interchangeable with URL, although a URL is really a special type of URI. A URI is simply any string that uniquely represents any resource (not necessarily an Internet resource). For example, this book has an ISBN (International Standard Book Number) which could be considered a URI for this book. Obviously, an ISBN is not a URL, but it is a URI.

URNs are also specialized URIs (defined, in part, in RFC 2141). URNs have the property of being persistent and location-independent. For example, suppose your Web site moves to different servers, but you want a single URL that will always bring users to your site. You can create a URN (in this case a Persistent URL or PURL) at **http://purl.oclc.org/** to provide a persistent URN that always points to your current URL.

Layers

Modern networks use the concept of layers, sometimes known as a *protocol stack*. You can imagine that each layer rests on top of all the lower-level layers, which is why it is sometimes called a stack. The classic Open Systems Interconnection (OSI) model has seven layers in its stack. However, for the Internet, you can logically consider only four layers: the application layer, the Transmission Control Protocol (TCP) layer, the IP layer, and the physical interface layer.

At the bottom of the stack is the physical interface layer. This is the software that drives your network interface card, modem, or whatever you use to connect to the network. On top of the physical layer is the IP layer. The IP layer handles the raw addressing and the formation of data packets, also known as *datagrams*.

The down side to datagrams is that there is no assurance that a datagram will ever arrive at its destination. You also may not receive packets in the order they were sent. A network error or problem with the destination computer will go undetected. On the plus side, datagrams are quite efficient.

To solve the inherent problems with datagrams, the next layer of the stack is the TCP layer. TCP actually manages the uncertainty associated with IP datagrams. When you send data via TCP, the TCP layer expects to receive acknowledgments from the destination computer. In the absence of an acknowledgment, the TCP layer will eventually retransmit the datagram.

The TCP layer not only ensures each packet arrives, but it also assembles them in the correct order so that the receiver finds the packets in the same order they were sent. As you might expect, for raw performance, TCP is not as efficient as IP. However, when you want an accurate logical stream of data between computers, TCP is the way to go. Some programs that require high performance, and have their own method for detecting missing and out-of-order packets, might well use this type of connection.

The top layer of the stack is the application layer. These are the protocols that will be the focus of this book. HTTP, FTP, and SMTP are all examples of application protocols.

If you read many traditional networking books, they'll point out that each layer of the stack only communicates with the layer above it and the layer below it. The application layer, for example, doesn't communicate to the physical network hardware. If you are writing the protocol stack for a computer, this is an important point. However, for normal programming tasks, the important point is this: Logically, each layer communicates with the corresponding layer on the other computer. Don't take that the wrong way. That doesn't mean that there is a direct connection between layers—far from it. But you can pretend that, for example, the TCP layer is just a direct connection to the TCP layer on the other machine, known as the *peer*. However, this isn't true. Opening a TCP connection might actually entail dialing a modem, generating X.25 packets, and beaming data to a TCP/IP satellite in Earth's orbit. But you don't care—the illusion is that the TCP socket is connected to the peer.

The Underlying Protocol

What's in a datagram? Each datagram has a short header and a payload of data. There is a maximum size for each datagram, although this is network-dependent. The current Internet uses IPv4 (version four), but the rapid growth in demand for IP addresses means that eventually everything will switch to IPv6 which has a different format and allows for longer addresses (JDK 1.4 adds support for IPv6).

The first part of the datagram contains a version number that—for today—is always four. Presumably, future network hardware will differentiate between version 6 and version 4 using this number.

The next portion of a datagram specifies the size of the header (maximum 60 bytes). There is also a field that contains the length of the entire datagram. Because a datagram may arrive more than once (due to network routing), each datagram also has an ID number to help identify duplicates.

Other fields in the datagram select the protocol type (a number assigned by ICANN), show the IP address of the source and destination, and also provide a checksum for the header. A variety of bits are used to select options, some of which aren't used very often. One other field in the header that you'll occasionally hear about is the Time to Live (TTL) field. The packet's TTL determines how many times the packet can be retransmitted before the system discards it. This field helps prevent infinite loops as your datagram travels between computers, routers, gateways, repeaters, and other network hardware. Each hop subtracts one from the TTL field until it reaches zero.

TCP is not efficient, but it is reliable. However, there are some applications where you want the best possible speed. For example, you might be streaming video, and missing some datagrams is less important than getting them at a high rate of speed. Because each layer only talks to the layers above and below, TCP allows you to create User Datagram Protocol (UDP) sockets. These sockets correspond very closely to raw IP sockets. They are not reliable, but they are efficient.

In addition to TCP and UDP, there are other protocols that can build on top of IP. For example, when you use the ping program to see if a host is reachable on the network, you are using ICMP (Internet Control Message Protocol). However, in versions prior to the JDK version 1.4, Java doesn't allow you to directly access IP, nor does it support sockets other than TCP and UDP sockets. If you wanted to write, for example, a ping program in Java, you'd need to resort to code in another language, such as C, and add it to your Java program (or you could use JDK 1.4).

Network Hardware

Logically, when you connect your Web browser to a remote server, you have a direct connection between your PC and the server. In real life, however, the route may be much more complex than you'd suspect.

Your computer probably connects to the Internet through some sort of gateway computer and perhaps a router. Besides that, your Internet provider doubtlessly employs a staggering array of routers, switches, and other esoteric hardware to make a connection to one of the major Internet backbones. The server you wish to connect to is probably behind a similar amount of hardware.

The good news is that you don't have to care. Other than decreasing your data transfer speed, these routers, gateways, and switches, are usually invisible.

The Internet is a two-way street. When you connect to the Internet, you open up a wealth of information. However, you also open up your computer to potential snooping or outright attack. This is especially true if you have a fixed IP address. In truth, even if you have a dynamically assigned IP address, you are still subject to attack, but people will have a harder time if they are looking for you specifically.

Firewalls

To protect themselves, many companies and even some individual users install a firewall between their computers and the public Internet. This firewall may be a dedicated piece of hardware, or it may be software running on one computer.

As a computer on your local network attempts to interact with the network, the firewall will intercept the datagrams. It may pass or kill these datagrams based on a set of rules set up by the person operating the firewall. These rules can filter on just about anything in the datagram header. For example, you might only allow FTP requests from certain IP addresses. Some protocols (Telnet, for example) might be shut off completely. Some firewalls also perform Network Address Translation (NAT) to place a private network on the public Internet. That way, a site with a single class C address might connect dozens of computers to the Internet.

Proxy Servers

Firewalls work at the low levels of the network stack, so they won't bother your Java programs except when you are behind one that is blocking you! However, there is a similar device—a proxy server—that operates at the application layer. These proxy servers route requests for specific items across the network and therefore have specific knowledge of the protocol in use.

For example, suppose you are responsible for a company network, and the company wants to monitor and control access to Web sites. You might block port 80 (using a firewall) and then install a proxy server on the same computer that operates the firewall. The proxy server might use—for example—port 8888. Now everyone in the office will have to set their proxy server to port 8888. The proxy server will then relay requests from port 8888 to port 80 and back.

This would allow you to log all Web page accesses—something that many people feel is an invasion of privacy. You could also block access to addresses you wanted to blacklist. Many proxy servers have some additional function that depends on its knowledge of the underlying protocol. For example, a Web proxy server might cache content (for faster reloads), prefetch links (again, to attempt to speed up Web browsing), or block advertisements.

Although HTTP proxy servers are most common, you can have a proxy server for any defined protocol, such as FTP or SMTP. Even though some proxy servers understand multiple protocols, none handle arbitrary ones. This is a big disadvantage to programmers. If you want your program to work behind a proxy server, you had better make it use a protocol the proxy understands.

There is a standard called SOCKS that allows you to tunnel through a proxy server, but not all proxies adhere to this standard. If you are using a common proxy protocol, such as HTTP or FTP, or you have a SOCKS proxy, you can set Java to automatically handle the proxy for you. This makes proxy servers painless to use, if you know how to set Java's properties correctly (see the "Immediate Solutions" section).

Learning about Protocols

The Internet is very democratic. All the standard protocols are really just suggestions that everyone uses to communicate. The main body that maintains these standards is the Internet Engineering Task Force (IETF). When someone wants to define a new standard for the Internet, he or she can submit an Internet draft to the IETF. Many of the documents define standards, but some others are informational documents.

Eventually, the IETF may approve a draft and make it an RFC (Request For Comments). All IETF-approved standards are RFCs. However, some RFCs are not actual standards. Once published, RFCs rarely change. Most changes require a new RFC. Some protocols—such as the standard for formatting email—have changed many times and have many different RFCs associated with them.

Very few RFCs become STD (standard) documents. Many of the protocols you use every day are not at the STD level and may never become STD documents because of political reasons. Standards have requirement levels. A few protocols, such as IP, are required. All Internet hosts must implement IP. Some standards are recommended but not required. Even such seemingly basic protocols as TCP are only recommended. Other RFCs are elective, limited use, or not recommended.

Another similar organization is the WWW Consortium (W3C). This is an organization run by several vendors (not an open body, such as IETF) and it keeps the standards for such Internet *lingua francas* as HTML and XML (Extensible Markup Language). Although anyone can submit an IETF document, only a W3C member can propose new W3C standards.

In addition to standards, you can find a large amount of open source software relating to Web development in Java. Open source software is a great boon to developers. Not only do you get working software, but you also get access to the source code. If you are so inclined, you can even pitch in and help develop the software.

Plenty of Java software is available under some sort of open source arrangement. Here are a few places to start looking:

- *Jakarta*—**jakarta.apache.org**
- *Sourceforge*—**www.sourceforge.net**
- *Java Boutique*—**javaboutique.internet.com**
- *Giant Java Tree*—**www.gjt.org**
- *GNU Java Programs*—**www.gnu.org/software/software.html#Java**

Immediate Solutions

Determining Your True IP Address

Often when you are developing programs you need to know your own IP address. Of course, you can always use the loopback address (usually 127.0.0.1). Your operating system probably supports a program called ipconfig or winipconfig that can tell you the IP addresses of the various network adapters in your computer.

However, sometimes these results are misleading. If you are behind a NAT firewall, for example, your public address might not match the address on your machine. Some Internet connections, such as satellite and some cable systems, also give you an IP address that is hard to figure out.

In cases like these, you can turn to a Web-based service to report your IP address to you. A quick search on any search engine for "IP Reflector" should turn up plenty. The one in the "Tools" section of **www.dslreports.com** seems to work well.

These services are just simple scripts that make the Web server reveal the address you appear to be using. In cases where you are behind a NAT translation, this address may be hard to figure out any other way.

WARNING! If you use a satellite or cable modem that uses a regular phone modem for transmission and a special cable modem for reception, many reflectors will report an incorrect IP address. That's because your system actually has two IP addresses—one for your transmissions and another for reception. The reflector at DSLReports works, but some others will return your transmission address, which isn't generally useful.

Using Dynamic Redirection

If your computer has a static IP address, you can host a Web server directly from your computer. This is handy for testing or just showing off your work to the world at large. However, if you have a dial-up connection, or some type of DSL, wireless, or satellite connection, your IP address changes from time to time—usually every time you connect to the Internet. This makes it hard for people to find you, or even for you to find yourself.

One answer is to use an IP redirection service. There are several free ones on the Web. When you connect to the Internet, you either have to manually update your

IP address, or in some cases, the service has a program that automatically does the job.

This type of service gives you a name in the DNS system that people can locate in the usual way. However, when a Web browser tries to find your site by name, the service redirects it to your last known address. Of course, that assumes that your computer is still connected at that address. Some of the services can figure out that you are not present and redirect the visitor to an alternate Web page (sort of like an answering machine that picks up the phone when you don't).

A few of these services that are popular are at **www.cjb.net**, **www.dns2go.com**, **and www.dyndns.org**. Of course, if you have a Web site that is accessible to the public, you could easily update a small redirect page each time you log in, perhaps with a Java program, to bring users to your updated IP address.

At its simplest, you could have an HTML document such as this:

```
<HTML>
<HEAD>
 <META HTTP-EQUIV=REFRESH CONTENT="http://199.28.1.1;0">
</HEAD>
<BODY>
 <H1>Redirecting...</H1>
</BODY>
</HTML>
```

You'd change the IP address in the **<META>** tag each time you logged in and learned your new IP address. There are many programs available on the Internet to automate this process. Browse the "IP Address Tools" section (under Shareware or Freeware) at **www.webattack.com** to see what is available.

You might find the list of DNS providers at **http://dir.yahoo.com/Business_ and_Economy/Business_to_Business/Communications_and_Networking/ Internet_and_World_Wide_Web/Forwarding/** useful. It covers both free services and those that charge a fee.

Determining the Class of an IP Address

How can you determine the class of an IP address? Just by looking at it. Table 1.1 shows a simple table that can help you determine the type of address you are using. The key is to consider the IP address as a 32-bit binary number instead of 4 separate octets. The first bit or two will tell you which class the address is. In Table 1.1, the most significant bit is bit 31, whereas the least significant bit is bit 0.

Table 1.1   Identifying an IP address's class.

Class	First Bit (Bit 31)	Second Bit (Bit 30)	Network Portion	Host Portion
A	0	Doesn't matter	Bits 30-24	Bits 23-0
B	1	0	Bits 29 through16	Bits 15 through0
C	1	1	Bits 29 through 8	Bits 7 through 0

Selecting a Port Number

There are two ways to use a port number. If you are designing a server, you'll need to select a port that is either commonly used for your server type or is one that you can use to communicate in some way to the clients that wish to connect to you. If you are working on a client, you don't really care what port number you use—instead, you care about the server's port number. Table 1.2 shows some common port assignments. Keep in mind that TCP ports and UDP ports are separate, although many servers listen on both TCP and UDP ports with the same number.

TIP: You can find a complete list of assigned port numbers in RFC 1700.

WARNING! On Unix and similar systems, only the root user can open low-numbered ports. That means that only root can start standard network services or they must run in SetUID mode, which allows the program to assume the identity of its owner—presumably root, in this case.

Table 1.2   Common port numbers.

Server Name	Port Number	Protocol	Description
echo	7	TCP/UDP	Testing service—echoes data back to the sender
daytime	13	TCP/UDP	Retrieves the current time and date (ASCII)
quote	17	TCP/UDP	Returns a quote of the day
FTP (data)	20	TCP	File Transfer Protocol (data channel)
FTP	21	TCP	FTP commands
ssh	22	TCP	Secure Shell (secure replacement for Telnet)
Telnet	23	TCP	Log in to a remote machine
SMTP	25	TCP	Simple Mail Transfer Protocol sends and forwards email

(continued)

Table 1.2   Common port numbers *(continued)*.

Server Name	Port Number	Protocol	Description
time	37	TCP/UDP	Returns the time since January 1, 1900, in integer format
DNS	53	TCP/UDP	Domain Name Server Resolves hostnames to IP addresses
finger	79	TCP	Returns information about a system or user
HTTP	80	TCP	Hypertext Transfer Protocol (Web)
POP3	110	TCP	Post Office Protocol 3—reads email
NNTP	119	TCP	Network News Transfer Protocol (Usenet)
NTP	123	TCP/UDP	Network Time Protocol

Using **Ping** and Other Tools

One of the most useful network tools around is **ping**. This simple command allows you to tell if a network computer is available and reachable. It can also resolve names to IP addresses—and back again—and shows you basic routing information.

The simplest way to use **ping** is to issue the following command line:

```
ping www.coriolis.com
```

This will result in output similar to this:

```
Pinging www.coriolis.com [38.187.128.10] with 32 bytes of data:

Reply from 38.187.128.10: bytes=32 time=828ms TTL=119
Reply from 38.187.128.10: bytes=32 time=813ms TTL=119
Reply from 38.187.128.10: bytes=32 time=703ms TTL=119
Reply from 38.187.128.10: bytes=32 time=781ms TTL=119

Ping statistics for 38.187.128.10:
    Packets: Sent = 4, Received = 4, Lost = 0 (0% loss),
Approximate round trip times in milli-seconds:
    Minimum = 703ms, Maximum =  828ms, Average =  781ms
```

Notice that **ping** resolves the hostname to the correct IP address and displays it.

However, what happens if you ping an IP address, as in:

```
ping 38.187.128.10
```

In this case, **ping** won't resolve the IP address into a hostname. However, if you add the -**a** option, the **ping** command will perform reverse DNS lookup and display the name just like in the first example.

Another trick **ping** can do is show you the route your packets take from your computer to the remote destination. Simply add the -**r** option and the number of hops you want to record (from 1 to 9).

An even more powerful way to trace routes is with the **traceroute** (or **tracert** if you are a Windows user) command. The output of the **traceroute** command shows you each portion of the network that your packet travels, the time required to reach that host (the program sends three test packets and therefore displays three times), and the resolved hostname of each computer in the path. Here is a typical **traceroute** session:

```
Tracing route to www.coriolis.com [38.187.128.10]
over a maximum of 30 hops:

 1    282 ms    125 ms    125 ms   twhou-5800-1.ev1.net [216.88.77.2]
 2    109 ms    110 ms    109 ms   216.88.77.1
 3    110 ms    109 ms    125 ms   twhou-7200-1.ev1.net [207.218.245.1]
 4    110 ms    110 ms    125 ms   216.90.223.81
 5    141 ms    141 ms    141 ms   64.242.22.97
 6    234 ms    156 ms    235 ms   204.6.142.50
 7    203 ms    250 ms    219 ms   sw.transit.tier1.us.psi.net [154.13.2.98]
 8    219 ms    500 ms    234 ms   rc10.sw.us.psi.net [38.1.24.202]
 9    219 ms    219 ms    265 ms   salt-lake.psi.net [38.1.44.249]
10    250 ms    282 ms    453 ms   38.2.190.24
11    313 ms    390 ms    453 ms   www.coriolis.com [38.187.128.10]
```

Sometimes a computer along the way won't respond to traces—then the time will appear as an asterisk. Also, if you are behind certain firewalls or proxies, you may not be able to get a trace. The **traceroute** program works by sending three datagrams for each hop. The datagram's TTL is set so that the relay point for that hop will kill the datagram. Most network computers will send a message back to the datagram's originator if the TTL expires. Therefore, **traceroute** gets messages from each computer along the path and can identify them.

These tools can be invaluable when you are trying to figure out why something isn't working. The **traceroute** command in particular can show you firewalls, routers, and other equipment that you would never realize were in your network path any other way.

Manually Exercising a Protocol

When you are trying to understand a protocol, it is often helpful to try it your-self—that is, without the benefit of a client program. The standard Telnet pro-gram allows you to access many servers directly because many servers build on a Telnet-style protocol.

For example, suppose you want to try fetching a Web page without a Web browser. You can Telnet to the host computer and simulate a Web browser. You simply have to direct the Telnet program to use port 80 instead of the customary Telnet port (port 23).

Try these steps:

Start your Telnet client. From a Unix command prompt, enter:

```
telnet www.coriolis.com 80
```

You can replace **www.coriolis.com** with the name of the computer you want to connect to (don't include **http://**). If you are running under Windows, you can use the same command (in fact, you have to under Windows 2000). If you use Win-dows 98 or ME, you can start Telnet and use the menus to select the hostname and port if you prefer.

Once the Telnet client connects to the host, type the following:

```
GET http://www.coriolis.com
```

If your Telnet client doesn't echo characters, you might be typing blind (you can set local echo in the program's options). When you hit Enter, the server will spew out the data the Web browser would see. You'll learn more about this format in other parts of the book (in particular, see Chapters 7, 10, and 12), but you can probably see that the first part contains HTTP headers, followed by a blank line, followed by the HTML code that corresponds to the default Web page.

Depending on your Telnet client, you may not be able to scroll back to the begin-ning of the page, although good clients will let you select how many lines to save.

The utility of this isn't really fetching Web pages. This is a good way to experiment with any TCP server that you can exercise with text commands. A surprising number of servers are responsive to commands that are nearly human-readable.

Locating an RFC

If you want to dig into the dark details of the Internet, you have to read the RFCs. The main source for RFCs is **www.ietf.org/rfc.html**. You might prefer **www.faqs.org/rfcs** that also has RFCs and a variety of other FAQ documents.

TIP: *RFC1000 is an index that can help you find a specific RFC you are seeking.*

Table 1.3 shows a few of the more interesting RFCs.

Some of the RFCs are actually geek humor, such as in RFC2549 ("IP Over Avian Carriers with Quality of Service") or RFC2324 ("Hyper Text Coffee Pot Control Protocol"). Some are merely informational, such as RFC1936 ("What is the Internet Anyway?").

Table 1.3   Useful RFCs.

RFC	Title	Description
RFC1700	Assigned numbers	Assigned port numbers and other assigned constants
RFC1122, RFC1123	Host requirements	Defines what Internet hosts must implement
RFC791, RFC919, RFC922, RFC950	Internet Protocol	Defines IP
RFC768	User Datagram Protocol	UDP standard
RFC792	Internet Control Message Protocol	The ICMP standard used by programs like ping
RFC793	Transmission Control Protocol	TCP standard
RFC821	Simple Mail Transfer Protocol	SMTP (sending and relaying email)
RFC822	Format of Electronic Mail Messages	The format for ASCII text email messages
RFC854, RFC855	Telnet Protocol	Standard for remote logins via Telnet
RFC862	Echo Protocol	Test protocol
RFC865	Quote of the Day	Returns a quote (or message) of the day
RFC867	Daytime Protocol	Defines the daytime service
RFC868	Time Protocol	Defines the time service
RFC959	File Transfer Protocol	Defines FTP
RFC977	Network News Transfer Protocol	Defines NNTP, which handles Usenet messages

(continued)

Table 1.3   Useful RFCs *(continued).*

RFC	Title	Description
RFC1000	RFC Reference Guide	Guide to other RFCs
RFC1034, RFC1035	Domain Name System	Defines DNS services
RFC1153	Digest Message Format for Mail	Defines a way to combine multiple email messages into one digest
RFC1288	Finger Protocol	Defines the finger service
RFC1303	Network Time Protocol (version 3)	A service that allows precise synchronization of two clocks
RFC1350	Trivial File Transfer Protocol	The TFTP service that transfers files between computers
RFC1738	Uniform Resource Locators	Defines fully qualified URLs
RFC1808	Relative Uniform Resource Locators	Defines relative URLs
RFC1939	Post Office Protocol (version 3)	Allows computers to retrieve email
RFC1945, RFC2068	Hypertext Transfer Protocol	Defines the basic protocol for Web browsing
RFC2045, RFC2046, RFC2047	Multipurpose Internet Mail Extensions	Defines MIME types that allow ASCII encoding of binary data; used for email and Web browsing
RFC2141	Uniform Resource Names Syntax	URNs—a scheme similar to URLs
RFC2396	Uniform Resource Identifiers	URIs—another scheme to identify and locate resources

Setting Up Java for Proxy Servers

If your client software is behind a proxy server, you may not be able to access the public Internet without a little extra effort. Java allows you to set properties either in a properties file or using the **-D** command-line option to the Java virtual machine. Table 1.4 shows the options you can use:

Table 1.4   Java proxy settings.

Property	Description
proxySet	True or false to indicate if Java should always use a proxy
proxyHost	Hostname or IP address of proxy
proxyPort	Proxy port for generic proxy
ftpProxySet	True or false to indicate if Java should use proxy for FTP

(continued)

Table 1.4   Java proxy settings *(continued)*.

Property	Description
ftpProxyHost	Hostname or IP address of FTP proxy
ftpProxyPort	Proxy port for FTP
gopherProxySet	True or false to indicate if Java should use proxy for gopher (an older method of retrieving documents)
gopherProxyHost	Hostname or IP address of gopher proxy
gopherProxyPort	Proxy port for gopher
http.proxySet	True or false to indicate if Java should use proxy for HTTP
http.proxyHost	Hostname or IP address of HTTP proxy
http.proxyPort	Proxy port for FTP
socksProxyHost	Hostname or IP address for SOCKS proxy server
socksProxyPort	Port for SOCKS proxy server

Some proxy servers require you to use a password to access them. Because proxy servers work at the application level, the exact method you'll use to do this varies. For example, an HTTP proxy might want you to add the user ID and password to the content headers of your HTTP request (something you'll read about later in the book).

Chapter 2

Java Network Programming

In Depth

Houston has a lot in common with Los Angeles and several other larger cities I've seen. In particular, everyone drives everywhere. When I was a kid growing up in a small town, we'd walk to the store, and we went everywhere else on bicycles. Here in Houston, there's no place to go within walking distance. For a city its size, Houston has practically no public transportation.

When you live in a city like Houston, you really live in your car, and you get to know it. As a software developer, you probably feel that way about your favorite programming tool and language. After all, you probably spend at least as much time behind your keyboard as you do behind the wheel.

However, no matter how much time you spend in your car, there are probably some things you don't use very often. I once spent 30 frantic seconds searching for my emergency blinkers. Every time daylight savings time arrives, I have to puzzle out the procedure to set my clock. I vaguely remember that there is a fuel shutoff reset switch somewhere around the spare tire, but I couldn't tell you exactly where.

Programming languages can make you feel the same way. Some things you use every day, and they are second nature to you. But there are always things you don't use very often, and you have to puzzle them out when you do need them.

Before you can tackle Internet protocols in Java, you'll need a few tricks out of the Java toolkit. This book assumes you already know the basics of Java. However, network programming techniques might be something you don't normally use, so this chapter will show you how to use Java features that are important for these sorts of programs.

Java has excellent support for network sockets, and using them is so simple. But you may not have had occasion to exercise all of their features. In addition, once you have a socket, you need to encode and decode data in meaningful ways. If you are writing a server, you'll find that threads are a necessary element because without threads, you can't readily handle multiple clients.

Essential Socket Programming

Traditional socket programs use C. However, Java offers many high-level ways to handle sockets that make writing network programs much easier. The downside is that it is very difficult to circumvent this built-in support. For example, Java sockets support UDP and TCP connections. If you want something else—for example, Internet Control Message Protocol (ICMP) for a ping program—you'll have to resort to native method calls (probably written in C) or JDK 1.4 or later.

Java's network support—not surprisingly—is in the **java.net** package. Many of the classes in this package aren't meant for your ordinary use. You'll likely use the following classes:

- **DatagramPacket**—A packet of data to send (or receive) via a UDP socket (implemented by **DatagramSocket**)
- **DatagramSocket**—A socket that communicates via UDP
- **HttpURLConnection**—A class to communicate specifically with HTTP servers
- **InetAddress**—Representation of an IP address by name or number
- **JarURLConnection**—A class to work with JAR files from a local file, a Web server, or an FTP server
- **MulticastSocket**—A socket designed for multicasting (i.e., sending and receiving to more than one remote socket)
- **ServerSocket**—A socket that listens for connections from clients
- **Socket**—A general-purpose socket
- **URL**—A class that represents a URL address
- **URLDecoder**—Decodes data formatted as a URL
- **URLEncoder**—Encodes URL data

Some of these classes I'll address in future chapters. The primary classes of interest in this chapter deal directly with sockets.

The basic idea behind socket communications is simple. A client establishes a connection with a server. Once the connection is made, the client can write to the socket to send data to the server. Conversely, the server sends data that the client will read to the socket. It's almost that simple; the details can be complex, but the idea is just that simple.

There are three main types of socket classes that Java provides. **DatagramSocket** is the class that implements the UDP protocol. Recall from Chapter 1 that UDP sockets don't use connections and don't ensure data delivery or preserve the data's sequence. Data in and out of the socket resides in a **DatagramPacket** object.

The other two socket classes are **Socket** and **ServerSocket**, and they both support TCP connections. If you are connecting to a server, you'll use **Socket**. If you are writing a server, you'll use **ServerSocket**. Why the difference? A client socket doesn't really care what port it uses locally. It does need to connect to a specific port on another computer. On the other hand, a server is very concerned with its local port assignment (that's how clients find it). Servers also have to listen for incoming connections.

Listening for an incoming connection isn't a very intuitive process. Suppose you are a Web server listening on port 80. When a client connects to you, it makes sense to think that you'd be using port 80 to talk to the client, right? That's not how it works, however. If it did work this way, only one client would be able to connect at a time. Internally, the networking software arranges it so that when a client connects on a port, the request goes to another socket that has a randomly assigned port. The client doesn't really care as long as it connects to the server and the server's main socket is free to continue listening for incoming connections.

Addressing

No matter what kind of socket you plan to use, you'll need a way to specify the address of the socket. You might think you could just pass a hostname or an IP address to the socket's constructor, but that's not quite the case. Instead, you'll use **InetAddress** to represent the remote computer's address.

InetAddress doesn't have any public constructors. So how do you get an instance of the object? You can use one of three static methods to create a new instance for you:

- The **getLocalHost** method returns an **InetAddress** object that refers to your local computer.

- The **getByName** method returns an object for the specified host. The name can be a string that represents the IP address, or it can be the actual host name.

- The **getAllByName** method finds all addresses that match a specified a name. This method returns an array.

Making any of these calls will either return an **InetAddress** object (or objects, in the case of **getAllByName**) or will throw an **UnknownHostException** if the name is not resolvable. Usually, you'll just pass the **InetAddress** object to a socket constructor. However, you can also use the object as a way to resolve hostnames to IP addresses (sort of an interface to DNS). You can call the instance methods **getHostName** and **getHostAddress** to return the hostname and IP address. You can also use **getAddress** to return the IP address as a byte array, not a string.

Listing 2.1 shows a simple console program that can resolve a name or IP address. When you pass an IP address on the command line, the program will work, but it may or may not look up the corresponding name. If Java can't resolve the hostname, the socket's name is simply a string that represents its IP address.

Listing 2.1 This program will convert a hostname to the equivalent IP address.

```
import java.net.*;

public class GetIP
  {
  public static void main(String [] args) {
    InetAddress address=null;
    if (args.length==0) {
      System.out.println("usage: GetIP host");
      System.exit(1);
      }
    try {
      address=InetAddress.getByName(args[0]);
      }
    catch (UnknownHostException e) {
      System.out.println("I can't find " + args[0]);
      System.exit(2);
      }
    System.out.println(address.getHostName() + "="
      + address.getHostAddress());
    System.exit(0);
    }
  }
```

Listing 2.2 shows how to use the **getAllByName** method. This returns an array of all the **InetAddress** objects that apply to the host. Armed with that array, you can iterate through the array and determine the characteristics of all the **InetAddress** objects.

Listing 2.2 A machine may have multiple IP addresses and this program will display them.

```
import java.net.*;

public class GetAllIP {
  public static void main(String [] args) throws Exception {
    InetAddress[] addr = InetAddress.getAllByName(args[0]);
    for (int i=0;i<addr.length;i++)
      System.out.println(addr[i]);
    }
  }
```

The **InetAddress** class is not very complex, but you can use it when you connect to another machine using a socket. The constructors also accept hostnames, so you rarely have to use this class, but it is useful when you want to resolve addresses yourself.

A TCP Client

When you want to connect to a server, you use the **Socket** class. The simplest way to create a **Socket** is to provide a hostname (or **InetAddress** object) and a port number to the constructor. The program in Listing 2.3 shows a very simple program that connects to a Web server. You supply the hostname or IP address on the command line. The program doesn't transfer any data, but it does check to see if some server, presumably a Web server, is listening on port 80 and connects to it.

Listing 2.3   Connecting with a Web server proves it exists, even if you don't transfer any data from it.

```
import java.net.*;
import java.io.*;

public class WebPing {
  public static void main(String[] args) {
    try {
      InetAddress addr;
      Socket sock=new Socket(args[0],80);
      addr=sock.getInetAddress();
      System.out.println("Connected to " +
        addr);
      sock.close();
      }
    catch (java.io.IOException e) {
      System.out.println("Can't connect to " + args[0]);
      System.out.println(e);
      }
    }
  }
```

If you are running a Web server on your local machine, you can test this program against the localhost computer. The output will look something like this:

```
Connected to localhost/127.0.0.1
```

Notice that the implicit call to **InetAddress.toString** (made by **println**) prints out the hostname and the IP address automatically. You could, of course, obtain the hostname and the IP address and format them yourself.

A TCP Server

The most common type of socket you'll use is a TCP socket. When using TCP, one computer acts as a server and the other acts as a client. You'll use **ServerSocket** to write a server. You construct a **ServerSocket** object by calling the constructor with a port number. If you are writing a standard server, you'll use the well-known port number associated with that server type. For example, a Web server would use port 80. If you aren't writing a standard server, you can select a port number that isn't in use on your system (typically above 1023).

Try issuing the following command:

```
telnet localhost 8123
```

It is very likely that the program will report that it can't connect to that port. If the port is in use, just select another number. Now, look at the program in Listing 2.4. This program provides a server on port 8123. The server doesn't do anything, but if you run this program, the Telnet program will be able to connect to port 8123.

Listing 2.4   This simplistic server will allow connections on socket 8123.

```java
import java.net.*;
import java.io.*;

public class Techo {
  public static void main(String[] args) {
    try {
      ServerSocket server=new ServerSocket(8123);
      while (true) {
        System.out.println("Listening");
        Socket sock = server.accept();
        InetAddress addr=sock.getInetAddress();
        System.out.println("Connection made to "
            + addr.getHostName() + " ("
            + addr.getHostAddress() + ")");
        pause(5000);
        sock.close();
        }
      }
    catch (IOException e) {
      System.out.println("Exception detected: " + e);
      }
    }
  private static void pause(int ms) {
    try {
      Thread.sleep(ms);
      }
    catch (InterruptedException e) {}
    }
  }
```

The constructor for **ServerSocket** accepts the port number. You could easily modify the code to accept a port number from a property file or from the command line, if you thought it might change. Once you have the server socket, you can call **accept** to listen for incoming connections. This call will block, so the program will halt until a client computer connects. If this is unacceptable, you'll have to make the call from within a thread, a topic covered later in this chapter.

Because this server doesn't do anything, it just pauses for 5 seconds once someone connects. If you try to run two copies of the server, the second copy will throw an exception. Only one program can listen to a port at once. If you make a connection to the host while it is busy, the system will complete the connection once the server calls **accept** again. The limit on how many clients can be waiting for the server varies by system. You can ask for a certain queue size by using a different **ServerSocket** constructor, but the underlying system is not obligated to fulfill your request.

If the port number you want is already in use, the constructor will throw an **IOException**. You can use this to discover the ports that are already in use on your machine (see Listing 2.5).

WARNING! *If you are running under Unix, you'll probably need to be running as root to start servers on reserved port numbers (those less than 1024).*

Listing 2.5   You can scan your computer for ports in use using this program.

```java
import java.net.*;

public class LocalScan {
  public static void main(String [] args) {
    for (int i=1;i<1023;i++) {
      testPort(i);
      }
    System.out.println("Completed");
    }
  private static void testPort(int i) {
    try {
      ServerSocket sock=new ServerSocket(i);
      }
    catch (java.io.IOException e) {
      System.out.println("Port " + i + " in use.");
      }
    }
  }
```

Stream I/O

Connecting to a remote machine is fine, but the real goal is to send and receive data. Java allows you to access I/O streams—just like the streams you use to perform file I/O. You can also add filters to any stream to convert it to a reader or writer and to handle special data types.

The **Socket** class has two methods that return streams: **getInputStream** and **getOutputStream**. You can use these streams directly. They are of type **java.io. InputStream** and **java.io.OutputStream**, respectively. However, you may want to add one or more filters to handle data in special ways. More recent versions of Java favor reader and writer classes over plain streams and you can use **InputStreamReader** and **OutputStreamWriter** to convert a stream into a reader or writer.

You might want to use several stream-related classes with a socket, including the following:

- **BufferedInputStream**—Allows you to buffer incoming data (you can also use **BufferedReader**).
- **BufferedOutputStream**—Adds an output buffer to the stream (you can also use **BufferedWriter**).
- **DataInputStream**—Allows you to read primitive Java data types in a way that is portable between machines.
- **DataOutputStream**—Writes primitive Java data types in a way that is portable between machines.
- **InputStreamReader**—Creates a reader object from an **InputStream**.
- **OutputStreamWriter**—Creates a writer object from an **OutputStream**.
- **ObjectInputStream**—Reads objects that implement **Serializable** or **Externalizable**.
- **ObjectOutputStream**—Writes objects that implement **Serializable** or **Externalizable**.
- **PrintStream**—Writes text-representations of data onto an **OutputStream** (this is the same stream type used with the **System.out** stream).
- **PrintWriter**—A writer object that corresponds to a **PrintStream**.
- **PushbackInputStream**—Allows you to push back a specified number of input characters.
- **PushbackReader**—A reader object that corresponds to a **PushbackInputStream**.
- **StreamTokenizer**—Breaks an input stream from a **Reader** object into tokens.

I especially like **BufferedInputReader** because it has the **readLine** method for reading an entire line at a time. What's the difference between a reader and an input stream (or a writer and an output stream)? The older stream classes deal in bytes. The newer reader and writer classes deal with Unicode characters (2-byte characters).

Consider the server in Listing 2.6. This is a simple server that only allows a single connection. When you connect to the server, it displays a few messages and exits.

Listing 2.6   This server displays messages to a single client.

```
import java.net.*;
import java.io.*;

public class BeerServer {
  public static void main(String args[]) throws Exception {
    ServerSocket ssock=new ServerSocket(1234);
    System.out.println("Listening");
    Socket sock=ssock.accept();
    ssock.close(); // no more connects

    PrintStream pstream=new PrintStream(
      sock.getOutputStream());
    for (int i=100;i>=0;i--) {
      pstream.println(i + " bottles of beer on the wall");
      }
    pstream.close();
    sock.close();
    }
}
```

Once the server is running, use a Telnet program to connect to your computer's port 1234. For example, type:

```
telnet localhost 1234
```

Notice that the **PrintStream** object all by itself doesn't do anything. You have to attach it to a stream (in this case, the socket's outbound stream). Although **PrintStream** is handy for this example, you should think carefully about using it in a real network program. One problem is that **PrintStream** handles the ends of lines differently on different platforms. Also, **PrintStream** may handle encoding differently on different platforms, and it has a nasty habit of gobbling up any exceptions that occur. If you want to check for errors, you have to call **checkError**.

Of course, a server or a client may want to accept data as well as provide it. Listing 2.7 shows a variation of the previous server that prompts the client for a starting number. You can connect to it via Telnet just like before, but this time you'll have to enter a number (depending on your Telnet program, you might not see an echo of what you type). Hit Enter and the program will proceed as before, but it will use the supplied count.

Listing 2.7   The client can specify information to control the output of this server.

```
import java.net.*;
import java.io.*;

public class BeerServer1 {
  public static void main(String args[]) throws Exception {
    ServerSocket ssock=new ServerSocket(1234);
    System.out.println("Listening");
    Socket sock=ssock.accept();
    ssock.close(); // no more connects

    PrintStream pstream=new PrintStream(
      sock.getOutputStream());

// ask for count
    pstream.print("count? ");
    BufferedReader input =
      new BufferedReader( new InputStreamReader(
        sock.getInputStream()));

// read and parse it
    String line = input.readLine();
    pstream.println("");
    int count = Integer.parseInt(line);
    for (int i=count;i>=0;i--) {
      pstream.println(i + " bottles of beer on the wall");
      }
    pstream.close();
    sock.close();
    }
  }
```

Working with strings is handy when the other side of the socket is a user. However, when two Java programs are talking, you might prefer using data or object streams. Listing 2.8 shows a simple server that returns the value of pi. Instead of providing this value as text, however, it uses a **DataOutputStream**.

Listing 2.8   A Java-specific server can use specialized streams to deliver typed data or objects.

```java
import java.net.*;
import java.io.*;

public class DataServer {
  public static void main(String args[]) throws Exception {
    ServerSocket ssock=new ServerSocket(1234);
    while (true ) {
      System.out.println("Listening");
      Socket sock=ssock.accept();

      DataOutputStream dstream=new DataOutputStream(
        sock.getOutputStream());
      dstream.writeFloat(3.14159265f);
      dstream.close();
      sock.close();
      }
    }
  }
```

Of course, the data streams only handle basic data types. If you want to pass a whole object, you'll need to use **ObjectInputStream** and **ObjectOutputStream**. These stream types will only work with objects that implement the **Serializable** or **Externalizable** interfaces. Listing 2.9 shows a simple client that fetches the value PI. This is a very useful way to transmit values between Java programs.

Listing 2.9   This client can retrieve the floating point data from the DataServer program in Listing 2.8.

```java
import java.net.*;
import java.io.*;

public class DataClient {
  public static void main(String[] args) throws Exception {
    Socket sock=new Socket(args[0],1234);
    DataInputStream dis=new DataInputStream(
      sock.getInputStream());
    float f=dis.readFloat();
    System.out.println("PI=" + f);
    dis.close();
    sock.close();
    }
  }
```

The **Serializable** interface has no methods; it simply marks a class that is willing to serialize itself (i.e., stores itself in a persistent manner). Some classes want more control of the serialization process, and these classes must implement the **Externalizable** interface, which has two members. Classes can also customize serialization by overriding **readObject** and **writeObject**.

You'll find an example server and client in Listings 2.10 and 2.11. In these cases, the server serializes one object—a **Hashtable**—however, you can serialize multiple objects easily and reconstitute them over the network.

Listing 2.10   You can serve entire objects using **ObjectOutputStream**.

```
import java.net.*;
import java.io.*;
import java.util.*;

public class ObjServer {
  public static void main(String args[]) throws Exception {
    ServerSocket ssock=new ServerSocket(1234);
    Hashtable hash = new Hashtable();
    hash.put("Dog","Madison");
    hash.put("Cat","Lacey");

    while (true ) {
      System.out.println("Listening");
      Socket sock=ssock.accept();

      ObjectOutputStream ostream=new ObjectOutputStream(
          sock.getOutputStream());
      ostream.writeObject(hash);
      ostream.close();
      sock.close();
      }
    }
  }
```

Listing 2.11   A Java-specific client can read objects from Java servers.

```
import java.net.*;
import java.io.*;
import java.util.*;

public class ObjClient {
    public static void main(String[] args) throws Exception {
      Socket sock=new Socket(args[0],1234);
      ObjectInputStream ois=new ObjectInputStream(
          sock.getInputStream());
      Hashtable hash=(Hashtable)ois.readObject();
      System.out.println(hash);
```

```
        ois.close();
        sock.close();
        }
    }
```

Notice how the Java I/O classes stack on each other. You start with an **InputStream**, and you can add an **InputStreamReader** layer. Then you can add more layers to add further processing. For example, you might use the classes in java.util.zip to compress data (and decompress it on the other side, of course). The methods in the **javax.crypto** package allow you to encrypt and decrypt secure messages.

Advanced Socket Methods

If the last section convinced you that working with sockets isn't very hard, you're right! Of course, you can make it more complicated if you like. However, for most of your programs, sockets are simple to use.

One thing that simplified the last few programs was that I allowed **main** to throw exceptions. That way, I didn't have to wrap each socket call in a **try** block. In real life, of course, you'd want to watch for these exceptions and take appropriate action.

I did catch the exceptions caused by **InetAddress**. However, many of the methods in the **Socket** and **SocketServer** classes can throw an **IOException**. Some of the methods (but none that you've seen so far) can throw a **SocketException**, also.

The following are some common subclasses of **SocketException**:

- **BindException**—Occurs when you attempt to create a socket on a port that is already in use

- **ConnectException**—Occurs when you attempt to connect a socket, and the connection fails

- **NoRouteToHostException**—Indicates that you have asked for an IP address that is unreachable

Socket Options

There are several options you can set on normal **Socket** objects. The **setSoTime-out** call sets a maximum time (in milliseconds) for **read** calls to wait for data. If you set this option, any read that can't complete within the prescribed time will throw an **InterruptedIOException**. The default setting is zero, which means **read** waits until it completes. A similar call for **ServerSocket** that affects how long **accept** will wait before throwing an **InterruptedIOException** is also called **setSoTimeout**.

Although not normally necessary, you can suggest a buffer size for the socket by calling **setSendBufferSize** and **setReceiveBufferSize**. These might allow you to improve performance on certain systems, depending on the platform in use and your application specific behavior.

Speaking of performance, Java tries to minimize the amount of data sent through a socket. If you want data to flow as soon as possible, which may have a negative impact on performance, call **setTcpNoDelay**. If you set this parameter to **false**— or leave it alone)—the system will try to use Nagle's algorithm (see RFC896) to optimize data transmission. That means the system tries to accumulate small chunks of data before sending a packet. Then, it accumulates data until the remote system acknowledges the first packet. However, for interactive programs, this may make the network connection seem sluggish.

Because of buffering, it is possible to close a socket before all the data you've sent through it has actually been transmitted. If this is a problem, you can call **setSoLinger**. This call specifies a number of seconds to wait before returning from **close** to attempt to clear any unsent data.

You can set the sockets to exchange keep alive packets periodically by calling **setKeepAlive** with a value of **true**. A keep alive packet is just a small amount of meaningless data exchanged between computers during otherwise idle periods. This is useful when you want to know quickly if one computer has crashed without closing its socket.

Normally, when you no longer need a socket, you call **close**. However, you can also call **shutdownInput** or **shutdownOutput** to close half of the socket instead of closing it completely.

It is possible that some socket implementations won't support certain socket options. That's why you may have to handle a **SocketException** when making calls like **setTcpNoDelay**.

Socket Constructors

The constructors used in the example programs are all you usually need. For a server, you specify the port. For a client, you specify the hostname as a string or as an **InetAddress**. You also specify the port. However, both classes have more sophisticated constructors available if you want to use them.

The **ServerSocket** class has a constructor that takes a **backlog** value and an optional binding address. The **backlog** allows you to specify how big a queue you'd like to create for incoming connections. This queue holds client connection requests while the server is busy handling another request. However, the system may place an upper limit on this queue size, so you should consider this parameter carefully.

The binding address allows you to specify which IP address you want the server to use for connections. This is useful when a single machine has more than one IP address (either because it has multiple network adapters or a single adapter has more than one address).

An ordinary socket provides extra constructors that allow you to specify the local address and the local port you want to use when opening the socket. This can be useful when the machine has more than one IP address.

Using UDP

Once you are used to using TCP sockets, UDP sockets (in the form of a **DatagramSocket**) seem difficult. Instead of connecting to a particular machine, you specify the local port the socket should use. If you don't specify a port, the system will randomly assign one for you. You can only send and receive byte arrays via a **DatagramSocket**.

Place the data you wish to send in a **DatagramPacket**. This packet not only contains the data but also the destination address and port. You pass the packet to the **DatagramSocket.send** method. You can call **DatagramSocket.receive** to fill in a packet.

If you have multiple transactions with one server, it is a good idea to call **connect** on the **DatagramSocket** object. This can save time because any security checks and other overhead only occur once. You'll need to call **disconnect** if you want to talk to another server.

Like TCP sockets, the **DatagramSocket** allows you to call **setSoTimeout** to make reading time out. You can also call **setSendBufferSize** and **setReceiveBufferSize** to suggest buffer sizes to the underlying operating system.

Because UDP sockets don't have a connection, you can't just simply reply to an incoming request. If you want to reply to a sender, you can extract the sender's address and port number (using **getAddress** and **getPort**), form another packet, and send it.

Why use UDP? For one thing, it is more efficient. Also, you can broadcast to multiple sockets at once. Consider Listing 2.12. If you run this program with **r** on the command line, the program will listen for UDP packets on port 1111. If you use **w** on the command line followed by an IP address and a word to send, the program will send a word to the host's UDP port 1111. In this case, the program uses a randomly assigned local port.

You can try the program using your server's IP address. However, if you run multiple copies of the receiver on different machines, you can broadcast by using a special IP address. To figure out what that IP address is, you have to look at your network number and determine its class (see Chapter 1). You can also look at your net mask (using the **ipconfig** command, for example). The idea is to use 255 in place of all the nonnetwork octets. Therefore, a class A broadcast address might be 10.255.255.255. If you are viewing your net mask, it will tell you what you need to know, also. For example, suppose your IP address is 169.254.39.44, and your net mask is 255.255.0.0. The broadcast address for your network, then, would be 169.254.255.255.

When you send to the broadcast address, all UDP listeners on the network will potentially receive a copy of the data. *Potentially* is the key word here—don't forget that UDP data is not guaranteed for delivery.

Listing 2.12   You can use two copies of this program to experiment with UDP sockets.

```java
import java.net.*;

public class UDP0 {
// command line arguments:
// r  -- read an incoming packet
// w hostname word -- write word to hostname
  public static void main(String[] args) throws Exception {
    byte [] ary= new byte[128];
    DatagramPacket pack=new DatagramPacket(ary,128);
    if (args[0].charAt(0)=='r') {
    // read
      DatagramSocket sock=new DatagramSocket(1111);
      sock.receive(pack);
      String word=new String(pack.getData());
      System.out.println("From: " + pack.getAddress()
        + " Port: " + pack.getPort());
      System.out.println(word);
      sock.close();
    } else { // write
      DatagramSocket sock=new DatagramSocket();
      pack.setAddress(InetAddress.getByName(args[1]));
      pack.setData(args[2].getBytes());
      pack.setPort(1111);
      sock.send(pack);
      sock.close();
    }
  }
}
```

TIP: *If you don't have very demanding requirements, you can use the **URL** class to retrieve data given a URL—assuming Java understands the protocol you specify. You can construct a **URL** object by simply passing a string that represents the URL to the **URL** object's constructor. If you just want to fetch the data from the URL, you can call **openStream**. You can also call **openConnection** to get a **URLConnection** object that gives you more control over the process. You'll read more about these objects in Chapter 10.*

Threads

When you are writing a server, you usually don't want to have clients waiting for other clients. The best way to handle clients is to create a new thread for each client. Because Java has built-in thread handling this is relatively straightforward.

You have two choices for constructing a thread. First, you can extend the **Thread** object to form a new object that creates a thread. If that isn't possible, you can make your object implement **Runnable** and write the corresponding **run** method. If you use the first method, you can start the thread using **start** (don't call **run** directly). However, if you use the second method (implementing **Runnable**), you'll have to create a **Thread** object and pass your object to the **Thread** constructor.

You can find an example server that uses threads in Listing 2.13. Note that the **MTThread** object extends **Thread**. The **main** routine still creates the **ServerSocket** and calls **accept**. However, when a client connects, the **main** routine creates a new instance of the **MTThread** object and, therefore, a new thread. The new thread needs to know the client's socket, so the **main** function passes it to the object's constructor. Finally, a call to **start** kicks off the new thread. If you run this server, you can start several Telnet sessions at once, and each one will receive data.

Listing 2.13   Using threads allows a server to handle multiple client requests at once.

```
import java.net.*;
import java.io.*;

public class MTServer extends Thread {
    Socket csocket;
    MTServer(Socket csocket) { this.csocket = csocket; }
  public static void main(String args[]) throws Exception {
    ServerSocket ssock=new ServerSocket(1234);
    System.out.println("Listening");
    while (true) {
      Socket sock=ssock.accept();
      System.out.println("Connected");
      new MTServer(sock).start();
      }


    }
```

```
public void run() {
  try {
    PrintStream pstream=new PrintStream(
      csocket.getOutputStream());
    for (int i=100;i>=0;i--) {
      pstream.println(i + " bottles of beer on the wall");
      }
    pstream.close();
    csocket.close();
    }
  catch (IOException e) {
    System.out.println(e);
    }
  }
}
```

Passing arguments into a thread can be tricky. The **Thread** object doesn't begin execution until you call **start**. That means that you could dispense with the object constructor, although the constructor is a neater way to pass in an argument. Instead, you could write the following:

```
MTServer svr = new MTServer();
svr.csocket = sock;
svr.start();
```

What you don't want to do is something like this:

```
MTServer svr = new MTServer();
svr.start();
svr.csocket = sock;
```

The problem with this is that the **run** method may already be executing by the time the main program sets **csocket**. Unless you have some way to synchronize the main thread and the new thread, you might crash your program.

A few other interesting methods exist in the **Thread** class, including the following:

- **sleep**—You can cause the thread to pause for a specified number of milliseconds. This is very efficient and allows other threads to execute while the thread is sleeping.

- **yield**—Most systems give threads a certain amount of time to execute. If the thread does not need its time slice, it can give it up with **yield**. This is especially important on systems that don't preemptively multitask. On these systems, only certain calls will switch to another thread.

- **setDaemon**—You can use the **setDaemon** call to mark a thread as a daemon thread (**true**) or a user thread (**false**). A Java program runs as long as at least one user thread is still running. A daemon thread will not stop the program from exiting.

- **setPriority**—Threads take turns running on the system's processors. Threads with higher priority will execute more often than threads with lower priorities. In Java, the higher the priority number, the higher the priority (this is backwards from many operating systems where lower numbers indicate higher priority). Priorities range between 1 and 10.

- **join**—In many cases one thread needs to wait for another to complete. That's the purpose behind the **join** method. When you call a thread's **join** method, you'll block until the thread completes. You can specify an optional time-out so you don't wind up waiting forever.

In addition, there are a few items in Java that support threads. In the **Object** class (which is another way of saying in every class), you'll find **wait** and **notify** methods. When you **wait** on an object, your thread will stop until a time-out occurs or the thread calls **notify**.

Another topic related to threads is the **synchronized** keyword that allows you to build methods that only one thread can execute at one time. Suppose two threads are going to call a **synchronized** method. When the first thread calls it, things proceed as normal. However, because the method is **synchronized**, the first thread acquires a lock. When the second thread tries to call, it blocks because the first thread has the lock. When the first thread completes the method execution, the lock becomes available, and the second thread can proceed.

As mentioned earlier, you don't have to extend **Thread** to create a thread. You can implement the **Runnable** interface in your object. Then the main program will create a **Thread** object and pass your object to the thread's constructor:

```
Thread t = new Thread(runnableObject);
```

Listing 2.14 shows a complete example of a server using this technique.

Listing 2.14   A multithreaded server does not have to extend Thread, as this example shows.

```
import java.net.*;
import java.io.*;

public class MTServer1 implements Runnable {
   Socket csocket;
   MTServer1(Socket csocket) { this.csocket = csocket; }
   public static void main(String args[]) throws Exception {
     ServerSocket ssock=new ServerSocket(1234);
     System.out.println("Listening");
     while (true) {
```

```
      Socket sock=ssock.accept();
      System.out.println("Connected");
      new Thread(new MTServer1(sock)).start();
    }
  }

  public void run() {
    try {
      PrintStream pstream=new PrintStream(
      csocket.getOutputStream());
      for (int i=100;i>=0;i−) {
        pstream.println(i + " bottles of beer on the wall");
        }
      pstream.close();
      csocket.close();
      }
    catch (IOException e) {
      System.out.println(e);
    }
  }
}
```

If you create a brand-new thread for every client, you may find that you spend a lot of time creating and destroying threads. A better idea is to use a pool of threads that you create once and never destroy. Instead, you reuse the threads as you need them.

You can keep a pool of thread objects ready to work in a queue, a stack, or some sort of list. The code in Listing 2.26 shows an example system that keeps a linked list of threads that handle incoming requests.

Immediate Solutions

Resolving a Hostname

If you have a hostname and you wish to transform it to an IP address, you can use the **InetAddress** class. In many cases, this same class can resolve an IP address to a hostname, although this is not always possible. You can't construct an **InetAddress** object directly. Instead, you call one of three static member functions: **getLocalHost**, **getByName**, and **getAllByName**.

Once you have an **InetAddress** object, you can call **getHostName** or **getHostAddress** to find the corresponding name or IP address. You can also call **getAddress** to get the IP address as an array of bytes. Listing 2.15 shows an excerpt of the code required to use **InetAddress**.

Listing 2.15   Finding a hostname or IP address using **InetAddress**.

```
try {
  address=InetAddress.getByName("www.coriolis.com");
  }
catch (UnknownHostException e) {
  System.out.println("I can't find host");
  System.exit(1);
  }
System.out.println(address.getHostName() + "="
   + address.getHostAddress());
```

Opening a TCP Socket to a Server

When you create a **Socket** object, you specify the destination address and port in the constructor. You can specify the destination address as a string or as an **InetAddress** object. If the computer has multiple network interfaces, you can also specify the local port and the outgoing interface to use, either as a string or as **InetAddress**.

When you construct a socket, you may trigger an exception if the hostname is unknown or if any other error occurs. Listing 2.16 shows an example of opening the Web server at **www.coriolis.com**.

Listing 2.16   Opening a socket requires exception handling code.

```
try {
  Socket sock = new Socket("www.coriolis.com",80);
  }
catch (UnknownHostException e) {
 // not found
  }
catch (java.io.IOException ioe) {
 // other error
  }
```

Opening a Server Socket

When you want to start a server, you can instantiate a **ServerSocket** object. The minimal constructor requires a port number that the socket will use to listen for incoming requests. If you wish, you can also suggest a queue size for incoming requests. Also, if there are multiple network interfaces, you can specify an **InetAddress** object to select a specific address.

Once a **ServerSocket** is instantiated, you can wait for a connection with **accept**. This will return a **Socket** object that you can use to communicate with the client. Client connections are only possible when the server calls **accept**; then, a single client will connect. If no clients are waiting to connect, the call will block (subject to any time-out set by **soSetTimeout**).

Industrial-strength servers usually create separate threads to handle incoming requests so that other clients will not have to wait to connect. You'll find an example in Listing 2.17.

Listing 2.17   The ServerSocket class makes it easy to accept client connections.

```
try {
ServerSocket ssock = new ServerSocket(2222); // port 2222
while (true) {
  Socket sock=ssock.accept();
  HandleClient(sock);
  }
 }
 catch (java.io.IOException e) {
 }
```

Creating a UDP Socket

For some protocols, or for maximum efficiency, you may wish to use UDP sockets instead of TCP. These sockets do not assure data delivery. There is also no guarantee that when data does arrive that it will arrive in the order it was sent. If you use these sockets, you'll have to provide an alternate way to deal with transmission loss and sequencing.

When you send and receive data via UDP, you use a **DatagramPacket** object. This object allows you to set an IP address, which could be a broadcast address, and a port number. It also contains a byte array that contains the data to send or receive. You pass the packet object to the **DatagramSocket** object's **send** or **receive** method.

If you are doing multiple transactions with one server, consider calling **DatagramSocket.connect** to set a connection to the remote computer. This reduces the overhead involved with sending each packet to the remote computer. However, then you can't send to other computers until you call **disconnect**.

UDP sockets don't use streams. You simply send and receive arrays of bytes. You'll find an example in Listing 2.18.

Listing 2.18   UDP sockets use **DatagramPacket** objects to send and receive data.

```
byte [] ary= new byte[128];
DatagramPacket pack=new DatagramPacket(ary,128);
if (reading) {
// read
  DatagramSocket sock=new DatagramSocket(portnum);
  sock.receive(pack);
  String word=new String(pack.getData());
  System.out.println("From: " + pack.getAddress()
    + " Port: " + pack.getPort());
  System.out.println(word);
  sock.close();
} else { // write
  DatagramSocket sock=new DatagramSocket();
  pack.setAddress(InetAddress.getByName(hostname);
  pack.setData(dataString.getBytes());
  pack.setPort(portnum);
  sock.send(pack);
  sock.close();
}
```

Sending Data to a TCP Socket

Once you have a **Socket** object (either from constructing one or as a result of a **ServerSocket.accept** call) you can fetch a stream that you can write to by calling **getOutputStream**. This is part of the **java.io** package and allows you to write bytes (or a byte array) to the socket for reading by the other computer.

You normally won't use the stream directly. Instead, you'll add one or more stream filters to make things simpler. For example, you might use **BufferedOutput-Stream** to buffer bytes to improve performance. A **DataOutputStream** object allows you to write primitive data types or an **ObjectOutputStream** object can write entire objects, as long as they are serializable. Listing 2.19 shows a simple example that opens a socket on a remote computer and sends an integer using a **DataOutputStream** filter.

Listing 2.19   A TCP socket uses streams to send data.

```
void sendToSocket(String host, int port) throws Exception {
  Socket sock = new Socket(host,port);
  DataOutputStream os = new DataOutputStream(sock.getOutputStream());
  os.writeChar('X');
  os.writeChar('Y');
  os.close();
  os.sock();
  }
```

Receiving Data from a TCP Socket

Receiving data requires you to call **getInputStream**. Once you have this input stream object you can use it to read raw bytes from the socket. If you issue a **read** and no data is available, the **read** call will block unless you've set a time-out.

You may wish to use filters to provide extra features, such as buffering (**Buffered-InputStream**) or data reception (**DataInputStream**). Listing 2.20 shows a simple function that receives data from a TCP socket.

Listing 2.20   TCP sockets deliver data via streams.

```
void sockRcv(Socket sock) throws Exception {
  char c1,c2;
  DataInputStream is = new DataInputStream(sock.getInputStream());
  c1=is.readChar();
  c2=is.readChar()();
  is.close();
  }
```

Compressing Socket Data

Because you can add filters to input and output streams, you can perform sophisticated processing, such as compression and decompression, with relative ease. The **java.util.zip** package has several stream classes you can use to compress and decompress data on the fly.

Listing 2.21 shows a program that receives data from a socket and decompresses it using **GZIPInputStream**. This server only accepts one connection and terminates when the transaction completes. Start the server with a port number on the command line.

Listing 2.21   You can use Java's compression classes to reduce the amount of data sent over a socket.

```
import java.net.*;
import java.io.*;
import java.util.zip.*;

public class CompRcv {
  public static void main(String[] args) throws Exception {
    ServerSocket ssock = new ServerSocket(
        Integer.parseInt(args[0]));
    System.out.println("Listening");
    Socket sock=ssock.accept();
    GZIPInputStream zip = new GZIPInputStream(
      sock.getInputStream());
    while (true) {
      int c;
      c = zip.read();
      if (c==-1) break;
      System.out.print((char)c);
      }
    }
  }
```

Listing 2.22 contains a companion client that sends a file to the server in Listing 2.21. Start the client with the hostname, the port number, and a file to send on the command line. This client and server work just the same as if they did not compress the data stream. The only difference is that they filter their streams with the special classes that compress data.

Listing 2.22   This client sends a compressed file to the server in Listing 2.21.

```java
import java.net.*;
import java.io.*;
import java.util.zip.*;

public class CompSend {
  public static void main(String[] args) throws Exception {
    Socket sock=new Socket(args[0],Integer.parseInt(args[1]));
    GZIPOutputStream zip = new GZIPOutputStream(
      sock.getOutputStream());
    String line;
    BufferedReader bis = new BufferedReader(
      new FileReader(args[2]));
    while (true) {
      try {
        line=bis.readLine();
        if (line==null) break;
        line=line+"\n";
        zip.write(line.getBytes(),0,line.length());
        }
      catch (Exception e) { break; }
      }
    zip.finish();
    zip.close();
    sock.close();
    }
  }
```

Setting a Socket Read Time-Out

When you make any call to read from a socket, the call normally blocks until the read completes. If you want a different behavior, you can call **Socket.setSo-Timeout**. The time-out is in milliseconds and defaults to 0, which indicates no time-out at all. If there is a time-out value and the read does not complete in the specified interval, the read will throw an **InterruptedIOException**.

As an example, suppose you made this call to set a 1 second (1000 millisecond) time-out:

```java
Sock.setSoTimeout(1000); // may throw SocketException
```

Then, assuming you have an input stream named **is**, you might write:

```
try {
   c=is.read();
   }
catch (InterruptedIOExecption e) { /* Time out! */ }
```

If you find yourself using **setSoTimeout**, you should think about using threads instead. Usually, doing reads in one thread and processing in another leads to a more robust solution. You can also use **getSoTimeout** to read the value back.

Setting a Server Accept Time-Out

When you call **ServerSocket.accept**, your program will stop until a client connects. If you want to set a time-out, you can call **ServerSocket.setSoTimeout** to set a time-out in milliseconds. However, if you find yourself doing this, you should attempt to rethink your design to use threads. Using threads, you can wait for client connections without stopping your processing. You can call **getSoTimeout** to read the value. Here's an example:

```
ssock.setSoTimeout(1000);   // may throw SocketException
```

Then, a call to **accept** will throw an **IOExeception** if a connection is not made within 1 second.

Setting **SoLinger**

Sometimes, you may close a socket before all the data you've sent has been transmitted to the other computer. In this case, you can call **setSoLinger** on the **Socket** object to set a time (in seconds) to wait for the data to clear before closing the socket. You can call **getSoLinger** to retrieve the value. The following will set the linger time to 5 seconds, and it may throw a **SocketException**:

```
sock.setSoLinger(true,5);
```

If you set the first parameter to **false**, you'll turn the linger feature off, which is the default state. Obviously, this call only applies to TCP sockets because UDP sockets don't have a connection to close.

Setting Socket Delay Behavior

To make data transmission more efficient, the underlying operating system usually buffers data and does not send a packet until the other computer acknowledges the previous transmissions. For some applications—notably those that are interactive—this may not be appropriate. If you want to change this behavior, call **socket.setTcpNoDelay(true)**. Call **getTcpNoDelay** if you want to determine the current value of this flag.

TIP: *RFC896 defines Nagle's algorithm which is the algorithm used to determine when to send packets.*

Setting Keep Alive Options

Consider the case where a client and server connect and then infrequently exchange data. The server could crash, and the client wouldn't notice until the next time the client sends data. By calling **Socket.setKeepAlive** and passing **true** as an argument, the sockets will periodically send meaningless data just to see if the connection is still alive. Here's an example:

```
sock.setKeepAlive(true); // may throw SocketException
```

Your program won't see this data, but if the sockets stop communicating, your program will receive an exception, even if you're not actively transmitting data. You can call **getKeepAlive** to find the current setting.

Setting Buffer Sizes

TCP sockets can buffer data, although the exact details are platform-dependent. You can make a suggestion to the operating system by calling **Socket.setReceiveBufferSize** and **Socket.setSendBufferSize**. These values are only suggestions. You can also call **getReceiveBufferSize** and **getSendBufferSize** to read the buffer sizes. Here's an example:

```
sock.setSendBufferSize(sock.getSendBufferSize+1024);
```

Of course, these calls may throw a **SocketException**.

Handling Socket Exceptions

Many socket operations can throw exceptions. Four common exceptions you may want to handle include the following:

- **java.io.IOException**—Occurs when there is a general I/O error
- **java.net.BindException**—Occurs when the requested port is in use
- **java.net.ConnectException**—Occurs when a client is unable to connect to the server
- **java.NoRouteToHostException**—Occurs when a network problem prevents the program from finding the host

You can catch the last three exceptions by handling **SocketException**, which is the base class for all three.

Creating a Multithreading Server

The basic procedure for a simple server is the following:

1. Create a **ServerSocket** class.
2. Call **accept**.
3. Perform necessary processing.
4. Go back and call **accept** again.

However, if there is any significant processing, this isn't efficient. You'd like to let the server handle each client in a separate thread. The easiest way to do that is to make your class extend **Thread**. Then you can write your processing in the **run** method. In the main routine (usually **static**), you can call **accept**, create a new instance of your class (probably passing it the socket returned by **accept**, and then call **start** to run the thread. You can find an example of this in Listing 2.23.

Listing 2.23   A basic multithreaded server.

```
import java.net.*;
import java.io.*;

public class AMTServer extends Thread {
    Socket csocket;
    AMTServer(Socket csocket) { this.csocket = csocket; }
    public static void main(String args[]) throws Exception {
      ServerSocket ssock=new ServerSocket(1234);
      while (true) {
        new AMTServer(ssock.accept()).start();
      }
```

```
    }

  public void run() {
// client processing code here
    }
  }
```

Automating the Multithreaded Server

Because the logic behind a multithreaded server is so predictable, you might be tempted to write a common base class for all multithreaded servers. That's a great idea, but there is a problem. You'd like to create a single base class that can instantiate your classes, with its custom client processing. However, that's hard to do without some special tricks.

You'll see that the code in Listing 2.24 uses an unusual technique to allow that one static member to create an instance of the class—even if that class is a subclass of the **MTServerBase** class. The idea is to pass a **Class** object into **startServer**. The method then uses the **newInstance** method to actually create the object. This assumes that your subclass has a default constructor, although you can use the reflection functions in **java.lang.reflection.Constructor** to call a nondefault constructor, if you wanted to modify the base class code.

This allows you to extend **MTServerBase** without providing a custom version of **startServer**. You can find a class object for a particular class type by appending **.class** to the ordinary name. If you have an instance of an object, you can use **getClass** to do the same thing. Because you pass the **startServer** method your class object, it can create an instance of your object using the **newInstance** method. Therefore, you don't have to replace the **startServer** method in your subclass.

Listing 2.24 You can use this base class to build multithreaded servers easily.

```
import java.net.*;
import java.io.*;

public class MTServerBase extends Thread {
    // client
    protected Socket socket;

    // Here is the thread that does the work
    // Presumably you'll override this in the subclass
    public void run() {
```

```
      try {
        String s = "I'm a test server. Goodbye";
        socket.getOutputStream().write(s.getBytes());
        socket.close();
        }
      catch (Exception e) {
        System.out.println(e);
        }
      }


  static public void startServer(int port,Class clobj) {
  ServerSocket ssock;
  Socket sock;
      try {
        ssock=new ServerSocket(port);
        while (true) {
          Socket esock=null;
            try {
              esock=ssock.accept();
// create new MTServerBase or subclass
              MTServerBase t=(MTServerBase)clobj.newInstance();
              t.socket=esock;
              t.start();
              } catch (Exception e) {
                try { esock.close(); } catch (Exception ec) {}
            }
          }
        } catch (IOException e) {
      }
    // if we return something is wrong!
    }



// Very simple test main
  static public void main(String args[]) {
    System.out.println("Starting server on port 808");
    MTServerBase.startServer(808,MTServerBase.class);
    }
  }
```

Listing 2.25 shows an example of how you can use this server base class to form another server. This particular server, which accepts the port number on the command line, converts lowercase input (from a Telnet program, for example) to uppercase. You can end the server by entering Control+C or Control+D.

Notice that the only code in the subclass is the **run** method and a new **main** to start the server properly. You can make any number of servers that derive from **MTServerBase** and focus on just the client interactions.

Listing 2.25   This example server uses the MTServerBase object.

```
import java.net.*;
import java.io.*;

public class UCServer extends MTServerBase {

  public void run() {
    try {
      InputStream is=socket.getInputStream();
      OutputStream os=socket.getOutputStream();
      while (true) {
        char c=(char)is.read();
// end on Control+C or Control+D
        if (c=='\003' || c=='\004') break;
        os.write(Character.toUpperCase(c));
        }
      socket.close();
      }
    catch (Exception e) {
      System.out.println(e);
      }
    }
  public static void main(String[] args) {
    int n = Integer.parseInt(args[0]);
    System.out.println("Starting server on port " + n);
    startServer(n,UCServer.class);

    }
  }
```

Servicing Clients with a Thread Pool

For medium-sized servers, creating a thread for every client is a great idea. However, for larger servers, the overhead of constantly creating and destroying threads could be prohibitive.

Java has many data structures you can use to hold thread objects. There are several ways you might build such a system, but the easiest is to construct a certain number of threads and simply use them as necessary to satisfy client requests.

The code in Listing 2.26 builds a linked list, starting with the static **head** variable. Each object has a **next** field that points to the next thread in the list.

The **init** method lets you set the number of threads in the pool and the class to use. The code immediately creates the specified number of threads. Each thread starts executing the **run** method, which immediately goes in to a **wait** state, waiting on the **Thread** object itself.

The remainder of the code is very similar to **MTServerBase**. The big difference is that when a client connection arrives via **accept**, the program simply picks the first thread off the list, removes it from the list, and calls **notify**. The built-in **run** method calls **doClientProcessing**, which you'd override to perform useful work. When this method returns, the thread puts itself back in the list and resumes waiting for more work.

Listing 2.26   Instead of creating a thread for each client, it is possible to manage a pool of threads as this server does.

```java
import java.net.*;
import java.io.*;

public class PoolServerBase extends Thread {
    // client
    protected Socket socket;
    // linked list of threads
    static PoolServerBase head=null;
    protected PoolServerBase next=null;

    // start server with number of threads
    static protected boolean init(Class clobj,int threads) {
      try {
        for (int i=0; i<threads; i++) {
          PoolServerBase thread = (PoolServerBase)clobj.newInstance();
          thread.next=head;
          head=thread;
          thread.start();
          }
        }
      catch (Exception e) { return false; }
      return true;
      }

  // add a thread to the list
    static synchronized protected void addToList(PoolServerBase me) {
      me.next=head;
      head=me;
      }
```

```
// hold thread until client arrives
   synchronized protected void waitForSignal() {
       try {
         wait();
         }
       catch (InterruptedException e) { }
    }

// main routine that schedules threads
   public void run() {
     while (true) {
       waitForSignal();
       doClientProcessing();
       addToList(this);
       }
     }

// Start a thread for a client
   synchronized protected void handleClient(Socket s) {
     socket=s;
     notify();
     }




   // Here is the code that does the work
   // Presumably you'll override this in the subclass
   protected void doClientProcessing() {
       try {
         String s = "I'm a test server. Goodbye";
         s+="Thread: " + this.toString();
         socket.getOutputStream().write(s.getBytes());
         sleep(10000);  // simulate processing
         s="Complete";
         socket.getOutputStream().write(s.getBytes());
         socket.close();
         }
       catch (Exception e) {
         System.out.println(e);
         }
       }

// Test for an empty list
   static synchronized protected boolean listEmpty() {
       return head==null;
       }
```

```
// assign a thread to a client
   static protected void assignThread(Socket sock) {
       PoolServerBase t=head;
       head=head.next;
       t.socket=sock;
       synchronized (t) {
         t.notify();
          }
       }


// Start up the server
    static public void startServer(int port) {
        ServerSocket ssock;
        Socket sock;
        try {
            ssock=new ServerSocket(port);
            while (true) {
            Socket esock=null;
            try {
                esock=ssock.accept();
// wait for non-empty thread list
                    while (listEmpty()) yield();
                    assignThread(esock);
                    } catch (Exception e) {
                    try { esock.close(); } catch (Exception ec) {}
                }
             }
         } catch (IOException e) {
      }
         // if we return something is wrong!
      }


// Very simple test main
    static public void main(String args[]) {
        init(PoolServerBase.class,3);
        System.out.println("Starting server on port 808");
        startServer(808);
       }
}
```

To make it simpler to debug and test this program, I placed an arbitrary 10-second delay in the default processing. Because each connection dumps its **Thread** object, you can easily make several connections and see that a different thread handles each connection. If you set the number of threads to a low number, you can see how the client will wait for an available thread and then reuse one that was previously in use.

You'll find an example of using the **PoolServerBase** class in Listing 2.27. This is the server used in the multithreading example earlier in this chapter. Telnet to the server, and it will echo characters back in uppercase. Enter a Control+C or a Control+D to end the session.

Listing 2.27   This example server uses **PoolServerBase** to manage a pool of threads.

```
import java.net.*;
import java.io.*;

public class UCServerPool extends PoolServerBase {

  protected void doClientProcessing() {
     try {
        InputStream is=socket.getInputStream();
        OutputStream os=socket.getOutputStream();
        while (true) {
           char c=(char)is.read();
// end on Control+C or Control+D
           if (c=='\003' || c=='\004') break;
           os.write(Character.toUpperCase(c));
           }
        socket.close();
        }
     catch (Exception e) {
        System.out.println(e);
        }
      }
  public static void main(String[] args) {
    int n = Integer.parseInt(args[0]);
    init(UCServerPool.class,10);
    System.out.println("Starting server on port " + n);
    startServer(n);

    }
  }
```

Chapter 3

Simple Protocols

In Depth

I've been a ham radio operator for almost 25 years. In addition, I've taught many students from different parts of the world. So I'm painfully aware of the reputation that Americans have. You know what I mean. Americans can't be bothered to learn the metric system, for example. Americans don't like to deal in other people's currency either.

Language is an especially embarrassing problem. Very few Americans (myself included) are bilingual. Worse still, most Americans think that if you scream loudly enough you can penetrate the non-English shell surrounding the American inside everyone.

Of course, America is a powerful country. It's no surprise that many people who don't speak English as a native tongue take the time to learn English. Of course, this just makes the problem worse. After all, if you can always find someone overseas that speaks your language, why bother learning the local language?

Communicating with computers via the network is similar. Both sides need to speak the same language. Popular protocols like Hypertext Transport Protocol (HTTP) force many clients to speak their language. Less-popular servers still impose their peculiar dialects on you.

In the last chapter, you learned how to open a socket and create sockets that clients can use. However, this is only half the battle. You still have to master the language involved in communicating with the other side.

Before you tackle more demanding protocols, it's a good idea to look at some simple protocols that have been around for a while. These are not as glamorous as HTTP, for example, but the ideas you'll use to work with these protocols will apply to more sophisticated servers that you'll write later.

In particular, this chapter will look at the following:

- Echo servers and clients that are mainly used for testing on the network
- Protocols for setting the time of day over the network
- Protocols for learning about users and machines

One ubiquitous protocol that you won't see in Java is **ping**. That's because **ping** uses Internet Control Message Protocol (ICMP)—a protocol that Java doesn't support directly.

Echo

The *echo protocol* (defined in RFC862) uses Transmission Control Protocol (TCP) or User Datagram Protocol (UDP) port 7 and is one of the simplest protocols to understand. Some of the servers in the last chapter were practically echo servers. An echo server just returns exactly what is sent to it.

One interesting thing about an echo server is that it is not very sensitive to peculiarities of the client. For example, suppose a client sends three lines of test messages to an echo server. If the client terminates the lines with new line characters, so does the echo server. If the client ends lines with carriage returns and new lines, the echo server returns those too. There isn't really any logic in the server that does this. To say that the echo server speaks multiple protocols would be like saying that a tape recorder knows all languages.

A TCP echo server is trivial because of the connection made by TCP sockets. When a client connects, the server simply sends everything it receives back over the same socket. UDP is a bit more difficult to handle, however. You have to extract the data from the UDP datagram and find the originating Internet Protocol (IP) address and port. Then you'll form another datagram to reply to the originator.

If a server is running an echo server, you can connect to it using a Telnet client to test it. Of course, a Java program can easily send and receive replies. You can find a TCP echo server in Listing 3.1.

Listing 3.1 This echo server uses multiple threads and a TCP socket.

```java
import java.io.*;

public class TcpEchoServer extends MTServerBase {
  public void run() {
    try {
      InputStream is = socket.getInputStream();
      OutputStream os = socket.getOutputStream();
      int c=0;
      while (c!=-1) {
        c=is.read();
        if (c!=-1) os.write(c);
        }
      }
    catch (IOException e) {
      System.out.println(e);
      }
    try {
      socket.close();
      }
    catch (IOException e) {}
    }
```

```
    public static void main(String [] args) {
      startServer(7,TcpEchoServer.class);
      }


    }
```

A UDP server isn't as similar as you might expect. Because each UDP packet is unique, there is no need to spin off multiple threads. Instead, you simply handle each packet as it arrives. The **DatagramPacket** object contains the address and port number of the program that sent the request. Therefore, you can use the exact same packet to return the data to the sender. You can find the code in Listing 3.2.

Listing 3.2   An echo server can also use UDP sockets.

```
import java.net.*;
import java.io.*;

public class UdpEchoServer {
  static final int BUFFERSIZE = 256;
  public static void main(String [] args) {
    DatagramSocket sock;
    DatagramPacket pack=new DatagramPacket(
      new byte[BUFFERSIZE],BUFFERSIZE);
    try {
      sock=new DatagramSocket(7);
      }
    catch (SocketException e) {
      System.out.println(e);
      return;
      }
// echo back everything
    while (true) {
      try {
        sock.receive(pack);
        sock.send(pack);
        }
      catch (IOException ioe) {
        System.out.println(ioe);
        }
      }
    }
}
```

You'll need a special client to exercise the UDP server. You can find one in Listing 3.3. Because there is no connection, the client could wait forever for a reply. To keep that from happening, the code calls **setSoTimeout** so that the maximum wait is 5 seconds (5,000 milliseconds). If there is no reply within that time, the **read** call throws an **InterruptedIOException**.

One possible use for an echo server is to estimate the speed of a network connection. The client in Listing 3.3 estimates the round-trip time. Of course, the simplified approach used by this program ignores the overhead involved in creating the **Calendar** objects, but it will give you a relative idea of the speed between different hosts.

Listing 3.3 This echo client estimates the speed of the network connection to the server.

```java
import java.net.*;
import java.io.*;
import java.util.Calendar;
public class UdpEchoClient {
  static final String testString = "Greeks bearing gifts";
  public static void main(String [] args) {
    InetAddress address;
    try {
      address = InetAddress.getByName(args[0]);
    }
    catch (UnknownHostException host) {
      System.out.println(host);
      return;
    }
    DatagramPacket pack=new DatagramPacket(
      testString.getBytes(),testString.length(),
      address,7);
    DatagramPacket incoming=new DatagramPacket(
      new byte[256],256);
    DatagramSocket sock=null;
    try {
      Calendar start, end;
      sock = new DatagramSocket();
      start = Calendar.getInstance();
      sock.send(pack);
      sock.setSoTimeout(5000);
      sock.receive(incoming);
      end = Calendar.getInstance();
      String reply = new String(incoming.getData());
      reply=reply.substring(0,testString.length());
      if (reply.equals(testString)) {
        System.out.println("Success");
```

```
      System.out.println("Time = " +
          (end.getTime().getTime()-start.getTime().getTime()) +
          "mS");
        }
      else
        System.out.println("Reply data did not match");        }
    catch (SocketException socke) {
      System.out.println(socke);
        }
    catch (IOException ioe) {
      System.out.println(ioe);
        }
    finally {
      sock.close();
        }
      }
  }
```

One oddity about this echo server is that it can't distinguish between a specific request and one that was broadcast. So, if you run the server and then call the client program with a broadcast address (for example, 255.255.255.255), it will respond—along with any other copies running on other machines.

You could run two different echo servers—one to handle TCP and one to handle UDP. However, a real echo server should listen for both TCP and UDP requests. You can combine the two quite easily by writing a class that wraps both servers into a single class (see Listing 3.4).

Listing 3.4   This class joins the TCP and UDP echo servers into one program.

```
class EchoServerUdp extends Thread {
  public void run() {
    UdpEchoServer.main(null);
    }
  }

public class EchoServer extends TcpEchoServer {
 public static void main(String [] args) {
   new EchoServerUdp().start();  // start UDP thread
   TcpEchoServer.main(args);
   }

  }
```

The **EchoServerUdp** class is not declared **public**, so it can reside in the same file as **EchoServer**. It simply represents a thread that starts the existing **UdpEcho-**

Server object. The **EchoServer** object itself only extends **TcpEchoServer**. The only thing it does is replace the **main** function. The new **main** starts the UDP thread and then passes control back to the original **main**. It is allowed to open a UDP and TCP socket on the same port.

An even simpler protocol—the discard service—appears in RFC863. This service uses port 9 (TCP or UDP) and just discards everything sent to it.

Finger

The finger protocol (defined in RFC1288, which updates RFC1196 and RFC742) is very familiar to Unix users but perhaps less so to those who have roots in other operating systems. The idea is that a client can finger a host to find out information about that host (typically a list of users currently logged in to the machine). Additionally, you can finger a particular user to get information about that user. A typical Unix host will show some basic information about the user (his or her real name and location, for example) and information in the user's .plan file. Other operating systems may show other information (or even no information). Different hosts may elect to provide other information as a response to finger— the protocol doesn't really stipulate what data finger returns.

Finger servers use TCP port 79. The client sends a single-line request. The server replies and closes the connection. The RFC specifies that lines end with a carriage return and line feed. It also recommends that the client filter out any non-ASCII data.

To finger an entire host, the client simply sends a blank line. If you want to finger a particular user, the line should contain the user's ID. It is permissible to ask for more than one user by placing the IDs on the same line, separated by a space. The RFC specifies that you can add a **/W** option to the command line to get verbose output, although the server is free to ignore that option if it wants to do so.

In addition to querying a machine for a user, you can also request that a machine forward a finger request to another machine by adding an **@** sign to the hostname. Because several well-known worm programs have used finger, many sites no longer run finger servers. Of those that do, many restrict the use of finger. For example, very few servers allow forward requests to other machines. Many public servers will not show a list of all users, even if you send a blank request. The RFC requires that you return a refusal to a request you won't accept. The RFC also requires you to show at least the full name of the user, if you are processing requests. However, in practice, clients rarely expect a particular format of data.

A finger client is easy to write (see Listing 3.5). Because you can't be too sure about the format of the returned data, the client code just dumps the returned data as a **String**. The calling program (for example, the **main** function) can format and display the returned data as it sees fit.

Because different platforms use different line-ending combinations, the client code specifically uses **\r\n** to match the standard set by the specification. In addition, because only ASCII characters are allowed, the code uses a specific byte encoding by passing the name of the encoding (ISO8859_1) to the **getBytes** method.

Encoding

The **getBytes** method, along with other methods that work with bytes and characters, can take an encoding string to determine how to convert between Unicode characters and bytes. This is required because Unicode characters require two bytes. The programs in this chapter use the ISO8859_1 encoding—one of several character encodings supported by Java.

The following are basic encodings that Java supports:
- *ASCII*—American Standard Code for Information Interchange
- *Cp1252*—Windows Latin-1
- *ISO8859_1*—ISO 8859_1, Latin alphabet number 1
- *UnicodeBig*—Sixteen-bit Unicode Transformation Format (UTF), big-endian byte order, with byte-order mark
- *UnicodeLittle*—Sixteen-bit UTF, little-endian byte order, with byte-order mark
- *UnicodeLittleUnmarked*—Sixteen-bit UTF, little-endian byte order
- *UTF8*—Eight-bit UTF
- *UTF-16*—Sixteen-bit UTF, byte order specified by a mandatory initial byte-order mark

Up to (and including) HTML 3.2, the HTML specification called for using the ISO 8859_1 character set. Of course, many browsers didn't follow this exactly, and later versions of the HTML specification allow for other encodings. So, for Web work, ISO 8859_1 is usually safe. Other Internet protocols are usually mute about which character set or sets you should support. The safest bet would probably be ASCII, but many hosts will recognize ISO 8859_1 character sets also.

In addition, international versions of Java can support many other encodings. You'll find more about these encodings in the "Immediate Solutions" section.

Listing 3.5   This finger client allows you to query a remote host.

```
import java.net.*;
import java.io.*;

public class Finger {
    public String finger(String host, String users)
        throws IOException, SocketException {
        String outstring="";
```

3. Simple Protocols

```
        int c=0;
        Socket sock=new Socket(host,79);
        OutputStream os = sock.getOutputStream();
        InputStream is = sock.getInputStream();
        users = users + "\r\n";
        os.write(users.getBytes("iso8859_1"));
        try {
            while (c!=-1) {
              c=is.read();
              if (c!=-1) outstring+=(char)c;
            }
        }
        catch (IOException e) {}
        return outstring;
    }
    public static void main(String[] args) {
        String hostname = "";
        String ulist = "";
        if (args.length==0) {
            System.out.println("usage: finger host [user...]");
            System.exit(1);
        }
        if (args.length>=2)
            for (int i=1; i<args.length; i++)
              ulist+=args[i]+" ";
        hostname=args[0];
        Finger worker = new Finger();
        try {
          System.out.println(worker.finger(hostname,ulist.trim()));
        }
        catch (Exception e) {
            System.out.println(e);
        }
    }
}
```

This object would be easy to use in other Java programs. For example, Listing 3.6 shows a Java Server Page (JSP) that uses the object to provide a Web-based finger gateway (see Figure 3.1). To try this, you'll need a JSP Web server, such as Tomcat or Allaire's JRun. In addition, you'll need to put the compiled Finger.class file in a directory that is on the server's class path. If you have a JSP application directory, you can use the WEB-INF/classes directory, although this may vary depending on how your system is set up and which server it uses.

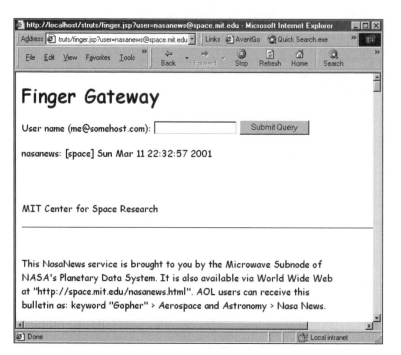

Figure 3.1   A web-based finger gateway.

Listing 3.6   This JSP provides a Web-based finger gateway.

```
<H1>Finger Gateway</H1>
<FORM SUBMIT=finger.jsp METHOD=GET>
User name (me@somehost.com): <INPUT NAME=user>
<INPUT TYPE=SUBMIT>
</FORM>
<%
if (request.getParameter("user")!=null) {
  Finger fing = new Finger();
  String inp = request.getParameter("user");
  String u;
  String host;
  int at = inp.indexOf('@');
  if (at==-1) {
     u="";
     host=inp;
     }
   else {
     host=inp.substring(at+1);
     u=inp.substring(0,at);
     }
```

```
      String s;
      try {
          s = fing.finger(host,u);
          }
      catch (Exception sexc) {
        s="Unknown host or network error";
          }

      int n0=0;
      do {
        int n=s.indexOf('\n',n0);
        if (n==-1) {
          out.print(s);
          break;
          }
        out.print(s.substring(n0,n) + "<BR>");
        n0=n+1;
        } while (n0!=s.length());
}
%>
```

You'll notice that the JSP page allows you to enter a typical email address (for example, **alw@coriolis.com**). The code automatically extracts the hostname and the user ID to pass to the **finger** method. The script converts new lines to **
** tags so the display will look better in the browser. The JSP file is self-contained. It submits data back to the same page and does processing as appropriate. This is handy for the developer because there is only one file to handle, and it's nice for the user because you can issue a new request from the same page that you use to view the previous request's data.

You might want to operate a custom finger server for a variety of reasons. For example, you might want to make network status available by using finger. A computer connected to real-world sensors might use finger to make that data available to other computers on the network. The server is a bit more difficult to write because you have to accept (or deny) the different requests defined by the protocol. Listing 3.7 shows a complete server implementation based on the **MTServerBase** object from Chapter 2.

Listing 3.7 This finger server uses a property file to control its responses.

```
import java.io.*;
import java.util.*;
import java.net.*;

public class FingerServer extends MTServerBase {
  static Properties prop=null;
```

```
public FingerServer() {
  if (prop==null) {
    prop = new Properties();
    try {
      prop.load(new FileInputStream("FingerServer.prop"));
      }
    catch (IOException e) {
      System.out.println("FingerServer.prop not present");
      }
    }
  }

void socketClose() {
  try {
    socket.close();
    }
  catch (IOException e) {}
  }

public void run() {
 BufferedReader is;
 OutputStreamWriter os;
 String s;
 String cmd;
 try {
   is = new BufferedReader(
     new InputStreamReader(socket.getInputStream()));
   os = new OutputStreamWriter(socket.getOutputStream(),
   " iso8859_1");
   }
 catch (Exception ioe) {
   System.out.println("Can't create streams\n" + ioe);
   socketClose();
   return;
   }
 // read command line
 try {
   cmd=is.readLine();
   }
 catch (IOException e) {
   socketClose();
   return;
   }

 // look up entry
```

```
    if (cmd.equals(""))
      cmd="*default";

// parse multiple requests
    StringTokenizer tok = new StringTokenizer(cmd);
    String token;
    while (tok.hasMoreTokens()) {
      token=tok.nextToken();
      if (token.equals("/W")||token.equals("/w"))
        continue;
      if (token.indexOf('@')==-1)
        s=prop.getProperty(token,"Not Found");
      else
        s="Finger forwarding service denied";
      // write it out
      try {
        s+="\r\n";
        os.write(s,0,s.length());
        os.flush();
        }
      catch (IOException we) {
        System.out.println("Write exception: " + we);
        }
      }

  socketClose();
  }

  public static void main(String [] args) {
    startServer(79,FingerServer.class);
    }

}
```

The **FingerServer** object provides a custom constructor. This constructor opens a properties file named FingerServer.prop (see Listing 3.8). This file contains keys that correspond to user names and values that indicate what you want to return in response to requests. The server denies forwarding requests. If a client makes a blank request, the server returns the ***default** property.

Again, the server uses the ISO8859_1 encoding. The server uses **readLine** to accept the command from the client. Then **StringTokenizer** breaks it into separate tokens for processing. The host ignores the **/W** option (it also checks for **/w**, just to be safe). Any token that contains an **@** character generates a denial message because the server doesn't support forwarding.

Listing 3.8   This property file defines two users and a default response for the finger server.

```
alw=Al Williams, League City TX
raya=Ray Argus, Houston TX
*default=This is the example Java finger server at AWC.
```

One interesting point about servers—they must provide information, but the information doesn't have to actually reside on that server. This idea forms the basis of n-tier systems and proxy servers (a topic you'll learn more about in Chapter 13). A server may delegate its responsibilities to another server.

Listing 3.9 shows a finger server that uses this idea. It simply forwards finger requests to another machine that you specify on the command line. This is—in a way—a proxy server. The Java server acts as a stand-in—a proxy—for the real server on another machine. To connect to the real server, the program uses the existing **Finger** class from Listing 3.6.

Listing 3.9   This class acts as a proxy, forwarding finger requests to a remote server.

```java
import java.net.*;
import java.io.*;

public class FingerProxy extends MTServerBase {
    static String parentHost;

    void socketClose() {
    try {
      socket.close();
      }
    catch (IOException e) {}
    }

    public void run() {
       Finger fing = new Finger();
       BufferedReader is;
       OutputStreamWriter os;
       String s;
       String cmd;
       try {
           is = new BufferedReader(
             new InputStreamReader(socket.getInputStream()));
           os = new OutputStreamWriter(socket.getOutputStream(),
             "iso8859_1");
           }
       catch (Exception ioe) {
           System.out.println("Can't create streams\n" + ioe);
           socketClose();
           return;
           }
```

3. Simple Protocols

```
   // read command line
   try {
     cmd=is.readLine();
     }
   catch (IOException e) {
     socketClose();
     return;
    }


   try {
      s=fing.finger(parentHost,cmd);
      os.write(s,0,s.length());
      os.flush();
      }
    catch (IOException we) {
      System.out.println("Write exception: " + we);
      }
   socketClose();
   }

   public static void main(String [] args) {
     parentHost=args[0];
     startServer(79,FingerProxy.class);
     }
}
```

Intercepting requests can serve many purposes—debugging a connection, for example. Some proxy servers act as an intermediary between two computers that can't normally communicate with each other because of security restrictions. A finger proxy is probably not the most practical proxy you'll ever see, but for some other protocols, proxies are very important.

Whois

Another protocol that can provide information about people is the whois command. The big difference between whois and finger is that information for whois resides in one of a few centralized servers. In particular, **whois.internic.net** is the main server that identifies data for domains. However, there are some other servers that supply whois data. Each domain registrar supplies their own whois server. For example, Network Solutions has a whois server at **whois.networksolutions.com**.

Data from a whois server is in an unspecified, human-readable format and is similar to an address book. The original specification appears in RFC954. With the proliferation of the Internet, and the advent of multiple registrars, a more robust system is needed. A proposal to replace whois with the system defined in RFC1913 and RFC1914 has been issued, but this new system is not in wide use.

The protocol is not much different from finger. You simply open a TCP socket on port 43 to the whois server (usually **whois.internic.net**). Once again, you send a single line (terminated by **\r\n**) to the server. This line contains a name, a list of names, a partial name, or a domain name.

The output of the whois command varies between different servers and changes from time to time, even on the same server (the command set is not especially fixed either). For the Internic server, every entity has a handle (for example, mine is AW1127). Searching on this handle will find an exact match. Anything else is likely to show multiple matches.

You can trim the output somewhat by adding one or more prefixes to your search string (see Table 3.1). For example, you can add the word domain to your search to restrict the output to domain names only. Different servers may recognize or ignore different commands. You can use Telnet to log in to the server and issue a **help** command to see the commands for a specific server.

Table 3.1   Common whois command prefixes.

Prefix	Effect
domain	Restrict to domains
handle	Restrict to handle
nameserver	Restrict to name servers
registrar	Restrict to registrars
expand	Show complete record for single match
full	Show long display for every record
host	Restrict to hosts
mailbox	Restrict to email addresses (or use an **@** in the query)
organization	Restrict to organizations
partial	Match starting portion of record (or end query with a period)
person	Restrict to persons
server	Restrict to servers
summary	Show summary only
=	Same as Expand
~	Never show subdisplays (opposite of expand)
!	Same as handle
$	Same as summary

Listing 3.10 shows a class that implements a whois client. By default, the **main** routine uses the Network Solutions server, but you can override this by naming the server as the first command line argument preceded by an % character.

Listing 3.10   This whois client defaults to the whois.internic.net server.

```
import java.net.*;
import java.io.*;

public class Whois {
    public void whois(String query) throws IOException {
    whois(query,"whois.internic.net");
    }

    public String whois(String query, String server) throws IOException {
        Socket sock = new Socket(server,43);
        int c=0;
        String outstring="";
        OutputStream os = sock.getOutputStream();
        InputStream is = sock.getInputStream();
        query += "\r\n";
        os.write(query.getBytes("iso8859_1"));
        try {
            while (c!=-1) {
              c=is.read();
              if (c!=-1) outstring+=(char)c;
            }
        }
        catch (IOException e) {}
        return outstring;
    }
    public static void main(String[] args) {
        String hostname = "";
        String ulist = "";
        if (args.length==0) {
            System.out.println("usage: whois [%host] query");
            System.exit(1);
        }
        int argn=0;
        hostname="whois.networksolutions.com"; // default
        if (args.length>1 && args[0].charAt(0)=='%') {
            hostname=args[argn].substring(1);
             argn++;
        }
         for (int i=argn; i<args.length; i++)
             ulist+=args[i]+" ";
```

```
                Whois worker = new Whois();
                try {
                    System.out.println(worker.whois(ulist.trim(),hostname));
                }
                catch (Exception e) {
                    System.out.println(e);
                }
            }
        }
```

Basic Time Protocols

If you have a network of computers, it is very annoying if they don't all have the same idea of the current time. Files that have the incorrect timestamps can cause program builds to work incorrectly and play havoc with any scheme to synchronize files.

It's no surprise that one service available on the network is a way to get another machine's idea of the time. If all machines on the network synchronize to a single time source, you'll have fewer problems with machines having time problems.

In fact, the RFCs don't define a single service. They define two different ones: RFC867 provides human-readable time in an undefined format, and RFC868 provides the time in a machine-readable form.

RFC867 calls for a server to send the time to any caller on TCP or UDP port 13. Because the time format is not specified (the RFC suggests two common formats), this requires little more than a finger client or server altered to report the time.

Several well-known servers keep their time synchronized to an atomic standard clock and can serve as a time reference for the network (see Table 3.2). Some of these servers are primary servers, but others are secondary servers that synchronize to the primary ones. For most purposes, the secondary servers are just as good as—and may have higher availability than—the primary ones.

Table 3.2   Some time servers.

URL	IP	Location
tock.usno.navy.mil	192.5.41.41	U.S. Navy
tock.usnogps.navy.mil	204.34.198.41	U.S. Navy
time-a.nist.gov	129.6.15.28	NIST, Gaithersburg, Maryland
time-b.nist.gov	129.6.15.29	NIST, Gaithersburg, Maryland
time-a.timefreq.bldrdoc.gov	132.163.4.101	NIST, Boulder, Colorado
time-b.timefreq.bldrdoc.gov	132.163.4.102	NIST, Boulder, Colorado

(continued)

3. Simple Protocols

Table 3.2   Some time servers *(continued)*.

URL	IP	Location
time-c.timefreq.bldrdoc.gov	132.163.4.103	NIST, Boulder, Colorado
utcnist.colorado.edu	128.138.140.44	University of Colorado, Boulder
time.nist.gov	192.43.244.18	NCAR, Boulder, Colorado
time-nw.nist.gov	131.107.1.10	Microsoft, Redmond, Washington
nist1.datum.com	63.149.208.50	Datum, San Jose, California
nist1.dc.glassey.com	216.200.93.8	Abovenet, Virginia
nist1.ny.glassey.com	208.184.49.9	Abovenet, New York City
nist1.sj.glassey.com	207.126.103.204	Abovenet, San Jose, California
nist1.aol-ca.truetime.com	207.200.81.113	TrueTime, AOL facility, Sunnyvale, California
nist1.aol-va.truetime.com	205.188.185.33	TrueTime, AOL facility, Virginia

It doesn't matter what, if anything, you send to the host (use Telnet to connect to port 13 of any of the servers in Table 3.2, and you'll see what I mean). Unfortunately, the format of the returned data varies wildly. Here's an output from one of the U.S. Naval Observatory servers:

```
Fri Mar  9 14:28:06 2001
```

However, here is one taken about a minute later from NIST (the National Institute of Standards and Technology):

```
51977 01-03-09 14:29:14 74 0 0 651.2 UTC(NIST) *
```

NIST documents its format on its Web site. Here are the elements of the response:

- **51977**—This is the modified Julian day. Modified means that it is the last 5 digits of the actual Julian day, which by convention begins at January 1, 4713 B.C. Adding 2.4 million to this number results in a proper Julian day.

- **01-03-09**—This is the date in year, month, day format.

- **14:29:14**—The time in hour, minute, second format. The time is always Coordinated Universal Time (UTC).

- **74**—This code indicates if the United States is, with some exceptions, observing daylight savings time. If the code is 00, then daylight savings time is not in effect. If the code is 50, then daylight savings time is in effect. If the current date is within a month of the daylight savings time changes, the number counts down the days to the change. So, in the current example, there are 23 days (50+23+1=74) until daylight savings time will be in effect.

3. Simple Protocols

- **0**—The first zero indicates that there will be no leap second correction applied to the clock at the end of this month. A 1 in this field indicates that there will be a leap second added to the clock at the end of this month. A 2 means the leap second will be subtracted instead.

- **0**—The second zero indicates the server's current health. A zero indicates that the server is operating properly. If the field is a 1, the time may be off by up to 5 seconds. A 2 indicates a possible error of more than 5 seconds. A 4 here means something is wrong, and the time could be totally wrong.

- **651.2**—This is the number of milliseconds added to the time to attempt to mitigate network delays (this was done over a TCP/IP satellite, which has a long delay).

- **UTC(NIST)**—This time zone indicator indicates Coordinated Universal Time. You might wonder why UTC is the abbreviation for Coordinated Universal Time. When the International Telecommunications Union standardized UTC, the Americans wanted to use CUT as an abbreviation. The French, however, wanted to use TUC to reflect the word ordering in French. Because neither side would budge, UTC is a compromise. In the past, UTC was known as Greenwich Mean Time (GMT), or zulu time.

- *****—When you call a time-of-day service on the phone, the operator will say, "At the tone, the time will be . . . " The asterisk is—for practical purposes—the tone. The time indicated is valid when you receive this character. Of course, with network delays and other problems, this could be off by a bit, but it will be close.

A simple client for this protocol appears in Listing 3.11. This is little more than a stripped-down version of one of the finger clients presented earlier. By default, the program uses a U.S. Naval Observatory server, but you can change that by naming a different server on the command line. Because the time server doesn't require any input, there is no need for the client to send anything at all. Simply making the connection is sufficient to retrieve the time data using TCP.

You can perform the same task using UDP (also on port 13), but then you do have to send a meaningless data packet to the server. This packet allows the server to answer because UDP has no connection to signal that a client is requesting data.

Listing 3.11   This server retrieves the time using the RFC867 protocol.

```
import java.net.*;
import java.io.*;

public class Time867 {
    public static void main(String[] args) {
        String hostname = "tock.usno.navy.mil";
        if (args.length==1) hostname=args[0];
```

```
    try {
    int c;
    Socket sock=new Socket(hostname,13);
    InputStream is = sock.getInputStream();
    do {
      c=is.read();
      if (c!=-1) System.out.print((char)c);
      } while (c!=-1);
    }
    catch (IOException e) { System.out.println(e); }
  }
}
```

Writing the server is a little trickier but only because the **Date** class that Java supplies is so awkward to use. The **DateFormat** class (from the **java.text** package) allows you to format a **Date** object, and the server uses this to generate the string required. If you are a stickler, you should be aware that the Java classes that deal with dates usually don't account for things such as leap seconds, so this server is not as precise as, for example, the NIST server. However, for most purposes, it is close enough.

Although this server only handles TCP requests, it would be easy to modify the UDP echo server to perform the same task (see Listing 3.12). Then you could join the two servers, just like the dual echo server does in Listing 3.4.

Listing 3.12   This server provides time data to RFC867 clients using TCP.

```
// Server for RFC867 time (TCP only)
import java.io.*;
import java.util.*;
import java.text.DateFormat;

public class Server867 extends MTServerBase {
    public void run() {
        try {
          OutputStream os = socket.getOutputStream();
          Date cal = new Date();
          DateFormat df=DateFormat.getDateTimeInstance(
              DateFormat.FULL,DateFormat.FULL);
          df.setTimeZone(TimeZone.getTimeZone("GMT"));
          String output=df.format(cal)
              +"\r\n";;
          os.write(output.getBytes("iso8859_1"));
          os.flush();
          socket.close();
          }
        catch (IOException e) {}
    }
```

```
        public static void main(String[] args) {
            startServer(13,Server867.class);
        }
    }
```

Another service defined by RFC868 exists and is more apt to be useful for machines. In this protocol, clients that connect to port 37 (either TCP or UDP) will receive the current date and time as a 32-bit number. This number represents the number of seconds since midnight, January 1, 1900.

WARNING! In 2036, this service will roll over. Perhaps this will trigger another Y2K-like crisis. Of course, I'll be 73 by then and hopefully retired!

The **Date** object can return the number of milliseconds since midnight, January 1, 1970, using **getTime**, so there is a bit of a mismatch here. For practical purposes, you can just divide the result by 1000 (to get seconds) and then add 2,208,988,800 seconds (the number of seconds in 70 years after accounting for leap years). You can find an example server (again, TCP only) in Listing 3.13.

Listing 3.13   This class implements an RFC868 time server.

```
// Server for RFC868 time
import java.io.*;
import java.util.*;
import java.text.DateFormat;

public class Server868 extends MTServerBase {
    public void run() {
      try {
       OutputStream os = socket.getOutputStream();
          long tick = new Date().getTime()/1000;
          byte [] outarray = new byte[4];
          tick+=2208988800L;
          outarray[0]=(byte)((tick & 0xFF000000L)>>24);
          outarray[1]=(byte)((tick & 0xFF0000L)>>16);
          outarray[2]=(byte)((tick & 0xFF00L)>>8);
          outarray[3]=(byte)(tick & 0xFFL);
          os.write(outarray);
          os.flush();
          socket.close();
          }
       catch (IOException e) {}
      }
    public static void main(String[] args) {
        startServer(37,Server868.class);
    }
}
```

The client, however, presents a unique problem. Java is not very good at handling unsigned arithmetic. However, when you try to form a **long** from the array of bytes you receive from the server, you'll wind up with negative numbers that will cause all sorts of trouble.

One possible solution appears in Listing 3.14. The code strips the topmost bit to ensure the result will be positive. Then, before adjusting the time between 1970 and 1900, the program determines if the topmost bit was set. If it is, it subtracts 0x80000000 from the adjustment number. This has the same effect but avoids accidentally making the number negative.

Listing 3.14   You can use this client to find the time from an RFC868 server.

```
import java.util.*;
import java.net.*;
import java.io.*;
import java.text.DateFormat;

public class Client868 {
    public static void main(String [] args) {
        Socket sock=null;
        try {
          sock=new Socket(args[0],37);
          byte [] inarrayb=new byte[4];
          int [] inarray=new int[4];
          Date date=new Date();
          long tick;
           InputStream is=sock.getInputStream();
          is.read(inarrayb);
// convert array to integers
        for (int i=0;i<4;i++) {
            inarray[i]=inarrayb[i];
            inarray[i]&=0xFF;
        }
        int tmp=inarray[0];
// make positive
        inarray[0]&=0x7F;
        tick=(inarray[0]<<24)+(inarray[1]<<16)+(inarray[2]<<8)+inarray[3];
        long adj=2208988800L;
// if original number was >=0x80000000, adjust the adjustment
        if ((tmp&0x80)==0x80) {
            adj-=0x7FFFFFFF;
            adj--;
        }
          tick-=adj; // convert between 1900/1970
          tick*=1000;  // convert to mS
          date.setTime(tick);
```

```
            DateFormat df=DateFormat.getDateTimeInstance(
                DateFormat.FULL,DateFormat.FULL);
            System.out.println(df.format(date));
        }
        catch (IOException e) {
            System.out.println(e);
            return;
        }
        finally {
            try {
                    sock.close();
            }
            catch (IOException e) {}
        }
        }
    }
```

All this extra work is simply a function of the lack of an unsigned data type in Java. C programs don't have this problem. Another solution, which is somewhat cleaner, involves using the **BigInteger** class in the **java.math** package. You'll find this approach in the "Immediate Solutions" section.

For more precise timekeeping, you can use the more advanced Network Time Protocol (NTP). RFC1305, and a few earlier documents, define NTP, which allows you to connect to multiple time servers and continuously update the correct time.

Immediate Solutions

Using the Echo Protocol

The echo protocol is one of the simplest possible protocols to use and is often a good way to perform a pseudo-ping (Java versions prior to 1.4 can't directly implement **ping** because they do not handle the ICMP protocol).

To use an echo server, simply open a socket (TCP or UDP) to port 7. Whatever you send to the server will return to you. You can use this for testing, timing network operations, or estimating loss over a UDP socket.

For an example, you can find an echo client that uses UDP in Listing 3.3.

WARNING! Because UDP does not ensure delivery—or even that the remote server exists—the program sets a time-out so that it doesn't wait forever for a host that will never answer.

Writing a TCP Echo Server

Writing an echo server may not seem very exciting. However, a simple echo server can serve as a basis for more complicated servers because the mechanisms used to connect, receive, and transmit data are present in all servers.

1. Use the **MTServerBase** object from Chapter 2 to concisely write a TCP echo server (see Listing 3.1). The server, of course, uses port 7.

2. Send everything you receive immediately back to the client using the following:

```
while (c!=-1) {
  c=is.read();
  if (c!=-1) os.write(c);
  }
```

Related solution:	Found on page:
Automating the Multithreaded Server	53

Writing a UDP Echo Server

A UDP server for the echo protocol is a bit different from the TCP variety. You don't need threads because each packet is a single independent request. Furthermore, you don't have a connection to send the data back to the client, so you'll have to pick out the correct IP address and port number from the **Datagram-Packet** object. Luckily, if you use the same packet to send as you do to receive, this isn't a problem. You can find the complete code for a UDP echo server in Listing 3.2.

The echo portion is quite simple:

```
while (true) {
  try {
    sock.receive(pack);
    sock.send(pack);
    }
  catch (IOException ioe) {
    System.out.println(ioe);
    }
```

However, for a different kind of server, you'd want to extract the address and port number from the packet using **getAddress** and **getPort**.

Joining a TCP and UDP Server

If you were writing a real echo server, you'd want to make it listen on the TCP and UDP ports simultaneously. Many other types of servers require this type of dual port operation as well.

Often, it is simpler to get each portion of the server working separately (perhaps using a common object to perform processing). Then, once everything is working properly, it is a simple matter to join them together. Typically, you'll use the TCP code as is but you'll add code to the **main** method to start a new thread that will run the UDP server.

Consider the two echo servers mentioned in the last two sections. One does TCP and the other does UDP. To join these two servers, simply do the following:

1. Make a new class that turns the UDP server into a thread. This class doesn't add any network functions; it simply calls the server's **main** routine when the thread starts.

```
class EchoServerUdp extends Thread {
  public void run() {
    UdpEchoServer.main(null);
    }
  }
```

2. Modify the TCP server to start the thread:

```
public class EchoServer extends TcpEchoServer {
  public static void main(String [] args) {
    new EchoServerUdp().start();  // start UDP thread
    TcpEchoServer.main(args);
    }
  }
```

Using this modular approach, you can develop and debug the two servers independently. If there is significant work to be done, the two server objects can share a third object that does the work, so you don't have to recode the actual logic.

Using a Finger Server

The finger protocol allows you to learn about a machine or user on a machine. You can request general information, usually a list of users or perhaps a list of user IDs, or information about a specific user.

WARNING! Many servers restrict finger or disallow it completely because it may represent a security hole. In particular, very few sites allow you to get a list of users because this is useful to hackers trying to find passwords.

To open a connection to a finger server, do the following:

1. Use TCP port 79.
2. The client sends a single-line request (terminated by a carriage return and line feed). A blank line indicates that the client wants information about the machine.
3. The server returns information about each user.

Of course, what the server returns depends on the operating system and the finger server in use. The RFC (RFC1288) indicates that the server must return at least the user's real name. Of course, some systems use finger for other purposes, so that's not always true, either. On a Unix system, the server will return some statistics about the user plus the content of the user's .plan file, if it exists.

Because Java uses Unicode strings, you'll need to convert those to ASCII bytes. Instead of relying on the default encoding scheme, it is often a good idea to provide a specific mapping between Unicode and ASCII. You'll also want to explicitly add the carriage return and line feed to the request because this is not standard on all operating systems.

Assuming you have a list of users in the **String users** and the name of the remote machine in **host**, the following code will write the request:

```
Socket sock=new Socket(host,79);
OutputStream os = sock.getOutputStream();
InputStream is = sock.getInputStream();
users = users + "\r\n";
os.write(users.getBytes("iso8859_1"));
```

This uses the ISO8859_1 encoding. Other possible choices include ASCII or CP1252.

The server will reply with data, but there is no set format for the response. You can simply display it as it arrives if you are writing an interactive finger client. Finger servers also support a forward request, where the remote computer fingers another computer at your request. However, very few sites allow this because there is no good reason for it and it represents a security risk.

Another possible option on the request is a **/W** flag. If the client provides this flag, the server can interpret it as a request for detailed information. However, the server is not obligated to actually provide any more information or change its format.

You'll find a complete example in Listing 3.5. Also, in Listing 3.6, you can find a JSP finger gateway that uses the class in Listing 3.5.

Writing a Finger Server

Writing a finger server requires you to accept and parse the command sent by the client and formulate an appropriate response. Exactly what that response is will be up to you. For example, fingering **nasanews@space.mit.edu** will display NASA-related news.

When writing a finger server, you'll need to:

- Look for a **/W** argument, even if you don't plan to process it. User IDs that contain an @ character are requests for forwards, which most servers will not allow.

TIP: *The **StringTokenizer** class is useful for breaking apart the command line you receive from the client.*

- Create a map between Unicode characters and bytes. It's a good idea to specify an explicit encoding (for example, **iso8859_1**) when creating a **Writer** object or obtaining bytes from a **String** object to send through an **OutputStream**.

You'll find a complete finger server in Listing 3.7. The **readLine** method of **Input-StreamReader** gets the command line. Once the server formulates and sends the output, it flushes the output stream to ensure all characters are sent. Then it closes the socket as required by the specification for finger.

Related solution:	Found on page:
Automating the Multithreaded Server	53

Creating a Simple Proxy

Many protocols, notably HTTP and FTP, are used through proxy servers. A *proxy server* is a server that acts as a middleman for a client. This is useful, for example, on corporate networks where you don't want direct access between the client (on the network) and a server (on the public Internet).

You'll find an HTTP proxy in Chapter 12. However, you can easily make a finger proxy from what you know now. Although a finger proxy is unusual, it is a good proxy to study because of its simplicity.

A proxy has knowledge of the underlying protocol it is passing. In this case, the finger proxy acts just like a finger server, but instead of directly formulating the reply to client commands, it delegates the responsibility to another host.

Take the following steps to create a finger proxy:

1. Reuse the finger client from Listing 3.5 to get the correct output.

2. Once the output appears from the true finger server, relay it to the origina-tor. From the client's point of view, you are a finger server because it made a request, and you replied. The fact that you asked another server for the correct response isn't immediately apparent. You can find the code for this proxy in Listing 3.9.

3. The proxy sends incoming requests to the parent finger server and displays the results:

```
s=fing.finger(parentHost,cmd); // ask parent
os.write(s,0,s.length());  // send output
os.flush();  // flush the output
```

Related solution:	Found on page:
Writing a Proxy Server	434

Using Whois

The **whois** protocol is similar to finger, but it queries a master server for many different entity types. The master whois database is at whois.internic.net. Network Solutions, the original registrar, has a server at whois.networksolutions.com. This protocol (defined by RFC954) is similar to finger. You open a TCP socket to port 43 and send a single-line command terminated by a carriage return and line feed.

What the server exactly is searching for depends on the server. Also, you can use a server-specific set of commands to restrict the search in different ways (see Table 3.1). If you Telnet to a server (using port 43) and issue a **help** command, you will probably see a list of accepted commands and other information about the server.

Listing 3.10 shows a whois client that can query any whois server. Because the command format can vary from server to server, the program simply sends whatever you place on the command line and prints whatever the server returns.

Finding the Time in Human-Readable Form

Machines that support RFC867 allow you to fetch the time in human-readable format, using either TCP or UDP on port 13. To find the time, do the following:

1. For TCP, simply make a connection. The server will send the time back (in whatever format it likes) and close the connection.

2. For UDP, send a datagram, although the contents of the datagram are unimportant.

You can find a list of popular time servers in Table 3.2. Many of these servers are set regularly from an atomic clock and offer very accurate time. Of course, network delays and other factors may make the time you read off by a bit, although the most sophisticated servers try to account for this.

Here is a short snippet of code to read the time from the U.S. Naval Observatory using TCP:

```
try {
 int c;
 Socket sock=new Socket("tock.usno.navy.mil",13);
```

```
    InputStream is = sock.getInputStream();
    do {
     c=is.read();
     if (c!=-1) System.out.print((char)c);
    } while (c!=-1);
    }
    catch (IOException e) { System.out.println(e); }
  }
```

Decoding a NIST Time String

NIST has a well-defined format for the string it returns for time. Here's the format:

```
JJJJJ YR-MO-DA HH:MM:SS TT L H msADV UTC(NIST) *
```

- **JJJJJ**—This is the modified Julian day. Modified means that it is the last 5 digits of the actual Julian day, which by convention begins at January 1, 4713 B.C. Adding 2.4 million to this number results in a proper Julian day.

- **YR-MO-DA**—This is the date in year, month, day format.

- **HH:MM:SS**—The time in hour, minute, second format. The time is always UTC.

- **TT**—This code indicates if the United States is, with some exceptions, observing daylight savings time. If the code is 00, then daylight savings time is not in effect. If the code is 50, then daylight savings time is in effect. If the current date is within a month of the daylight savings time changes, the number counts down the days to the change.

- **L**—The character indicates if a leap second correction will be applied to the clock at the end of this month. A 1 in this field indicates that there will be a leap second added to the clock at the end of this month. A 2 means the leap second will be subtracted instead. A 0 means there is no leap second this month.

- **H**—This character indicates the server's current health. A zero indicates that the server is operating properly. If the field is a 1, the time may be off by up to 5 seconds. A 2 indicates a possible error of more than 5 seconds. A 4 here means something is wrong, and the time could be totally wrong.

- **msADV**—This is the number of milliseconds added to the time to attempt to mitigate network delays.

- **UTC(NIST)**—This time zone indicator indicates Coordinated Universal Time. In the past, UTC was known as Greenwich Mean Time (GMT), or zulu time.

- *****—This is the on-time marker. When you receive this character, the time specified by the package is correct. Of course, with network delays and other problems, this could be off by a bit, but it will be close.

Finding the Time in Machine-Readable Form

The general strategy to find the time in machine-readable format follows:

1. Read the bytes and subtract 2,208,988,800 (the number of seconds between 1900 and 1970, accounting for leap years).

2. Multiply by 1,000 to convert to milliseconds.

3. Call the **Date** object's **setTime** method to arrive at the correct date and time.

Listing 3.15 implements these ideas—as does Listing 3.14, although Listing 3.14 uses bit manipulations to overcome the large number problem, a strategy that closely models what you might do in C. Listing 3.15 takes a more Javalike approach by using the **BigInteger** class. This class is meant to handle numbers larger than the normal Java data types.

The program uses a special form of the **read** method to load the last four bytes of a 5-byte array with the incoming data. Then, it sets the first byte to zero. In this way, the **BigInteger** constructor will accept it as a 5-byte integer that is positive. If you try to use a 4-byte array, the constructor may create a negative number.

Of course, once the number is in **BigInteger** format, you'll have to do the other operations using **BigInteger** also. When it is time to load the **Date** object, you can call **longValue** to get a corresponding **long** from the **BigInteger** object.

Listing 3.15   This RFC868 client uses the BigInteger class to handle the incoming time.

```java
import java.util.*;
import java.net.*;
import java.io.*;
import java.math.*;
import java.text.DateFormat;

public class Client868big {
    public static void main(String [] args) {
        Socket sock=null;
        try {
          sock=new Socket(args[0],37);
          byte [] inarray=new byte[5];
          Date date=new Date();
           InputStream is=sock.getInputStream();
          is.read(inarray,1,4);
          BigInteger tick;
          inarray[0]=0; // make sure number is positive
          tick = new BigInteger(inarray);
          //number of second between 1900 and 1970
           // convert between 1900/1970
```

```
    tick=tick.subtract(new BigInteger("2208988800"));
    // convert to mS
    tick=tick.multiply(new BigInteger("1000"));
       date.setTime(tick.longValue());
       DateFormat df=DateFormat.getDateTimeInstance(
         DateFormat.FULL,DateFormat.FULL);
       System.out.println(df.format(date));
     }
     catch (IOException e) {
         System.out.println(e);
         return;
     }
     finally {
         try {
             sock.close();
         }
         catch (IOException e) {}
     }
   }
}
```

Writing a Time Server

You can write a time server that handles incoming requests for human-readable times or machine-readable times. Simply do the following:

1. Watch for incoming connections (or datagrams).

2. Reply with the time in the appropriate format.

3. Close the connection once you finish sending the data (if you're a TCP server).

You can find an example RFC867 TCP server in Listing 3.12. Because the **Date-Format** object can create any format you like, you can use it to generate a string that you'll serve to the client. The string should end with a carriage return and line feed.

An example RFC868 server, also TCP, appears in Listing 3.13. Here the **getTime** method retrieves the current date and time as the number of milliseconds since January 1, 1970. To write this server, do the following:

1. Convert this number to seconds (divide by 1,000).

2. Add the number of seconds that elapsed between 1900 and 1970 (counting leap years but not counting leap seconds, about 2,208,988,800).

3. Extract each byte into a byte array that you can send to the output of the socket. This is easy to do with standard bit-manipulation (the **&** and **>>** operators).

Here's a portion of a typical time server that splits the result into bytes:

```
long tick = new Date().getTime()/1000;
byte [] outarray = new byte[4];
tick+=2208988800L;
outarray[0]=(byte)((tick & 0xFF000000L)>>24);
outarray[1]=(byte)((tick & 0xFF0000L)>>16);
outarray[2]=(byte)((tick & 0xFF00L)>>8);
outarray[3]=(byte)(tick & 0xFFL);
os.write(outarray);
os.flush();
```

Selecting a Unicode to Byte Mapping

Java uses Unicode characters that use 16 bits to represent characters. Because network transmission usually takes place in bytes, you'll need to convert the Unicode characters into bytes. When writing to an **OutputWriter**, the system will use a default encoding, if you don't specify one. However, for network protocols, you are best served by selecting one yourself.

There are several ways you can specify the encoding:

• For an **OutputStreamWriter**, you can specify the encoding in the constructor, for example.

• If you are working with bytes directly, you can call the **String** object's **getBytes** method with an encoding specified.

The encoding method is a string that the system attempts to match. All Java installations support a few basic encodings, although newer versions may support more than older versions. The i18n.jar file adds support for many other encodings (see Table 3.3).

Keep in mind that all normal printable ASCII characters are themselves in Unicode, so the mapping is usually not a big deal. The problem is when you use characters that appear in other languages or odd contexts (special characters on a PC, for example). UTF provides a special way to encode Unicode characters over 8-bit channels. However, unless the receiver is expecting UTF, this format doesn't make much sense.

Table 3.3   Encodings recognized by Java.

Name	Encoding
ASCII	American Standard Code for Information Interchange
Cp1252	Windows Latin-1
ISO8859_1	ISO 8859-1, Latin alphabet No. 1
UnicodeBig	16-bit UTF, big-endian byte order, with byte-order mark
UnicodeBigUnmarked	16-bit UTF, big-endian byte order
UnicodeLittle	16-bit UTF, little-endian byte order, with byte-order mark
UnicodeLittleUnmarked	16-bit UTF, little-endian byte order
UTF8	8-bit UTF
UTF-16	16-bit UTF, byte order specified by a mandatory initial byte-order mark
Big5	Big5, Traditional Chinese
Cp037	USA, Canada (Bilingual, French), Netherlands, Portugal, Brazil, Australia
Cp273	IBM Austria, Germany
Cp277	IBM Denmark, Norway
Cp278	IBM Finland, Sweden
Cp280	IBM Italy
Cp284	IBM Catalan/Spain, Spanish Latin America
Cp285	IBM United Kingdom, Ireland
Cp297	IBM France
Cp420	IBM Arabic
Cp424	IBM Hebrew
Cp437	MS-DOS United States, Australia, New Zealand, South Africa
Cp500	EBCDIC 500V1
Cp737	PC Greek
Cp775	PC Baltic
Cp838	IBM Thailand extended SBCS
Cp850	MS-DOS Latin-1
Cp852	MS-DOS Latin-2
Cp855	IBM Cyrillic
Cp856	IBM Hebrew
Cp857	IBM Turkish
Cp858	Variant of Cp850 with Euro character
Cp860	MS-DOS Portuguese

(continued)

3. Simple Protocols

Table 3.3   Encodings recognized by Java *(continued)*.

Name	Encoding
Cp861	MS-DOS Icelandic
Cp862	PC Hebrew
Cp863	MS-DOS Canadian French
Cp864	PC Arabic
Cp865	MS-DOS Nordic
Cp866	MS-DOS Russian
Cp868	MS-DOS Pakistan
Cp869	IBM Modern Greek
Cp870	IBM Multilingual Latin-2
Cp871	IBM Iceland
Cp874	IBM Thai
Cp875	IBM Greek
Cp918	IBM Pakistan (Urdu)
Cp921	IBM Latvia, Lithuania (AIX, DOS)
Cp922	IBM Estonia (AIX, DOS)
Cp930	Japanese Katakana-Kanji mixed with 4370 UDC, superset of 5026
Cp933	Korean Mixed with 1880 UDC, superset of 5029
Cp935	Simplified Chinese Host mixed with 1880 UDC, superset of 5031
Cp937	Traditional Chinese Host mixed with 6204 UDC, superset of 5033
Cp939	Japanese Latin Kanji mixed with 4370 UDC, superset of 5035
Cp942	IBM OS/2 Japanese, superset of Cp932
Cp942C	Variant of Cp942
Cp943	IBM OS/2 Japanese, superset of Cp932 and Shift-JIS
Cp943C	Variant of Cp943
Cp948	OS/2 Chinese (Taiwan), superset of 938
Cp949	PC Korean
Cp949C	Variant of Cp949
Cp950	PC Chinese (Hong Kong, Taiwan)
Cp964	AIX Chinese (Taiwan)
Cp970	AIX Korean
Cp1006	IBM AIX Pakistan (Urdu)
Cp1025	IBM Multilingual Cyrillic: Bulgaria, Bosnia, Herzegovinia, Macedonia (FYR)

(continued)

Table 3.3 **Encodings recognized by Java** *(continued).*

Name	Encoding
Cp1026	IBM Latin-5, Turkey
Cp1046	IBM Arabic—Windows
Cp1097	IBM Iran (Farsi)/Persian
Cp1098	IBM Iran (Farsi)/Persian (PC)
Cp1112	IBM Latvia, Lithuania
Cp1122	IBM Estonia
Cp1123	IBM Ukraine
Cp1124	IBM AIX Ukraine
Cp1140	Variant of Cp037 with Euro character
Cp1141	Variant of Cp273 with Euro character
Cp1142	Variant of Cp277 with Euro character
Cp1143	Variant of Cp278 with Euro character
Cp1144	Variant of Cp280 with Euro character
Cp1145	Variant of Cp284 with Euro character
Cp1146	Variant of Cp285 with Euro character
Cp1147	Variant of Cp297 with Euro character
Cp1148	Variant of Cp500 with Euro character
Cp1149	Variant of Cp871 with Euro character
Cp1250	Windows Eastern European
Cp1251	Windows Cyrillic
Cp1253	Windows Greek
Cp1254	Windows Turkish
Cp1255	Windows Hebrew
Cp1256	Windows Arabic
Cp1257	Windows Baltic
Cp1258	Windows Vietnamese
Cp1381	IBM OS/2, DOS People's Republic of China (PRC)
Cp1383	IBM AIX People's Republic of China (PRC)
Cp33722	IBM-eucJP—Japanese, superset of 5050
EUC_CN	GB2312, EUC encoding, Simplified Chinese
EUC_JP	JIS X 0201, 0208, 0212, EUC encoding, Japanese
EUC_KR	KS C 5601, EUC encoding, Korean

(continued)

Table 3.3   Encodings recognized by Java *(continued)*.

Name	Encoding
EUC_TW	CNS11643 (Plane 1-3), EUC encoding, Traditional Chinese
GBK	GBK, Simplified Chinese
ISO2022CN	ISO 2022 CN, Chinese (conversion to Unicode only)
ISO2022CN_CNS	CNS 11643 in ISO 2022 CN form, Traditional Chinese (conversion from Unicode only)
ISO2022CN_GB	GB 2312 in ISO 2022 CN form, Simplified Chinese (conversion from Unicode only)
ISO2022JP	JIS X 0201, 0208 in ISO 2022 form, Japanese
ISO2022KR	ISO 2022 KR, Korean
ISO8859_2	ISO 8859-2, Latin alphabet No. 2
ISO8859_3	ISO 8859-3, Latin alphabet No. 3
ISO8859_4	ISO 8859-4, Latin alphabet No. 4
ISO8859_5	ISO 8859-5, Latin/Cyrillic alphabet
ISO8859_6	ISO 8859-6, Latin/Arabic alphabet
ISO8859_7	ISO 8859-7, Latin/Greek alphabet
ISO8859_8	ISO 8859-8, Latin/Hebrew alphabet
ISO8859_9	ISO 8859-9, Latin alphabet No. 5
ISO8859_13	ISO 8859-13, Latin alphabet No. 7
ISO8859_15_FDIS	ISO 8859-15, Latin alphabet No. 9
JIS0201	JIS X 0201, Japanese
JIS0208	JIS X 0208, Japanese
JIS0212	JIS X 0212, Japanese
JISAutoDetect	Detects and converts from Shift-JIS, EUC-JP, ISO 2022 JP (conversion to Unicode only)
Johab	Johab, Korean
KOI8_R	KOI8-R, Russian
MS874	Windows Thai
MS932	Windows Japanese
MS936	Windows Simplified Chinese
MS949	Windows Korean
MS950	Windows Traditional Chinese
MacArabic	Macintosh Arabic
MacCentralEurope	Macintosh Latin-2

(continued)

Table 3.3 Encodings recognized by Java *(continued).*

Name	Encoding
MacCroatian	Macintosh Croatian
MacCyrillic	Macintosh Cyrillic
MacDingbat	Macintosh Dingbat
MacGreek	Macintosh Greek
MacHebrew	Macintosh Hebrew
MacIceland	Macintosh Iceland
MacRoman	Macintosh Roman
MacRomania	Macintosh Romania
MacSymbol	Macintosh Symbol
MacThai	Macintosh Thai
MacTurkish	Macintosh Turkish
MacUkraine	Macintosh Ukraine
SJIS	Shift-JIS, Japanese
TIS620	TIS620, Thai

3. Simple Protocols

Chapter 4

TFTP

In Depth

I'm always amazed when I hear someone talking about how wonderful it would be to live in the old days. I don't mean someone who is longing for youth (I suppose most of us do that eventually). No, I mean someone who wants to live in the Old South, or the Wild West, or even in medieval Europe. Anyone who thinks that would be a good thing probably doesn't know much about what went on in those days!

Every year a local park puts on an exhibit where people show you what it was like in the days of the early settlers to this part of Texas. It's nothing short of amazing how much work was involved in these early days; people had to make their own soap, spin cloth, sew clothes, and produce every mouthful of food they ate. That's a full-time job. Somehow, the ladies would even find time to make their own lace—a luxury I'd probably forego if I had to make my own soap!

Today, most of us don't produce any of our own food. Soap, clothes, and everything else is courtesy of the local WalMart store. Even if you grow your own food, you probably buy ready-made fertilizer, packaged seed, and have plenty of power tools to help you.

Although many technically inclined people build their own PCs, that only goes so far, too. Most of us can put a motherboard into a ready-made case. But how many of us could create all the parts that go on that motherboard, solder them in place, and then install our handmade creation into a case we built using metal smelted in our backyard forge? I'm guessing no one raised a hand.

In the last chapter, the protocols you used were quite simple. You could exercise most of them with Telnet—that's how simple they were. However, practical protocols are often much more complex. Just as you wouldn't try to make your own Pentium IV processor, you might not really want to write every line of code required to handle some of these more complicated protocols.

In this chapter, you'll investigate a protocol that is relatively simple but more complex than the ones in Chapter 3. To make life easier, you'll see how open source software can simplify your task when faced with a complex protocol.

In particular, this chapter covers the Trivial File Transfer Protocol (TFTP) as defined by RFC1350. If you think about transferring files, you probably think about FTP (File Transfer Protocol). As the name implies, FTP is more complex than TFTP (Chapter 6 will cover FTP).

Many diskless workstations use TFTP to load files they require from a server. TFTP is appropriate for any case in which one computer needs to request a file from another computer and there is no need for logging in to the remote machine. Typically, a TFTP server only provides a limited number of files, and anyone who wants them is welcome to them.

About TFTP

The TFTP protocol is deliberately designed to be easy to handle. It uses User Datagram Protocol (UDP) sockets, which are efficient, but this means that TFTP must account for the unreliable nature of the data transport.

TFTP servers listen on port 69 for incoming packets. A client simply uses a random port number. The initial exchange of packets allows the server to move the client to a different port number.

Each datagram has an opcode (a 16-bit word) that tells what type of packet it is. There are only five different types of packets (see Table 4.1). The small number of possible packets is one reason the protocol is simple. However, several other features make it easy to write TFTP software:

- *Each packet sent elicits a response.* You can't proceed until you receive this response. If a timeout occurs, you resend the packet. Therefore, you only have to remember one packet of data at a time.

- *Each data packet has 512 bytes of the file.* A smaller packet indicates the end of file.

- *Almost all errors cause the transfer to terminate.* The server returns an error code and optional description and terminates the transaction.

- *There are only three file types recognized by the protocol.* One file type is obsolete, so in practice, you only need to worry about two file types.

When one computer wants to read a file to another, it sends a read request (RRQ) to port 69 of the remote computer. To write a file, the computer sends a write request (WRQ). The packet includes the packet type code (known as the opcode),

Table 4.1   TFTP packet types.

Code	Name	Description
1	RRQ	Read request (request for a file)
2	WRQ	Write request (request to send file)
3	DAT	File data
4	ACK	Acknowledge, clear to proceed
5	ERR	Error occurred

the file name (terminated by a zero byte), and a mode string (also terminated by a zero byte). The mode can be netascii for a text file or octet for binary files. A third legal mode, mail, is now considered obsolete.

When reading a file, the remote computer will respond with a DATA packet. Write requests will generate an ACK. The remote computer will send its response using a port other than port 69. This is the port the client should use for future transmissions.

DATA packets contain a 2-byte block number (the block numbers begin at 1). Normally, 512 bytes of data follow the block number. However, a lesser number of bytes may occur (including zero bytes). A short block indicates the end of file. Because the block number is only 2 bytes, and each block has 512 bytes, TFTP won't handle files larger than 32 megabytes.

An ACK packet also has a block number. If the ACK refers to a WRQ packet, the block number will be zero. Otherwise, the block number must correspond to the last DATA packet's block number.

At any time, either machine can send an ERR packet. This contains a 2-byte error code (see Table 4.2), plus a zero-terminated error string. For example, if the server wants to reject a connection request, it can send an ERR packet.

ERR packets are not acknowledged. However, it is possible for the error sender to wait for a short period to see if it continues to receive packets from the other computer. In this case, you can assume the other computer did not receive the error, and you should retransmit it. This is not strictly necessary, however.

In practice, then, you need some sort of time-out period and a retry count. Suppose you send data packet 100 to the receiver. You wait for an ACK packet, but it doesn't arrive within a predetermined amount of time. You can then resend it. Of course, the receiver may have read the packet the first time. In that case, the ACK

Table 4.2   Error types.

Code	Description
0	Undefined (see error string)
1	File not found
2	Access violation
3	Disk full
4	Illegal TFTP operation
5	Unknown transfer ID (port number)
6	File already exists
7	No such user

must have been lost. The receiver simply discards the duplicate packet and reissues an ACK packet. You could also assume that the absence of a DATA packet means the ACK was lost, and you could retransmit it to aggressively attempt to complete the transfer.

What this means, in practice, is that both sides of the transaction must implement a time-out mechanism and be prepared to receive duplicate packets. Because only one packet at a time can be outstanding, this is easy to implement.

WARNING! Don't make the mistake of thinking that only ACK packets form an acknowledgment. In fact, every packet either computer sends expects a certain packet in response. So, for a sent DATA packet, you should receive an ACK. But from the other side's point of view, an ACK packet causes another DATA packet to arrive.

The only ACK that does not generate a response is the final one (in response to a DATA packet with less than 512 bytes in it). Once the receiver sends the final ACK, it is free to close down. However, you may want to wait a short interval to see if the sender retransmits the DATA packet. If it does, you can assume the final ACK was lost and retransmit it. This behavior is optional, but a good idea nonetheless.

Play by Play

Consider a typical TFTP transaction as shown in Table 4.3. Computer A is a workstation that wants to read a file from Computer B. Computer B is running a TFTP server on the usual port, port 69.

In this example, the server has moved the client to port 3242 (a random choice) leaving port 69 open for more RRQ (or WRQ) requests. In this example, the file must be between 1,024 and 1,535 bytes in length. If the file were 1,024 bytes long, the final DATA packet would have zero data bytes in it and would simply signify the end of the file. If the file had 1,536 bytes, the final DATA packet would contain 512 bytes. Then the receiver would expect yet another DATA packet, even if it was a zero-length packet. Therefore, the file must be at least 1,024 bytes long, but it can't be any longer than 1,535 bytes.

If Computer A were writing to the server, the transaction would look like Table 4.4.

Table 4.3   Computer A reading from Computer B.

| Computer A | | Computer B |
Data	To Remote Port	Response
RRQ	69	DATA
ACK	3242	DATA
ACK	3242	DATA
ACK	3242	

Table 4.4   Computer A writing to Computer B.

Computer A		Computer B
Data	To Remote Port	Response
WRQ	69	ACK
DATA	3242	ACK
DATA	3242	ACK

In this example, the file must be between 512 bytes and 1,023 bytes in length. If either side decides it has waited too long for a response, it can retransmit its data. Because there is only one possible outstanding packet at any given time, this is straightforward to program.

A TFTP Client

Armed with an understanding of the protocol, you can tackle writing a simple client class. A client can send or receive a file, and because it doesn't have to handle multiple requests, there isn't any reason to deal with multiple threads and sockets.

In the "Immediate Solutions" section later in this chapter, you'll find a complete TFTP client (see Listing 4.5). The class (**TftpSocket**) derives from **DatagramSocket**. This works well, although you could easily have made it so that the class encapsulated a socket instead.

The new class has constructors that mirror the constructors available for **DatagramSocket**. However, the logic required by the **TftpSocket** class is the same in any case. So, the private **create** function takes care of all the constructors.

In addition to the arguments that the normal **DatagramSocket** constructors require, each **TftpSocket** constructor also requires a file name, a file type (netascii or octet), and a network hostname. Although it would be easy to try to deal with end-of-line issues in the case of netascii files, this client makes no such attempt.

The constructor doesn't actually begin a transaction. It does resolve the hostname to an **InetAddress** object. It also converts the string arguments into bytes because the server will expect bytes—not Unicode strings.

Once you've constructed a **TftpSocket** object, you'll call either **fsend** or **freceive** to carry out the operation you wish. Consider the case where you wish to receive a file first.

All of the logic required for requesting and receiving a file is in the **freceive** method. However, the details are buried in two specialized routines: **sendPacket** and

rcvPacket. These routines hold all the specialized knowledge of the packet transactions, whereas the **freceive** method controls the sequence of packets and the
time-out logic. You can find the **freceive** method in Listing 4.1.

Listing 4.1 The freceive method receives a file via TFTP.

```
// Get a file
    public boolean freceive() throws SocketException {
    boolean rv;
    int n;
    try {
        fileout=new FileOutputStream(fnstring);
    }
    catch (Exception e) { return false; }
    try {
        int retry=0;
        block=1;
        rv=sendPacket(RRQ);
        if (!rv) return rv;
        while (!EOF) {
            do {
                n=rcvPacket();
                if (n==TIMEOUT) {
                    if (retry++>5) return false;
                    continue;
                }
                retry=0; // reset retry count
                if (n==ERR) return false;
                if (n==UNKNOWN) {
                    sendErrPacket(0,"Unknown error");
                    return false;
                }
            } while (n!=DAT);
        }
        return true;
    }
    finally { // close in all cases
        if (!streamClose(fileout)) return false;
        }
    }
```

In the case of error packets, the **sendPacket** routine creates a generic error.
However, you can also call **sendErrorPacket** to create a specific error. In a similar fashion, calling **sendPacket** creates an acknowledgment for the current block.
However, if the server retransmits a block, you may need to repeat a previous
acknowledgment, so the **sendAck** method will create a specific acknowledgment packet.

The **freceive** method is responsible for creating a **FileOutputStream** that the **rcvPacket** uses to write to the output file. Of course, this file should be closed no matter what happens, so **freceive** implements a **finally** clause to ensure that even if an error occurs, the program will close the stream.

The **fsend** method is very similar to **freceive** (see Listing 4.2). It opens a **FileInputStream** object, of course, because in this case, the program is reading an existing file. Again, the **sendPacket** and **rcvPacket** methods handle all the low-level details.

Listing 4.2   This method sends a file.

```
// Send a file
    public boolean fsend() throws SocketException {
    boolean rv;
    try {
        filein = new FileInputStream(fnstring);
    }
    catch (Exception e) { return false; }
    try {
        int n;
        int retry=0;
        block=0;
        rv=sendPacket(WRQ);
        if (!rv) return rv;
        while (!EOF) {
            do {
                n=rcvPacket();
                if (n==TIMEOUT) {
                    if (++retry>5) return false;
                    if (block!=0)
                        if (!sendPacket(DAT)) return false;
                    continue;
                }
                if (n==ERR) return false;
                if (n==UNKNOWN) {
                    sendErrPacket(0,"Unknown error");
                    return false;
                }
            } while (n!=ACK);
            if (!sendPacket(DAT)) return false;
        }
        return true;
    }
        finally {
        streamClose(filein); // close no matter what
        }
    }
```

The **rcvPacket** method returns the type of packet received. However, the calling routine needs to know a few more details. Therefore, the class defines a few private return codes that don't overlap with the packet code numbers, particularly the following:

- *NONE*—A packet was received, but it was not the one expected. For example, this could indicate that a duplicate acknowledgment arrived for a packet.

- *UNKNOWN*—A sequence error occurred. For example, the server sent an acknowledgment for a packet that the client did not send yet.

- *TIMEOUT*—Indicates that a time-out has occurred.

The **TftpSocket** class has a test **main** function you can use for testing. If you supply no arguments, the class will start as a server. However, you can supply a file name, the file type (netascii or octet), and a hostname. You can also add an **S** as the final argument if you wish to send the file (the default is to receive the file).

Single stepping this code with a debugger can be very instructive. The class has several instance variables that the client-side code uses, including the following:

- **String fnstring**—This is the target file name as a Java string.

- **byte[] fn**—The client also needs the file name as a byte array.

- **byte[] ftype**—When you specify the file type, the client stores it in this byte array.

- **InetAddress hostaddr**—The remote computer (the server, in this case).

- **int port**—The port number to use. Initially, this will be 69, but when the server responds, it will specify a different port number to use.

- **int block**—The client uses this variable to track the block it expects to receive.

- **FileInputStream filein**—This stream is used when sending a file.

- **FileOutputStream fileout**—This stream is active when receiving a file.

- **boolean EOF**—When the file operation is complete, this flag will become true.

When receiving a file, the client expects a particular block, determined by the **block** variable. However, it is possible that—because of network losses—the server might resend a block the client has already processed. The client must reacknowledge these old packets so that the server will continue to send new packets. Here's the code that does the work:

```
case DAT:
// check block # and store
blockin=(byt[2]<<8)+byt[3];
if (blockin>block) return UNKNOWN;  // higher than expected
```

```
        if (blockin<block) {                 // packet re-sent
              sendAck(blockin);  // re-send ACK
              return NONE;
              }
        // block number matches
        try {
          fileout.write(byt,4,pack.getLength()-4);
        }
        catch (IOException e) { }
// DAT packet <516 bytes means end of file
        if (pack.getLength()<516) EOF=true;
            sendPacket(ACK);  // ack current
        block++;
        return DAT;
```

Notice that if a block arrives that has a higher number than expected, that's just an error. Because the server isn't allowed to send a packet until the client acknowledges the last packet, this error should not be able to occur.

A Server

What's the difference between a TFTP server and client? Very little. The server listens on port 69, of course. It also allocates a port to handle each client request. Otherwise, the transactions are just the same. The server responds to RRQ and WRQ instead of generating them. Once the client issues one of these commands, the remaining transactions are just the same as the client's transactions—that is, the server must either issue ACK packets in response to DAT packets, or it must send DAT packets and wait for ACK packets to arrive.

Because the server and client are so similar, it makes sense to try to use the same class for both sides of the conversation. The class provides a static member function (**tftpd**) that handles the server logic (see Listing 4.3). This function will block, so you'll probably call it from within a thread.

Listing 4.3   This method acts as a server, responding to WRQ and RRQ packets.

```
public static void tftpd() {
    DatagramSocket sskt;
    try {
      sskt = new DatagramSocket(69);
    }
    catch (SocketException e) {
    System.out.println("Unable to start server: " + e);
    return;
    }
    byte [] buf = new byte[1024];
```

```
DatagramPacket pkt=new DatagramPacket(buf,1024);
while (true) {
try {
        // wait for WRQ or RRQ -- all others are errors
    sskt.setSoTimeout(0);
    sskt.receive(pkt);
    int port=pkt.getPort();
    byte[] byt=pkt.getData();
    int code=(byt[0]<<8)+byt[1];
    if (code!=WRQ && code!=RRQ) {
      byte[] errary = new byte[4];
      errary[0]=(byte)((ERR>>8)&0xFF);
      errary[1]=(byte)(ERR & 0xFF);
      errary[2]=(byte)0;
      errary[3]=(byte)0;
      errary[4]=0;
      pkt.setData(errary);
      sskt.send(pkt);
      continue;
    }
    // Start new thread (use private constructor)
    TftpSocket worker=new TftpSocket();
    int zlen,zlen1;
    worker.port=pkt.getPort();
    worker.hostaddr=pkt.getAddress();
    for (zlen=0;byt[zlen+2]!=0;zlen++);
    worker.fnstring=new String(byt,2,zlen);
    worker.fn=worker.fnstring.getBytes();
    for (zlen1=0;byt[zlen+zlen1+2]!=0;zlen1++);
    worker.ftype=new String(byt,zlen+2,zlen1).getBytes();
    worker.serverCode=code;
    new Thread(worker).start();
  }
  catch (IOException e) { /* ignore */ }
  }
}
```

When used as a client, the socket provides constructors that correspond to the normal **DatagramSocket** constructors. One of the main functions of these constructors is to convert **String** arguments into byte arrays. However, as a server, the file name and other information arrive from the client as a byte array already, so there is no reason to perform these conversions. For that reason, the class provides a private default constructor. This allows the **tftpd** function to fill in the necessary data itself. Because the constructor is private, only members of the **TftpSocket** class can use it.

The server waits for an incoming RRQ or WRQ packet. When it receives one, it starts a new thread based on the **TftpSocket** object (that's why **TftpSocket** implements **runnable**). The **run** method is only running when a particular instance of **TftpSocket** is servicing a client (see Listing 4.4).

The server thread uses the same **rcvPacket** and **sendPacket** routines that the client uses. Of course, the active file stream is the opposite in the server compared with the client. So, where the client has a **FileInputStream**, the server has a **FileOutputStream** and vice versa. That makes sense because if one side is reading, the other side has to be writing.

Listing 4.4   The TFTP server thread services clients.

```
public void run() {  // this is the server "thread"
    if (serverCode==WRQ) {
    // Set up output stream
    try {
      fileout=new FileOutputStream(fnstring);
    }
    catch (IOException e) {
        sendErrPacket(2,"Access violation");
        return;
    }
    // send ACK0
    sendAck(0);
    // wait for DATA
    int n;
    do {
        try {
            n=rcvPacket();
        }
        catch (SocketException e) { n=ERR; }
        if (n==ERR) {
            streamClose(fileout);
            return;
        }
        if (n!=DAT&&n!=NONE) {
            sendErrPacket(0,"?");
            streamClose(fileout);
            return;
        }
    } while (!EOF);
    }
    if (serverCode==RRQ) {
    // set up input stream
```

```
    try {
        filein=new FileInputStream(fnstring);
    }
    catch (IOException e) {
        sendErrPacket(1,"File not found");
        return;
    }
    // send DATA
    block=1;
    int retry=0;
    do {
        int n;
        if (!sendPacket(DAT)) {
            sendErrPacket(0,"?");
            streamClose(filein);
            return;
        }
        do {
            try {
                n=rcvPacket();
            }
            catch (SocketException e) { n=ERR; }
            if (n==ERR) {
                streamClose(filein);
                return;
            }
            if (n==UNKNOWN||n==RRQ||n==WRQ||n==DAT) {
                sendErrPacket(4,"Illegal");
                streamClose(filein);
                return;
            }
            if (n==TIMEOUT && ++retry>5) {
                sendErrPacket(0,"Timeout");
                streamClose(filein);
                return;
            }
            if (n==ACK) {
                block++;
                retry=0;
            }
        } while (n!=ACK&&n!=TIMEOUT);
    } while (!EOF);
    }
}
```

An Easier Way

All that work just to make a TFTP server and client? Yes, and TFTP is one of the easier protocols used on the Internet. However, if you search, you might be able to find a little help on the Web.

In particular, the GNU project has a TFTP class, written by Mark Benvenuto, at **http://www.gnu.org/software/java/java-software.html**. This set of classes works in a similar fashion to the code presented in this chapter, although the details are different.

The **gnu.inet.tftp** package contains several useful classes (all with source code, of course):

- **Tftp**—This simple class is nothing more than a **main** function, a function to print a help message (**usage**), and a constructor. The constructor creates a **TftpConnection** that does all the work. This class is essentially the user interface for the **TftpConnection** class and forms a usable command-line client program.

- **TftpConnection**—In this class, you'll find the code that handles the client's connection.

- **TftpLogStream**—The GNU TFTP server can create a log file and display informational messages. This class handles that logging.

- **TftpReadConnection**—This class is code that manages reading a file.

- **TftpServerConnection**—This class represents a server's side of a TFTP connection.

- **TftpWriteConnection**—This class is code that manages writing to a file.

- **Tftpd**—This is a user interface class for **TftpServerConnection**.

- **LineBufferedOutputStream**—This is a general-purpose buffering class used by the TFTP classes.

The real key portions of the package are **TftpConnection** and **TftpServer-Connection**. The actual work occurs in **TftpReadConnection** and **TftpWrite-Connection**. The other classes are either for user interface (**Tftp** and **Tftpd**) or I/O support (**TftpLogStream** and **LineBufferedOutputStream**).

TFTP vs. FTP

In Chapter 6, you'll read about FTP. This is the service users often use to transfer files between computers. Why even consider TFTP? For one, TFTP is very simple and is often used by simple computers in diskless workstations to retrieve necessary files. However, the security of TFTP is nonexistent.

You could alter the TFTP server, for example, to only accept requests from known Internet Protocol (IP) addresses. This wouldn't be foolproof, but it would provide some protection. Of course, nothing is perfect; hackers can assume bogus IP addresses (a process known as spoofing), but this would certainly keep out the casual hacker.

However, the TFTP protocol is easily extended for customized applications. Suppose you have a computer that gathers information from a temperature sensor and stores it in a file. Every night you want to send that file to a remote computer via the network. TFTP will do this very easily. Besides that, you could easily extend the TFTP protocol to provide any amount of security you want to implement.

For example, changing the port number the server uses for listening would provide a very mild form of security. You could also make the client append a password to the WRQ or RRQ packet. For maximum security, you might decide to encrypt the contents of DAT packets using a simple cipher or a more advanced form of encryption. Why reinvent a new protocol for transferring files when TFTP already exists?

On the companion CD-ROM you'll find another TFTP class named **TftpCustom**. This class is identical to the **TftpSocket** class except it provides a simple form of encryption. In particular, this line appears near the top of the file:

```
final static byte crypt=(byte)0xA5;
```

Both the client and the server must agree on this number. Then, when forming a data packet, the new code looks like this:

```
for (int idx=0;idx<1;idx++)
    bytes[len+idx]=(byte)(fbuf[idx]^crypt);
// This line was from the old code
//System.arraycopy(fbuf,0,bytes,len,1);
```

In the original code, **arraycopy** moves the bytes from **fbuf** to the **bytes** array that makes up the datagram's data. The encrypted version uses a **for** loop and exclusive-ors each byte as it copies it.

On the receiving end, the program reverses the process:

```
for (int idx=4;idx<pack.getLength();idx++)
    byt[idx]=(byte)(byt[idx]^crypt);
try {
  fileout.write(byt,4,pack.getLength()-4);
}
catch (IOException e) { }
```

This encryption scheme, of course, is quite simpleminded. However, it will foil a casual hacker. You are free to devise more elaborate schemes if you need a higher level of security.

Immediate Solutions

Finding the TFTP Specification

TFTP is defined in RFC1350, which replaced RFC783. One place to locate this document is at **http://www.faqs.org/rfcs/rfc1350.html**.

Creating a TFTP Class

Because TFTP servers and clients are nearly identical, it usually makes sense to write one class to handle both cases (see Listing 4.5). The **TftpSocket** class has an **fsend** and **freceive** method for client use and a **tftpd** entry point for making the class act as a server.

The class also has a simplified **main** function, so you can test it out. With no arguments, the class behaves as a server. If you want the program to function as a client, provide a file name, a file type (netascii or octet), and a hostname. This receives the file from the server. If you add an **S** argument, the program sends the file to the server instead.

Listing 4.5   The complete TFTP class.

```
// TFTP Class -- Williams
import java.net.*;
import java.util.*;
import java.io.*;

    public class TftpSocket extends DatagramSocket
            implements Runnable {
    final static int NONE=0;  // local
    final static int RRQ=1;
    final static int WRQ=2;
    final static int DAT=3;
    final static int ACK=4;
    final static int ERR=5;
    final static int UNKNOWN=6; // local code
    final static int TIMEOUT=7; // local code
    protected String fnstring;
    protected byte[] fn;
```

```java
    protected byte[] ftype;
    protected InetAddress hostaddr;
    protected int port=69;
    protected byte[] bytes = new byte[516];
    protected byte[] bytesin = new byte[1024];
    protected int block=0;
    protected FileInputStream filein;
    protected FileOutputStream fileout;
    protected boolean EOF=false;
    protected int serverCode=0;   // operation requested

// Constructors (same as DatagramSocket)

    public TftpSocket(String filen, String type, String host)
      throws UnknownHostException, SocketException {
    create(filen,type,host);
    }

    public TftpSocket(int sport, String filen, String type, String host)
      throws UnknownHostException, SocketException {
    super(sport);
    create(filen,type,host);
    }

    public TftpSocket(int sport, InetAddress ia,
                String filen, String type, String host)
       throws UnknownHostException, SocketException {
       super(sport,ia);
       create(filen,type,host);
    }

    // private constructor (used by server only)
    private TftpSocket() throws SocketException { }

    // this private function does the work for
    // all the client constructors
    private void create(String filen, String type, String host)
       throws UnknownHostException, SocketException {
    try {
      fn=filen.getBytes("ISO-8859-1");
      ftype=type.getBytes();
    }
    catch (Exception e) {
        fn=filen.getBytes();
        ftype=type.getBytes();
    }
```

```
        fnstring=filen;
        setSoTimeout(1500);   // 1.5 second time-out
        hostaddr=InetAddress.getByName(host);
    }


// Send a specific error packet
    protected boolean sendErrPacket(int code,String msg) {
    bytes[0]=(byte)((ERR>>8)&0xFF);
    bytes[1]=(byte)(ERR & 0xFF);
    bytes[2]=(byte)((code>>8)&0xFF);
    bytes[3]=(byte)(code & 0xFF);
    System.arraycopy(msg.getBytes(),0,bytes,4,msg.length());
    bytes[4+msg.length()]=0;
    DatagramPacket pack =
            new DatagramPacket(bytes,5+msg.length(),hostaddr,port);
    try {
      send(pack);
    }
    catch (Exception e) {
        return false;
    }
    return true;
    }


// Send a specific acknowledgment
    protected boolean sendAck(int block) {
    bytes[0]=(byte)((ACK>>8)&0xFF);
    bytes[1]=(byte)(ACK & 0xFF);
    bytes[2]=(byte)((block>>8)&0xFF);
    bytes[3]=(byte)(block & 0xFF);
    DatagramPacket pack = new DatagramPacket(bytes,4,hostaddr,port);
    try {
      send(pack);
    }
    catch (Exception e) {
        return false;
    }
    return true;
    }

// Send a packet (generic error or current block ACK)
    protected boolean sendPacket(int ptype) {
    int len=2;
        bytes[0]=(byte)((ptype>>8)&0xFF);
    bytes[1]=(byte)(ptype & 0xFF);
    switch (ptype) {
```

4. TFTP

```
    case RRQ:
    case WRQ:
        System.arraycopy(fn,0,bytes,2,fn.length);
        bytes[2+fn.length]=0;
        System.arraycopy(ftype,0,bytes,3+fn.length,ftype.length);
        bytes[3+fn.length+ftype.length]=0;
        len+=fn.length+ftype.length+2;
        break;

    case DAT:
    case ACK:
        int l;
        bytes[2]=(byte)((block>>8)&0xFF);
        bytes[3]=(byte)(block&0xFF);
        len+=2;
        // more for file
        if (ptype==DAT) {
            byte [] fbuf=new byte[512];
            try {
              l=filein.read(fbuf,0,512);
            }
            catch (IOException e) {
                l=0; // assume EOF
            }
            // load data
            System.arraycopy(fbuf,0,bytes,len,l);
            len+=l;
            if (l!=512) EOF=true;
        }
        break;

    case ERR:
        bytes[2]=bytes[3]=bytes[4]=0;
        len=5;
        break;

default:
    return false;
}
DatagramPacket pack = new DatagramPacket(bytes,len,hostaddr,port);
try {
  send(pack);
}
catch (Exception e) {
    return false;
}
```

```
       return true;
        }

// Process a received packet
    protected int rcvPacket() throws SocketException {
        DatagramPacket pack = new DatagramPacket(bytesin,1024);
        byte [] byt;
        boolean status=false;
        try {
        receive(pack);
        status=true;
          }
        catch (IOException e) { }
        if (!status) return TIMEOUT;
        // we only process ACK, DAT, ERR
        port=pack.getPort();
        byt=pack.getData();
        int code=(byt[0]<<8)+byt[1];
        int blockin;
        switch (code) {
        case RRQ:
        case WRQ:
        return code;
        case ACK:
        // check block #
        blockin=(byt[2]<<8)+byt[3];
        if (blockin!=block) return NONE;
        block++;
        return ACK;
        case DAT:
        // check block # and store
        blockin=(byt[2]<<8)+byt[3];
        if (blockin>block) return UNKNOWN;
        if (blockin<block) {
                sendAck(blockin);  // resend ACK
                return NONE;
                }
        // block number matches
        try {
          fileout.write(byt,4,pack.getLength()-4);
        }
        catch (IOException e) { }
        if (pack.getLength()<516) EOF=true;
            sendPacket(ACK);  // ack current
        block++;
            return DAT;
```

```
                case ERR:
                // should do something smart with the error message
                String errm = new String(byt,4,pack.getLength());
                System.out.println(errm);
                return ERR;
                default:
                return UNKNOWN;
                }


        }

    // Send a file
        public boolean fsend() throws SocketException {
        boolean rv;
        try {
            filein = new FileInputStream(fnstring);
        }
        catch (Exception e) { return false; }
        try {
            int n;
            int retry=0;
            block=0;
            rv=sendPacket(WRQ);
            if (!rv) return rv;
            while (!EOF) {
                do {
                    n=rcvPacket();
                    if (n==TIMEOUT) {
                        if (++retry>5) return false;
                        if (block!=0)
                            if (!sendPacket(DAT)) return false;
                        continue;
                    }
                    if (n==ERR) return false;
                    if (n==UNKNOWN) {
                        sendErrPacket(0,"Unknown error");
                        return false;
                    }
                } while (n!=ACK);
                if (!sendPacket(DAT)) return false;
            }
            return true;
        }
        finally {
        streamClose(filein); // close no matter what
        }
        }
```

```
// Get a file
    public boolean freceive() throws SocketException {
    boolean rv;
    int n;
    try {
        fileout=new FileOutputStream(fnstring);
    }
    catch (Exception e) { return false; }
    try {
        int retry=0;
        block=1;
        rv=sendPacket(RRQ);
        if (!rv) return rv;
        while (!EOF) {
            do {
                n=rcvPacket();
                if (n==TIMEOUT) {
                    if (retry++>5) return false;
                    continue;
                }
                retry=0; // reset retry count
                if (n==ERR) return false;
                if (n==UNKNOWN) {
                    sendErrPacket(0,"Unknown error");
                    return false;
                }
            } while (n!=DAT);
        }
        return true;
    }
    finally { // close in all cases
        if (!streamClose(fileout)) return false;
        }
    }


// this is the server "thread"
    public void run() {
        if (serverCode==WRQ) {
        // Set up output stream
        try {
          fileout=new FileOutputStream(fnstring);
        }
        catch (IOException e) {
            sendErrPacket(2,"Access violation");
            return;
        }
```

```
// send ACK0
sendAck(0);
block=1;
// wait for DATA
int n;
do {
    try {
        n=rcvPacket();
    }
    catch (SocketException e) { n=ERR; }
    if (n==ERR) {
        streamClose(fileout);
        return;
    }
    if (n!=DAT&&n!=NONE) {
        sendErrPacket(0,"?");
        streamClose(fileout);
        return;
    }
} while (!EOF);
}
if (serverCode==RRQ) {
// set up input stream
try {
    filein=new FileInputStream(fnstring);
}
catch (IOException e) {
    sendErrPacket(1,"File not found");
    return;
}
// send DATA
block=1;
int retry=0;
do {
    int n;
    if (!sendPacket(DAT)) {
        sendErrPacket(0,"?");
        streamClose(filein);
        return;
    }
    do {
        try {
            n=rcvPacket();
        }
        catch (SocketException e) { n=ERR; }
```

```
                    if (n==ERR) {
                        streamClose(filein);
                        return;
                    }
                    if (n==UNKNOWN||n==RRQ||n==WRQ||n==DAT) {
                        sendErrPacket(4,"Illegal");
                        streamClose(filein);
                        return;
                    }
                    if (n==TIMEOUT && ++retry>5) {
                        sendErrPacket(0,"Timeout");
                        streamClose(filein);
                        return;
                    }
                    if (n==ACK) {
                        block++;
                        retry=0;
                    }
                } while (n!=ACK&&n!=TIMEOUT);
            } while (!EOF);
        }
    }

// Interface for server
public static void tftpd() {
    DatagramSocket sskt;
    try {
        sskt = new DatagramSocket(69);
    }
    catch (SocketException e) {
    System.out.println("Unable to start server: " + e);
    return;
    }
    byte [] buf = new byte[1024];
    DatagramPacket pkt=new DatagramPacket(buf,1024);
    while (true) {
    try {
            // wait for WRQ or RRQ -- all others are errors
        sskt.setSoTimeout(0);
        sskt.receive(pkt);
        int port=pkt.getPort();
        byte[] byt=pkt.getData();
        int code=(byt[0]<<8)+byt[1];
        if (code!=WRQ && code!=RRQ) {
          byte[] errary = new byte[4];
          errary[0]=(byte)((ERR>>8)&0xFF);
```

4. TFTP

```
                    errary[1]=(byte)(ERR & 0xFF);
                    errary[2]=(byte)0;
                    errary[3]=(byte)0;
                    errary[4]=0;
                    pkt.setData(errary);
                    sskt.send(pkt);
                    continue;
                }
                // Start new thread (use private constructor)
                TftpSocket worker=new TftpSocket();
                int zlen,zlen1;
                worker.port=pkt.getPort();
                worker.hostaddr=pkt.getAddress();
                for (zlen=0;byt[zlen+2]!=0;zlen++);
                worker.fnstring=new String(byt,2,zlen);
                worker.fn=worker.fnstring.getBytes();
                for (zlen1=0;byt[zlen+zlen1+2]!=0;zlen1++);
                worker.ftype=new String(byt,zlen+2,zlen1).getBytes();
                worker.serverCode=code;
                new Thread(worker).start();
            }
        catch (IOException e) { /* ignore */ }
        }
    }


    // Handy function to close a stream
    private boolean streamClose(InputStream s) {
        boolean rv=true;
        try {
            s.close();
        }
        catch (Exception e) { rv=false; }
        return rv;
    }

    // Handy function to close a stream
    private boolean streamClose(OutputStream s) {
        boolean rv=true;
        try {
            s.close();
        }
        catch (Exception e) { rv=false; }
        return rv;
    }
```

```
// Test main
// provide file name, file type, host on command line
// follow with an S to send R (or nothing) to receive
    public static void main(String [] args) throws Exception {
    if (args.length==0) {
        System.out.println("Starting server");
        new Tftpd().start();
        return;
    }
    TftpSocket sock=new TftpSocket(args[0],args[1],args[2]);
    if (args.length<=3||!args[3].equals("S")) {
        System.out.println("Client request "+sock.freceive());
    }
        else {
        System.out.println("Client request " + sock.fsend());
    }
  }
}


// Helper thread for test main
class Tftpd extends Thread {
    public void run() {
    TftpSocket.tftpd();
    }
}
```

Creating a TFTP Client

If you want to modify the TFTP code in Listing 4.5, you can remove all the server-related code by removing the **Tftpd** class, the **TftpSocket.run** method, and the **TftpSocket.tftpd** method.

If you plan on writing your own code, the client must perform the following steps:

1. Send an RRQ or WRQ request to port 69 of the server.

2. Wait for a DAT (if reading) or ACK packet (if writing). This packet will contain a new port number to use other than 69.

3. Upon receipt of a DAT packet, reply with an ACK. Upon receipt of an ACK packet, send the next DAT packet.

4. Be prepared to handle time-out errors or ERR packets.

Creating a TFTP Server

You can modify the TFTP code in Listing 4.5 so that it only acts as a server. Simply remove the **main**, **fsend**, and **freceive** methods. If you want to create your own server, here are the steps involved:

1. Listen on port 69 for RRQ or WWQ requests.

2. For each valid request, create a new socket (and probably a new thread, as well). For RRQ requests, respond with an initial DAT packet. For WWQ requests, acknowledge block zero.

3. Respond to ACK packets with the next DAT packet. Respond to DAT packets with ACK packets.

4. Be prepared to handle time-out errors or ERR packets.

Using the GNU TFTP Classes

You can also find an implementation of TFTP at **http://www.gnu.org/software/ java/java-software.html**. These classes also perform client and server TFTP functions.

To create a client connection, you can write:

```
conn = new TftpConnection(address, rFilen, lFilen, requesttype, debug);
conn.setSocketTimeout(5000);  // 5 second time-out
Thread th = new Thread(conn);
Th.start();
```

Of course, you must **import gnu.inet.tftp** for this code to work. The parameters to the **TftpConnection** constructor are:

- **address**—The remote server's address (an **InetAddress** object)

- **rFilen**—Remote file name

- **lFilen**—Local file name

- **requesttype**—One of TFTP_ReadRequest or TFTP_WriteRequest

- **debug**—The debug level (zero for no debugging)

To create a server, the following code will suffice:

```
Tftpd server;
server = new Tftpd();
server.processConnections();
```

Configuring the GNU TFTP Server

The GNU server uses a properties file to specify its operating parameters. In particular:

- **rootDirectory**—The directory that serves as the root for all file requests
- **logging**—Set to 1 to enable logging
- **logFile**—Name of log file
- **logStdout**—If 1, only log to stdout and not to a file
- **socketTimeout**—The amount of time to wait for input on a socket before timing out (milliseconds)
- **maxRetries**—Number of times to retry a packet
- **debugMode**—Set to 1 to enable debugging messages

Chapter 5

Telnet

In Depth

I've never fully accepted the WIMP (Windows Icon Mouse Pointer) interface. If you really think a mouse is intuitive, try teaching a small child how to use one. They want to lift it off the desk, put it on the screen, and otherwise mishandle it. Even my Mother—who is now a bona fide computer wizard—had trouble with the idea of the mouse at first.

I've softened a bit over the years, and I do use the mouse a lot more often. Of course, you can hardly avoid using a mouse these days. But times used to be different—especially when the Internet was just starting. In those days, it wasn't uncommon to use a TeleType terminal with a 110 baud modem (the kind where you pushed the phone's handset into the foam cups).

That seems hopelessly slow today, but many people did quite a bit of work in these conditions. Even when glass TeleType terminals (that is, terminals with a screen instead of a printer) appeared, each one operated a bit differently. With no clear standard, it was difficult to get terminals from one vendor to talk to computers from another company. Some terminals (notably those from IBM) didn't even use ASCII characters.

Today, terminals are much more standardized. If your experience with terminals is mainly with PC-based terminal emulators, you've probably encountered VT-style terminals. This style of terminal uses control codes popularized by Digital Equipment Corporation's (DEC) VT terminals; of course, Compaq has since bought DEC. These terminals use escape sequences—that is, an escape character followed by one or more commands—to control the cursor and the screen display.

The most important characteristic of these terminals, however, is that when you press a key, you can expect it to immediately transmit a character to the host computer. This is not the case with some terminals. Some HP and IBM computers favor terminals that collect an entire screen of data and then transmit it all at once. Also, some terminals are not able to handle full-duplex operation. A half-duplex terminal will allow you to type or allow the host computer to access the screen or printer, but not both at the same time.

To accommodate all these different types of terminals, the Internet defines the Telnet protocol in RFC854 (and a few other RFCs that refine the specification). Telnet allows an arbitrary terminal to log in to an arbitrary remote computer over the network. Many developers use Telnet to log in to remote servers. However, many other protocols use some or all of the Telnet protocol as a base.

Telnet relies on some special socket operations that Java does not support, so it isn't possible to completely implement Telnet in Java. However, for practical purposes, you can usually live without the parts you can't do in Java.

Telnet Overview

At first glance, it seems trivial to implement Telnet. Just open a socket on port 23 and exchange data, right? If there was a universal terminal, it might be that simple. However, because terminals (and host computers) vary, things are a bit more complex.

In theory, Telnet doesn't distinguish between a terminal and a host computer. It is rarely seen, but two terminals can communicate with each other via Telnet with no intervening computer. Upon connecting, both sides pretend to be a network virtual terminal (NVT). The NVT is a bare-bones terminal with features that should be available on any terminal, although the Telnet program may have to translate NVT codes and commands to local equivalents. The two parties can negotiate over what special features they will use. Although the NVT has limited capabilities, the two parties can use any features as long as they both agree.

NVT Overview

The NVT is a simulation of a basic terminal. What are the characteristics of this terminal? Conceptually, the terminal has a keyboard and a printer. Each uses 7-bit ASCII code in an 8-bit byte. By default, the NVT sends any typed character to the Telnet connection and the printer. That means the opposite end of the Telnet connection does not have to echo characters back.

The default NVT buffers characters until the end of a line, until the NVT has no more buffer, or until a program or user generates some locally defined signal to transmit (for example, a send key).

The NVT is a half-duplex device, by default. This is one place where the specification does distinguish between a host computer and a terminal. Hosts should send a special go ahead (GA) signal when they require more input. This allows true half-duplex terminals to unlock their keyboards. The specification states that it doesn't intend for terminals to send a GA signal at the end of each line. However, if two terminals are directly communicating, they would need to send GA signals to each other after each line (in the absence of other options). The RFC suggests providing the user a manual way to send a GA signal.

The RFC provides for only three special characters that the NVT must handle. The NUL (code 0), Line Feed (LF; code 10), and Carriage Return (CR; code 13) characters have their usual meanings. In particular, the NUL character does nothing. The LF character moves the print head down, keeping the same horizontal position. A CR moves the print head to the left margin of the current line.

The NVT takes into account the differences in line-ending conventions by defining CR and LF together as a new line. If you want to send an actual CR (that is, move the carriage to the left margin without starting a new line), you must send a CR and a NUL character together. In this way, systems that have to simulate a true CR (for example, through backspacing) will not have to do so in the usual case where the CR pairs with an LF. The Telnet program should remove any incoming NUL character if it follows a CR and not pass the extra byte to any underlying program.

In addition, the NVT may respond to several other commands (see Table 5.1). The specification, however, is silent on several interesting points, such as where the location of the tab stops on the terminal or how to change them.

Beyond these special characters, Telnet also defines a series of special Telnet commands. These are sequences of bytes that begin with an Interpret-As-Command (IAC) byte. This byte has a value of 255. If you really need to send 255 in the data stream, simply send it twice. Otherwise, the next byte (and possibly subsequent bytes) will constitute a special Telnet command. Many of these are for negotiating mutually agreeable options. Others allow you to interrupt the output and perform other special functions that are not specifically related to the display of data on the terminal.

Special Commands

The Telnet protocol supports 16 special commands that you can find in Table 5.2. The **DO**, **DONT**, **WILL**, **SB**, **SE**, and **WONT** commands relate to negotiation. You'll later read how they work.

The **GA** command, as mentioned earlier, informs the receiver that it may transmit at will. You'll see that in modern use, usually the sender and receiver will

Table 5.1   Optional NVT characters.

Character	Code	Description
BEL	7	Produces a signal (usually audible) without moving the cursor
BS	8	Moves the cursor one position left
HT	9	Moves to the next horizontal tab stop
VT	11	Moves to the next vertical tab stop
FF	12	Form feeds (moves to next page); often clears the screen on nonprinting terminals

Table 5.2   Telnet commands.

Command	Code	Description
IAC	255	Interpret-as command (to send 255 in data, double the character)
DONT	254	Request to receiver to stop performing an option
DO	253	Request to receiver to start performing an option
WONT	252	Refuse to perform an option
WILL	251	Agree to perform an option
SB	250	Suboption negotiation
GA	249	Go ahead (half duplex)
EL	248	Erase line
EC	247	Erase character
AYT	246	Are you there
AO	245	Abort output
IP	244	Interrupt process
BRK	243	Break
DM	242	Data mark
NOP	241	No operation
SE	240	End of suboption negotiation

5. Telnet

negotiate so that neither side sends **GA** commands. I don't suppose you'll see the **NOP** (no operation) command very often either.

The **EC** and **EL** commands cause the erasure of the last character or line. Not all terminals can effectively perform these commands, so you can't be sure what effect they will produce. For example, some old printing terminals might represent an **EL** by printing a backslash at the end of the current line and starting a new line.

The **AYT** command stands for "Are you there." This is simply an inquiry to make sure the other end is still receiving. The receiver should generate some printable response.

The remaining commands typically originate from a terminal. **BRK**, **IP**, and **AO** allow you to attempt to exercise control over a program running on a remote host. The host should react to these commands as soon as possible.

These immediate commands cause Java a bit of a problem. The RFC specifies that when you send an immediate command, you should also send a **DM** command using an urgent TCP packet (sometimes known as out-of-band data). Unfortunately, Java—at least as of the JDK 1.3—doesn't have a way to handle these urgent packets.

The problem arises when an errant process is not responding, and the terminal has already sent data that the Telnet program is buffering. When the Telnet program sees an urgent **DM** command, it should examine the buffer for **AYT**, **IP**, and **AO**. This also has the side effect of discarding buffered characters.

A Java program can't send or receive out-of-band data, so a Java-based Telnet program can only handle these special characters as they arrive in the data stream. If data is buffered, the priority commands will simply have to wait until they appear in the data stream.

Don't forget that all the Telnet commands must follow an **IAC** prefix (255). If you want to send a 255 in the data stream, you can double the character.

Negotiation

Either side of a Telnet connection can request a change in the default NVT parameters. However, the specification does not allow either side to force any options. Simply handling the NVT simulation is enough to satisfy the RFC.

Consider character echo, for example. Many serial terminals expect the host computer to echo characters back to the terminal. That gives the user positive feedback that the character arrived correctly. However, over a slow network connection—or when the terminal buffers lines—echoing characters doesn't make sense. However, with a fast network connection and a character-oriented terminal, you may want to enable echo processing.

RFC857 defines an option code of **1** for echo processing. To ask the other side of the connection to echo, you could send the special command **DO 1**. The other side can indicate its willingness to echo by sending **WILL 1**.

It's important to realize that either side can request this echo procedure. In other words, the host can advertise its willingness to echo by sending **WILL 1** before the terminal sends the **DO** command. The order is unimportant. If the host is not willing to echo, it would send a **WONT** command. The terminal could also send notice that it does not wish characters echoed by sending **DONT 1**.

Keep in mind that the Telnet specification doesn't distinguish between the host and the terminal. Therefore, it is just as legitimate for the host to request echoing from the terminal. Usually, the host computer doesn't want echo. So upon connection, you might see the following exchange:

```
HOST: WILL ECHO
TERMINAL: DO ECHO
TERMINAL: WILL ECHO
HOST: DONT ECHO
```

The previous sequence causes the host to echo characters to the terminal, but the terminal does not echo characters to the terminal. Keep in mind that it would be just as legitimate for the terminal to request echoing first:

```
TERMINAL: DO ECHO
HOST: WILL ECHO
```

In the first example, you can consider the **DO** command as an acknowledgment to the **WILL** command. In the second example, the **DO** is an imperative, and the **WILL** serves as an acknowledgment.

Loop Prevention

Because **WILL** and **DO** are almost interchangeable, you must be careful to prevent endless loops. For example, suppose the host sends a **WILL**, and the terminal sends a **DO** to acknowledge it. The host should not further acknowledge the **DO** with another **WILL** (which would cause the terminal to issue another **DO** command in a classic endless loop).

To prevent these loops you should observe the following rules:

- Only request a change in option status. Don't simply announce your current status.

- If you receive a request to change to a state that you are already in, don't acknowledge the request. In other words, if you are currently echoing characters and you receive a **DO ECHO** command, ignore it.

Naturally, any request to change status only affects the characters transmitted after the command. You probably won't change the echo status except at the beginning of the connection. However, it might make sense to change certain other options in the middle of a transaction.

Like any other Telnet command, these commands require the **IAC** prefix. Therefore, a **WILL ECHO** command, for example, is actually 255, 251, 1 (**WILL** is command 251).

Other Options

There are a myriad of RFCs that define a variety of possible options a Telnet server and client can agree on (see Table 5.3). If the terminal (or host) wants to process data a line at a time, you can attempt to negotiate option 34 (defined by RFC1184). This supercedes the older kludge line mode. Kludge line mode is an understanding that if echo is on or if suppress-go-ahead option is on (but not both), then Telnet would send single lines at a time.

Table 5.3   Common Telnet options.

Option Number	RFC	Description
1	857	Echo characters
3	858	Suppress GA
5	859	Status
6	860	Timing mark
24	1091	Terminal type
31	1073	Window size
32	1079	Terminal speed
33	1372	Remote flow control
34	1184	Line mode
36	1408	Environment variable

TIP: You can often make a Telnet client show you the commands it sends and receives. Most Unix Telnet programs (and the Cygwin Telnet program for Windows) will display the negotiations between the client and the host. Exactly how this works varies depending on your Telnet program.

Here is some sample output from the Cygwin Telnet program after issuing a toggle options commands:

```
$ telnet
telnet> toggle option
Will show option processing.
telnet> open guardian
Trying 192.244.69.30...
Connected to guardian
Escape character is '^]'.
SENT DO SUPPRESS GO AHEAD
SENT WILL TERMINAL TYPE
SENT WILL NAWS
SENT WILL TSPEED
SENT WILL LFLOW
SENT WILL LINEMODE
SENT WILL NEW-ENVIRON
SENT DO STATUS
RCVD DO OLD-ENVIRON
SENT WONT OLD-ENVIRON
RCVD DO TERMINAL TYPE
RCVD WILL SUPPRESS GO AHEAD
RCVD DO NAWS
SENT IAC SB NAWS 0 80 (80) 0 25 (25)
RCVD DO TSPEED
RCVD DO LFLOW
```

```
RCVD DONT LINEMODE
RCVD DONT NEW-ENVIRON
RCVD WONT STATUS
RCVD IAC SB TERMINAL-TYPE SEND
SENT IAC SB TERMINAL-TYPE IS "xterm"
RCVD IAC SB TERMINAL-SPEED SEND
SENT IAC SB TERMINAL-SPEED IS 38400,38400
RCVD WILL ECHO
SENT DO ECHO
RCVD DO ECHO
SENT WONT ECHO
RCVD DONT ECHO
login:
```

Suboptions

Some options require additional information once they are in force. First, the two sides negotiate the option. After both sides agree, they can exchange **SB** commands (suboptions). For example, the terminal may want to communicate it's terminal type to the host. This will allow the host to send terminal-specific command sequences to alter the display.

First, the client will signify its willingness to provide the information (using option 24):

```
IAC WILL 24
```

The host then can acknowledge and accept this option by issuing a **DO** command:

```
IAC DO 24
```

Next, the host will request the suboption value using the **SB** command. A **1** in the request indicates that the host wishes to know the suboption value. After any **SB** command, you'll see an **SE** (suboption end) command:

```
IAC SB 24 1
IAC SE
```

The terminal will respond with the following (data in quotes are string literals):

```
IAC SB 24 0 "VT52"
IAC SE
```

The zero in the **SB** command indicates that the terminal is supplying the value (**VT52**, in this case). Of course, different subcommands will have different data.

Telnet in Practice

The Telnet RFCs paint a bare-bones picture of Telnet. However, most modern Telnet programs provide much more than the basics. In particular, it is rare to find a practical Telnet client that doesn't emulate some popular terminal (or even many different types of terminals). This is so prevalent that many hosts will assume you have at least some capabilities to display special characters or move the cursor.

Also, sometimes the program you connect to will affect how you receive data. For example, even if Telnet does not echo characters back to your terminal, the program you connect to might.

Typically, you think of the program a Telnet client connects to as a Unix shell. However, there are other cases where a Telnet connection is useful. For example, a database server might accept queries via Telnet. Many conferencing systems and MUD (Multi-User Dungeon) games can use Telnet.

With increased awareness of security problems, many sites are trying to phase out Telnet. By default, Telnet doesn't hide any of your data (including passwords) on the network. This means that anyone who can intercept your network traffic can compromise your security. You can encrypt socket data in several ways (for example, Secure Socket Layer or SSL), and these can work with Telnet. However, in practice, most sites use SSH (Secure Shell) to facilitate secure logins.

SSH uses special encryption techniques to encode all the data between a server and the client. It can also authenticate both parties proving that, for example, someone is not simply pretending to be the computer you think you are using.

A Basic Java Client

A proper Telnet client should be prepared to send and receive data at any time, so it makes sense that you'll have to use a thread. I wanted to create a general-purpose class that handles all the protocol concerns so that you could derive new classes that only contain the specialized processing you need. The result is the **TelnetTTY** class in Listing 5.1.

Listing 5.1   This base class allows you to easily create Telnet clients.

```
/* Telnet TTY class -- Williams
   This class provides a base for writing objects
   that do the telnet protocol.

   Bare minimum options. Assumes host will accept
   "go ahead suppression"
```

```
*/
import java.io.*;
import java.net.*;


public class TelnetTTY extends Thread {
    // Telnet constants
    final static int IAC=255;
    final static int DONT=254;
    final static int DO=253;
    final static int WONT=252;
    final static int WILL=251;
    final static int NOP=241;
    final static int OP_ECHO=1;
    final static int OP_SGA=3;

    // default NVT has echo off, go ahead on in both directions
    // however, we assume Suppress GA will work



    protected Socket sock;
    protected InputStreamReader rdr;
    protected OutputStreamWriter wrt;
    protected boolean errflag=false;
    protected IOException ioerror; // if an error, what was it?
    private boolean crflag=false;
    private boolean echoflag=false;
    protected boolean stopthread=false;
    // Constructor
    public TelnetTTY(String host, int port) throws IOException,
       UnknownHostException {
       TelnetTTYCons(host,port);
    }
    // Constructor
    public TelnetTTY(String host) throws IOException,
       UnknownHostException {
       TelnetTTYCons(host,23);
    }

    // Core code for constructors
    public void TelnetTTYCons(String host, int port) throws IOException,
       UnknownHostException {
       sock=new Socket(host,port);
       rdr=new InputStreamReader(sock.getInputStream());
       wrt=new OutputStreamWriter(sock.getOutputStream());
       start();
```

```
            // some hosts won't do anything until you start talking
                sendc(IAC); sendc(DO); sendc(OP_SGA);
                sendc(IAC); sendc(WILL); sendc(OP_SGA);
                }

            // read error flag and information
            public boolean getErrorFlag() {
              return errflag || (ioerror!=null);
            }

            public IOException getErrorException() {
              return ioerror;
            }

            // send a character to the remote
            public void send(int c) throws IOException {
              if (c=='\n') wrt.write('\r');    // LF=>CR LF
              wrt.write(c);
              if (c=='\r') wrt.write(0);       // CR=>CR NUL
              if (c==IAC) wrt.write(IAC); // double IACs in stream
              wrt.flush();
            }

            // Send an entire string
            public void send(String s) throws IOException {
              for (int i=0;i<s.length();i++) {
                  int c=(int)s.charAt(i);
                  if (c=='\n') wrt.write('\r');    // LF=>CR LF
                  wrt.write(c);
                  if (c=='\r') wrt.write(0);       // CR=>CR NUL
                  if (c==IAC) wrt.write(IAC);
              }
              wrt.flush();
            }

            // This thread listens for incoming characters
            public void run() {
              int c;
              while (!stopthread) {
                  c=getChar();
                  if (c==-1||ioerror!=null) break;
                  if (c==IAC) {
                  processCmd();
                  if (ioerror!=null) return;
                  }
```

```
      else
        processChar(c);
    }
    errflag=true;
  }

// Get a character from the stream
protected int getChar() {
  try {
      int c;
      if (crflag) {
         crflag=false;
         c=rdr.read();
         if (echoflag) wrt.write(c);
         if (c!=0) return c; // ignore CR NUL
         }
      c=rdr.read();
      if (echoflag) wrt.write(c);
      if (c=='\r') crflag=true;
      return c;
  }
  catch (IOException e) {
      ioerror=e;
      return -1;
  }
}

// Send a "bare" character
private void sendc(int c) {
  try {
      wrt.write(c);
      wrt.flush();
  }
  catch (IOException e) {
      ioerror=e;
  }
}

// Process a command
protected synchronized void processCmd() {
  int c;
  c=getChar();
  if (ioerror!=null) return;
  switch (c) {
  case IAC:
      processChar(IAC);  // escaped 8-bit character
```

```
    case NOP: // nop
        return;
    case DO:  // DO
        int state=WONT; // wont
        c=getChar();
        if (ioerror!=null) return;
        if (c==OP_SGA) {
          state=WILL; // will
        }
        if (c==OP_ECHO && !echoflag) {
          state=WILL; // will
          echoflag=true;
        }
        sendc(IAC);
        sendc(state);
        sendc(c);
        return;

    case WILL:  // WILL
        c=getChar();
        return;

    case WONT:  // WONT
        c=getChar();
        if (c==OP_SGA) {
       // hmm... we have to have SGA
        }
        return;

    case DONT:
        c=getChar();
        if (c==OP_ECHO && echoflag) {
        echoflag=false;
        sendc(IAC);
        sendc(WONT);
        sendc(OP_ECHO);
        }
        if (c==OP_SGA) {
        // hmm... we have to have SGA
        }
        return;

    // do more IAC commands
    default:        // just for debugging purposes
        System.out.println("\n[CMD: " + c + "]");
    }
  }
```

```
  // process incoming characters - subclass will override
  protected synchronized void processChar(int c) {
   if (c<32 && c != 10 && c !=13 && c !=9 && c !=8)
     return;
   System.out.print((char)c);
   }

  // Test main
  public static void main(String args[]) throws Exception {
   int c;
   TelnetTTY tty = new TelnetTTY(args[0]);
   while ((c=System.in.read())!=-1) {
     if (tty.getErrorFlag()) break;
     tty.send(c);
   }
   System.out.println("Finished");
   }
}
```

The object has two constructors. The first requires a hostname and assumes you want to use port 23. The second constructor allows you to specify a port number explicitly. Because the actual work is the same, a private function contains the actual logic for starting the client processing.

There are several places where the Telnet client may asynchronously detect errors or a broken socket. The **getErrorFlag** method returns **true** if an error occurred. If the error was due to an exception, the **getErrorException** method will return the **IOException** object.

When an application program wants to send data to the remote end of the connection, it can use the **send** method to send either an individual character or a string. The methods handle doubling any **IAC** characters so they are not mistaken for commands.

The **run** method is the receiving thread. The thread waits for a character and either calls **processChar** or **processCmd**. Most subclasses will override **processChar**, but few if any will override **processCmd**. The example **processChar** simply prints the character to the system console, but a subclass might elect to put the character into a text field that belongs to a graphical user interface panel.

The **processCmd** method handles the **WILL, WONT, DO, DONT** logic. It assumes that the remote will allow it to dispense with the go ahead characters. I haven't found a server yet that would not work like this.

The remaining functions are simple support functions. There is also a test **main** function that will connect to the host you specify on the command line. Even this simple main works relatively well as a bare-bones Telnet client. It reads characters from the system console and allows the default **processChar** method to print incoming characters.

You may notice doubled characters if you use this simple client to log in to a shell. That's because the program has no choice but to display the characters you type. There is no portable way to make the system console not echo characters as you type.

Creating a Telnet Server

There is very little difference between a Telnet server and a client. From the protocol's point of view, there is no difference. Of course, a server will manage its socket differently because it will listen for incoming connections. A server application, of course, will also want to provide some service such as database access.

I decided to modify the existing **TelnetTTY** object so that it could create servers as well (see Listing 5.2). This involved a few new functions, particularly the following:

- A new constructor that accepts a **Socket** object.

- **TelnetTTYServer** methods that create a **ServerSocket** object and accept connection requests. Each connection instantiates the object and calls its **connected** method.

- A **connected** method that subclasses can override. Typically, a server would prompt for a login or display a sign-on message in this method.

The **TelnetTTYServer** method can't directly instantiate a **TelnetTTY** object because you will typically want it to create a subclass. Therefore, the method requires a **Class** object to specify which class to instantiate. The program uses the **getConstructor** method to find a **Constructor** object that corresponds to your object. Then the program calls **newInstance** to actually create your object. This is the same technique used in Chapter 2 in the **MTServerBase** object.

Listing 5.2   A few modifications to the **TelnetTTY** object allows you to also create
Telnet servers.

```
/* Telnet TTY class -- Williams
   This class provides a base for writing objects
   that do the telnet protocol.

   Bare minimum options. Assumes host will accept
   "go ahead suppression"
```

```
*/
import java.io.*;
import java.net.*;


public class TelnetTTY extends Thread {
    // Telnet constants
    final static int IAC=255;
    final static int DONT=254;
    final static int DO=253;
    final static int WONT=252;
    final static int WILL=251;
    final static int NOP=241;
    final static int OP_ECHO=1;
    final static int OP_SGA=3;

    // default NVT has echo off, go ahead on in both directions
    // however, we assume Suppress GA will work



    protected Socket sock;
    protected InputStreamReader rdr;
    protected OutputStreamWriter wrt;
    protected boolean errflag=false;
    protected IOException ioerror; // if an error, what was it?
    private boolean crflag=false;
    private boolean echoflag=false;
    protected boolean stopthread=false;
    // Constructor
    public TelnetTTY(String host, int port) throws IOException,
       UnknownHostException {
       TelnetTTYCons(host,port);
    }
    // Constructor
    public TelnetTTY(String host) throws IOException,
       UnknownHostException {
       TelnetTTYCons(host,23);
    }

    // Core code for constructors
    public void TelnetTTYCons(String host, int port) throws IOException,
       UnknownHostException {
       sock=new Socket(host,port);
       rdr=new InputStreamReader(sock.getInputStream());
       wrt=new OutputStreamWriter(sock.getOutputStream());
       start();
```

```
// some hosts won't do anything until you start talking
    sendc(IAC); sendc(DO); sendc(OP_SGA);
    sendc(IAC); sendc(WILL); sendc(OP_SGA);
}


// Server constructor
public TelnetTTY(Socket skt) throws IOException {
    sock=skt;
    rdr=new InputStreamReader(sock.getInputStream());
    wrt=new OutputStreamWriter(sock.getOutputStream());
    start();
// some hosts won't do anything until you start talking
    sendc(IAC); sendc(DO); sendc(OP_SGA);
    sendc(IAC); sendc(WILL); sendc(OP_SGA);
}


// Static call to start server
public static void TelnetTTYServer(Class c) throws IOException {
TelnetTTYServer(c,23);
}

// Static call to start server on any port
public static void TelnetTTYServer(Class c,int port)
  throws IOException {
  ServerSocket ssock=new ServerSocket(port);
  java.lang.reflect.Constructor cons;
  Class [] arg = new Class[1];
  arg[0]=Socket.class;
// find constructor for user's class
  try {
      cons=c.getConstructor(arg);
  }
  catch (NoSuchMethodException e) {
    System.err.println("Can't find constructor");
     return;
  }
  while (true) {
    Socket [] args = new Socket[1];
    TelnetTTY svr;
    args[0]=ssock.accept();
   // create user's class
    try {
      svr = (TelnetTTY)cons.newInstance((Object [])args);
    }
    catch (Exception e) { continue; }
    svr.connected();
    }
```

```
}

// called when a client connects -- subclass will override
protected void connected() {
}

// read error flag and information
public boolean getErrorFlag() {
  return errflag || (ioerror!=null);
}

public IOException getErrorException() {
  return ioerror;
}

// send a character to the remote
public void send(int c) throws IOException {
  if (c=='\n') wrt.write('\r');   // LF=>CR LF
  wrt.write(c);
  if (c=='\r') wrt.write(0);      // CR=>CR NUL
  if (c==IAC) wrt.write(IAC); // double IACs in stream
  wrt.flush();
}

// Send an entire string
public void send(String s) throws IOException {
  for (int i=0;i<s.length();i++) {
    int c=(int)s.charAt(i);
    if (c=='\n') wrt.write('\r');   // LF=>CR LF
    wrt.write(c);
    if (c=='\r') wrt.write(0);      // CR=>CR NUL
    if (c==IAC) wrt.write(IAC);
  }
  wrt.flush();
}

// This thread listens for incoming characters
public void run() {
  int c;
  while (!stopthread) {
    c=getChar();
    if (c==-1||ioerror!=null) break;
    if (c==IAC) {
      processCmd();
      if (ioerror!=null) return;
    }
```

```
          else
            processChar(c);
      }
      errflag=true;
}

// Get a character from the stream
protected int getChar() {
    try {
        int c;
        if (crflag) {
          crflag=false;
          c=rdr.read();
          if (echoflag) wrt.write(c);
          if (c!=0) return c; // ignore CR NUL
        }
        c=rdr.read();
        if (echoflag) wrt.write(c);
        if (c=='\r') crflag=true;
        return c;
      }
    catch (IOException e) {
      ioerror=e;
      return -1;
    }
}

// Send a "bare" character
private void sendc(int c) {
    try {
      wrt.write(c);
      wrt.flush();
    }
    catch (IOException e) {
        ioerror=e;
    }
}

// Process a command
protected synchronized void processCmd() {
    int c;
    c=getChar();
    if (ioerror!=null) return;
    switch (c) {
    case IAC:
        processChar(IAC);  // escaped 8-bit character
```

```
        case NOP: // nop
           return;
        case DO:  // DO
           int state=WONT; // wont
           c=getChar();
          if (ioerror!=null) return;
          if (c==OP_SGA) {
          state=WILL; // will
          }
          if (c==OP_ECHO && !echoflag) {
            state=WILL; // will
            echoflag=true;
          }
          sendc(IAC);
          sendc(state);
          sendc(c);
          return;

      case WILL:  // WILL
        c=getChar();
        return;

      case WONT:  // WONT
        c=getChar();
        if (c==OP_SGA) {
// hmm... we have to have SGA
        }
        return;

      case DONT:
        c=getChar();
        if (c==OP_ECHO && echoflag) {
          echoflag=false;
          sendc(IAC);
          sendc(WONT);
          sendc(OP_ECHO);
        }
        if (c==OP_SGA) {
  // hmm... we have to have SGA
        }
        return;

// do more IAC commands
      default:        // just for debugging purposes
        System.out.println("\n[CMD: " + c + "]");
      }
   }
```

```
      // process incoming characters - subclass will override
      protected synchronized void processChar(int c) {
        if (c<32 && c != 10 && c !=13 && c !=9 && c !=8)
          return;
        System.out.print((char)c);
      }


      // Test main
      public static void main(String args[]) throws Exception {
        int c;
        if (args.length==0) {
            TelnetTTYServer(TelnetTTY.class);
        }
        TelnetTTY tty = new TelnetTTY(args[0]);
        while ((c=System.in.read())!=-1) {
            if (tty.getErrorFlag()) break;
            tty.send(c);
        }
        System.out.println("Finished");
      }


    }
```

Customizing the Server

By default, the server doesn't do anything interesting, but it does accept connections. To have it perform some useful function, you'll have to create a subclass, such as in Listing 5.3.

Listing 5.3 This simplistic Telnet server can provide a status message and the current time and also obey **help** and **quit** commands.

```
import java.net.*;
import java.io.*;

public class TelnetServe extends TelnetTTY {
    StringBuffer buf = new StringBuffer();
// This constructor just calls the base class
    public TelnetServe(Socket s) throws IOException {
      super(s);
    }
// on connection, print a sign on message
    protected void connected() {
      try {
        send("Welcome to the Java Telnet Server\n");
      }
```

```
       catch (IOException e) {}
     }
// process an incoming line
   protected void processLine(String line) {
   try {
      // this is just a simple example
      if (line.equals("status"))
       send("\nStatus OK\n");
      else if (line.equals("time"))
       send("\n"+new java.util.Date().toString()+"\n");
      else if (line.equals("help"))
       send("\nCommands are: status, time, help, quit\n");
      else if (line.equals("quit")) {
       send("\nGoodbye\n");
      sock.close();
      stopthread=true;
      }
      else
     send("Unknown command\n");
   }
   catch (Exception e) {}
   }
// This overrides the base class and builds a line
// that will be handled by processLine
   protected synchronized void processChar(int c) {
     if (c=='\r') {
      String line=buf.toString();
      buf=new StringBuffer();
      // process line
      processLine(line);
     }
     else {
       if (c!='\n') buf.append((char)c);
   }

   }

// Test main
   public static void main(String args[]) throws Exception {
   TelnetTTYServer(TelnetServe.class);
   }
}
```

This class provides override functions for **processChar** and **connected**. The **processChar** method builds a line in the **buf** (a **StringBuffer**). Once a complete line is ready, the method calls **processLine** to perform the actual work. The **connected** method simply prints a sign-on message.

For this example, **processLine** only responds to a handful of commands. The **time** command is the only one that performs any significant processing.

Telnet Open Source

There are many Java Telnet implementations available on the Web. Perhaps one of the most complete is the Telnet Applet (at **http://www.mud.de/se/jta/**). Don't let the name fool you. This is a powerful piece of Java code that implements Telnet in a very reusable way. It supports a plug-in architecture and includes code for handling SSH. Although the authors (Matthias L. Jugel and Marcus Meißner) use it to build an applet, there is no reason you can't use the base code as a foundation for any kind of Telnet application.

The **de.mud.telnet** package contains a simple class, **TelnetWrapper** that you can use to write programs without having to plumb the depths of the Telnet class. Listing 5.4 shows how simple it is to use.

Listing 5.4   The **TelnetWrapper** class (from the open source **de.mud.telnet** package)
makes it simple to interact with a host via Telnet.

```
import de.mud.telnet.*;
public class JtaTest {
    public static void main(String args[]) {
      TelnetWrapper telnet = new TelnetWrapper();
      try {
        telnet.connect(args[0], 23);
        telnet.login("alw", "xxx");
        telnet.setPrompt("/users/alw ->");
        telnet.waitfor("TERM =");
        telnet.send("dumb");
        System.out.println(telnet.send("ls -l"));
        } catch(java.io.IOException e) {
          e.printStackTrace();
        }
    }
  }
```

The sequence of events is straightforward:

- **connect**—This causes the object to connect to the named host, on a specified port.

- **login**—Making a call to log in causes the object to log in with the given user name and password.

- **setPrompt**—This call tells the object which string the host will send when prompting for input.

- **waitfor**—Use this call to cause the object to pause until the host sends the specified string.

- **send**—This sends the string you provide and returns the data received up to (and including) the prompt.

You can find the most useful methods in Table 5.4.

Table 5.4   Useful methods for TelnetWrapper.

Method	Description
connect	Connect to a remote machine
disconnect	Disconnect from remote computer
getTerminalType	Get the current terminal type for TTYPE Telnet option
getWindowSize	Get the current window size of the terminal
login	Log in to remote host
send	Send a command to the remote host; returns text sent back up to (and including) prompt text, if the prompt text is set (see **setPrompt**)
setLocalEcho	Set the local echo option
setPrompt	Set the prompt string that the object will wait for when you call **send**
waitfor	Wait for a string to come from the remote host and return all characters received up to (and including) the string

5. Telnet

Immediate Solutions

Finding the Telnet Specification

The Telnet specification is spread among many different RFCs. RFC854 (also known as STD0008) defines the core Telnet protocol and the characteristics of the NVT that Telnet programs must emulate. However, in practice, most Telnet programs will negotiate one or more options, each covered by a different RFC. RFC855 (also part of STD0008) defines the options in general, whereas specific RFCs cover particular options.

The most common options follow:

- *Binary*—This mode allows the parties to negotiate binary transmission. Although it might seem like Telnet always uses 8 bits, keep in mind that without a binary option, some Telnet implementations might translate incoming 8-bit NVT characters into another character set (for example, EBCDIC). In binary mode, this conversion would cease. However, you still must double bytes with the value 255, and Telnet commands are still in force (RFC0856).

- *Echo*—This causes the remote host to echo characters (RFC0857/STD0028).

- *Suppress Go Ahead*—This sets up a full-duplex connection (RFC0858/STD0029).

- *Status*—A Telnet program can use this option to request the options in force on the other side (RFC0859/STD0030).

- *Timing Mark*—When one Telnet program sends another a **DO TM** command, the other will respond (typically with a **WILL TM**) after processing any data that preceded the **DO** command. Even if the remote host sends **DONT TM**, it still serves the same purpose (RFC0860/STD0031).

- *Extended Option*—This option actually introduces 255 more options for future expansion (RFC0861/STD0032).

- *Window Size*—Known as NAWS (Negotiate About Window Size), this option lets the two parties agree on the width and height of the Telnet window, in characters (RFC1073).

- *Terminal Speed*—Using this option the Telnet program can set an effective baud rate, which the host can use to control how much data it sends at once (RFC1079).

5. Telnet

- *Terminal Type*—The Telnet client can use this option to announce the type of terminal it emulates. The host can use this to select special characters to effect text appearance, set the cursor position, and perform other special operations (RFC1091).

- *Line Mode*—Computers can agree to transfer data a line at a time using this option (RFC1184).

- *Remote Flow Control*—If the terminal wants to control the output flow from the remote host, it can use this option (RFC1372).

- *Environment*—This option allows a Telnet session to set environment variables on the remote host (RFC1572).

In addition, RFCs 652–658 define options that allow the sender and the receiver to agree on the disposition of special characters (for example, line feeds, carriage returns, tabs, and other similar characters).

Sending Telnet Commands with Data

Each Telnet command begins with a special **IAC** code (255). This makes it simple to send 8-bit data through Telnet because only bytes with a value of 255 require special treatment. If you want to send a byte with that value, simply send it twice.

WARNING! Be sure to double any data byte with the value of 255 that is not an IAC. For example, if you are involved in suboption negotiation, and a data value contains 255, double that byte. Even if you have negotiated binary mode, you still double any bytes with a value of 255 (unless, of course, you mean to send an IAC).

Each Telnet command (see Table 5.2) requires a different number of bytes, and many require further transactions with the suboption command.

Simulating the NVT

Each side of the Telnet transaction simulates an NVT. This terminal should buffer characters as much as possible (up to the end of the line, where possible). It does not require the remote side to perform character echo. The character set is 7-bit ASCII in an 8-bit byte.

The NVT recognizes only a few special characters, NUL (0), LF (10), and CR (13). To help terminals that don't distinguish between CR and the end of line, an end of line is explicitly sent as a CR and an LF character. Any CR that is not a true end of line is sent as CR NUL.

In modern practice, most Telnet programs are more capable than the NVT. By using option negotiation, both Telnet programs can agree on what special features to use.

Negotiating Telnet Options

If a Telnet program wishes to use features not present in the NVT (or suppress NVT features), it must negotiate with the remote Telnet program. No Telnet program is obligated to support anything beyond the NVT.

Two possible situations can occur:

1. You may want the remote system to start (or stop) performing some action. In this case, you send a **DO** (or **DONT**) command.

2. You may want to perform some action yourself (or, conversely, you may want to stop performing an action). In this case, you send a **WILL** (or **WONT**) command.

In either case, you must allow the other end to agree or disagree with your request. If you send a **DO** command, the opposite side may send a **WILL**, indicating that it will comply with your request, or a **WONT** if it does not wish to satisfy the request. If you have sent a **WILL** command, the remote will reply with a **DO** or **DONT** (depending, of course, on its desire to have you actually perform the indicated action).

Preventing Negotiation Loops

The symmetry of the **DO/DONT** and **WILL/WONT** commands leads to a possible problem. If one Telnet program issues a **DO**, the other side may acknowledge with a **WILL**. However, the original Telnet program may mistakenly further acknowledge with another **DO**, which will cause the generation of yet another **WILL**, and lead to a classic endless loop.

Follow these rules to prevent negotiation loops:

- *Only request a change in option status.* Don't simply announce your current status.

- *If you receive a request to change to a state that you are already in, don't acknowledge the request.* In other words, if you are currently echoing characters and you receive a DO ECHO command, ignore it.

Handling Suboptions

Many options require data. For example, if the Telnet client wants to indicate the type of terminal it emulates, at some point, it must send the terminal's ID (for example, TTY or VT52).

Consider the terminal type option (option 24). The exchange might look like this:

IAC WILL 24	*I will provide terminal information (sent from terminal to host).*
IAC DO 24	*I will accept terminal information (sent from host to terminal).*
IAC SB 24 1	*Send me the suboption for terminal type (sent from host to terminal).*
IAC SE	*End of SB command (sent from host to terminal).*
IAC SB 24 0 "VT52"	*I am a VT52 (sent from terminal to host).*
IAC SE	*End of SB command (sent from terminal to host).*

The **SB** command contains a 1 if the sender is requesting the value and a 0 if it is supplying the value. The VT52 in quotes is simply the ASCII bytes that make up the string.

TIP: If the data in the SB command contains a byte with the value of 255, be sure to double the byte so it is not confused with an IAC command.

Creating a Telnet Client from a Base Class

Listing 5.1 shows a base class suitable for creating a Telnet client (Listing 5.2 shows a variation on that class that could be a server or a client). Using this object to handle the protocol requirements makes it easy to create a Telnet client application by simply subclassing the **TelnetTTY** object.

The subclass can provide a **processChar** method to handle incoming characters. The **send** method allows the subclass to send characters to the remote machine. The server name and (optionally) the port number pass to the base class constructor.

Listing 5.5 shows a trivial subclass that shifts all incoming characters to uppercase. The **main** function simply reads input from the system console and sends it directly to the remote host.

Listing 5.5   This Telnet client shifts all incoming characters to uppercase.

```
import java.io.*;

public class TelnetTest extends TelnetTTY {
    public TelnetTest(String host) throws IOException {
    super(host);
    }
    public synchronized void processChar(int c) {
    char cu=Character.toUpperCase((char)c);
    System.out.print(cu);
    }
    public static void main(String args[]) throws Exception {
    int c;
    TelnetTest tty=new TelnetTest(args[0]);
    while ((c=System.in.read())!=-1) {
       if (tty.getErrorFlag()) break;
       tty.send(c);
    }
  }
}
```

Creating a Telnet Server from a Base Class

Because the Telnet protocol is quite symmetrical, a few modifications to the **TelnetTTY** class (from Listing 5.1) will allow you to create a client or a server. The updated code appears in Listing 5.2.

Creating a new server is very easy. You simply do the following:

1. Override **TelnetTTY**.

2. Provide a constructor for your object that accepts a **Socket** object.

In addition, you can override **connected** to handle any tasks you want to perform when a client makes a connection and **processChar** to handle incoming characters.

Listing 5.6 shows a Telnet server that prints a palindrome when a client connects and then forces the connection to close. You can find another Telnet server in the "In Depth" section of this chapter (see Listing 5.3).

Listing 5.6   This Telnet server also uses **TelnetTTY**.

```
import java.io.*;
import java.net.Socket;

public class TServer extends TelnetTTY {
    public TServer(Socket s) throws IOException {
    super(s);
    }
    public void connected() {
    try {
        send("A man, a plan, a canal, Panama!\n");
        sock.close();
        stopthread=true;
    }
    catch (IOException e) { }
    }

    public static void main(String args[]) throws Exception {
    TelnetTTYServer(TServer.class);
    }

}
```

Using **TelnetWrapper**

The Open Source Telnet Applet (at **http://www.mud.de/se/jta/**) contains a class that makes it easy to write sophisticated Telnet clients. The class **TelnetWrapper** is similar to the **TelnetTTY** class, but it has scripting features that allow you to wait for certain characters to arrive from the remote computer's output.

In Listing 5.7, you'll find a simple Telnet client that uses **TelnetWrapper**. The **connect** method specifies the machine name and port. The **login** method provides a user name and password. The scripting part of the application occurs when the program calls **setPrompt**. Now the **TelnetWrapper** object understands that data that occurs before this string is the output of some command (presumably from a Unix shell). The **waitfor** call causes the object to wait for the host to inquire about the terminal type. After the program replies (using **send**), it issues a **df** command (to check disk space). Because of the prior call to **setPrompt**, the **send** command will return the output from the command.

Listing 5.7   The TelnetWrapper class makes it simple to write a Telnet client that waits for responses from the host.

```java
import de.mud.telnet.*;
public class JtaScript {
    public static void main(String args[]) {
        TelnetWrapper telnet = new TelnetWrapper();
        String username="alw";
        String hostname="colossus";
        try {
            telnet.connect(hostname, 23);
            telnet.login(username, "password");
            telnet.setPrompt("/users/" + username + " ->");
            telnet.waitfor("TERM =");
            telnet.send("dumb");
            System.out.println(telnet.send("df"));
        } catch(java.io.IOException e) {
            e.printStackTrace();
        }
    }
}
```

To use the **TelnetWrapper**, follow these steps:

1. Instantiate a **TelnetWrapper** object.

2. Call **connect** to specify the remote host and port.

3. Call **login** to establish your user name and password.

4. Use **waitfor**, **setprompt**, and **send** to interact with the host.

5. You can use **disconnect** to break the connection with the host.

Chapter 6

FTP

In Depth

At last count six working PCs were distributed throughout my house. My computer, of course, is in my home office. I have an old laptop that isn't worth selling and a newer laptop that is nearly as fast as my desktop computer. Then, both of my sons have computers in their rooms. Finally, there is an old computer out in my electronics lab (well, OK, it's really my garage).

Not long after having two computers I put a network backbone in the attic and set up a small network. However, for some reason, I didn't run the cable over to the garage. Invariably, whatever file I happened to need would either be on the network when I was in the garage, or in the garage when I was on one of the network computers. I suppose that's a computer variation of Finagle's law.

Until I finally snaked some cable to my ersatz lab, I'd use what's affectionately known as Nike Net to transfer files (you know, you slip on your Nike shoes and run down the hall carrying a floppy). I imagine that back before the Internet, people had the same experience on a major scale. I can remember being part of a group of Hewlett Packard computer users that would send a magnetic tape around in the mail. You'd keep it a few days, take what you wanted, add anything you had to the end, and mail it to the next site.

That's why FTP (File Transfer Protocol) is one of the earliest Internet standards. Its job is to allow computers (sometimes dissimilar computers) to transfer files. Like many of the Internet protocols, the interaction is almost usable by a human, but it is really made for machines.

In a way, FTP uses the same ideas as Telnet. You are expected to look like a Network Virtual Terminal (NVT) and a few other Telnet protocol items appear in FTP. However, where Telnet attempts to bridge between terminals with different modes, FTP is worried more about differences in files. In today's relatively homogenized world, you think of files as a big stream of bytes. However, some computers store files using records, odd word lengths, or unique data structures. Even some modern computers, such as the Macintosh, have oddball files that don't translate well into a simple string of bytes (each Mac file can really have two subfiles known as forks).

The Basics

FTP is a peculiar protocol because it uses two sockets. The main socket (TCP port 21) handles the commands the FTP client sends to the server as well as the associated response from the server. The other port, which is at port 20 by default but can be changed, handles data.

With the modern Internet, this mechanism might seem strange. However, the control port doesn't need to handle binary data, for example. In addition—although few FTP programs support it—you can theoretically use the control port to set up a data transfer between the server and a third machine.

If you read RFC959 (the basic specification for FTP) you'll find that a great deal of it is concerned with translation between different character encodings and storage representations. For example, the RFC mentions that the DEC TOPS-20 stores ASCII text in five 7-bit characters, left-justified in a 36-bit word. IBM mainframes, of course, use Extended Binary-Coded Decimal Interchange Code (EB-CDIC). Some computers don't represent files as a stream of bytes. The RFC covers all of these details.

Luckily, in the modern world, a lot of this is antiquated baggage. Even if you work with a computer that has an odd way of dealing with files and characters, the Internet has forced most platforms to make concessions so that there is much less variety today.

You might wonder why you even care about these details. Suppose you have a Joint Photographic Experts Group (JPEG) file from your vacation on a remote server, along with a text file describing the contents of the picture. If you download the JPEG, you expect it to come over the network with each byte intact. However, if you load an ASCII text file to an IBM mainframe, you can't easily read it. That's why FTP distinguishes between files that contain text and files that it should copy verbatim.

In practice, the biggest reason users want to distinguish these file types is because MS-DOS and Windows use two characters (a carriage return and a line feed) at the end of lines, whereas Unix and most other systems use only a single line feed. Most FTP servers will convert the line endings as appropriate in text mode, but they won't modify binary files.

Another infrequently used option allows the user to specify the type of printing control codes in a text file. Presumably, you could use FTP to send a file from a server to a printer that listens to a socket on some remote machine. Very few modern implementations will have to deal with printing control codes.

6. FTP

Transfers

When a user asks to send or receive a file, the server will typically open a socket on the user's machine. That means that every FTP client can also be a server of sorts. By default, the data socket is socket 20, but typically, the client will select another port (especially because only one user can listen on port 20 at a time).

When the user asks for a list of available files the server uses a separate data connection to deliver the results. There are two ways the server can supply the list: as just a list of file names, one per line, or as a complete listing that can contain details such as file size and any date and time information that is available. People like to see the full listing; however, there is no standard format, so if a program is reading the list, it will probably prefer the bare formatted listing.

Some FTP clients can't act as a server for the data socket. This is usually the case when the client is behind a firewall. The firewall would reject incoming connection requests, and that would make it impossible to use FTP.

To remedy this, you can ask the server to use passive mode. In passive mode, the server creates a separate data socket and informs the client of the port number it should use for the data connection. Then the server listens on this port for a connection from the client.

Usually FTP programs use the default stream mode. However, you can also select block mode (where you send data with a header that indicates the length of the block) or compressed mode. Compressed mode uses a form of run-length encoding. Naturally, if you really want compression, you'd be better off using a more efficient encoding on the file (such as zip, for example) before you send it via FTP.

The FTP programs, by the way, don't perform any error detection or correction because they use TCP ports. The underlying network should prevent scrambled data problems.

Replies

As I mentioned earlier, FTP is made to be useful for a program to use but still be intelligible for a human, if necessary. This is especially evident in the replies that the server sends in response to commands (over the control connection).

The first four characters of the response are important. The first three are a special code that indicates, in detail, the server's response. The next character is a space if there is only one line of response text or if this line is the last line of a multiline response. If the fourth character is a hyphen, expect more lines of responses to follow this one (all of them will have the same three-digit code).

Following these four special characters, the remainder of the line can contain any descriptive text necessary for the reply. In most cases, these are only of interest to human users. However, there are a few replies that have information embedded in them that an FTP client program would need to interpret.

The numeric codes are always in the range of 100 through 599. Each digit has a special meaning that the FTP client can use to guide its actions. The first digit gives the client a rough idea of success or failure:

- *100 through 199*—A positive preliminary reply. This means that the server acknowledges the receipt of a command, and, at this point, everything is correct. However, the client must continue to wait for another reply before sending any further commands.

- *200 through 299*—The requested action is complete and successful.

- *300 through 399*—A positive intermediate reply. Any of these codes indicate that the server accepted the command, but it needs more information from the client to continue.

- *400 through 499*—This range of codes indicates that there was a failure, but the failure may be temporary. For example, suppose the server can't open any more sockets because of the current number of users. If you attempt the exact same transfer later, it might succeed.

- *500 through 599*—These codes indicate a permanent error. Retrying the exact same commands will only generate another error.

The second digit further narrows the meaning of the message. If the second digit of a message is 0, the server is complaining about the syntax of the command. A 1 indicates an informational message. Replies that concern control and data connections (that is, socket-related messages) will have a 2 in the second place. Messages relating to user logins have a 3 in the middle digit, and file system messages use a 5 in the same spot. The RFC does not define any messages that use a 4 in the second position.

The third digit specifies an exact message within the constraints set by the other two digits. You can find a table of common messages in Table 6.1. Entries marked as Fixed Format must conform to a particular format in the text area.

You'll notice that a few of the error codes (for example, 450 and 550) seem to be the same. Remember that the first digit determines if the error is temporary or permanent. For example, if you try to perform an operation and someone else had the file open, then that would be a 450 response. After all, you could try it again, and it might work. However, if the file is not accessible to that user, a 550 response would be more appropriate.

6. FTP

Table 6.1   The FTP Server responds with one of these codes for each operation requested.

Code	Meaning	Fixed Format
110	Restart marker reply	Yes
120	Service ready later	No
125	Data connection already open	No
150	File status OK, about to open data connection	No
200	Command OK	No
202	Command not implemented because it isn't necessary on this server	No
211	System status or help reply	No
212	Directory status	No
213	File status	No
214	Help	No
215	System type (for example, Unix)	Yes
220	Service ready for login	No
221	Service closing control connection	No
225	Data connection open; no transfer in progress	No
226	Closing data connection (success)	No
227	Entering passive mode	Yes
230	User logged in	No
250	Requested file action complete	No
257	Path created	No
331	User name OK, need password	No
332	Need account information	No
350	Requested action pending further information	No
421	Service not available	No
425	Can't open data connection	No
426	Connection closed (aborted)	No
450	File unavailable	No
451	Aborted due to local error	No
452	Aborted due to lack of space	No
500	Syntax error in command	No
501	Syntax error in parameters	No
502	Command not implemented	No
503	Bad sequence of commands	No

(continued)

Table 6.1 The FTP Server responds with one of these codes for each operation requested *(continued)*.

Code	Meaning	Fixed Format
504	Command not implemented for that parameter	No
530	Not logged in	No
532	Need account for storing files	No
550	Failed because file is not available	No
551	Failed because page type is unknown	No
552	Failed because storage allocation exceeded	No
553	Failed because of bad file name	No

Logging In

FTP servers usually want users to authenticate themselves. The exact details of how the server will verify the user's ID and password is, of course, system specific (unless you use your own private authentication scheme, such as a list of users in a properties file, for example).

When a client makes an initial connection to the server, the server will usually send a 220 response to indicate its readiness. The client should respond with a **USER** command, which includes the user's ID. The client will then usually receive a 331 response. The first digit is a three, so you know this means the server expects more information. That information is the password (sent with the **PASS** command). Once the server accepts both the user ID and the password, it will respond with a 230 response.

Some systems also require an account either for logging in or for certain operations. The client can specify this with the **ACCT** command at any time. If the server requires the account information, it can issue a 332 response to the client.

Making the Connection

Although managing the control connection is the same as making any other socket connection, the data connection is quite different. The data connection may come and go at different times throughout the life of the conversation between the client and the server.

Usually, the server expects the client to be listening on port 20. Because this is usually not practical for most clients, it is common for the client to issue a **PORT** command. This command requires six decimal numbers (represented in ASCII form). The first four numbers are the parts of the client's Internet Protocol (IP) address. The last two numbers represent the 16-bit port number. The first number is the most-significant 8 bits, and the last number is the least-significant byte. The command requires you to separate the numbers with commas.

Therefore, if the client were at IP address 10.1.1.5 and listening on port 513, the **PORT** command would look like this:

```
PORT 10,1,1,5,2,1
```

Interestingly, the IP address does not have to match the client's address. It is legal to use a **PORT** command to direct the server to send or receive data with a third computer. Of course, that third computer would have to be listening on the specified port. This is uncommon in modern usage.

Forming the **PORT** command in a Java program requires a little reformatting of the IP address and port number available from the control socket (see Listing 6.1). The **getLocalAddress** method (part of **Socket**) returns an **InetAddress** object. You can then call **getHostAddress** to find the local address you are using to talk to the FTP server. However, you have to convert all the periods to commas to conform to the **PORT** command's syntax. Placing the IP address in a **StringBuffer** makes that easy to accomplish. Finally, you can call **append** to insert the port number (don't forget to break it into 2 bytes first).

In Listing 6.1, the code follows the **PORT** command (sent with **sendCmd**, a method elsewhere in the program) by a **LIST** command, which asks the server to send a listing of available files on the data port. Then the code has to listen on the **ServerSocket** (using **accept**).

Listing 6.1   This Java code forms a PORT command.

```
// ctlskt is the FTP control socket
// datskt is the FTP data socket
ServerSocket datsktsvr = new ServerSocket(0); // pick a port
StringBuffer cmd = new StringBuffer("PORT ");
cmd.append(ctlskt.getLocalAddress().getHostAddress());
for (int i = 0; i < cmd.length(); i++) {
   if ('.' == cmd.charAt(i))
   cmd.setCharAt(i, ',');
}
cmd.append(",");
cmd.append(Integer.toString(port/256));
cmd.append(",");
cmd.append(Integer.toString(port&0xFF));
status=sendCmd(cmd.toString());
if (status!=200) return -1;
status=sendCmd("LIST");
// wait for remote connection (could time out)
datskt=datsktsvr.accept();
```

6. FTP

Of course, the **PORT** command assumes you want the server to make the connection to the client. If you want to connect to the server, you can issue a **PASV** command. This will respond with code 227, if the server supports passive mode. The response will also have the IP address and port, using the same format as the **PORT** command, embedded in the return string. For example, here's a reply from a real FTP server on the Internet:

```
227 Entering Passive Mode (208,146,45,13,17,47)
```

The client then has to parse through the string for the correct parameters. You can find an example of this in Listing 6.2. Here, the **lastResponse** variable holds the response from the server following a **sendCmd** call. Here the code has to replace the commas with periods, reconstitute the port number, and then it constructs a **Socket** object.

Passive mode will work behind most firewalls, with little downside to using it in any situation. Very few servers don't support passive mode, so a smart strategy would be to try passive mode, and if you get an error return, you can always try sending a **PORT** command instead (RFC1579 recommends this approach).

Listing 6.2   This code fragment issues a **PASV** command to initiate passive mode.

```
status=sendCmd("PASV");
if (status<200||status>299) return -1;
// find IP/port
for (i=4;i<lastResponse.length();i++)
    if (Character.isDigit(lastResponse.charAt(i))) break;
if (i==lastResponse.length()) return -1; // not found
token=new java.util.StringTokenizer(lastResponse.substring(i),",) ");
if (token.countTokens()!=6) return -1; // unknown IP/port
    for (i=0;i<4;i++) {
IP.append(token.nextToken());
if (i!=3) IP.append(".");
    }
port=Integer.parseInt(token.nextToken())*256;
port+=Integer.parseInt(token.nextToken());
datskt=new Socket(IP.toString(),port);
status=sendCmd("LIST");
```

Once you have **datskt** set, either from the **accept** call (in normal mode) or from the **Socket** constructor (in passive mode), you can easily send data to the socket (or read data from the socket). You can find code in Listing 6.3 that reads from the socket and writes to a **writer** in variable **w** (presumably a file).

6. FTP

Listing 6.3   Writing to the data socket is easy using a stream or writer class.

```
datReader=new InputStreamReader(datskt.getInputStream());
// transfer data until socket closes
int ch;
do {
    ch=datReader.read();
    if (ch!=-1) w.write((char)ch);
} while (ch!=-1);
w.flush();
datskt.close();
```

FTP Command Details

The RFC defines quite a few commands that FTP servers may implement. Of course, you are free to leave many commands unimplemented. You have to return the correct error responses for commands you don't want to support. However, many FTP clients assume there will be certain commands available (**USER**, **PORT**, **LIST**, and **NLST**, for example). Many clients don't gracefully handle missing commands.

Table 6.2 shows the available commands. Some of these don't get much use in modern programs. If you want to experiment with these commands by hand, you can always use a Telnet program to connect to an FTP server (be sure to use port 21). Of course, you can't open a data port, so you won't be able to meaningfully use commands such as **RETR**, **LIST**, or other commands that need a data connection.

Many command-line FTP clients use similar commands. So when you enter **SITE** or **PWD**, the client is really just forwarding that to the server. Many clients also support a **QUOTE** command so that you can send any command directly to the server. So typing **HELP** might show the help messages for your local FTP program, but typing **QUOTE HELP** will show you the server's help messages.

Table 6.2   FTP commands specified by the FTP RFC.

Command	Arguments	Description	Possible Initial Replies
USER	User name	Specify username.	230, 530, 500, 501, 421, 331, 332
PASS	Password	Specify password.	230, 202, 530, 500, 501, 503, 421, 332
ACCT	Account information	Specify user account.	230, 202, 530, 500, 501, 503, 421
CWD	Directory name	Change working directory.	250, 500, 501, 502, 421, 530 , 550

(continued)

Table 6.2   FTP commands specified by the FTP RFC *(continued)*.

Command	Arguments	Description	Possible Initial Replies
CDUP	None	Change to parent directory (same as CWD for many systems).	250, 500, 501, 502, 421, 530, 550
SMNT	Mount information	Structure mount (change file systems—for example, mounting a tape or removable disk).	202, 250, 500, 501, 502, 421, 530, 550
REIN	None	Reinitialize (start over); requires a new **USER** command to continue.	120, 220, 421, 500, 502
QUIT	None	End session.	221, 500
PORT	IP address and port number	Specify data port.	200, 500, 501, 421, 530
PASV	None	Request passive mode.	227, 500, 501, 502, 421, 530
TYPE	File type code	Select ASCII, EBCDIC, or Image (A, E, I) file types.	200, 500, 501, 504, 421, 530
STRU	Structure code	Select type of file structure (typically the default, F for File, is used).	200, 500, 501, 504, 421, 530
MODE	Mode code	Select the transfer mode (typically the default, S for Stream, is used).	200, 500, 501, 504, 421, 530
RETR	File name	Retrieve file.	125, 150, 450, 550, 500, 501, 421, 530
STOR	File name	Store file.	125, 150, 532, 450, 452, 553, 500, 501, 421, 530
STOU	None	Store as a unique file name; the server's response will contain the file's name.	125, 150, 532, 450, 452, 553, 500, 501, 421, 530
APPE	File name	If the file specified does not exist, this is essentially the same as **STOR**. However, if the file does exist, the current file adds to the end of the existing file (append mode).	125, 150, 532, 450, 452, 553, 500, 501, 421, 530

(continued)

6. FTP

Table 6.2   FTP commands specified by the FTP RFC *(continued)*.

Command	Arguments	Description	Possible Initial Replies
ALLO	Size	Allocate the specified number of bytes for the next **STOR**, **STOU**, or **APPE** command; usually only implemented on machines that require file allocation.	200, 202, 500, 501, 504, 421, 530
REST	Marker	Inform the server that the next transfer should restart at a checkpoint (indicated by the marker argument).	500, 501, 502, 421, 530, 350
RNFR	File name	Specify the existing file name of a file you wish to rename; always followed by **RNTO**.	450, 550, 500, 501, 502, 421, 530, 350
RNTO	File name	Specify the new name of a file you wish to rename; always preceded by **RNFR**.	250, 532, 553, 500, 501, 502, 503, 421, 530
ABOR	None	Abort current transfer (usually sent with urgent Telnet message).	225, 226, 500, 501, 502, 421
DELE	File name	Delete a file.	250, 450, 550, 500, 501, 502, 421, 530
RMD	Directory name	Remove a directory.	250, 500, 501, 502, 421, 530, 550
MKD	Directory name	Make a directory.	257, 500, 501, 502, 421, 530, 550
PWD	None	Print the current directory.	257, 500, 501, 502, 421, 550
LIST	Path name	Transfer a human-readable list of files in the specified directory or file; uses the current directory if the argument is not present.	125, 150, 450, 500, 501, 502, 421, 530
NLST	Path name	Similar to **LIST**, this command transfers a list of file names only, one per line.	125, 150, 450, 500, 501, 502, 421, 530

(continued)

Table 6.2   FTP commands specified by the FTP RFC *(continued)*.

Command	Arguments	Description	Possible Initial Replies
SITE	Command	Send site-specific commands (for example, many Unix FTP servers use this to allow you to execute **chmod** on your files).	200, 202, 500, 501, 530
SYST	None	Return a standard name for the system type and possibly a default byte size.	215, 500, 501, 502, 421
STAT	File name	If a transfer is in progress (and this was sent using the Telnet urgent protocol) the server returns information about the transfer in progress. If there is no transfer in progress, and a pathname is provided, the server will return details about the file name.	211, 212, 213, 450, 500, 501, 502, 421, 530
HELP	Command	Return help text for the specified command (or a summary if there is no argument).	211, 214, 500, 501, 502, 421
NOOP	None	No operation.	200, 500, 421

Client Considerations

Writing a client isn't too difficult if you understand the underlying FTP protocol. In the Immediate Solutions section of this chapter, you'll find a simple client that does a directory listing on the server of your choice. Because directory listings and file transfers are more or less the same, you can write just a few functions that will cover all the common tasks required.

In particular, a typical design will have the following methods:

- **connect**—Connects to the server and provide a user name and password
- **dataSocketIn**—Opens the data socket and reads data from it to another stream (probably a file)
- **dataSocketOut**—Opens the data socket and writes data to it from another stream
- **dataSocket**—Creates a data socket or connects to the server's data socket when using passive mode; used by **dataSocketIn** and **dataSocketOut**

- **getResponse**—Retrieves a response code from the server, taking into account the possibility of multiline responses

- **sendCmd**—Sends a command to the server and await a reply

Armed with these methods, it is simple to exercise the server using the standard FTP commands. The **dataSocketIn** command is especially interesting. You pass it a command that will result in data transfer. It handles the data connection, using **dataSocket**, and then transfers data from the socket to a stream of your choice. This is very versatile because the stream can represent a file, the console, or even a string. You can find **dataSocketIn** in Listing 6.4. The **dataSocketOut** method is quite similar. However, as you'd expect, it reads data from a stream you select and then sends it to the data socket.

Listing 6.4   The **dataSocketIn** method transfers data from the FTP server to a stream of your choice.

```
public int dataSocketIn(String datCmd,Writer w) throws IOException {
 int status;
 status=dataSocket(datCmd);
 if (status!=0) return status;
 datReader=new InputStreamReader(datskt.getInputStream());
 // transfer data until socket closes
 int ch;
 do {
     ch=datReader.read();
     if (ch!=-1) w.write((char)ch);
 } while (ch!=-1);
 w.flush();
 datskt.close();
 return getResponse();
 }
```

Server Considerations

Writing an FTP server requires you to listen on the control connection and parse the incoming command lines. This requires some way to read lines and some sort of parsing. Of course, you can just use the simple methods in **String** to skip blanks, isolate the first word of the input, and then compare the word with known words until you find a match. A slightly more sophisticated approach will use **String-Tokenizer** to isolate the first word of the input.

Either way, however, you wind up with an ugly bunch of **if** statements, and it is cumbersome to add more items. Many servers have this same problem, so I decided to try to create some reusable classes to make it easier to write an FTP server.

The first class I wrote was **LineServer** (see Listing 6.5). This class, which derives from **MTServerBase**, handles the case where the server expects lines of input. That doesn't solve the parsing problem, but it does give you a reasonable framework to use.

To use **LineServer**, you extend your own class and override **process** and **init**. The server calls **process** for each line you receive. You can return **false** from this method if you want to end the connection with the current client. When a client connects, you get a call to **init**. That way you can send any messages required to prime the client.

Listing 6.5 The **LineServer** class is useful for any server that reads input line by line.

```
// Line server -- generic line-oriented server
// Al Williams
import java.io.*;
import java.net.*;

public class LineServer extends MTServerBase
{
    protected BufferedReader iread;
    protected BufferedWriter owrite;
    public boolean running=false;
    public void run() {
        try {
            iread=new BufferedReader(new
            InputStreamReader(socket.getInputStream()));
            owrite=new BufferedWriter(new
            OutputStreamWriter(socket.getOutputStream()));
            if (!init()) {
                socket.close();
                return;
            }
            running=true;
            while (true) {
            String line = iread.readLine();
            if (!process(line)) {
              running=false;
              socket.close();
              return;
             }
           }
         }
        catch (IOException ioe) {
        running=false;
        }
```

```
    }
    // You'll override this (and provide a main that calls startServer)
    public boolean process(String line) throws IOException {
// this line is here just so we can throw IOExceptions
// from subclasses
      if (line==null) throw new IOException();
      return false; // return true to end connection
    }

    // You'll override this if you want any custom start processing
    public boolean init() throws IOException {
      if (running) throw new IOException(); // just for subclass
      return true; // false to abort
    }
  }
```

In my C programming days, I might have solved the parsing problem with a simple table. The table would match strings and function pointers, so when a string matches an entry in the table, you could call the function directly. However, Java doesn't have function pointers, right?

Of course, Java doesn't have function pointers, but it does have a **Method** object that can do nearly the same thing in this case. The **Method** object is part of the reflection API that Java objects can use to learn about other classes (or themselves) at runtime. I decided I'd use **Method** to map command names to methods in a simple way.

This led to the class that appears in Listing 6.6. Each instance of **ParseTableEntry** contains a **String** (in the **word** field) and a **Method** object in the **func** field (both fields are private). The constructor takes three arguments: the word to match, the class that owns the method you wish to call, and the name of the method as a string.

There are two methods you can call to make **ParseTableEntry** useful. First, you can call **equals**. As you'd expect, this attempts to match a string to the entry's word. In the way I wrote the class, the match is not case sensitive, although you could easily change it (or even better, make it an option).

The second method you can call is the **call** method. This code encapsulates the dirty work of actually calling the method. The first argument is the instance you want to use for the call. The other two arguments are the arguments to the method you specified (a **String** and a **StringTokenizer**). Of course, that means the methods you call must expect those arguments. It also must return a **boolean**, which the **call** method returns.

Of course, it doesn't make any sense to use just one **ParseTableEntry** object. Instead, you want an array of them. The object has a static method (**parse**) that accepts an array, an object instance, the word to parse, the line you are examining, and the **StringTokenizer** instance you've used to get the word. This method searches the table until it finds an entry that matches or an entry for the empty string, which matches everything and should be the last entry. It makes the call for you and returns the return value.

Listing 6.6 The **ParseTableEntry** class allows you to build arrays that map command names to method calls.

```
// Helper class for SFtpServer
// or any program that needs a simple first word parse
import java.lang.reflect.*;
import java.util.StringTokenizer;

public class ParseTableEntry {
    private String word;
    private Method func;

    public static boolean parse(ParseTableEntry [] parseTable,
            Object othis,
            String word,String line,
            StringTokenizer token) {
    for (int i=0;i<parseTable.length;i++) {
       if (parseTable[i].equals(word)
       || parseTable[i].equals(""))
       return parseTable[i].call(othis,line,token);
    }
    // should never get here unless no "" case in table
    return false;
     }

    public ParseTableEntry(String word, Class c, String methd) {
    Class [] cary = new Class[2];
    this.word=word;
    cary[0]=String.class;
    cary[1]=StringTokenizer.class;
    try {
        func=c.getMethod(methd,cary);
    }
    catch (Exception e) {
        System.err.println("ParseTable: " + e);
    }
     }
```

```
 public boolean equals(String s) {
return word.compareToIgnoreCase(s)==0;
 }
 public boolean call(Object thisptr,String line, StringTokenizer token) {
Object arg[] = new Object[2];
arg[0]=(Object)line;
arg[1]=(Object)token;
try {
    Boolean bv;
    bv=(Boolean)func.invoke(thisptr,arg);
    return bv.booleanValue();
}
catch (Exception e) {
    System.err.println("Invoke: " + e);
}
return false; // error
 }
}
```

This simple class takes the pain out of using the **Method** class by hiding all the ugly details. In particular, you'll notice that the class has to package the method's arguments in an **Object** array, and then pick the **boolean** return value out of a **Boolean** object. This isn't that difficult, but it is boring and messy looking, so why not wrap it in a class?

The calling program simply sets up the array of entries like this:

```
ParseTableEntry parseTable[] = {
  new ParseTableEntry("LIST",SFtpServer.class,"listCmd"),
  new ParseTableEntry("NLST",SFtpServer.class,"listCmd"),
// always make this the last entry
  new ParseTableEntry("",SFtpServer.class,"unknownCmd")
  };
```

Armed with this, it is relatively easy to build an FTP server. You simply create a **LineServer** subclass. In the **process** routine, you can use an array of **Parse-TableEntry** objects to jump to the correct routine in your class. You can find an example of this in Listing 6.7.

The server in Listing 6.7 (**SFtpServer**) isn't very complex, yet it can still interact with most FTP clients. The server only serves two files that it names a.txt and b.txt. The program actually reads its own source code and sends that, although you could easily use another file or change the program to make it work with the real file system.

Because the server doesn't really serve a true file system, it doesn't have to handle directories, text modes, or any other system-specific issues. The user can't store files, and all users log on as the anonymous user.

Listing 6.7 This simple FTP server illustrates how easy it is to build a server with the tools in this chapter.

```java
// Simple FTP server
import java.io.*;
import java.net.*;
import java.util.*;




// **** MAIN CLASS
public class SFtpServer extends LineServer {

    private ParseTableEntry parseTable[] = {
      new ParseTableEntry("USER",SFtpServer.class,"userCmd"),
      new ParseTableEntry("QUIT",SFtpServer.class,"quitCmd"),
      new ParseTableEntry("PASS",SFtpServer.class,"passCmd"),
      new ParseTableEntry("ACCT",SFtpServer.class,"unimplCmd"),
      new ParseTableEntry("SMNT",SFtpServer.class,"unimplCmd"),
      new ParseTableEntry("CWD",SFtpServer.class,"unimplCmd"),
      new ParseTableEntry("CDUP",SFtpServer.class,"unimplCmd"),
      new ParseTableEntry("REIN",SFtpServer.class,"reinCmd"),
      new ParseTableEntry("PASV",SFtpServer.class,"unimplCmd"),
      new ParseTableEntry("STRU",SFtpServer.class,"unimplCmd"),
      new ParseTableEntry("MODE",SFtpServer.class,"unimplCmd"),
      new ParseTableEntry("TYPE",SFtpServer.class,"unimplCmd"),
      new ParseTableEntry("STOU",SFtpServer.class,"unimplCmd"),
      new ParseTableEntry("APPE",SFtpServer.class,"unimplCmd"),
      new ParseTableEntry("ALLO",SFtpServer.class,"unimplCmd"),
      new ParseTableEntry("REST",SFtpServer.class,"unimplCmd"),
      new ParseTableEntry("RMD",SFtpServer.class,"unimplCmd"),
      new ParseTableEntry("MKD",SFtpServer.class,"unimplCmd"),
      new ParseTableEntry("PWD",SFtpServer.class,"pwdCmd"),
      new ParseTableEntry("SITE",SFtpServer.class,"unimplCmd"),
      new ParseTableEntry("SYST",SFtpServer.class,"systCmd"),
      new ParseTableEntry("HELP",SFtpServer.class,"helpCmd"),
      new ParseTableEntry("NOOP",SFtpServer.class,"noopCmd"),
      new ParseTableEntry("STAT",SFtpServer.class,"unimplCmd"),
      new ParseTableEntry("RNFR",SFtpServer.class,"unimplCmd"),
      new ParseTableEntry("RNTO",SFtpServer.class,"unimplCmd"),
      new ParseTableEntry("DELE",SFtpServer.class,"unimplCmd"),
```

6. FTP

```
        new ParseTableEntry("PORT",SFtpServer.class,"portCmd"),
        new ParseTableEntry("RETR",SFtpServer.class,"retrCmd"),
        new ParseTableEntry("LIST",SFtpServer.class,"listCmd"),
        new ParseTableEntry("NLST",SFtpServer.class,"listCmd"),
// always make this the last entry
        new ParseTableEntry("",SFtpServer.class,"unknownCmd")
    };

    int loginstate=0; // 0=none, 1=user OK, 2= user/pw ok, 3=user Not OK
    String dataportip;
    int dataport=20;

    public void writeString(String s) throws IOException {
      owrite.write(s,0,s.length());
      owrite.write("\r\n");
      owrite.flush();
    }

    public boolean init() throws IOException {
    // set default initial IP
      dataportip=socket.getInetAddress().getHostAddress();
      writeString("220-SFtp. Anonymous logins accepted");
      writeString("220-Your IP: " + dataportip);
      writeString("220-Default data port: " + dataport);
      writeString("220 Server ready");
      return true;
    }

    public boolean process(String line) throws IOException {
        boolean rv=false;
        StringTokenizer token=new StringTokenizer(line);
        String word=null;
        try {
           word=token.nextToken();
           }
        catch (NoSuchElementException nsee) {} // just a blank line
        if (word==null) return true; // ignore blank lines
        String output;
        rv=ParseTableEntry.parse(parseTable,this,word,line,token);
        owrite.flush();
        return rv;
    }

    // getMethod only works on public methods
    public boolean unknownCmd(String line,StringTokenizer token)
```

```
throws IOException {
      writeString("500 Unknown command ");
      return true;
      }

   public boolean quitCmd(String line,StringTokenizer token)
throws IOException {
      writeString("221 Goodbye");
      return false;
   }

   public boolean unimplCmd(String line,StringTokenizer token)
throws IOException {
      writeString("202 Command not implemented.");
      return true;
   }

   public boolean pwdCmd(String line,StringTokenizer token)
     throws IOException {
     if (loginstate!=2) return loginerr();
     writeString("257 \"/\" is the current working directory.");
     return true;
   }

   public boolean loginerr() throws IOException {
     writeString("530 Please login");
     return true;
   }

   public boolean reinCmd(String line,StringTokenizer token)
throws IOException {
      writeString("200 Command OK.");
      loginstate=0;
      return true;
      }

   public boolean systCmd(String line,StringTokenizer token)
throws IOException {
      if (loginstate!=2) return loginerr();
      writeString("215 UNIX Type: L8");
      return true;
      }

   public boolean passCmd(String line,StringTokenizer token)
throws IOException {
      String pw=token.nextToken();
```

```
            if (loginstate==0) {
              writeString("503 Login with USER First");
              return true;
              }
          if (loginstate==1 && pw!=null && !pw.equals("")) {
              System.err.println("Login from " + pw);
              loginstate=2;
              writeString("230 User logged in");
              return true;
              }
          loginstate=0;
          writeString("530 Login incorrect");
          return false;
      }
    public boolean userCmd(String line,StringTokenizer token)
  throws IOException {
  // we only allow anonymous
        if (token.nextToken().equals("anonymous")) {
            loginstate=1;
            }
        else {
            loginstate=3;
            }
        writeString("331 Send e-mail as password");
        return true;
        }


    public boolean noopCmd(String line,StringTokenizer token)
  throws IOException {
        writeString("200 Command OK");
        return true;
        }


    public boolean portCmd(String line,StringTokenizer token)
  throws IOException {
        StringBuffer b=new StringBuffer();
        try {
          for (int i=0;i<4;i++) {
            String tmp=token.nextToken(" ,");
            if (tmp==null) throw new Exception();
            int n=Integer.parseInt(tmp); // throw if not integer
            if (n<0||n>255) throw new Exception();
            b.append(tmp);
            if (i!=3) b.append(".");
            }
          dataportip=b.toString();
```

```
              String tmp=token.nextToken(" ,");
              dataport=Integer.parseInt(tmp)*256;
              tmp=token.nextToken();
              dataport+=Integer.parseInt(tmp);
              }
         catch (Exception e) {
            writeString("501 Illegal Port Command");
            return true;
            }
         writeString("200 Command OK");
         return true;
         }


   public boolean retrCmd(String line,StringTokenizer token)
 throws IOException {
         String fn=token.nextToken();
         if (fn.equals("a.txt")) {
            sendData(new FileReader("SFtpServer.java"));
         }
         else if (fn.equals("b.txt")) {
            sendData(new FileReader("ParseTableEntry.java"));
            }
         else {
             writeString("550 No such file");
             }
         return true;
   }


   public boolean listCmd(String line,StringTokenizer token)
 throws IOException {

       sendData(new StringReader("a.txt\r\nb.txt\r\n"));
       return true;
   }



   public boolean helpCmd(String line,StringTokenizer token)
 throws IOException {
         writeString("214-Simple Java Server by alw@al-williams.com");
         writeString("214 No further help available.");
         return true;
         }



   public boolean sendData(Reader r) throws IOException {
     int c;
```

```
        Socket s=null;
        try {
           writeString("150 Opening Data connection");
           s=new Socket(dataportip,dataport);
           OutputStreamWriter w=new OutputStreamWriter(s.getOutputStream());
           do {
              c=r.read();
              if (c!=-1) w.write((char)c);
              } while (c!=-1);
           w.flush();
           writeString("226 Transfer Complete");
           s.close();
           return true;
           }
     catch (Exception e) {
        writeString("426 Transfer error");
        s.close();
        return true;
        }
     }

     static public void main(String args[]) {
       SFtpServer.startServer(21,SFtpServer.class);
       }
     }
```

Immediate Solutions

Finding the FTP Specification

The FTP specification is primarily in RFC959 (also known as STD0009). This document defines the main portions of FTP. You'll also find additional information in RFC2577 (security) and RFC2428 (IPV6).

Connecting to an FTP Server

Nearly all FTP servers require some sort of user login and password. Even though some servers will accept anonymous users, that literally means using the username "anonymous" and usually providing your email address as a password.

Here are the steps required to connect to an FTP server:

1. Wait for a 220 response code indicating the server is ready to receive commands.

2. Send a **USER** command, specifying the user ID.

3. Wait for a reply. If it is reply 331, send a **PASS** command specifying the password.

4. If the reply from **USER** or **PASS** is 230, you are ready to send commands to the server. Any other reply means there is a problem.

Listing 6.8 shows a bit of code that does the job (this is an excerpt from the client code in Listing 6.9).

Listing 6.8   This code logs in to an FTP server.

```
do {
    status=getResponse();
} while (status!=220 && status!=-1);
if (status==-1) {
    return false;
}
status=sendCmd("USER " + user);
if (status==331) status=sendCmd("PASS " + pw);
if (status==332) return false; // no ACCT
if (status!=230) return false;
return true;
```

6. FTP

Interpreting FTP Responses

Each response from the FTP server is in the form of one or more lines. Each line has a three-digit numeric response code at the very beginning. The fourth character will indicate if there are more lines to follow. A hyphen in the fourth character tells the client to expect more lines. A space means this is the last (or the only) line the server will send. All the lines in a multiline response will start with the same code.

The first digit of the reply code informs the client that either the code is a failure code or a success code and whether the client should take further action. Because reply codes range from 100 through 599, there are five groups of codes:

- *Group 1*—Command OK; wait for further response codes
- *Group 2*—Command OK and complete
- *Group 3*—Command OK; send more information to complete
- *Group 4*—Command failed; try again later
- *Group 5*—Command failed; permanent error

The second digit further narrows the meaning of the message as follows:

- *Digit 0*—Syntax error in command
- *Digit 1*—Informational message
- *Digit 2*—Socket-related messages
- *Digit 3*—User login messages
- *Digit 5*—File system messages

You can find a complete list of the response codes defined by the RFC in Table 6.1.

Managing the Current Directory

You can change the server's idea of the current directory with the **CWD** command. **CDUP** also changes the directory by moving to the parent directory of the current directory. The **PWD** command responds with the current directory.

Reading a File Directory

One of the first things the user wants to know when connecting to an FTP server is what files are available. The **LIST** and **NLST** commands provide this information in different formats (the **LIST** command has more details, but the **NLST** output is easier for programs to parse).

Both of these commands provide their output as pseudo file. As far as the client can tell, this is just a request for a special file that happens to list the contents of the specified directory (or the current directory if you don't provide one).

The steps required to read a directory listing are similar to receiving an ordinary file:

1. Send a **PORT** command to indicate which port you are using for a data port. (Of course, if you are using passive mode, you'll send **PASV** instead.)

2. Wait for a 200 response.

3. Send a **LIST** command.

4. Expect a connection on the data socket and a 150 response code.

5. At the end of the list, the server will send a 226 response code.

Listing 6.9 shows a simple FTP client that retrieves a directory listing. You provide the server name, a username, and password on the command line. You can also supply a directory name as the final argument if you wish.

The **connect** function handles the login. When the program wants to send a command, it uses **sendCmd**, which returns the status code and leaves the last line of the response in **lastResponse**. The real key, however, is **dataSocketIn**. This method sets up a data port (either actively or passively, depending on the **passive** field's value). Then it issues the command you supply and reads data from the data port.

Listing 6.9   This program retrieves a directory listing.

```java
// FTP LS
import java.net.*;
import java.io.*;

public class FtpLS {
    final public static boolean debug=true; // true for debug trace
    protected Socket ctlskt;  // control socket
    protected Socket datskt;  // data socket
    protected Reader datReader;  // IO Stream for data socket
    protected Writer datWriter;
    protected BufferedReader ctlin;  // Control port reader
    protected OutputStream ctlout;  // Control port writer
    public String lastResponse;  // Last response from host
    public boolean passive = false; // passive mode
```

```
// Connect to host -- we don't do ACCT
public boolean connect(String host,String user, String pw)
  throws UnknownHostException, IOException {
  int status;
  ctlskt=new Socket(host,21);
  ctlin=new BufferedReader(
  new InputStreamReader(ctlskt.getInputStream()));
  ctlout=ctlskt.getOutputStream();
  do {
   status=getResponse();
   } while (status!=220 && status!=-1);
  if (status==-1) {
    return false;
    }
  status=sendCmd("USER " + user);
  if (status==331) status=sendCmd("PASS " + pw);
  if (status==332) return false; // no ACCT
  if  (status!=230) return false;
  return true;
  }

// This creates a data socket
protected int dataSocket(String datCmd) throws IOException {
 int port;
 int status;
 ServerSocket datsktsvr;
 if (passive) {
   java.util.StringTokenizer token;
   StringBuffer IP=new StringBuffer();
   int i;
   status=sendCmd("PASV");
   if (status<200||status>299) return -1;
  // find IP/port
   for (i=4;i<lastResponse.length();i++)
     if (Character.isDigit(lastResponse.charAt(i))) break;
     if (i==lastResponse.length()) return -1; // not found
     token=new java.util.StringTokenizer
       (lastResponse.substring(i),",) ");
     if (token.countTokens()!=6) return -1; // unknown IP/port
     for (i=0;i<4;i++) {
       IP.append(token.nextToken());
       if (i!=3) IP.append(".");
       }
     port=Integer.parseInt(token.nextToken())*256;
     port+=Integer.parseInt(token.nextToken());
     datskt=new Socket(IP.toString(),port);
     status=sendCmd(datCmd);
     }
```

6. FTP

```
else {
    datsktsvr=new ServerSocket(0);
    port=datsktsvr.getLocalPort();
   //set host/port
   StringBuffer cmd = new StringBuffer("PORT ");
   cmd.append(ctlskt.getLocalAddress().getHostAddress());
   for (int i = 0; i < cmd.length(); i++) {
     if ('.' == cmd.charAt(i))
         cmd.setCharAt(i, ',');
   }
   cmd.append(",");
   cmd.append(Integer.toString(port/256));
   cmd.append(",");
   cmd.append(Integer.toString(port&0xFF));
   status=sendCmd(cmd.toString());
   if (status!=200) return -1;
   status=sendCmd(datCmd);
  // wait for remote connection (could time out)
  datskt=datsktsvr.accept();
   }
return 0;
}
// This function pipes everything from the
// data port to the specified writer (which could
// be the console, or a string, or a file)
public int dataSocketIn(String datCmd,Writer w) throws IOException {

  int status;
  status=dataSocket(datCmd);
  if (status!=0) return status;
  datReader=new InputStreamReader(datskt.getInputStream());
  // transfer data until socket closes
  int ch;
  do {
    ch=datReader.read();
    if (ch!=-1) w.write((char)ch);
    } while (ch!=-1);
  w.flush();
  datskt.close();
  return getResponse();
  }

// Get a response accounting for possible mutliline responses
protected int getResponse() throws IOException {
  int n;
  String tmp;
```

```
                         do {
                           lastResponse=ctlin.readLine();
                           if (debug) System.out.println("DEBUG Received: " + lastResponse);
                         } while (lastResponse.charAt(3)=='-');
                         tmp=lastResponse.substring(0,3);
                         try {
                           n=Integer.parseInt(tmp);
                           }
                         catch (NumberFormatException e) {
                           n=-1;
                         }
                         return n;
                        }


                    // Send a command and return status code
                    public int sendCmd(String cmd) throws IOException {
                     if (debug) System.out.println("DEBUG Sent: " + cmd);
                     String tmp=cmd+"\r\n";
                     int n;
                     ctlout.write(tmp.getBytes());
                     ctlout.flush();
                     return getResponse();
                    }


                    // Main driver

                    public static void main(String [] args) throws Exception {
                        if (args.length<3||args.length>4) {
                          System.out.println(
                            "usage: EZftp host user password [directory]");
                          System.exit(1);
                        }
                        FtpLS obj= new FtpLS();
                        obj.passive=true;
                        if (!obj.connect(args[0],args[1],args[2])) {
                          System.out.println("Can't connect");
                          System.exit(1);
                        }

            // Last argument is directory if present
                        if (args.length==4)
                        obj.sendCmd("CWD " + args[3]);

            // print directory (chop off response code)
                        obj.sendCmd("PWD");
                        System.out.println(obj.lastResponse.substring(4));
```

```
// Do a directory
      obj.dataSocketIn("LIST",new OutputStreamWriter(System.out));

      System.exit(0);
   }
}
```

Transferring Files

Transferring a file is mostly the same as transferring a file directory. The only difference is you issue a **STOR** command to send a file to the server and a **RETR** command to retrieve a file from the server. Obviously, in the case of a **STOR** command, you have to provide the data over the data connection. That requires a **dataSocketOut** method to complement **dataSocketIn**. Listing 6.10 shows such a method you can add to the program in Listing 6.9.

Listing 6.10   Add this code to Listing 6.9 to enable transferring data to the server.

```
 public int dataSocketOut(String datCmd,Reader r) throws IOException {
 int status;
 status=dataSocket(datCmd);
 if (status!=0) return status;
 datWriter=new OutputStreamWriter(datskt.getOutputStream());
 int ch;
 do {
     ch=r.read();
     if (ch!=-1) datWriter.write((char)ch);
 } while (ch!=-1);
 datWriter.flush();
 datskt.close();
 return getResponse();
  }
```

6. FTP

To see this in action, replace Listing 6.9's **main** function with the one in Listing 6.11. This will read a file from the server named ftp.test and then write it back to the server as ftp1.test. Notice that because **dataSocketIn** and **dataSocketOut** both accept streams, it is easy to send a file or receive a directory listing to the console because you can represent both as streams. It would be equally easy to create a **StringReader** or **StringWriter** object to use a string instead of a file as the data's source or destination.

Listing 6.11   Here is a **main** function that will send and receive a file using the code in Listings 6.9 and 6.10.

```
public static void main(String [] args) throws Exception {
    if (args.length<3||args.length>4) {
    System.out.println("usage: EZftp host user password [directory]");
    System.exit(1);
}
FtpLS obj= new FtpLS();
obj.passive=true;
if (!obj.connect(args[0],args[1],args[2])) {
    System.out.println("Can't connect");
    System.exit(1);
}

FileWriter f = new FileWriter("ftp.test");
obj.dataSocketIn("RETR readme",f);
System.out.println(obj.lastResponse);

// Write test
FileReader fw = new FileReader("ftp.test");
obj.dataSocketOut("STOR ftp1.test",fw);
System.out.println(obj.lastResponse);


System.exit(0);
  }
}
```

Choosing Active or Passive Mode

If you examine the code in Listing 6.9, you'll notice that the **dataSocket** routine handles making the actual data connection. The operation of this function differs depending on the state of the **passive** flag.

Take the following steps when using active mode (that is, **passive** is false):

1. Create a **ServerSocket**. An argument of **zero** causes the object to pick an available port.

2. Determine the port used by the socket (call **getLocalPort**).

3. Locate the IP address you are using to communicate with the server by calling **getLocalAddress** on the control socket. You can further reduce this to a simple IP address by calling **getHostAddress**.

4. Build a **PORT** command string. The arguments (separated by commas) are each octet of the IP address, the high 8 bits of the 16-bit port number (from Step 2) and the bottom 8 bits of the port number. Send the command and wait for a positive reply (reply 200).

5. Call **accept** to wait for a data connection. You may want to provide a time-out in case the server never opens the connection.

In passive mode, take these steps:

1. Send a **PASV** command and wait for a positive reply.

2. The reply will contain the IP address and port that you should use in the same format you would use for the **PORT** command. Parse the data from the response.

3. Create an ordinary **Socket** instance using the IP address and port number from Step 2.

Using the **PORT** command may not work from behind a firewall. Therefore, it is a good idea to try passive mode if **PORT** fails, or even start with passive mode. Of course, some FTP servers may not implement passive mode (although that should be rare), so be prepared to fall back to using the **PORT** command if necessary.

Using Open Source FTP

There are several open source FTP packages available. One that seems very ro-bust is at the Giant Java Tree (**www.gjt.org**). This package strongly encapsulates the FTP logic.

To use the **org.gjt.tst.net.ftp.client** package, you simply instantiate the **FtpClient-ExtraProtocol** class. This allows you to use methods such as **user**, **password**, **download**, and **upload**. It also provides an enumeration to handle directory lists. You can also use **FtpClientProtocol** if you don't need the extra functions in the **FtpClientExtraProtocol** class (directory manipulation functions, primarily).

Listing 6.12 shows a simple program that uses **FtpClientExtraProtocol** to down-load a file. The methods correspond to user commands, so it is easy to work with this class. You can also create FTP servers with this package, although that is a bit more work.

Listing 6.12   This program downloads a file using an open source FTP class.

```
import java.io.PrintWriter;
import java.io.OutputStreamWriter;
import java.io.FileOutputStream;
import java.io.File;
```

```java
import java.io.IOException;
import org.gjt.tst.net.ftp.client.*;


public class FtpClient {
    private FtpClientExtraProtocol ftp;
    // This does the actual download
    private static void downloadTheFile()
        throws IOException, InterruptedException {

        File file = new File("test.txt");
        FileOutputStream out = null;
        try {
            out = new FileOutputStream(file);
            ftp.download(out, "test.txt");
        }
        finally {
            if (null != out) {
                out.close();
                out = null;
            }
        }

    }


    public static void main(String[] args)  {

        PrintWriter trace =
            new PrintWriter(new OutputStreamWriter(System.err),true);

        try {
            ftp = new FtpClientExtraProtocol("localhost", trace);
            ftp.setTimeout(2000);
        }
        catch (IOException e) {
            trace.println("Cannot connect to server");
            return;
        }

        ftp.setDataConnectionActiveServer();
        try {
            ftp.user("kirk");
            if (!ftp.isLoggedIn())
                ftp.password("enterprise");
                downloadTestFile(ftp);
        }
```

```
        catch (InterruptedException ex) {
            trace.println(ex.getMessage());
        }
        catch (IOException ex) {
            trace.println(ex.getMessage());
        }
        finally {
            try {
                ftp.logout();
                ftp.close();
            } catch (IOException e) {}
        }
    }
}
```

Chapter 7

SMTP

In Depth

My wife says I'm obsessed with mail. Why not? Mail means that someone wants to tell you something and—excluding junk mail—it was something important enough to put in a letter. When I was a kid, I used to send off for free things and anxiously wait for the postman every day (we didn't have video games).

Some people think that mail has become antiquated—everything is done by phone. But I think the phone is the cause of many societal problems. When you call someone and get a busy signal, that's a subtle form of rejection. Of course, call waiting shifts the rejection from the second caller back to the first caller—now you can pick which caller you want to insult.

Fortunately, email has brought new life to the art of letter writing. People don't wait for the mailman anymore; they wait to hear their incoming mail notification. That's probably why AOL is so popular. "You've got mail!" is instant gratification, a subtle reinforcement of your worth as a person.

When you send email, you connect to a Simple Mail Transfer Protocol (SMTP) host computer on port 25. This host delivers mail to local users and forwards it if the recipient is a user on another computer. You can find all the technical details about SMTP in the Internet RFC2821, which updates RFCs dating back to 1982. Reading the protocol, you get the idea that the author wanted to let someone dial in to an SMTP host using a TeleType (this was 1982, remember) and manually conduct business with the software. You can also use SMTP to send what amounts to an early form of instant message. You don't see that used much today because there are many P2P (peer-to-peer) solutions for instant messaging.

If the entire goal of SMTP was to send a message from a sender to a recipient, you might well use File Transfer Protocol (FTP) for that. However, the author also allows for one SMTP host to forward mail to another. Therefore, the protocol is amenable to machine interpretation as well as manual entry. If you use a Telnet program to log in to an SMTP host (on port 25), you'll see a response like this one:

```
220 smtp1b.mail.yahoo.com ESMTP
```

This response is from the Yahoo! SMTP server at **smtp.mail.yahoo.com**.

Every line the host sends begins with a three-digit response code. The fourth character is a hyphen if more lines related to this response are forthcoming. If the fourth character is a space, this is the last line, or—as is usually the case—the only line of a multiline response. Programs usually read only the first four characters and ignore the rest of a line. As you might expect, the rest of the line is more useful for humans than the codes. You can find a list of response codes and their meanings in Table 7.3 in the "Immediate Solutions" section. These codes are similar to the FTP codes (see Chapter 6), and as you'd expect, they follow the same pattern. Codes that start with 2 indicate success. Codes that start with a 3 require more information. The 4XX and 5XX groups indicate a failure (with the 5XX failures being the severe ones).

As in FTP, the second digit of the response also has special meaning. A 0 means a syntax error occurred. Informational messages have a 1 in the middle position. Messages with a 2 in the middle are connection related. Finally, responses that have their second digit set to 5 refer to the status of the mail system.

There are many possible commands you can send to an SMTP server (see Table 7.1). However, many of these are not often needed. The command order is important. The basic sequence is as follows:

1. **HELO** Identifies the sender's machine
2. **MAIL FROM:** Starts mail from the sender
3. **RCPT TO:** Identifies the recipient (may occur more than once)

Table 7.1   There are only a few SMTP commands, and even fewer are required for most programs.

Command	Description	Required
DATA	Begins the actual contents of the email message (ends with a line containing only a period)	X
EXPN	Expands a mailing list	
EHLO	Identifies sender and triggers extended SMTP options	X
HELO	Identifies sender via hostname or Internet Protocol (IP) address	X
HELP	Sends a help response	
MAIL FROM:	Starts a mail transaction from a sender	X
NOOP	Elicits a positive response, but takes no action	X
QUIT	Ends session	X
RCPT TO:	Indicates a single recipient for the email	X
RSET	Aborts current transaction	X
SEND	Sends data directly to a terminal	
SOML	Sends data to a terminal or via email	
SAML	Sends data to a terminal and via email	
TURN	Causes the sender to become the receiver and vice versa	
VRFY	Verifies an email address	

7. SMTP

4. **DATA** Specifies email message

5. **QUIT** Terminates session with server

Each command has only one or two possible responses that aren't errors. Most email programs let you specify multiple recipients, as well as carbon-copy recipients and blind-carbon-copy recipients (CC and BCC). As far as SMTP cares, all of these are recipients that you specify with separate **RCPT TO:** commands.

The difference between a CC recipient and a BCC recipient is whether the recipient's address appears in the email's headers or not. Like a Web document, email has a header and a body (you can find the details in RFC2821). You can send many headers, including the subject, a reply path, and other headers that particular email programs might interpret in different ways. SMTP doesn't care which headers you include (if any).

Verification

In addition to sending email, an SMTP host can verify email addresses using the **VRFY** command. This command causes the host to look up the user and provide a full address. However, some sites don't allow this because it simplifies things for hackers trolling for user IDs.

For example, here is an attempt to verify an address at **smtp.mail.yahoo.com**:

```
220 smtp016.mail.yahoo.com ESMTP
VRFY jtkirk
252 send some mail, i'll try my best
```

Not an especially helpful message.

There are several SMTP features you don't see very often. One is the **EXPN** command. It lets you expand a mailing list (usually generating a multiline reply). The other feature is that SMTP addresses can have routes where you specify that the SMTP server sends your email to another machine, and that machine sends it to another machine, and so on. This was useful when computer connections were spotty, but now that nearly all computers are connected to the public Internet in some way, you rarely see it.

Timeouts, Multiple Lines, and Transparency

When I looked at other SMTP examples on the Web, I noticed that many of them did not follow the RFC to the letter. They would work in most cases, but a few odd conditions might cause failure. I tried to avoid these in my code. In particular, I noticed that many examples didn't correctly handle the following situations:

7. SMTP

- *Time-out*—For any number of reasons, the server might fail to respond. It's prudent to allow the server a certain amount of response time before terminating the connection. Some code didn't allow for this possibility. Others allowed for time-outs but did so inefficiently by simply looping.

- *Multiple Lines*—As I mentioned earlier, some servers will reply with multiple lines for a single response. Each response begins with the three-digit code, but the fourth character will be a hyphen for all but the last line. Some examples of SMTP code do not consider this possibility.

- *Transparency*—When processing mail messages, the SMTP server looks for a line containing only a period to terminate the message. However, what if the message has a line that really contains a single period? To prevent this problem, ordinary SMTP clients always add an extra period to any line in your message that begins with a period. If the server examines a line and finds two periods at the beginning, it knows to strip off the first one—(because it was secretly added by the client program—and to continue processing more lines.

Extended SMTP

Newer versions of SMTP allow extra features without sacrificing backward compatibility. If a client identifies with **EHLO** instead of **HELO**, the server recognizes that the extended SMTP protocol is in effect.

When you issue an **EHLO** (Extended Hello) you can expect a multiline response in return. The server will reply with all the extensions it knows about (for example, 8BITMIME indicates the server can accept 8-bit attachments).

Headers

SMTP doesn't care what you send in the body of your email message. However, many email programs expect you to send headers that have specific meanings. You can find a complete list in RFC2822. Here are some of the more common headers you'll encounter:

- *Subject*—The subject of the message.

- *From*—The sender's email address.

- *To*—The primary recipient of the message.

- *CC*—Carbon copy recipients. These people will appear in the address list and receive a copy of the message.

- *BCC*—Blind carbon copy recipients. These people will receive a copy but will not appear in the address list.

- *Return-Path*—The email address that should receive administrative messages.

- *Received*—The date and time received.

- *Reply-To*—The email address that should receive any reply.

- *Date*—The date and time the message was sent.

A blank line separates the headers from the message body. Here is a typical mail message with a minimum of headers:

```
Date:      26 Jul 99 1429 EDT
From:      alw@al-williams.com
To:        admin@al-williams.com

The server is down again - Al
```

Headers are the key to sending formatted email and to mailing attachments. Consider this email message (including headers):

```
Subject: html test
mime-version: 1.0
content-type: text/html
content-transfer-encoding: 7bit

<H1>Hello Al</H1>
<hr>
<P>This is not spam.... it's wham!</P>
```

This message will appear in most email programs as a formatted Web page. You can find details about these headers (known as MIME or Multipurpose Internet Mail Extensions) in RFC2045 through RFC2049.

Because some email gateways only accept 7-bit ASCII text, any binary data, such as an image attachment, has to be encoded using some scheme that maps 8-bit bytes into 7-bit characters.

Encoding

Because some machines and communications lines that handle email may not allow 8-bit data, several schemes defined in RFC1521 allow you to convert 8-bit bytes to 7-bit characters. As you might expect, doing this encoding will inflate the size of the data. If you just converted each byte into two hex digits, you'd double the size of the data. That's not very efficient, so each scheme tries to minimize the impact.

Quotable Printable

This simple scheme is not very efficient, unless 8-bit characters only occasionally appear in the mail message. This method does not normally change characters with hex values of 21 to 3C and 3E to 7E (the printable characters). However, any byte can have an alternate representation of an equal sign and a two-character hex number. So, although you don't have to encode an A (41 hex) in this way, you can write it as =41. A BEL character (07) would be =07 and must be encoded.

You can also leave white space alone (space and tab) unless they are at the end of the line. Some systems may add spurious spaces at the end of lines, so the recipient will strip ordinary blanks at the end of lines. If you want a hard-line break, you must encode this as a carriage return and a line feed, regardless of what your local system thinks is an end of line. In addition, no line can be longer than 76 characters (excluding the carriage return and line feed but counting any escaped characters as 3 characters). If you have a longer line, you can break it into multiple lines and end the extra lines with an equal sign. This is known as a soft-line break because the receiver can elect to ignore it.

If you use this style of encoding, you'll set the Content-Transfer-Encoding header to quotable printable.

Base 64

The quotable printable encoding is useful for messages that are mostly plain text, but it quickly inflates a binary file (in the worst possible case, it would triple the file size). Base 64 is more complex to implement, but it only inflates the file size by 33 percent.

Base 64 uses 65 characters from the ASCII set. That means each character can represent 6 bits (1 character—the equal sign—does not represent data). The algorithm joins three bytes together to form a 24-bit word. Then it breaks the 24-bit word into four 6-bit tokens (still 24 bits). Each possible token has an ASCII character representation (see Table 7.2). The RFC calls for the first bits to be the most significant bit of the first word, so nothing is left to chance.

To accommodate the mail system, output lines are never greater than 76 characters. Line breaks don't count, so you just chop the lines up to fit. At the end of the file, you may not have enough bytes to make up a group of three bytes. In this case, you add zeros to the end of the number until you have a whole number of 6-bit groups. If you have one extra character, you'd add four zero bits and perform the encoding to get two base 64 characters. To keep the encoding group at four characters, you'll pad the output with two equal signs. If you have two extra characters, you'll add two zeros, encode, and pad with a single equal sign. Of course, if your file size happens to be evenly divisible by three, you won't have to pad at all.

Table 7.2   You can use this table to encode 6-bit groups into ASCII characters for the base 64 encoding algorithm.

Hex Value Encoding	Hex Value Encoding	Hex Value Encoding	Hex Value Encoding
00 A	11 R	22 i	33 z
01 B	12 S	23 j	34 0
02 C	13 T	24 k	35 1
03 D	14 U	25 l	36 2
04 E	15 V	26 m	37 3
05 F	16 W	27 n	38 4
06 G	17 X	28 o	39 5
07 H	18 Y	29 p	3A 6
08 I	19 Z	2A q	3B 7
09 J	1A a	2B r	3C 8
0A K	1B b	2C s	3D 9
0B L	1C c	2D t	3E +
0C M	1D d	2E u	3F /
0D N	1E e	2F v	
0E O	1F f	30 w	
0F P	20 g	31 x	
10 Q	21 h	32 y	

You'll see a class that can perform this encoding in the Immediate Solutions section of this chapter.

Implementation

Before tackling the SMTP class itself, I wrote two small helper classes. The first class, **MailMessage** (see Listing 7.1), simply encapsulates the strings that make up a typical email message. The second class, **SMTPResults** (in Listing 7.2), is a container for static integers that represent the response codes from Table 7.3.

The main class, **SMTP** (see Listing 7.3), has only two important methods. The constructor you'll use to create an instance of SMTP requires a hostname or IP address of an SMTP server. The other method is **sendMail**. You simply pass a filled-in **MailMessage** object to **sendMail**, and it does the rest. If **sendMail** returns 0, then everything went well. If an error occurs, you'll find the SMTP response code in the return value.

The internal details of SMTP are a bit more interesting. The **sendMail** function simply opens a socket and then calls **sendMailEngine**. Even if **sendMailEngine** returns an error, the **sendMail** function can properly close the socket (you could also do the same thing with a **finally** clause). The **sendAddress** method breaks up the list of email addresses and sends separate **RCPT TO:** commands.

Perhaps the most interesting routine, however, is **getResponse**. This function reads a complete response from the SMTP server and verifies it against the expected response codes. If the code matches one of the expected responses, the function returns 0. Otherwise, it returns the response code in question.

The problem with this function relates to time-outs; the function should wait only a certain amount of time before it gives up. One way to handle it would be to check the socket for available characters until a certain amount of time expires. However, this would make your program run continuously while waiting, consuming system resources. Instead, I decided to make a small private class, **TimeoutRead**, which extends **Thread**. This object executes in a separate thread, which calls **readLine** on the socket. Once the code finds the end of the response, the thread ends.

The main program, then, must wait for the thread to end, or a time-out period to expire. That's exactly what the **Thread.join** function does. The main code calls **join**, passing it the number of milliseconds it's willing to wait. When **join** returns, either the thread is completed, or the time-out has expired.

The only problem with this design is that the thread doesn't end just because the time-out expires. Although the **Thread** object has stop and suspend methods, they're deprecated. Besides, there are no guarantees that these methods would interrupt **readLine**, anyway. If the thread is still running, it may interfere with the program shutting down (not to mention it will waste system resources). Calling **System.exit** ends the thread, but that might not be appropriate for all programs.

That's why it's important that **sendMail** close the socket under all conditions. When the socket closes, the **readLine** function throws an exception and this ends the thread.

The **SMTP** class also has a main function you can use to test the class. It takes an email address as a command-line argument and sends a short test message to that address. Of course, if you're using the class as part of a larger system, nothing will ever call **main**, so you could safely delete it.

The **MailMessage** class has two members that you can use for advanced features. The **addHeader** method allows you to add additional headers to your message. This is useful if you want to send, for example, HTML. The other advanced field is a reference to a **Writer** class object that will encode the message body (using base 64 encoding, for example). If you leave this reference as **null** (the default) the class won't encode the message. If you provide a class reference (for example, **B64Encode.class**), you must also use **addHeader** to add the required headers.

Listing 7.1   The MailMessage class contains the information the SMTP class uses to send an email.

```java
import java.util.Hashtable;
import java.io.Writer;

/**
 * This is just a collection of data that makes up a mail message.
 * @author Al Williams
 * @version 1.0
 * @see SMTP#sendMail
 */
public class MailMessage
{
    /**
     * Default constructor.
     * @param None
     */
    public MailMessage()
    {
    }
    /**
     * Constructor that initializes.
     * @param _from The sender's e-mail address.
     * @param _to The recipient's e-mail address (separate
     *        multiple addresses with semicolons).
     * @param _cc Carbon copy addresses (separate multiple addresses
     *        with semicolons).
     * @param _bcc Blind copy addresses (separate multiple addresses
     *        with semicolons).
     * @param _subject The email subject.
     * @param _body The body of the email.
     */
    public MailMessage( String _from, String _to,
    String _cc, String _bcc, String _subject, String _body )
    {
        sender = _from;
        to = _to;
        cc = _cc;
        bcc = _bcc;
        subject = _subject;
        body = _body;
    }
```

```
/**
 * Constructor with commonly required arguments.
 * @param _from The sender's e-mail address.
 * @param _to The recipient's e-mail address
 *    (separate multiple addresses with semicolons).
 * @param _subject The e-mail subject.
 * @Param _body The body of the e-mail.
 */
public MailMessage( String _from, String _to, String _subject,
    String _body)
{
    sender = _from;
    to = _to;
    subject = _subject;
    body = _body;
}
/**
 * The sender's e-mail address.
 */
public String sender;
/**
 * The recipient's e-mail address (separate multiple addresses
 *with semicolons).
 */
public String to;
/**
 * The Carbon Copy addresses (separate multiple addresses with
 *   semicolons).
 */
public String cc;
/**
 * The Blind Carbon Copy addresses (separate multiple addresses
 *with semicolons).
 */
public String bcc;
/**
 * The e-mail's subject.
 */
public String subject;
/**
 * The e-mail's body.
 */
public String body;
/**
 * Extra headers
 */
```

```
public Class encoder=null;
public Hashtable headers=null;
public void addHeader(String header,String value) {
if (headers==null) headers=new Hashtable();
headers.put(header,value);
}
}
```

Listing 7.2   This class provides the SMTP result codes.

```
/**
 * Static values for SMTP result codes
 * @author Al Williams
 * @version 1.0
 */
public class SMTPResults
{
    /**
     * Syntax error, command unrecognized
     */
    static final public int SMTP_RESULT_UNRECOG = 500;
    /**
     * Syntax error in parameters or arguments
     */
    static final public int SMTP_RESULT_PARAM = 501;
    /**
     * Command not implemented
     */
    static final public int SMTP_RESULT_UNIMPLEMENTED = 502;
    /**
     * Bad sequence of commands
     */
    static final public int SMTP_RESULT_SEQUENCE = 503;
    /**
     * Command parameter not implemented
     */
    static final public int SMTP_RESULT_PARAMNI = 504;
    /**
     * System status, or system help reply
     */
    static final public int SMTP_RESULT_SYSTEM = 211;
    /**
     * Help message
     */
    static final public int SMTP_RESULT_HELP = 214;
    /**
     * <domain> Service ready
```

```java
    */
   static final public int SMTP_RESULT_READY = 220;
   /**
    * <domain> Service closing transmission channel
    */
   static final public int SMTP_RESULT_CLOSING = 221;
   /**  <
    * domain> Service not available, closing transmission channel
    */
   static final public int SMTP_RESULT_SERUNAVAILABLE = 421;
   /**
    * Requested mail action okay, completed
    */
   static final public int SMTP_RESULT_COMPLETED = 250;
   /**
    * User not local; will forward to <forward-path>
    */
   static final public int SMTP_RESULT_FORWARD = 251;
   /**
    * Requested mail action not taken: mailbox unavailable
    */
   static final public int SMTP_RESULT_MBXUNAVAILABLE = 450;
   /**
    * Requested action not taken: mailbox unavailable
    */
   static final public int SMTP_RESULT_NOTTAKEN = 550;
   /**
    * Requested action aborted: error in processing
    */
   static final public int SMTP_RESULT_ABORTED = 451;
   /**
    * User not local; please try <forward-path>
    */
   static final public int SMTP_RESULT_USER_NOT_LOCAL = 551;
   /**
    * Requested action not taken: insufficient system storage
    */
   static final public int SMTP_RESULT_STORAGE = 452;
   /**
    * Requested mail action aborted: exceeded storage allocation
    */
   static final public int SMTP_RESULT_EXSTORAGE = 552;
   /**
    * Requested action not taken: mailbox name not allowed
    */
   static final public int SMTP_RESULT_NOT_ALLOWED = 553;
```

7. SMTP

```
        /**
         * Start mail input; end with <CRLF>.<CRLF>
         */
        static final public int SMTP_RESULT_MAIL_START = 354;
        /**
         * Transaction failed
         */
        static final public int SMTP_RESULT_TRANS_FAILED = 554;
}
```

Listing 7.3   The SMTP class makes it easy to send email from a Java program.

```java
import java.awt.*;
import java.net.*;
import java.util.*;
import java.io.*;
import SMTPResults;
import MailMessage;




/**
 * SMTP Class. You can use this class to
 * send e-mail via a SMTP server.
 * You can find more info about Email and SMTP via the RFCs particularly
 * <A HREF=http://www.faqs.org/rfcs/rfc821.html>RFC821</A> and
 * <A HREF=http://www.faqs.org/rfcs/rfc822.html>RFC822</A>
 * @author Al Williams
 * @version 1.0
 */
public class SMTP
{
    // things you might want to change
    // 30 seconds timeout
    final static boolean debug = true;
    final static int WAIT_TIMEOUT = ( 30 * 1000 );
    final static int smtpPort = 25;
    final static String addressSep = ";";  // separates e-mail addresses
// SMTP server for testing
    final static String testServer = "mail.direcpc.com";

    String smtpServer;
    // could hardcode this
    MailMessage message;
    String hostname;
    BufferedReader input;
    OutputStream output;
```

```java
String errorText;       // copy of last response -- in case of error
Socket sock;


final String crlf = "\r\n";
/**
 * Get the last response message. Useful for displaying error
 *   from SMTP server.
 * @returns String containing last response from server.
 */
public String getLastResponse()
 {
 if (errorText==null) return "Unable to connect or unknown error";
 return errorText;
 }


/**
 * Constructor. Requires SMTP server name.
 * @param host An SMTP server. Remember, the server must be accessible
 *    from this code.
 * In particular, applets can usually only connect back
 *   to the same host they originated from.
 */


public SMTP( String host )
{
    smtpServer = host;
}

//read data from input stream to buffer String

private int getResponse( int expect1 ) throws IOException
{
    return getResponse( expect1, -1 );
}

synchronized private int getResponse( int expect1, int expect2 )
  throws IOException
{
    boolean defStatus;
    long startTime;
    int replyCode;

    TimeoutRead thread = new TimeoutRead( input );
    thread.setBuffer("");
```

```
            thread.start();
            try
            {
                thread.join( WAIT_TIMEOUT );
            }
            catch( InterruptedException e )
            {
            }
            if( thread.isComplete() && thread.getBuffer().length() > 0 )
            {
                try
                {
// if there is an error, this is it.
                    errorText = thread.getBuffer();
                    replyCode = Integer.valueOf(
                      errorText.substring( 0, 3 ) ).intValue();
                    if( replyCode == 0 ) return -1;
                    if( replyCode == expect1 || replyCode == expect2 )
                        return 0;
                    return replyCode;
                }
                catch( NumberFormatException e )
                {
                    error(e);
                    return -1;
                }
            }
            return -1;
            // nothing in buffer
        }



    private void writeString( String s ) throws IOException
    {
        output.write( s.getBytes() );
    }
    private int sendAddresses(String pfx, String addr) throws IOException
    {
        int n0=0;
        int n;
        int rv=0;
        while (rv==0 && (n=addr.indexOf(addressSep,n0))!=-1)
            {
            writeString(pfx+addr.substring(n0,n)+crlf);
            n0=n+1;
```

```
        rv=getResponse( SMTPResults.SMTP_RESULT_COMPLETED,
          SMTPResults.SMTP_RESULT_FORWARD );
    }
  if (rv==0)
  {
    writeString(pfx+addr.substring(n0)+crlf);
    rv=getResponse( SMTPResults.SMTP_RESULT_COMPLETED,
      SMTPResults.SMTP_RESULT_FORWARD );
  }
  return rv;
}




/**
 * Use sendMail to actually send an e-mail message.
 * @param MailMessage This is a filled-in MailMessage object that
 *    specifies the text, subject, and recipients.
 * @return Zero if successful. Otherwise, it returns the SMTP
 *    return code.
 * @see SMTPResults
 */

public int sendMail( MailMessage msg)
{
    String inBuffer;
    String outBuffer;
    int rv;
    message = msg;
    if( msg.to == null || msg.to.length() == 0 )
    {
        error("Must supply To field");
        return -1;
    }
    // Create connection
    try
    {
        sock = new Socket( smtpServer, smtpPort );
        hostname = "[" + sock.getLocalAddress().getHostAddress() + "]";
    }
    catch( IOException e )
    {
        error(e);
        return -1;
    }
    //Create I/O streams
```

```
        try
        {
            input = new BufferedReader( new InputStreamReader(
            sock.getInputStream() ) );
        }
        catch( IOException e )
        {
            error(e);
            return -1;
        }
        try
        {
            output = sock.getOutputStream();
        }
        catch( IOException e )
        {
            error(e);
            return -1;
        }
        rv=sendMailEngine();
// end connection
        try
        {
            sock.close();
        sock=null;
        }
        catch( IOException e )
        {
            error(e);
            return -1;
        }
        return rv;
    }


// this is a separate routine so the main sendMail can always close the
socket
private int sendMailEngine()
{
        try
        {

            int replyCode;
            int n;
            Date today = new Date();
            replyCode = getResponse( SMTPResults.SMTP_RESULT_READY );
            if( replyCode != 0 ) return replyCode;
```

```
        //Send HELO
        writeString( "HELO " + hostname + crlf );
        replyCode = getResponse( SMTPResults.SMTP_RESULT_COMPLETED );
        if( replyCode != 0 ) return replyCode;
        // Identify sender
        writeString( "MAIL FROM: " + message.sender + crlf );
        replyCode = getResponse( SMTPResults.SMTP_RESULT_COMPLETED );
        if( replyCode != 0 ) return replyCode;
        // Send to all recipients
        replyCode = sendAddresses("RCPT TO: ",message.to);
        if( replyCode != 0 ) return replyCode;
        // Send to all CC's (if any)
        if( message.cc != null && message.cc.length() != 0 )
        {
            replyCode = sendAddresses("RCPT TO: ",message.cc);
            if( replyCode != 0 ) return replyCode;
         }
            // Send to all BCC's (if any)
         if( message.bcc != null && message.bcc.length() != 0 )
         {
           replyCode = sendAddresses("RCPT TO: ",message.bcc);
           if( replyCode != 0 ) return replyCode;
          }

            // Send mesage
            writeString( "DATA" + crlf );
            replyCode = getResponse( SMTPResults.SMTP_RESULT_MAIL_START );
            if( replyCode != 0 ) return replyCode;

            //Send mail content CRLF.CRLF
            // Start with headers
            writeString( "Subject: " + message.subject + crlf);
            writeString( "From: " + message.sender + crlf);
            writeString( "To: " + message.to + crlf);
            if( message.cc != null && message.cc.length() != 0 )
                writeString( "Cc: " + message.cc + crlf);
            writeString( "X-Mailer: SMTP Java Class by Al Williams" +
                crlf);
            writeString( "Comment: Unauthenticated sender" + crlf );
        if (message.headers!=null) {
            Enumeration key=message.headers.keys();
            while (key.hasMoreElements()) {
                String keystring=(String)key.nextElement();

writeString(keystring+":"+(String)message.headers.get(keystring)+crlf);
            }
        }
```

```
        writeString( "Date: " + today.toString() +crlf + crlf );
    String bodybuf=message.body;
    if (message.encoder!=null) {
        StringWriter wbuf = new StringWriter();
        Writer xform;
        try {
            Class[] args = new Class[1];
            args[0]=Writer.class;
            java.lang.reflect.Constructor c=
                message.encoder.getConstructor(args);
            Object[] cargs=new Object[1];
            cargs[0]=wbuf;
            xform=(Writer)c.newInstance(cargs);
            xform.write(message.body);
            xform.flush();
        }
        catch (Exception e) {
            error(e);
            return -1;
        }
        bodybuf=wbuf.toString();
    }


        StringBuffer body=new StringBuffer(bodybuf);
    // chop lines to 76 characters
    int sbindex=0;
    int lineindex;
    do {
        String bodyline=body.substring(sbindex);
        String line;
        lineindex=bodyline.indexOf('\n');
        if (lineindex==-1)
            line=bodyline;
        else
            line=bodyline.substring(0,lineindex);
        while (line.length()>76) {
            if (line.charAt(0)=='.') writeString(".");
            writeString(line.substring(0,76));
            line=line.substring(76);
        }
        if (line.charAt(0)=='.') writeString(".");
        writeString(line); // write rest
        sbindex+=lineindex+1;
        writeString(crlf);
    } while (lineindex!=-1);
```

```
                    writeString( "." + crlf );  // end mail
                    replyCode = getResponse(
                        SMTPResults.SMTP_RESULT_COMPLETED);
                    if( replyCode != 0 ) return replyCode;
                    // Quit
                    writeString( "QUIT" + crlf );
                    replyCode = getResponse( SMTPResults.SMTP_RESULT_CLOSING );
                    if( replyCode != 0 ) return replyCode;
            }
        catch( IOException e )
        {
        error(e);
            return -1;
        }
    return 0;
    }

    protected void finalize() throws Throwable
    {
      if (sock!=null) sock.close();
      super.finalize();
    }

    private void error(Exception e) {
    if (debug) error(e.getMessage());
    }
    private void error(String s) {
    if (debug) {
        System.out.println(s);
    }
    }

    public static void main( String args [] )
    {
        int rc;
        Date today = new Date();
        if (args.length!=1)
        {
          System.out.println("Usage: SMTP e-mail address");
          System.exit(1);
        }
        System.out.println("Sending test message to " + args[0]);
        MailMessage msg = new MailMessage( "alw@al-williams.com", args[0],
"Test",
            "<h1>Sent at " + today.toString()+"</h1><hr>Thanks!");
    msg.addHeader("MIME-Version","1.0");
```

7. SMTP

```
        msg.addHeader("Content-Type","text/html");
        msg.addHeader("Content-Transfer-Encoding","Base64");
        msg.encoder=B64Encoder.class;
            SMTP smtp = new SMTP( testServer);
            rc = smtp.sendMail( msg );
            if( rc != 0 )
            {
              System.out.println( "Error " + rc );
              System.out.println(smtp.getLastResponse());
            }
            else
             System.out.println( "OK" );
        }


    }


    // private class to handle the reading in a thread
    class TimeoutRead extends Thread
    {
        private String buffer = new String( "" );
        private BufferedReader input;
        private boolean complete = false;
        synchronized String getBuffer() { return buffer; }
        synchronized void setBuffer(String s) { buffer=s; }
        synchronized public boolean isComplete()
        {
            return complete;
        }
        public TimeoutRead( BufferedReader i )
        {
            input = i;
        }
        public void run() // do input in thread
        {
            try
            {
                do
                {
                    setBuffer(input.readLine());
                } while (getBuffer().charAt(3)=='-'); // loop on multi-line
response
// This line is useful for debugging
                if (SMTP.debug) System.out.println(buffer);
            }
            catch( IOException e )
```

```
        {
            setBuffer("");
        }
        complete = true;
    }


}
```

Using SMTP

You'll find a JSP page that uses the **SMTP** component in Listing 7.4. It reads a list of group names from a property file. The user fills in the email fields and selects a group name from a drop-down box. The JSP file sends the mail to everyone in the list. If the list members change, you have to alter only the property file. With a little extra work, you could write a Web-based interface using JSP to view and update the property file.

Of course, the SMTP.class file, and all the class files that it depends on, will need to be in a directory that appears in the server's CLASSPATH. For many servers, that will mean placing it in the WEB-INF/classes directory in the application's main directory. You can make a simple JSP page to reveal the class path with just a few lines:

```
<%
out.println(System.getProperty ("java.class.path"));
%>
```

Listing 7.4.   You can use SMTP from within a JSP page to send email.

```
<%@ page import="java.io.InputStream" %>
<%@ page import="java.util.Properties" %>
<%@ page import="java.util.Enumeration" %>



<%!
  Properties database;
%>
<%
  ServletContext ctx;
  InputStream is;
  String dfile;
  dfile="/maillist/addresses.prop";
  database=new Properties();
  ctx=getServletContext();
  is=ctx.getResourceAsStream(dfile);
  if (is==null)
    out.println("Internal server error " + dfile);
```

```
    else
      {
      database.load(is);
      is.close();
      }
%>
<HTML>
<HEAD>
</HEAD>
<BODY BGColor=CornSilk>
<% if (request.getContentLength()==-1) { %>
<H1>Send mail to a group</H1>
<FORM METHOD=POST>

Group: <SELECT NAME=group>
<%
  Enumeration e=database.keys();
  while (e.hasMoreElements())
    {
    String s=(String)e.nextElement();
    out.println("<OPTION VALUE='" + s + "'>"+s);
    }
%>

</SELECT>
<BR>
From: <INPUT NAME=From SIZE=40><BR>
Subject: <INPUT NAME=Subj SIZE=40><BR>
<TEXTAREA ROWS=25 COLS=80 Name=msg>
</TEXTAREA>
<BR>
<INPUT TYPE=SUBMIT VALUE=Send>
</FORM>

<% } else {
 String elist;
 // really this could come from a database...
 elist=(String)database.getProperty(request.getParameter("group"));
 MailMessage msg=new MailMessage(request.getParameter("From"),elist,
     request.getParameter("Subj"),request.getParameter("msg"));
  SMTP smtp=new SMTP("smtp.myserver.com");  // use yours
  if (smtp.sendMail(msg)==0) {
%>
  Message sent.
<% } else { %>
  An error occurred. Please try again.
```

```
<%
   }
 }
%>
</BODY>
</HTML>
```

Attachments

As far as SMTP knows, all mail messages are a single entity. However, you've probably seen file attachments in email messages. This is purely a function of the email client interpreting a single email message as multiple files.

The multipart content type is the key to attachments. It also allows you to send alternate representations of the same message (for example, HTML and plain text). Here's a simple example message:

```
MIME-Version: 1.0
Content-Type: multipart/mixed; boundary="XXXYYYZZZ"
Subject: I have attachments

--XXXYYYZZZ
Content-Type: text/plain

This is the main message.
--XXXYYYZZZ
Content-Type: text/plain
Content-Description: test

This file will appear as test.txt!
--XXXYYYZZZ--
```

Each part of the message is separated by two dashes and the boundary text, which must not appear as part of the message. The last boundary has two dashes in front and another two dashes in the rear.

The text between the boundaries is an independent message. It can have its own headers, although the headers must start with Content- (the other headers don't mean anything in this context). A blank line separates these subheaders from the remaining message. Because no headers are necessary for ordinary text, it is permissible to start the attachment with a blank line if you don't need any special headers. In the example, because the attachment's Content-Description header is **test** and the Content-Type header is **text/plain**, the attachment will have a name of test.txt in most mail readers.

You can add more attachments by simply repeating the —XXXYYYZZZ separator (using only the two trailing dashes at the very end of all messages). Exactly how the mail client will present these attachments depends on the following subtypes:

- *multipart/mixed*—Each part is separate and should appear in the order provided.

- *multipart/alternative*—Each part is a different representation of the same message (for example, you might have one part as text, one part as HTML, and another part in some proprietary document format).

- *multipart/digest*—Each part is another mail message (often used by mailing list software).

- *multipart/parallel*—Each part is separate and should appear at once. This might be useful when one part is an HTML page, and the other part is a sound file you want to play while viewing the HTML page. In fact, few mail programs will actually do this. Most will treat this type as multipart/mixed.

Selecting the separator can be tricky. The separator must appear on a line by itself and can't exceed 70 characters. The preceding carriage return and line feed are part of the boundary and not part of the preceding message.

Notice that the first thing in the message is a boundary separator. The area before the first boundary is a no man's land—there isn't enough information to interpret it, and most smart mail readers will silently discard anything there. Some mail programs will place in this area text that provides instructions to users who don't have a capable mail program, on the assumption that they are the only ones that will see the message.

A common type of attachment is an email message itself (usually of type message/rfc822). Because that message may have attachments too, it is permissible to nest multipart messages. In that case, each part must use a unique boundary identifier.

SMTP Twists

One of the main problems with SMTP is that anyone can connect to a server and send mail. This feature helps spammers and other people who want to send untraceable email. To combat this, many SMTP servers are no longer open. Many providers reject connection requests that don't originate on their own network, for example. Others keep a database of IP addresses from their POP (Post Office Protocol) server (see Chapter 8) and verify incoming requests against it. Because a POP server requires a password, you can assume any request from that IP (within a certain amount of time) probably came from an authorized user.

This can pose a problem for programs trying to send email. Very few servers require password authentication, but in practice these servers are rare.

Immediate Solutions

Finding the SMTP Specification

The main RFC that governs SMTP is RFC2821. This single document covers several older RFCs and documents recent practices.

Connecting to an SMTP Server

By default, the SMTP server listens on port 25. Once you open the port, you should expect a response code of 220. If you want to see exactly the response you can expect from your server, set the correct server name in the code below:

```
String server="mail.myserver.com";
Socket sock;
sock = new Socket(server, 25 );
BufferedReader reader = new
    BufferedReader(new InputStreamReader(sock.getInputStream()));
System.out.println(reader.readLine());
```

Sending Mail via SMTP

Using an SMTP server requires your program to issue a command to sign on to the server. The standard command is **HELO**, but if you want extended information and commands from the server, you should issue an **EHLO** command instead. You can then send an email by issuing these three commands (you can repeat them to send multiple mail messages):

1. **MAIL FROM:** Starts mail from the sender

2. **RCPT TO:** Identifies the recipient (may occur more than once)

3. **DATA:** Specifies email message

To exit the data mode, you send a single period at the start of a line. If a real period begins a line, you should double it so that the server will not interpret it as the end of the message. Receivers know to treat two periods at the start of a line as a single period.

Once you have no more mail to send, you can issue a **QUIT** command. Table 7.1 shows all the commands available. Here is a manual session with an SMTP server that sends some email (lines entered by the user are highlighted):

```
$ telnet mail.al-williams.com 25
Trying 206.244.69.140 ...
Connected to mail.al-williams.com.
Escape character is '^]'.
220 po2.al-williams.com ESMTP server ready Mon, 14 May 2001 19:06:33 -0400
HELO darkstar@al-williams.com
250 po2.al-williams.com
MAIL FROM: alw@al-williams.com
250 Sender <alw@al-williams.com> Ok
RCPT TO: stamps@al-williams.com
250 Recipient <stamps@al-williams.com> Ok
DATA
354 Ok Send data ending with <CRLF>.<CRLF>
This is a message with 2 lines
And this is the second line
.
250 Message received: 20010514230632.AAA7382@[206.71.104.186]
QUIT
Connection closed by foreign host.
```

Message lines should not exceed 78 characters. The RFC insists that they must not exceed 998 characters (not counting the carriage return and line feed at the end of the line).

Interpreting Response Codes

SMTP servers reply using a three-digit code reminiscent of the ones FTP servers return. The first digit indicates the type of message (2 is success, 3 is a request for more information, and a 4 or 5 indicates a failure). Table 7.3 shows the most common SMTP server reply codes.

Table 7.3   The SMTP server replies with numeric codes.

Code	Description
211	System status, or system help reply
214	Help message
220	<domain> Service ready
221	<domain> Service closing transmission channel

(continued)

Table 7.3   The SMTP server replies with numeric codes *(continued)*.

Code	Description
250	Requested mail action okay, completed
251	User not local; will forward to <forward-path>
354	Start mail input; end with <CRLF>.<CRLF>
421	<domain> Service not available, closing transmission channel
450	Requested mail action not taken: mailbox unavailable
451	Requested action aborted: local error in processing
452	Requested action not taken: insufficient system storage
500	Syntax error, command unrecognized
501	Syntax error in parameters or arguments
502	Command not implemented
503	Bad sequence of commands
504	Command parameter not implemented
550	Requested action not taken: mailbox unavailable
551	User not local; please try <forward-path>
552	Requested mail action aborted: exceeded storage allocation
553	Requested action not taken: mailbox name not allowed
554	Transaction failed

Forming Addresses

As you'd expect, you can use a normal email address when forming SMTP commands. However, sometimes you'd like to use a display name in addition to the normal email address. SMTP recognizes any string you'd like to use for an email address if you enclose the actual address in angle brackets. For example:

```
Al Williams <alw@al-williams.com>
```

The server will discard everything except for the address in angle brackets. Of course, what the user sees depends on what is in the From and To headers (see the next section). Most mail programs will perform the opposite step and display only the part of the address outside of the angle brackets.

7. SMTP

Selecting Headers

SMTP is the transport mechanism for email, and it doesn't really care how you format your mail. However, email programs expect a certain format. In particular, they expect a set of headers—that is, information about the message—followed by a blank line and the body of the text.

Nonstandard headers begin with X- (for example, X-MimeOLE: Produced By Microsoft MimeOLE V5.50.4133.2400). Headers that begin with Content- are specifically for MIME messages. You can find a list of common headers in Table 7.4.

Table 7.4   Common headers provide meta-information about the email message.

Subject	Subject of the Message
To	The primary recipient of the message.
From	The sender's email address.
CC	Carbon copy recipients. These people will appear in the address list and receive a copy of the message.
BCC	Blind carbon copy recipients. These people will receive a copy but will not appear in the address list.
Return-Path	The email address that should receive administrative messages.
Received	The date and time received.
Reply-To	The email address that should receive any reply.
Date	The date and time the message was sent.
Mime-Version	Identifies a message as Multipurpose Internet Mail Extension-compliant and also registers the version of MIME the message uses. MIME headers begin with Content-.
Content-Type	Identifies the type of data in the message (for example, text/html).
Content-Transfer-Encoding	Identifies the encoding of the message (for example, 7 bit or base 64).
Content-Description	Describes a part of a MIME message (used to generate an attachment's file name).

Formatting Message Text

By using the MIME standard, you can send messages that contain 8-bit characters, HTML, or even binary data, such as graphic interchange format (GIF) files. There are several steps required:

1. Include the Mime-Version header to mark the message as MIME-compliant.

2. Use the Content-Type header to mark the document's type (see Table 7.5).

Table 7.5   These MIME types are very common.

Type	Description
application/pdf	Adobe Acrobat
application/rtf	Rich Text Format
application/zip	ZIP compressed data
audio/midi	Music files
audio/mpeg	Sound files using MPEG encoding
audio/x-realaudio	RealAudio sound files
audio/x-wav	Wave file
image/gif	GIF picture
image/jpeg	JPEG (Joint Photographic Experts Group) picture
image/png	PNG (Portable Network Graphic) picture
message/rfc822	Email message (useful for messages within messages)
multipart/alternative	Email with different formats attached
multipart/digest	Email containing emails
multipart/mixed	Email with attachments
multipart/parallel	Email with attachments for simultaneous display
text/html	HTML text
text/plain	Ordinary ASCII text
video/mpeg	MPEG encoded video
video/quicktime	Apple QuickTime video
video/x-msvideo	Microsoft AVI-format video

3. If the content contains characters that are not 7-bit ASCII characters, you should encode the message body and set the Content-Transfer-Encoding header to indicate the method used to encode the data.

There are many other MIME types available because it is easy to make up additional types. By convention, any custom MIME types should start with x as in audio/x-realaudio.

7. SMTP

Encoding Message Text Using Quotable Printable Encoding

If messages contain nonstandard characters, you must encode them using some scheme to convert the bytes into 7-bit ASCII characters. One such scheme is the quotable printable encoding (Content-Transfer-Encoding: quotable-printable).

This method is simple to implement, but it's not efficient for data that contains many non-ASCII characters. Here's how to encode a message using this scheme:

1. Leave characters with hex values of 21 to 3C and 3E to 7E alone. These are all the usual printable characters, except for the space (20) and the equal sign (3D).

2. You can leave spaces and tabs as-is, unless they are at the end of the line. Then you must encode them as =20 (space) or =09 (tab).

3. All other characters (except for carriage returns and line feeds) must use the three-byte representation =XX, where XX is the hex code for the character. For example, to insert a BEL (hex 7) you'd use =07.

4. Each line can contain no more than 76 characters. You can break the lines by placing an equal sign before the carriage return and line feed. This will allow the receiver to treat the next line as a continuation of the current line. Any carriage return-line feed pairs that do not follow an equal sign are hard line breaks.

You can encode any character using the equal sign notation, but because it uses three bytes to represent each character, you usually won't encode characters that don't require it. For example =41 is an uppercase A even though you could just use the uppercase A anyway.

Encoding Message Text Using Base 64

The most common way to encode messages that may contain non-ASCII characters is to use base 64 encoding. Here's how you encode a message using base 64:

1. Group three bytes from the input stream together to form 24 bits (the first byte's most significant bit is the new 24-bit word's most-significant bit). So the ASCII text ABC is hex 414243 as a 24-bit word. In binary, that's 010000010100001001000011.

2. Break the 24-bit word into four 6-bit groups. Using the same example, you get 010000 010100 001001 000011 (or in hex, 10 14 09 03).

3. Replace each group with the ASCII character found in Table 7.2.

4. Break each line into 76 characters or fewer (any characters not in Table 7.2 are ignored, so you can insert line breaks anywhere).

The only place you might have trouble is at the end of the file. At the end you might wind up with one or two spare characters. In this case, add zeros to make up an integral number of 6-bit groups (because bytes are 8 bits, that means you'll have either 12 or 18 bits). Convert the two or three 6-bit groups into ASCII characters as before and use equal signs to fill in the one or two characters required to form a four-character group.

Listing 7.5 shows the logic as a **FilterWriter**. This stream writes data out (to another **Writer** subclass) using base 64 encoding. The SMTP classes you'll see in this chapter can accept this type of object to encode body text automatically.

Listing 7.5   This filter applies base 64 encoding to a stream.

```java
// Base 64 encoding
import java.io.*;

public class B64Encoder extends FilterWriter {
    public B64Encoder(Writer w) { super(w); }
    private int charctr=0;
    private int linectr=0;
    private int buffer=0;
    private int encodeByte(int byt) {
    if (byt<=25) return 'A'+byt;
    if (byt<=51) return 'a'+byt-26;
    if (byt<=61) return '0'+byt-52;
    if (byt==62) return '+';
    if (byt==63) return '/';
    return -1; // huh?
    }


    public void close() throws IOException {
    flush();
    super.close();
    }

    private void writeit(int c) throws IOException {
    if (linectr++>=76) {
        out.write("\r\n");
        linectr=1;
    }
    out.write(c);
    }
```

```
public void flush() throws IOException {
if (charctr==2) {
    buffer<<=2; // make 16 bits to 18 bits
    writeit(encodeByte((buffer&0x3F000)>>12));
}
if (charctr==1) buffer<<=4; // make 8 bits to 12 bits
if (charctr!=0) {
    writeit(encodeByte((buffer&0xFC0)>>6));
    writeit(encodeByte(buffer&0x3F));
    if (charctr==1) writeit('=');
    writeit('=');
}

charctr=0;
out.flush();
}

public void write(int c) throws IOException {
int[] code = new int[3];
int i;
buffer<<=8;
buffer+=c;
if (++charctr!=3) return;
charctr=0;
for (i=0;i<4;i++) {
    writeit(encodeByte((buffer&0xFC0000)>>18));
    buffer<<=6;
}
buffer=0;
return;
}

public void write(char[] c, int o, int l) throws IOException {
while (l--!=0) {
    write(c[o++]);
}
}
}

public void write(String s, int of, int l) throws IOException {
write(s.toCharArray(),of,l);
}


public static void main(String args[]) throws Exception {
B64Encoder filter=new B64Encoder(new OutputStreamWriter(System.out));
int x;
```

```
    filter.write("Hello");
    do {
        x=System.in.read();
        if (x!=-1) filter.write(x);
    } while (x!=-1);
    filter.flush();
    }

}
```

Formatting Multipart Messages

MIME allows you to break one SMTP mail message into multiple parts. You might want to do this for several reasons, including the following:

- *Multiple parts might show the same content in different ways (for example, HTML and plain text).* This is known as *alternate* representation.

- *A message might store different presentation elements in different parts.* For example, one part might be text, and another part might be background music or audio narration. This is a *parallel* message.

- *Attachments to a message should appear as a separate part.* This common case is known as a *mixed* type.

- *A message might contain multiple email messages (as in a mailing list digest, which gives rise to the name* digest *format).*

The key is to set the Content-Type header to multipart/alternate, multipart/mixed, multipart/parallel, or multipart/digest. In addition, you'll place a semicolon in the header and specify some unique boundary text. For example:

```
Content-Type: multipart/mixed ; boundary=":::NEXT PART:::"
```

The body of the message should be formatted as follows:

1. Start with two dashes and the boundary text. Any text in the body before the first boundary is ignored (some mailers put instructions for non-MIME mail readers in this area).

2. Immediately following the boundary text are any MIME headers that you want to use for this part of the message (MIME headers begin with Content-). In particular, you'll want to set Content-Type. You may also set Content-Description, which many mailers will use (along with the type) to set the file name of the attachment. You may also want to set Content-Transfer-Encoding if you are encoding this body part using any special encoding method.

3. After the headers, you have the usual blank line and the body for this subpart of the message. The end of the subpart occurs when the boundary line appears, including the two leading dashes. The new line preceding the boundary is part of the boundary and doesn't affect the message body.

4. The last subpart ends with two dashes, the boundary line, and two more dashes.

Here is an example multipart message:

```
MIME-Version: 1.0
Content-Type: multipart/mixed; boundary="NEXT_PART"
Subject: A Test Message

--NEXT_PART
Content-Type: text/plain

This is the main message.
--NEXT_PART
Content-Type: text/plain
Content-Description: attach1

This is my attachment.
--NEXT_PART--
```

Using the MailMessage Object

Listing 7.1 in this chapter shows the **MailMessage** object. You can use this object to create a mail message that you can use with the **SMTP** class in Listing 7.3. Here are the steps you'll need:

1. Construct an object using one of the two constructors provided. You must provide a from and to address, along with the body text and a subject, no matter which constructor you use. The verbose constructor allows you to add a CC and BCC list.

2. Use the **addHeader** method to add any extra headers you may need, such as Mime-Version. By default, SMTP will set the standard headers that identify the sender, the recipients, and the date.

3. If you want to encode the body text (for example, using base 64 encoding), you must set the **encoder** field to be a class reference. To use the **B64Encoder** class in Listing 7.5 you'd set the **encoder** field to **B64Encoder.class**, for example. You must also set any headers that are appropriate for your encoding.

Here is a code fragment that shows how to make a **MailMessage** object:

```
MailMessage msg = new MailMessage("editor@al-williams.com",
         "alw@al-williams.com", "You are late!", "<H1>Late!</H1>" +
         "<I>Please</I> try to get your tasks done " +
         "<FONT COLOR=RED>on time!");
msg.addHeader("Mime-Version: 1.0");
msg.addHeader("Content-Type: text/html");
msg.encoder = B64Encoder.class;
```

Using the SMTP Object

If you have a **MailMessage** object, it is easy to send it using the **SMTP** object from Listing 7.3. Here are the steps:

1. Construct an **SMTP** object using your SMTP server's name or IP address.

2. Call the **sendMail** method, passing the **MailMessage** object you want to send.

3. Examine the return value. If it is 0, you successfully mailed your message.

4. If the return value is not 0, you can get the error message using **getLastResponse**.

Here's a bit of code that will get the job done:

```
SMTP smtp = new SMTP( "yourserver.domain.com");
rc = smtp.sendMail( msg );
if( rc != 0 )
{
  System.out.println( "Error " + rc );
  System.out.println(smtp.getLastResponse());
}
else
 System.out.println( "OK" );
}
```

Chapter 8

POP3

In Depth

When I was a kid, my parents ran a small home-based business. In those days, the phone company had no competition, and it made all the phones. You couldn't connect anything to the phone lines without an expensive device you had to rent from it, which did little more than compensate Ma Bell for the lost potential income.

My parents didn't want to miss business calls, so they bought an expensive answering machine from Lafayette (a long defunct Radio Shack competitor). Because the machine couldn't connect to the phone lines, it was a real Rube Goldberg. The phone sat on top of the main box. The box connected to a cradle that sat on top of the phone and held the phone's handset. Another cable connected the box to an ordinary tape recorder.

The box had a little four-track tape, like you used to see in radio stations. When the phone rang, it would disturb some sensor in the box. The box would move a solenoid in the cradle, which would take the phone off the hook. The four-track tape would play into a speaker in the cradle that was under the handset's microphone. At the same time, the box would turn on the tape recorder (the recorder's microphone was in the cradle under the handset's earpiece). The box would hold this state of affairs for thirty seconds and then reset everything.

Needless to say, very few people had answering machines in those days. Not only was the machine expensive but also a slamming door or loud noise would trigger it. Today you can buy an all-digital machine for $10 that is much more advanced than this early unit.

In a way, email is a modern version of the telephone. The Simple Mail Transfer Protocol (SMTP) protocol specifies how to send mail to a user on another computer. When computers were large mainframes or minicomputers that hosted many users, that was all you needed. The problem is that the vast majority of Internet users today use a personal computer. It probably isn't on twenty-four hours a day. Even if it is, it may not be connected to the Internet at all times, and it may not have a permanent hostname or Internet Protocol (IP) address.

Without some scheme to handle this problem, email would be practically unusable. That's why POP3 (Post Office Protocol 3) exists. POP3 allows a remote computer (that is presumably on the Internet most or all of the time) to store mail for you.

Many email clients, such as Netscape Messenger, Microsoft Outlook, and Eudora Pro, use POP3 to download incoming messages from an email server. (A newer scheme called Internet Message Access Protocol can also be used, but POP3 is by far the most common.) Your email program communicates with a POP3-enabled server and retrieves email via a process outlined in RFC1939. Your email program still uses a separate SMTP server to send email.

The POP3 Protocol

Like many Internet protocols, POP3 expects commands on a single line terminated by a carriage return and line feed. The default port is port 110, and the protocol uses TCP (Transmission Control Protocol) connections. Commands you send will consist of three or four characters, and the server will not consider the case of the commands. Each command may have parameters, each separated by a single space. Each parameter must be forty characters long or less.

Responses are different from other protocols, such as FTP (File Transfer Protocol) or SMTP. The first character of the response will be a plus sign (+), which indicates a successful response, or a minus sign (–), which signifies a failure. In addition, the server will send an uppercase keyword. There is only one standard positive response (+OK) and one standard negative response (–ERR), although the protocol can accommodate other response keywords.

The response can contain other information (up to 512 bytes total) and will end with a carriage return and line feed. Some responses always consist of multiple lines. In this case, the server will send the additional lines and finish with a line containing a single period. An SMTP message terminates this same way. Likewise, the same escape mechanism applies. The server will insert an extra period if any line in a multiline response that begins with a period.

POP3 servers have more than one possible state. When you first connect, the server is in the authorization state. Before you can do anything, you'll have to provide credentials to the server (in other words, provide a user ID and password).

Once you've provided correct information, the server enters the transaction state. This allows the client to retrieve mail and information about mail and to mark mail for deletion. Typically, the server will lock the mailbox during this phase of operation. Finally, when the client issues a command to end the session, the server enters the update state, where it cleans up the incoming mailbox, releases the mailbox, and closes the socket.

POP3 has only a few commands (see Table 8.1). Some of the commands are not required for a basic implementation.

8. POP3

Table 8.1   Commands recognized by POP3 servers.

Command	Required	Legal Time of Use	Multiline Response	Description
USER	Yes	Authorization	No	Provide user ID.
PASS	Yes	Authorization	No	Provide password.
APOP	No	Authorization	No	Send user ID and MD5-encoded challenge string in lieu of password.
QUIT	Yes	Authorization, transaction	No	End session (begins update phase if currently in transaction).
STAT	Yes	Transaction	No	Cause response to contain number of messages and size in bytes.
LIST	Yes	Transaction	Possible	Return status for a numbered message, or a multiline response with status for all messages if no number is provided.
RETR	Yes	Transaction	Yes	Retrieve a numbered message.
DELE	Yes	Transaction	No	Mark message as deleted.
NOOP	Yes	Transaction	No	No action.
RSET	Yes	Transaction	No	Unmark any messages that were marked for deletion.
TOP	No	Transaction	Yes	Retrieve headers and specified number of lines from a numbered message.
UIDL	No	Transaction	Possible	Generate a unique hash code for each message (or a specific message). Useful for ignoring previously retrieved messages.

Authorization

When the server enters the authorization state, it sends a prompt that conforms to the response format. For example:

```
+OK POP3 darkstar.al-williams.com v2000.69 server ready
```

At this point, the client can send a **QUIT** command to abort, or it can use the **APOP** or the **USER** and **PASS** commands to enter the transaction state.

As you'd expect, the **USER** and **PASS** commands allow you to specify a username and password. Some servers also allow you to extract some text from the initial prompt, encrypt it using your password, and send the encrypted version using the **APOP** command. In addition, a server can provide other forms of authentication (for examples, read RFC1734).

WARNING! Notice that your password is sent in the clear unless you use APOP or an alternate authentication scheme specific to your server.

Transaction

The main commands of interest during the transaction phase are **STAT**, **LIST**, and **RETR**. The **STAT** command replies with the number of messages and the number of bytes in the mailbox. For example:

```
+OK 2 924
```

This response indicates that the mailbox contains two messages with a total length of 924 bytes. The **LIST** command replies with a message number (assigned by the server) and the size of the message. If you specify a message number, the reply is a single line:

```
+OK 2 418
```

The first number is, of course, the message number. The second number is the size of the message in bytes. If you don't specify a number, the server sends a multiline reply:

```
+OK 2 messages (924 bytes)
1 506
2 418
.
```

Of course, the main reason you log in to a POP3 server is to fetch messages. That's what the **RETR** command does. You specify a message number, and a multiline response returns the message text. As with all multiline responses, any line that begins with a period will have the period doubled. A single period on a line ends the message.

Using the **RETR** command does not delete the message from the server. To mark a message for future deletion, the client can send a **DELE** command. This doesn't really delete the message, but it does hide the message from future **LIST** and **RETR** commands. When the server completes the update state, it will actually delete the message. If the client breaks the connection during the transaction phase, or issues a **RSET** command, the server will not really delete the marked messages.

Update

The **QUIT** command causes the server to enter the update state. This is when the server really deletes messages. It also releases the lock on the user's mailbox. Many POP3 servers implement a time-out to prevent the server from holding a lock on the mailbox indefinitely. However, even if a time-out occurs, the server should not delete messages because a time-out is not the same as the update state.

A POP3 Class

Listing 8.2 in the "Immediate Solutions" section shows a simple class that can interact with a POP3 server. Because the SMTP classes in the last chapter used the **MailMessage** class to represent an email message, it makes sense to use the same class to hold incoming messages.

The class, **PopClient**, has a sample test **main** method that accepts input from the command line to determine the server, the user ID, and the password. The program simply prints out any waiting mail messages (with each message followed by its headers).

The code in the class is straightforward. The **output** method adds a carriage return and line feed to the output, sends it to the server, and then interprets the response.

The real heart of the class is the **readMail** method. This method reads all the lines in the response and decides which lines are headers and which are body text. It correctly assembles the headers and fills in the **MailMessage** object appropriately.

A Custom List Manager

One of the best ways to exercise your email handling skills is to build a simple mailing list manager. List managers generally reside on servers and process incoming messages. A user can send one email message to the list address, and the manager forwards this message to the rest of the list's subscribers. Additionally, users can send messages to a special administrator's address to subscribe to, or unsubscribe from, the list. One of the best-known list managers in use today is a program named Majordomo.

I've created a list manager called Seneschal (*seneschal* is a medieval word for the administrator of servants in a noble home). I had considered Minordomo or Captaindomo, but those were already taken. Instead of making Seneschal a true server program, I decided to make it a program that I occasionally run manually to process my email. This keeps the sample code simple and lets me focus on discrete actions, such as checking mail, scanning for mail addressed to the list, forwarding messages to list subscribers, and deleting old messages. If you don't want to run Seneschal manually, you can program it to run at set intervals with the help of a scheduling program like cron, under Unix.

Seneschal assumes you have a POP3 email account and that the account accepts email for more than one address. For example, my domain is **al-williams.com**, and I can use any POP3-enabled application to connect to my domain's mail server. Even though I use **alw@al-williams.com** as my primary email address, my inbox gathers messages sent to any arbitrary address on the domain. You could send email to **bogusmail@al-williams.com**, and the system would still deliver the message to me because I'm the domain administrator. To use Seneschal, designate one address at your domain as the admin interface and another as the list interface. These could look something like **admin@al-williams.com** and **list@al-williams.com**.

The program responds to messages sent to one of these two addresses only and ignores all other email in your in-box. This makes it possible for you to run two or more Seneschal lists, each with a different email address. Note that the inbox can be accessed by only one program at a time, though, so be careful not to schedule the programs so that they overlap.

The only command-line argument the program accepts is the name of a properties file, which contains program configuration options (see Table 8.2). One option is the name of another file. The second file holds the list of subscribers, whose email addresses are keys. Each key's value is a set of option flags that aren't currently in use but that can be extended to create a more functional application.

Table 8.2 Seneschal options reside in a property file.

Parameter	Meaning
addressEmail	List main address
adminAddress	Email list administration address
smtpserver	SMTP server address
SMTPPort	Port for SMTP server (usually 25)
list	Full path to mailing list property file
popserver	POP3 server address
popuser	POP3 username
poppw	POP3 password

The Code

You can write your own code to handle the POP3 and SMTP transactions, but with all of the open source libraries on the Web, there's no need. I found a set of POP3 classes, written by John Thomas, that looked complete and easy to use (the maintainer's site is at **www.geocities.com/SunsetStrip/Studio/4994/pop3.html**). Table 8.3 in the later section "Using the **com.jthomas.pop** Package" provides a summary of the POP3 package's useful methods. I also used the SMTP classes from Chapter 7. The Seneschal code appears in Listing 8.1.

The POP3 classes return email messages as an array of **String** objects. However, I decided it would be easier to work with the mail in a different format. When Seneschal receives a message, it parses the headers into a **Hashtable** object. Next, it builds a single **String** containing the mail message. Depending on which email address the message was sent to, the program calls one of two routines: The first is for normal email, and the second is for administration requests.

Using the POP3 classes to retrieve email isn't difficult. The basic steps are as follows:

1. Construct a **pop3** object providing a POP3 server, a user ID, and a password.
2. Call the object's **connect** method to establish a connection with the server.
3. Call the **login** method to complete the connection.
4. Use **List** to retrieve a list of available emails.
5. Use **Retr** to return the actual text of a message.
6. Use **Dele** to mark a message for future deletion.
7. Call **Quit** to disconnect from the server and process any pending delete operations.

The **pop3** object's methods return a **popStatus** object. Not only can you check for success or failure, you can also obtain the extended results—for example, the list of messages or the message text—using the **popStatus** object's **Responses** method, which returns an array of **String** objects.

When you call **retr**, you get the email message in the response array, one **String** per line of text. The first lines contain the message headers (such as, To: or Subject:). Then there's a single blank line, followed by the message text.

Seneschal uses three action methods in two tiers. The first tier's **action** method takes a **pop3** object as an argument, parses the data, and stores each header in a **Hashtable**. To do this, it splits the string at the colon. Everything up to—but not including—the colon then becomes a key in the table. The remainder of the line—not including the colon—becomes the key's value. The first tier then calls one of the second tier action methods (either **action** or **admin**). The second-tier **action** method and the **admin** method can easily locate the value of any particular header since the first tier method did all the work in advance. When the parsing code encounters a blank line, it stops populating the **Hashtable**.

This simple parsing method works well for the headers. However, the admin method has a bigger parsing challenge. It must recognize the **subscribe** and **unsubscribe** commands, even when they're embedded in the message text. I used **StringTokenizer**, which is similar to the **strtok** function found in C, to combat this problem. This class breaks a string into tokens using delimiters that you specify.

Another routine that performs custom parsing is **baseEmail**. The code in **baseEmail** finds the core email address from headers like this one:

Al Williams <alw@al-williams.com>

Without **baseEmail** you'd be unable to unsubscribe if you changed your display name or used a different mailer that didn't format the display name the same way.

Listing 8.1 The Seneschal class implements an email list manager.

```
// Seneschal e-mail list manager
// Williams
import com.jthomas.pop.*;
import com.al_williams.SMTP.*;
import java.util.*;
import java.io.*;

public class Seneschal {
    String smtpserver;
    Properties maillist;  // list of members
    static Properties options;  // options
    // helper functions to get addresses
    public static String getAddress() { return getOpt("address","list@al-
williams.com"); }
    public static String getAdmin() { return
getOpt("adminAddress","listadmin@al-williams.com"); }

    public static void main(String arg[]) {
        String cfgfile="maillist.cfg";
        if (arg.length>1) {
            System.out.println("Usage: Seneschal [configfile]");
            System.exit(1);
        }
        if (arg.length==1) cfgfile=arg[0];
        options=new Properties();
```

```
        try {
          options.load(new FileInputStream(cfgfile));
        }
        catch (IOException ioe) {
        // can't open setup file?
          System.out.println("Can't open configuration file "+ioe);
          System.exit(9);
        }

        // Everything is ready to go, so start
        new Seneschal().go(arg);
    }


  // Real main routine
  public void go(String [] arg) {
// set STMP port
SMTP.smtpPort=getIntOpt("SMTPPort",25);
maillist=new Properties();
// load subscribers list
try {
    maillist.load(new FileInputStream(getOpt("list","maillist")));
}
catch (IOException ioe) {
    System.out.println(ioe);
    System.exit(2);
}
// Set up pop server
pop3 pop = new pop3(getOpt("popserver"),
            getOpt("popuser"), getOpt("poppw"));
smtpserver=getOpt("smtpserver");
popStatus status=pop.connect(), xstatus;
if (status.OK())
      status = pop.login();
if (status.OK()) {
      status = pop.list();  // check mail
      String[] responses = status.Responses();
      String[] xresponses;
      int n;
// for each message....
      for(int i=0; i< responses.length; i++) {
      n=responses[i].indexOf(' ');
      n=Integer.parseInt(responses[i].substring(0,n));
// read it
      xstatus=pop.retr(n);
      if (xstatus.OK()) {
```

```
        xresponses = xstatus.Responses();
        // check for recipient
        for (int n1=0;n<xresponses.length;n1++) {
          String to;
          boolean adminflg=false;
          if (xresponses[n1].length()==0 ) break;
          if (!xresponses[n1].substring(0,3).equalsIgnoreCase("to:"))
            continue;
          if (xresponses[n1].indexOf(getAdmin())!=-1) adminflg=true;
          if (!adminflg && xresponses[n1].indexOf(getAddress())==-1)
            continue;
// this email message is for me
// do something with email message #n
// including delete it most likely
          if (action(pop,n,adminflg))
          pop.dele(n); // kill message
          }
      } else {
          System.out.println("RETR ERROR"); }


      }
      status = pop.quit(); // must quit to delete properly
  }
}


  // This is the low-level action that, by default,
  // builds a hashtable of the headers and a string of the message
  // only override this if you want greater control
  public boolean action(pop3 pop, int n,boolean adminflg) {
  boolean header=true;
  popStatus status=pop.retr(n);
  if (!status.OK()) return false;
  String [] responses = status.Responses();
  StringBuffer message = new StringBuffer();
  Hashtable headers = new Hashtable();
  for (int i=0;i<responses.length;i++) {
    if (responses[i].length()==0) {
    header=false;
    continue;
  }
  if (header) {
    int n1=responses[i].indexOf(':');
    if (n1!=-1) headers.put(responses[i].substring(0,n1).trim(),
            responses[i].substring(n1+1).trim());
  }
```

```
       else {
          message.append(responses[i]);
          message.append("\n");
          }
       }
    if (adminflg)
         return admin(headers,message.toString());
    else
         return action(headers,message.toString());
    }


    // This is the action routine for normal mail
    public boolean action(Hashtable headers, String message) {
     SMTP smtp=new SMTP(smtpserver);
     int rc;
     MailMessage msg;
     message+="\nSent by Seneschal by Al Williams\nTo unsubscribe " +
        "send unsubscribe to " + getAdmin();
// loop for all members
     msg=new MailMessage(getAddress(),"",
        (String)headers.get("Subject"),message);
     for (Enumeration e=maillist.keys();e.hasMoreElements();) {
        msg.to=(String)e.nextElement();
        rc=smtp.sendMail(msg);
        if (rc!=0) {
           System.out.println("Error " + rc);
           System.out.println(smtp.getLastResponse());
        }
      }
    return true;
    }


    // This is the admin routine that handles messages to the admin
    public boolean admin(Hashtable headers, String message) {
    // commands subscribe, unsubscribe
      boolean rv=true;
      StringTokenizer strtok = new StringTokenizer(message);
      while (strtok.hasMoreTokens()) {
        String tok=strtok.nextToken();
        if (tok.equalsIgnoreCase("subscribe")) {
           rv&=subscribe(baseEmail((String)headers.get("From")));
           }
        if (tok.equalsIgnoreCase("unsubscribe")) {
          rv&=unsubscribe(baseEmail((String)headers.get("From")));
           }
    }
```

8. POP3

```
  return rv;  // all commands must succeed or fail
}

// subscribe and send confirming email
private boolean subscribe(String email) {
  boolean rv;
  MailMessage msg=new MailMessage("list",email,"You are subscribed",
    "This message is to confirm that you have " +
    "subscribed to the list\nIf you wish to unsubscribe " +
    "send unsubscribe to " + getAdmin());
  SMTP smtp=new SMTP(smtpserver);
  maillist.put(email,"0");
  if (rv=saveList())
    rv&=smtp.sendMail(msg)==0;
  return rv;
}

// unsubscribe and send confirming email
private boolean unsubscribe(String email) {
  boolean rv;
  MailMessage msg=new MailMessage("list",email,"You have unsubscribed",
    "This message is to confirm that you have " +
    "unsubscribed to the list\nIf you wish to subscribe " +
    "send subscribe to " + getAdmin());
  SMTP smtp=new SMTP(smtpserver);
  maillist.remove(email);
  if (rv=saveList())
    rv&=smtp.sendMail(msg)==0;
  return rv;
}

// Strip email from within <>
private String baseEmail(String email) {
  int n,n1;
  n=email.indexOf('<');
  if (n==-1) return email;
  n1=email.indexOf('>');
  if (n1==-1) return email; //?
  return email.substring(n+1,n1);
}

// Save the list back to property file
private boolean saveList() {
  try {
    maillist.store(new FileOutputStream(getOpt("list","maillist")),"");
    return true;
    }
```

8. POP3

```
        catch (IOException e) {
          System.out.println("Can't save mail list: " + e);
          return false;
          }
      }


      // Get an option with a default value (String)
      private static String getOpt(String key, String def) {
        String s;
        s=(String)options.get(key);
        if (s==null || s.equals("")) s=def;
        return s;
      }

      // Get an option
      private static String getOpt(String key) {
        return (String)options.get(key);
      }

      // Get an integer option
      private static int getIntOpt(String key, int def) {
        String s=getOpt(key,"");
        if (s.equals("")) return def;
        return def;
        }


    }
```

Leverage

As it is, Seneschal isn't very sophisticated. For example, many mail list programs mark outgoing messages with special headers to prevent bounced mail from forming an endless loop. It would be easy enough to add a unique Seneschal header to an outbound message. Then you could examine inbound messages for this special header and refuse to forward any returned messages.

Obviously, there are other tests you could perform on the messages. You might refuse to forward email from addresses that aren't on the subscriber list. You could also refuse to accept mail with certain words or attachments in it.

Depending on your needs, you can change the way Seneschal sends out messages to several subscribers. Currently, the program sends one copy of a message to each address, resulting in numerous SMTP transactions. It would be simple enough to add each address to the BCC (blind carbon copy) list of the outbound message and send it all as one SMTP transaction. However, a failure in the SMTP transaction might then prevent all the recipients from receiving the email.

Further Development

Seneschal is primarily a list manager. But its basic structure—especially that of the **admin** method—would work well for a more robust email server.

Once you can send and receive email, you're ready to work on a host of service applications. You could let users send requests via email and reply in kind. You could even add an application that automatically replies to emails requesting prices, stock quotes, or news stories. Of course, you could also provide the traditional email services such as list servers, autoresponders, or remailing. Another place where email services are making a comeback is on email-enabled mobile devices. Many pagers and phones have email capabilities now, and offering your content via email may be the only way to reach the users of those devices.

About IMAP

Although POP3 is very popular, some servers also support IMAP (Internet Message Access Protocol, defined by RFC2060). IMAP is similar in operation to POP3, but has special features that make it well suited for managing a mailbox remotely.

Both POP3 and IMAP rely on a centralized server that accepts mail on behalf of the user. POP3 requires the user to download the messages to a local computer. IMAP can do this also. However, it also has provisions for managing the mailbox on the host computer. This allows you to work with your mail on many different machines. It is also useful for clients that don't have much space locally.

Although IMAP is useful in some situations, nearly all servers will at least support POP3. POP3 is also simpler to understand because it has far fewer commands than IMAP. If you really need IMAP support, you'll probably be just as happy to find a ready-made class library to handle it for you (for example, Sun's **JavaMail**).

Using JavaMail

Because email processing is a common task, Sun developed the **JavaMail API**. By itself, this is simply a specification that defines what mail-client objects should look like. The actual operation of the objects is not part of the specification. However, Sun provides a redistributable reference implementation that handles POP3 and IMAP (along with SMTP for sending email).

Because the **JavaMail** package tries to handle any mail system, it is somewhat more complex than the other classes you've examined so far. Rather than deal with concrete commands to a specific server, **JavaMail** abstracts the email system into functional objects.

For example, the **Session** object corresponds to a session with an email server and the **Message** object models an abstract email message. You won't use **Message** directly—instead, you'll work with a subclass like **MimeMessage**. An **Address** object allows you to address your message. An **Authenticator** represents your user ID and password.

When you have a connection to a POP3 or IMAP server, you can access the contents via a **Store** object. This object will allow you to access **Folder** objects (although the POP3 server will only have one **Folder**, named INBOX). Naturally, you can retrieve **Message** objects from the **Folder**.

Using **JavaMail** isn't as hard as installing **JavaMail**. You have to download the **JavaMail** package and the **JavaBean Activation Framework** (JAF) package. The **JavaMail** documentation explains this. That means you have to set at least three extra JAR files in your CLASSPATH.

JavaMail is capable of handling complex mail clients. However, a simple program is easy to create also. Listing 8.3 (in the "Immediate Solutions" section) shows a client that is comparable to the other client programs in this chapter. The program obtains a **Session** object and uses it to obtain a **Store** object. By calling **connect**, the program makes a connection between the server and the **Store** object. Finally, it is a simple matter of opening a folder to find the messages.

You'll notice that the code contains a line that assigns an array reference with all the messages. This may seem inefficient, but the **JavaMail** provider is supposed to not fetch the actual data from the server until necessary.

Immediate Solutions

Finding the POP3 Specification

The main RFC that governs POP3 is RFC1939. As usual, there are extensions and additions in several other RFCs. For example, extension of authentication schemes is mentioned in RFC1734.

Finding the IMAP Specification

Because POP3 is not well suited to manipulating mail that remains on the host computer, some hosts support a different specification known as IMAP (although they usually also support POP3). IMAP allows you to create mail folders on the server and leave mail on the server machine. The mail client then downloads headers and whatever messages it wants to read directly. IMAP has had several versions, but you can find the latest (version 4) in RFC1730.

Interpreting POP3 Server Responses

POP3 servers always respond with a +OK if an operation is successful or a –ERR if the operation failed. The text is always uppercase. The server may place a space after the response and then place other information on the line (for example, the results of an operation).

Some commands generate multiline results. In this case, the subsequent lines follow the result indicator line. The end of the multiline result will be a single period. To prevent data from prematurely terminating the result, the server will insert an extra period into any result that starts with a period.

If you have a response line in a variable named **line**, you might write this code:

```
    // check for end
if (line.length()!=0 && line.charAt(0)=='.' && line.length()==1)
return;  // whatever you need to do at the end
// check for escaped period
if (line.length()!=0 && line.charAt(0)=='.')
line=line.substring(1);
```

8. POP3

Authentication with POP3

Different POP3 servers may support various types of authentication. However, the basic method is to use the **USER** and **PASS** commands. After connecting to a POP3 server (usually on port 110), the server will issue a prompt in the form of a response. You can then use the **USER** and **PASS** commands like this (the server's output all begins with a plus sign):

```
+OK hello from popgate
USER wd5gnr
+OK password required.
PASS al
+OK maildrop ready, 153 messages (795545 octets) (890161 6291456)
```

Learning the Status of a Mailbox

You can issue a **STAT** command to find out how many messages a mailbox contains and how many bytes it requires. The response will indicate success and contains two numbers to indicate the two quantities:

```
STAT
+OK 12 81703
```

This indicates 12 messages and almost 82K of data. It is often useful to perform this command after logging in to the server and caching the results:

```
if (!output("STAT")) return false;
StringTokenizer tokens = new StringTokenizer(response);
tokens.nextToken(); // throw away first
messageCount=Integer.parseInt(tokens.nextToken());
totalSize=Integer.parseInt(tokens.nextToken());
```

The **output** method writes the command to the server and collects the result in the **response** variable (see Listing 8.2 for the entire program).

Determining Message Details

You can use the **LIST** command to learn the details about a specific message, or all messages. When you make a connection, the server arbitrarily numbers each message in the mailbox. If you provide a message number, the server responds on a single line:

```
+OK 1 13185
```

The first number is the message number, and the second is the size in bytes. Of course, if you ask for a message number that doesn't exist, you'll elicit an error response:

```
-ERR invalid message number
```

If you don't supply a message number, the server responds with a multiline response. The status line won't contain any message information itself. Each subsequent line will contain the two numbers corresponding to a different message.

Another way to find out some information about a mail message is to use the **TOP** command (although not all servers support it). The **TOP** command allows you to fetch the headers and a certain number of lines from a message. For example, to just retrieve the message headers for message number 3, you could issue this command:

```
TOP 3 0
```

This is useful for email programs that want to show just the sender and subject, for example, without downloading the entire message. The response is, of course, a multiline response, with the headers, a blank line, and the specified number of lines from the email message.

Reading a Mail Message

Once you have a mail message number you'd like to read, you simply issue a **RETR** command with the message number as an argument. The server will reply with the message headers, a blank line, and the message text, all in multiline reply format.

Deleting a Message

The **DELE** command allows you to delete a specific message. However, the message is not really deleted until you successfully issue a **QUIT** command. If the network connection drops, the server will not actually delete messages. This prevents accidental loss of email messages.

You can also ask the server to undo deletions you've issued before you issue a **QUIT** command. Simply send a **RSET** command and you will effectively undelete any messages you deleted during this session.

Building a POP3 Client Class

Armed with the knowledge of how the POP3 protocol works, it is simple enough to write a class to handle the transactions (see Listing 8.2). There are six important fields in the object:

- **skt**—The socket to the server
- **out**—The output stream that sends data to the server
- **in**—Input stream from the server
- **response**—The last response string from the server
- **messageCount**—The number of messages in the mailbox
- **totalSize**—The number of bytes in the mailbox

The **output** routine manages the transmission of commands to the server and interprets the response. A **false** return indicates an error response from the server.

The **connect** method allows you to log in to the server. It also initializes the **messageCount** and **totalSize** fields. Other methods include **readMail** to read a single mail message, and **readAll** to read an array of mail messages. The program uses the **MailMessage** class from the previous chapter to represent messages.

Listing 8.2 contains a simple test **main**, so you can see the class in action. Simply supply a server name, a username, and a password on the command line. Although the program displays the mail, it does not remove it from the server.

Listing 8.2   This class communicates with a POP3 server.

```
// POP3 class -- Williams
import java.io.*;
import java.net.*;
import java.util.StringTokenizer;
import java.util.Hashtable;
import java.util.Enumeration;
```

```
public class PopClient {
    protected Socket skt;
    protected OutputStreamWriter out;
    protected BufferedReader in;
    public String response;
    // mailbox stats
    public int messageCount=0;
    public int totalSize=0;

    // Write a string with CRLF and check response
    protected boolean output(String s) throws IOException {
     out.write(s+"\r\n");
     out.flush();
     response=in.readLine();
     if (response.charAt(0)!='+') return false;
     return true;

     }

    // Connect, login, and set the status variables
    public boolean connect(String host,String user,String pw,int port)
     throws UnknownHostException, IOException  {
        if (port==0) port=110; // default port
        skt=new Socket(host,port);
        out=new OutputStreamWriter(skt.getOutputStream());
        in=new BufferedReader(new InputStreamReader(skt.getInputStream()));
        response=in.readLine();
        if (response.charAt(0)!='+') return false;
        if (!output("USER " + user)) return false;
        if (!output("PASS " + pw)) return false;
        if (!output("STAT")) return false;
        StringTokenizer tokens = new StringTokenizer(response);
        tokens.nextToken(); // throw away first
        messageCount=Integer.parseInt(tokens.nextToken());
        totalSize=Integer.parseInt(tokens.nextToken());
        return true;
        }

    // Do a quit with or without an RSET
    public boolean quit(boolean delete) throws IOException {
       boolean rv=true;
       if (!delete)
       if (!output("RSET")) rv=false;
       if (!output("QUIT")) rv=false;
       try {
        skt.close();
        }
```

257

```
      catch (IOException e) {}
      return rv;
  }

  // Mark a message for deletion
  public boolean delete(int n) throws IOException {
    if (n>messageCount) return false; // catch overflow locally
    return output("DELE " + Integer.toString(n));
    }

  // Read all messages (could take a while!)
  public MailMessage[] readAll() throws IOException {
    MailMessage [] msgs = new MailMessage[messageCount];
    for (int i=0;i<messageCount;i++) {
       msgs[i]=readMail(i+1);
    }
    return msgs;
  }


  // Read a specific message
  public MailMessage readMail(int n) throws IOException {
    if (n>messageCount) return null; // catch overflow locally
    MailMessage mail;
    Hashtable headers=new Hashtable();
    String line;
    StringBuffer bodytext=new StringBuffer();
    boolean body=false;
    if (!output("RETR " + Integer.toString(n))) return null;
    String lastHeader = "";
// for each line of response...
    while (true) {
       line=in.readLine();
       if (line.length()==0 && !body) {
         body=true; // blank line in headers means body
         continue;
         }
       else {
  // check for end
          if (line.length()!=0 && line.charAt(0)=='.' &&
          line.length()==1)break;
     // check for escaped period
          if (line.length()!=0 && line.charAt(0)=='.')
             line=line.substring(1);
          }
```

```
    // if body, just build up lines
      if (body) {
        bodytext.append(line);
        bodytext.append("\n");
        }
      else {   // headers
      // if a wrap-around header, append it
        if (line.charAt(0)==' ' || line.charAt(0)=='\t') {
          headers.put(lastHeader,
            (String)headers.get(lastHeader)+" "+
            line.trim());
          continue;
          }
    // otherwise split header line at :
        int ndx=line.indexOf(':');
        if (ndx!=-1) {
          String key=line.substring(0,ndx).trim();
          String value=line.substring(ndx+1).trim();
          lastHeader=key.toLowerCase();
        // and store in hashtable
          headers.put(lastHeader,value);
        }
      }
}
// ok we got it all I think
mail=new MailMessage((String)headers.get("from"),
          (String)headers.get("to"),
          (String)headers.get("cc"),"",
          (String)headers.get("subject"),
          bodytext.toString());
// remove "standard headers"
headers.remove("from");
headers.remove("to");
headers.remove("cc");
headers.remove("subject");
mail.headers=headers;
return mail;
}

// Test main
public static void main(String args[]) throws Exception {
PopClient pop= new PopClient();
if (pop.connect(args[0],args[1],args[2],0)) {
    System.out.println(pop.messageCount + " messages");
    if (pop.messageCount!=0) {
```

```
                    MailMessage [] msgs=pop.readAll();
                    for (int i=0;i<msgs.length;i++) {
                        MailMessage msg=msgs[i];
                        System.out.println(msg.body);
                        System.out.println("---- Headers ----");
                        Enumeration keys=msg.headers.keys();
                        while (keys.hasMoreElements()) {
                          String iKey=(String)keys.nextElement();
                          System.out.println(iKey + ":" + msg.headers.get(iKey));
                          }
                        System.out.println("****** NEXT MESSAGE ******");
                      }
                    }
              }
              else {
                  System.out.println("Error : " + pop.response);
              }
              pop.quit(false);
              }
        }
```

Using the **com.jthomas.pop** Package

You can find another POP3 class written by John Thomas at **gate.cruzio.com/ ~jthomas/pop/readme.html** or **www.geocities.com/SunsetStrip/Studio/4994/ pop3.html**. He includes several classes (including source code) that you can use to handle incoming email:

- **pop3**—Handles most common mail operations. It does not support the **APOP** command for authentication.

- **apop**—Extends **pop3** and adds support for the **APOP** command. If you want to use the **apop** class, you also need **MD5** and **MailDigest** classes, which are not open source, from Sun.

- **testmain** and **testapop**—Tests the two main classes.

- **Convert** and **popStatus**—Perform utility functions required by the other classes.

In addition, the package has several examples (including an applet).

The **pop3** class is simple to use. You can find its useful methods in Table 8.3. The Seneschal mailing list manager in Listing 8.1 uses this class to handle incoming mail.

8. POP3

Table 8.3   The **com.jthomas.pop.pop3** object provides several useful methods.

Method	Description
connect	Connect to a POP3 server.
login	Provide user ID and password. Calls **stat** internally.
stat	Get status information about mailbox.
quit	End connection with server and process deletes.
list	Get information about messages.
uidl	Find unique ID for message.
retr	Retrieve entire message.
top	Retrieve top part of message.
dele	Mark message for deletion.
rset	Reset deletions.
noop	No operation.
get_TotalMsgs	Get number of waiting messages.
get_TotalSize	Get total mailbox size.
appendFile	Retrieve a message and append it to a local file.

Installing **JavaMail**

To install **JavaMail** over an ordinary JDK installation you need to download two packages:

1. The **JavaMail** package itself (**java.sun.com/products/javamail/index.html**).

2. The **JavaBean** Activation Framework package (**java.sun.com/beans/glasgow/jaf.html**).

Although the **JavaMail** specification is abstract, Sun includes a reference implementation that you can use and redistribute for POP3, IMAP, and SMTP services.

*TIP: Once you install both packages, you'll need to make sure that the mailapi.jar and mail.jar files are in your CLASSPATH. In addition, you'll need the pop3.jar, imap.jar, and smtp.jar if you plan to use all three protocols. The activation.jar file from the **JavaBean** Activation Framework package is also required.*

8. POP3

Working with **JavaMail Message** Objects

The **Message** object has many useful methods. However, you should recognize that the actual object you receive is usually an instance of a **Message** subclass, and therefore has extra methods available. Table 8.4 shows the most useful methods for the **Message** object.

Table 8.4   The Message object has these methods.

Method	Description
addFrom	Add an array of addresses to the sender header for this message.
addRecipient	Add a recipient to the message.
addRecipients	Add an array of recipients.
getAllRecipients	Return an array of recipients for the message.
getFolder	Return the folder that contains this message.
getFrom	Return the senders for this message.
getMessageNumber	Return this message's number.
getReceivedDate	Return date and time the message was received.
getRecipients	Return the recipients list.
getReplyTo	Return the reply to header.
getSentDate	Return the sent date.
getSubject	Return the message subject.
reply	Construct a message suitable for generating a reply.
setFrom	Set the sender header for this message.
setMessageNumber	Set the number of the message.
setRecipient	Set a recipient for the message.
setRecipients	Set an array of recipients.
setReplyTo	Set the reply to address header.
setSentDate	Set the date and time for sending.
setSubject	Set the message's subject.

Working with **JavaMail Session** Objects

The key to working with **JavaMail** is the **Session** object. You'll never instantiate one directly. Instead, you'll usually call **getDefaultInstance** to return an appropriate instance to use. At a minimum, you pass **getDefaultInstance** a **Properties** object. However, it only uses this object if it creates a new **Session**. You can leave the **Properties** object empty if you want to use the default settings.

8. POP3

However, you can also set properties to control different aspects of the session. For example, **mail.host** can set the default mail server and **mail.user** can set the USER ID. So to set a properties object to set the mail server, you might write:

```
prop.put("mail.host","darkstar.al-williams.com");
```

Using **JavaMail** with a POP Mail Server

You can find a simple program that uses **JavaMail** in Listing 8.3. The steps are simple:

1. Create a **Properties** object. The **Session** object accepts options via a **Properties** object. In this case, there are no options, but you still need a **Properties** object.

2. Create a **Session** object. You don't directly instantiate **Session**, but instead you call **getDefaultInstance**.

3. Use **session.getStore** to retrieve the server's POP3 store. You can also specify IMAP.

4. Use **store.connect** to make a live connection between the **store** object and the actual server.

5. Call **store.getFolder** to find the INBOX folder (the only folder in a POP3 store). For an IMAP server, you can access different folders.

6. Use **folder.open** to open the folder in read-only mode.

7. Call **folder.getMessages** to retrieve an array of messages. The array is efficient, so it does not transfer data unnecessarily.

*TIP: Remember, you can construct a **Message** object and use **JavaMail** to send it via SMTP, so if you are using **JavaMail** anyway, you might consider using it to send your email as well.*

Listing 8.3   This simple program fetches mail using **JavaMail**.

```
// JavaMail Demo -- Williams
import javax.mail.*;
import javax.mail.internet.*;
import java.util.Properties;

public class JMailDemo {
    public static void main(String args[]) throws Exception {
        String host = args[0];
        String username = args[1];
        String password = args[2];
```

```
// Create empty properties
   Properties props = new Properties();

// Get session
   Session session = Session.getDefaultInstance(props, null);

// Get the store
   Store store = session.getStore("pop3");
   store.connect(host, username, password);

// Get folder
   Folder folder = store.getFolder("INBOX");
   folder.open(Folder.READ_ONLY);

// Get directory
   Message message[] = folder.getMessages();

// print first sender, subject, and message
   for (int i=0, n=message.length; i<n; i++) {
       System.out.println(i + ": " + message[i].getFrom()[0]
               + "\t" + message[i].getSubject());
       System.out.println(message[i].getContent().toString());
   }

  // Close connection
  folder.close(false);
  store.close();
  }
}
```

Using **JavaMail** with an IMAP Mail Server

Using IMAP instead of POP with **JavaMail** is—superficially—as easy as changing the argument to **getFolder** to use IMAP. Of course, the real trick is that IMAP has many more capabilities (for example, multiple folders). That means that many of the **JavaMail** methods that don't make sense with POP are suddenly useful. For example, Listing 8.4 shows a mail listing program that also shows the subfolders available on the IMAP server.

Listing 8.4   This mail listing program uses an IMAP server and lists the available subfolders.

```
// JavaMail Demo -- Williams
import javax.mail.*;
import javax.mail.internet.*;
import java.util.Properties;

public class IMapMailDemo {
    public static void main(String args[]) throws Exception {
        String host = args[0];
        String username = args[1];
        String password = args[2];

        // Create empty properties
        Properties props = new Properties();

        // Get session
        Session session = Session.getDefaultInstance(props, null);

        // Get the store
        Store store = session.getStore("imap");
        store.connect(host, username, password);

        // Get folder
        Folder folder = store.getFolder("INBOX");
        folder.open(Folder.READ_ONLY);
        // print sub folders
        Folder [] folders = folder.list();
        if (folders.length==0) System.out.println("No sub folders");
        for (int ij=0;ij<folders.length;ij++) {
            System.out.println("Subfolder: " + folders[ij].getFullName());
        }


        // Get directory
        Message message[] = folder.getMessages();
        if (message.length==0) System.out.println("No mail");
        // print first sender, subject, and message
        for (int i=0, n=message.length; i<n; i++) {
            System.out.println(i + ": " + message[i].getFrom()[0]
                        + "\t" + message[i].getSubject());
            System.out.println(message[i].getContent().toString());
        }
}
```

```
            // Close connection
            folder.close(false);
            store.close();
        }
    }
```

Chapter 9

NNTP

In Depth

I live in Texas. You can't live in most parts of Texas for very long before you start picking up some Spanish. We have plenty of Spanish television and radio, and most large companies and government agencies have bilingual phone messages.

One of the things that I've always found interesting about any of the languages that have common roots in Latin is how familiar they appear to English speakers. If you look at Farsi, for example, you know you are looking at a different language. Even Russian uses a different alphabet. A quick glance at a Spanish newspaper, on the other hand, looks like you could puzzle out the meaning if you wanted to take the time.

Because the Romans (who spoke Latin) conquered much of the world they knew, it isn't surprising that they brought their language with them and spread it around. Even when other languages mutated, they tended to mutate in the same ways— sort of an evolution for languages. What works well stays, and what doesn't work as well gets changed. For example, of all the Latin-derived tongues, only Romanian retains multiple cases for nouns. No language I know of kept Latin's neutral gender, either.

Unlike the Romans, the Internet did conquer the whole world. New protocols are like new languages—they tend to keep what works and discard what doesn't. That means that many protocols seem similar, yet they are subtly different.

This is certainly the case with the Network News Transfer Protocol (NNTP). At first glance it seems almost identical to email protocols. However, the command structure is different and several subtle differences exist.

About News

The purpose of news is to allow people to post and read messages on a variety of topics. All the messages reside on a server, and the server organizes the messages into groups—each group corresponds to a topic.

Each group contains messages that are similar in format to email messages (see Chapter 8). Clients can connect to the server that contains these news messages, review the messages, and post new messages.

In addition to end users, servers may connect together and exchange messages. The idea is that users will connect to a nearby server to read news messages, thus reducing congestion on the network and loading on the server.

The NNTP protocol that RFC977 defines is, in theory, neutral on exactly what type of news messages you send and read. However, the system is geared toward handling Usenet news (itself defined in RFC850). Usenet news is an older system where computers traded news messages, often using private communication links and phone lines. Users of each computer could read and post messages with all other users, which is more efficient than, say, emailing hundreds or thousands of users with the same message.

Usenet groups are hierarchical in nature. So several ham radio groups might be under rec.radio.amateur (for example, rec.radio.amateur.homebrew and rec.radio.amateur.satellite).

Inside NNTP

Superficially, NNTP resembles SMTP. You send commands and receive response codes. The response codes are three digit codes that are similar to SMTP codes insomuch as the first digit determines if the code is successful or not.

A client would typically connect to a server and provide a user ID and password, if required (and on modern servers, it is practically always required). The client can request lists of groups, or even determine if there are new groups by providing a timestamp for the last time it read the groups from the server.

All of the message-related commands require the client to first issue a **GROUP** command to set the current group. Within the group, messages have a sequence number, and they also have a unique ID that does not change. The client can query the server for message IDs and then download all or part of particular messages.

There are only 15 basic commands:

- **ARTICLE**—You can issue this command to read the current article, or you can include an article number or a message ID surrounded by angle brackets. The number is simply a numeric sequence number, but the message ID is unique and constant. If you don't supply either, the server sends what it thinks is the current message for your session but does not advance the current message number.
- **BODY**—This command is the same as the **ARTICLE** command, except it only returns the body of the message and omits the headers.
- **GROUP**—When you send the **GROUP** command, you must include a group name. This allows the server to understand that you wish to work with the specified group. If you don't know the valid group names, you can issue a **LIST** command.
- **HEAD**—This command is the same as the **ARTICLE** command, except it only returns the headers for the indicated message. This can be useful for

clients that only show the headers and allow the user to pick specific articles to download.

- **HELP**—Like many of the Internet protocols, you could conceivably use NNTP from nothing more than a Telnet-style terminal. If such is the case, the **HELP** command can tell you which commands are legal.

- **IHAVE**—This allows the client to indicate that it has a copy of a message (specified by its unique message ID). This is mostly of use to subordinate servers that may have messages the main server would like to copy. This command is not for posting new messages.

- **LAST**—When a client sends a **LAST** command, the server moves the current article pointer back to the previous article.

- **LIST**—Use the **LIST** command to obtain a list of groups the server handles. Each line of the response will have a group name, the last message number in that group, the first message number in the group, and a flag. The flag will be a "y" if the server accepts postings for that group, or an "n" if the server does not accept postings for the group. Keep in mind that just because a server can accept postings does not mean it will accept them from you.

- **NEWGROUPS**—With this command, you supply a date and time, and the server replies with a list of groups newer than the arguments you specify. You can provide the date in YYMMDD format (the server will add 1900 for years above 50 and 2000 for years below, so 88 is 1988, but 20 is 2020). The time is in the server's local time zone (in HHMMSS format), unless you specify GMT after it, in which case it uses Greenwich Mean Time to evaluate the date and time. The server responds with the list terminated by a line containing only a period. If there are no new groups, that terminating line may be the only response.

- **NEWNEWS**—This command is similar to the **NEWGROUPS** command, but it lists new news messages for a particular group. The command's first argument is the group (using * as a wildcard character). Following the group is the date and time in the same format used by **NEWGROUPS**.

- **NEXT**—Using this command will cause the server to advance the current article pointer to the next article.

- **POST**—Issuing this command causes the server to post a message to the current group. Of course, if the server doesn't allow posting, you'll get an error message. If you receive a positive reply, you can send the message as you would an email message (that is, headers, a blank line, and a line containing only a period at the end). Like email, if a line starts with a period, you should double it so it won't be confused with an end of message marker.

- **QUIT**—As you'd expect, the **QUIT** command causes the server to disconnect.

9. NNTP

- **SLAVE**—Programs that are subordinate servers can send the **SLAVE** command to inform the server that it is not a user-oriented program. The master server is not obligated to do anything about this command—it is for information only. For example, a server might give a slave higher (or lower) priority than user programs, although it is not obligated to do so.

- **STAT**—This command has the same syntax as the **ARTICLE** command. However, this command doesn't return any headers or text. Instead, it simply returns information about the indicated message.

Each command has only a few possible response codes (see Table 9.1). The first digit is a classification: A one indicates help, two is a successful return, three means more information is required, and four is a failure. The codes in the table appear roughly in the order the server might send them to you. For example, if you post an article, the server might return code 340 to tell you to proceed. After you send the article, the server will return code 240.

Table 9.1   The responses you can expect depend on the command issued to the server.

Command	Response Code	Meaning
ARTICLE	220	Article follows (followed by article number and ID)
	412	No group selected
	420	No current article
	423	No article with this number in this group
	430	No article with this number
BODY	222	Body follows (followed by article number and ID)
	412	No group selected
	420	No current article
	423	No article with this number in this group
	430	No article with this number
GROUP	211	Group selected (response contains estimated number of articles, first number, last number, and name of group)
HEAD	221	Head follows (followed by article number and ID)
	412	No group selected
	420	No current article
	423	No article with this number in this group
	430	No article with this number
HELP	100	Help text follows (terminates with a single period on a line)

(continued)

9. NNTP

Table 9.1   The responses you can expect depend on the command issued to the server *(continued)*.

Command	Response Code	Meaning
IHAVE	335	Send article
	435	Do not send article
	235	Article received
	436	Transmission failed, try again
	437	Article rejected, do not try again
LAST	223	Article retrieved (followed by number and article ID)
	412	No group selected
	420	No current article
	422	No previous article
LIST	215	List of groups follows
NEWGROUPS	231	List of groups follows
NEWNEWS	230	List of article IDs follows
NEXT	223	Article retrieved (followed by number and article ID)
	412	No group selected
	420	No current article
	421	No next article
POST	340	Send post
	440	Posting not allowed
	240	Posting successful (server may still silently reject message later)
	441	Posting failed
QUIT	205	Goodbye
SLAVE	202	Slave status noted
STAT	223	Article exists, request text separately (followed by article number and ID)
	412	No group selected
	420	No current article
	423	No article with this number in this group
	430	No article with this number

News servers usually require user authentication because running a server requires a lot of storage and bandwidth. If you really want to find an open server, do a Web search for "open NNTP server"—there are several lists on the Internet, including a meta list at **http://dir.yahoo.com/Computers_and_Internet/ Internet/Chats_and_Forums/Usenet/Public_Access_Usenet_Sites/**. However, many open servers are actually closed servers that are improperly configured. Once the server operator notices the bandwidth congestion, they often close the server, so the lists change frequently.

The basic specification in RFC977 doesn't provide a way for the server to authenticate the user. However, nearly all servers implement one or more of the methods mentioned in RFC2980. Most often, you'll use the **AUTHINFO** command twice. The first use of the command will specify the user name, and the second specifies the password. For example:

```
AUTHINFO USER alw
AUTHINFO PASSWORD startrek
```

Encapsulating NNTP

Like most of the Internet protocols, you can write a class to hide the protocol complexity from the rest of your programs. Because a news article looks like an email message, you can use the **MailMessage** class from Chapters 7 and 8 to hold the actual message. After all, that class handles the basic format of a message that contains headers.

You can find the **NewsClient** class in Listing 9.1. The **connect** method uses port 119 by default and waits for the initial response from the server. A 200 response means the server will consider accepting postings. A 201 means the server will not accept posts at all. Once the code sees the response, it sends **AUTHINFO** commands to log in to the server.

Listing 9.1   The NewsClient class encapsulates the NNTP client logic.

```
// NNTP class -- Williams

import java.io.*;
import java.net.*;
import java.util.StringTokenizer;
import java.util.Hashtable;
import java.util.Enumeration;
import java.util.Date;

public class NewsClient {
    protected Socket skt;
    protected OutputStreamWriter out;
```

```java
    protected BufferedReader in;
    public String response;
    public int responseCode;
    public int first=-1;
    public int last=-1;
    public int count=-1;

    protected void write(String s) throws IOException {
        //        System.out.println(s);  // debug
        out.write(s+"\r\n");
        out.flush();
    }


    // Write a string with CRLF and check response
    protected boolean output(String s) throws IOException {
        write(s);
        response=in.readLine();
        //        System.out.println(response);  debug
        responseCode=Integer.parseInt(response.substring(0,3));
        return responseCode>=200 && responseCode<=399;

    }


    // Connect, login, and set the status variables
    public boolean connect(String host,String user,String pw,int port)
     throws UnknownHostException, IOException  {
        if (port==0) port=119; // default port
        skt=new Socket(host,port);
        out=new OutputStreamWriter(skt.getOutputStream());
        in=new BufferedReader(new InputStreamReader(skt.getInputStream()));
        response=in.readLine();
        if (!response.substring(0,3).equals("200")
            && !response.substring(0,3).equals("201"))
              return false;
        if (!output("AUTHINFO USER " + user)) return false;
        if (!output("AUTHINFO PASS " + pw)) return false;
        return true;
    }


    // Do a quit
    public boolean quit() throws IOException {
        boolean rv=true;
        if (!output("QUIT")) rv=false;
        try {
            skt.close();
        }
        catch (IOException e) {}
```

```
    return rv;
}

 public boolean setGroup(String group) throws IOException {
    if (!output("GROUP " + group)) return false;
     StringTokenizer token = new StringTokenizer(response);
     token.nextToken(); // skip code
    count=Integer.parseInt(token.nextToken()); // estimate count
    first=Integer.parseInt(token.nextToken());
    last=Integer.parseInt(token.nextToken());
    return true;
 }

// Read a specific message
public MailMessage readMessage(int n) throws IOException {
    return readMessage(n,"ARTICLE");
}

public MailMessage readMessage(int n,String cmd) throws IOException {
    MailMessage mail;
    Hashtable headers=new Hashtable();
    String line;
    StringBuffer bodytext=new StringBuffer();
    boolean body=false;
    if (n==-1) {
        if (!output(cmd)) return null;
    }
    else {
        if (!output(cmd + " " + Integer.toString(n))) return null;
    }
    String lastHeader = "";
    // for each line of response...
    while (true) {
        line=in.readLine();
        if (line.length()==0 && !body) {
            body=true; // blank line in headers means body
            continue;
        }
        else {
            // check for end
            if (line.length()!=0 && line.charAt(0)=='.'
              && line.length()==1) break;
            // check for escaped period
            if (line.length()!=0 && line.charAt(0)=='.')
                line=line.substring(1);
        }
        // if body, just build up lines
```

```
                if (body) {
                   bodytext.append(line);
                   bodytext.append("\n");
                }
                else {  // headers
                   // if a wrap-around header, append it
                   if (line.charAt(0)==' ' || line.charAt(0)=='\t') {
                       headers.put(lastHeader,
                                 (String)headers.get(lastHeader)+" "+
                                 line.trim());
                       continue;
                   }
                   // otherwise split header line at :
                   int ndx=line.indexOf(':');
                   if (ndx!=-1) {
                       String key=line.substring(0,ndx).trim();
                       String value=line.substring(ndx+1).trim();
                       lastHeader=key.toLowerCase();
                       // and store in hashtable
                       headers.put(lastHeader,value);
                   }
                }
            }
        }
        // get real message id (header may be blank)
        StringTokenizer token = new StringTokenizer(response);
        // throw away response
        token.nextToken();
        headers.put("X-server-number",token.nextToken());
        headers.put("X-actual-message-id",token.nextToken());
        // ok we got it all I think
        mail=new MailMessage((String)headers.get("from"),
                           (String)headers.get("Newsgroups"),
                           (String)headers.get("cc"),"",
                           (String)headers.get("subject"),
                           bodytext.toString());
        // remove "standard headers"
        headers.remove("from");
        headers.remove("Newsgroups");
        headers.remove("cc");
        headers.remove("subject");
        mail.headers=headers;
        return mail;
    }
```

```
public boolean postMessage(MailMessage msg) throws IOException {
    if (!output("POST")) return false;
    String id=response.substring(response.indexOf('<'));
    id=id.substring(0,id.indexOf('>')+1);
    // Note MS Outlook does not like these headers
    // lower case
    write("From: "+msg.sender);
    write("Newsgroups: "+msg.to);
    write("Subject: "+msg.subject);
    write("Message-ID:"+id);
    if (msg.headers!=null) {
        for (Enumeration e=msg.headers.keys();
            e.hasMoreElements();) {
            String hdr = (String) e.nextElement();
            String val = (String) msg.headers.get(hdr);
            write(hdr+": "+val);
        }
    }
    write("");   // end of headers
    try {
        String line;
        // want to split the input into lines so we can
        // put a CRLF at the end of each
        BufferedReader rdr = new BufferedReader(
            new StringReader(msg.body+"\n"));
        do {
            line=rdr.readLine();
            if (line!=null) {
                // do . escape
                if (line.length()>0 && line.charAt(0)=='.')
                    line="."+line;
                write(line);
            }
        } while (line!=null);
    }
    catch (Exception e) { }
    return output(".");
}


public boolean nextPost() throws IOException {
    if (!output("NEXT")) return false;
    return true;
}
```

```
public boolean lastPost() throws IOException {
    if (!output("LAST")) return false;
    return true;
}
public NewsClient() { }


public static void readdump(NewsClient news) throws Exception {
    MailMessage msg=news.readMessage(-1);
    System.out.println(msg.body);
    System.out.println("----- Headers -----");
    Enumeration keys=msg.headers.keys();
    while (keys.hasMoreElements()) {
        String iKey=(String)keys.nextElement();
        System.out.println(iKey + ":" + msg.headers.get(iKey));
    }


}

// Test main
public static void main(String args[]) throws Exception {
    NewsClient news= new NewsClient();
    if (news.connect(args[0],args[1],args[2],0)) {
        // Test posting
        MailMessage msg = new MailMessage("test@test.org",
            "alt.test",
            "Java BB test " + new Date().toString(),
            "This is just a test\nPlease ignore");
        System.out.println("Posting = " + news.postMessage(msg));
        System.out.println(news.response);


        // read something
        news.setGroup("alt.test");
        news.output("STAT " + Integer.toString(news.last));
        readdump(news);
        news.nextPost();
        readdump(news);
        news.quit();
    }
    else {
        System.out.println("Error : " + news.response);
    }

}
}
```

Most of the commands are straightforward. Many have to parse the server's response to pick up information. For example, the **setGroup** method picks apart the server's response to set the **count**, **first**, and **last** fields. The **count** is only an estimate of the number of articles, but the other two fields will tell you the range of messages the server has for the current group.

The method to read messages has a slight twist. The default call (**readMessage**) accepts a message number (or –1 to read the current message). However, an alternate form takes a command name as a second argument. This allows you to send a **HEAD** or **BODY** command, so you'll only get part of the message instead of the entire article. In practice, this is useful for getting just the headers, so you can avoid downloading entire messages unnecessarily. With the headers, you can display subject lines and only download messages of interest.

News articles may have a header that indicates the message ID, but some articles will lack this header. Therefore, **readMessage** creates a special header, **X-server-number** that contains the actual message ID from the server, not the message header. In addition, it also creates the **X-actual-message-id** header that contains the message number.

The **readdump** method is simply for debugging. The sample **main** method uses it to display some messages from the alt.test group. Of course, this isn't a very useful way to read news groups.

Posting is also simple using **MailMessage**. Instead of setting the recipient email addresses in the **MailMessage** object, you can set newsgroup names (separated by commas). The **postMessage** method will extract the necessary information from the **MailMessage** object and perform the posting.

NNTP on the Web

By coupling the **NewsClient** class with a Java Server Page (JSP) user interface, you can allow users to read newsgroups on the Web. You'll see an example of this in the "Immediate Solutions" section of this chapter.

To keep things simple, I created a front page that allows the user to select one of a fixed list of news groups (see Listing 9.2 in "Showing Articles on the Web"). Of course, you could use the **LIST** command to generate the list dynamically. However, many servers host hundreds or even thousands of groups, and you may not be willing to wait. Although, you could write a simple program to generate a local copy of the **LIST** command's output and use this local copy to populate the selection box. You could even arrange to run the program automatically once or twice a day. However, for this example, I just used a short list of Java-related newsgroups.

Once you've selected a group, the news.jsp page takes over (see Listing 9.3 in "Showing Articles on the Web"). From the NNTP point of view, this page is simple.

9. NNTP

**Welcome to WNews
(comp.lang.java)**

Message	From	Sent
NoClassDefFoundError	alexlong@earthlin...	Tue, 12 Jun 2001 16:10:40 GMT
Re: Runtime.exec() help	"Rish"	Tue, 12 Jun 2001 15:37:15 GMT
Permanent job - E-Commerce Developer Opportunity in Colorado!	"David Snow"...	Tue, 12 Jun 2001 15:31:43 GMT
Re: Best IDE for Java	"Claudio Par...	Tue, 12 Jun 2001 16:04:45 +0200
Re: InetAddress.getByName	Jim Sculley <n...	Tue, 12 Jun 2001 08:45:12 -0400
OutOfMemory problem	"JimmyMac" <...	Tue, 12 Jun 2001 13:14:31 GMT
		Tue, 12 Jun 2001

Figure 9.1   A Web interface (using JSP) makes it easy to read the news.

However, some HTML issues complicate things. The problem stems from the relatively slow nature of reading messages. I wanted to use tables to display the subject, sender, and posting date (see Figure 9.1). However, reading any significant number of headers can be slow depending on the speed of the server.

One way to make the page appear faster is to call **out.flush** after reading each article to force the data to the browser. Without this call, the browser may not receive any data until many messages (or even all of the messages) are ready. However, using a table foils this strategy. The browser will not format the table until it has all the rows in the table.

To combat this, I actually made each message reside in its own table. The tables have fixed widths, so visually it appears the tables are actually one table. This, unfortunately, leads to another problem. The width of a table column depends on the browser's ability to wrap the text to fit. If the text has no spaces, the browser will expand the column to fit. When all the messages are part of the same table, this isn't a problem. If a column grows, all the columns grow to match. With the individual tables, however, if one column gets wider, it won't match the others.

The column that proves to be troublesome is the sender's address. Some of the addresses can be quite long and have no blanks. Because the sender's address isn't that critical (most of them are phony anyway), I arbitrarily truncate the address so that it isn't likely to overflow the table column.

When you select a subject, the news.jsp file calls the newsread.jsp file (see Listing 9.4 in "Reading Articles on the Web"). This file actually retrieves the entire message and displays it.

Another potential problem for both scripts is handling content within the message parts that appear to be HTML. I wrote a simple class to encode HTML text (see Listing 9.5 in "Reading Articles on the Web"). Just about all of the parts of the message should undergo encoding so that special characters will display correctly.

Both news.jsp and newsread.jsp require the server name, user ID, and password. Therefore, I placed this information in the newscfg.jsp file and include it where necessary (see Listing 9.6 in "Reading Articles on the Web").

Immediate Solutions

Finding the NNTP Specification

The main RFC that governs NNTP is RFC977. As usual, there are extensions, and in fact authentication as defined in RFC2980 is almost mandatory in practice. The message format, including required headers, appears in RFC1036, with common extensions documented again in RFC2980.

Connecting to a News Server

If you know the name or IP address of the news server you want to connect to, you can simply open a TCP socket to begin communications. By convention, port 119 is the usual port you'll use. The server will respond with a 200 code if the server will consider **POST** commands or a 201 if the server never allows posting.

Very few news servers will allow you to connect without a user ID and password, so the usual sequence will look like this (server responses are highlighted):

```
200 207.218.205.199 DNEWS Version 5.5a3, S1, posting OK
AUTHINFO USER alw
381 PASS required
AUTHINFO PASS startrek
281 Ok
```

Of course, if your server does not require a user ID and password, you can skip the **AUTHINFO** commands and proceed to sending commands to the server.

Selecting a Group

Before you can retrieve any messages, you need to select a group. Not surprisingly, you use the **GROUP** command to do this. You'll supply a group name, which must be a valid group for this server (you can find the server's group with the **LIST** command). The name is not case sensitive. Here is a typical command and reply (the server's reply is highlighted):

9. NNTP

```
GROUP comp.lang.java
211 1049 24145 28225 comp.lang.java selected
```

The first number is the reply code, and the second number is an estimate of the total number of articles the server is holding. Although this number is an estimate, it will either be correct, or it will be larger than the actual number of articles. The last two numbers are the ID numbers of the first and last messages in the group. It is not unusual for servers to add leading zeros to these numbers. As a by-product, this command sets the server's idea of the current message to the first message in the group.

You can parse the response line using **StringTokenizer**:

```
StringTokenizer token = new StringTokenizer(response);
token.nextToken(); // skip code
count=Integer.parseInt(token.nextToken()); // estimate count
first=Integer.parseInt(token.nextToken());
last=Integer.parseInt(token.nextToken());
```

Listing Groups

You can use the **LIST** command to get a list of the groups the server supports. The reply will consist of group names, one per line, and a terminating line consisting of a single period:

```
215 list of newsgroups follows
24hoursupport.helpdesk 426988 348728 y
3b 3370 2825 y
3b.config 26535 25603 y
3b.misc 25953 25151 y
3b.tech 10834 10371 y
.
```

Each line contains the group name, the last message number in the group, the first message number in the group, and a flag. If the flag is "y", the server accepts posts from this group, although not necessarily from you. If the flag is "n", the server does not accept posts for this group at all.

Many servers recognize extensions to the **LIST** command defined in RFC2980. One commonly seen is the "m" flag, which indicates that the group is moderated. Your posts will be sent to the moderator rather than posted.

9. NNTP

Finding New Groups

You can issue a **NEWGROUPS** command to learn if any new groups have been added to the server since a certain date. This session asks for the new groups as of June 2, 2001, at midnight (00:00) GMT. The format of the replies is the same as the **LIST** command's replies.

```
NEWGROUPS 010602 00:00 GMT
231 list of new newsgroups follows
de.markt.arbeit.biete.misc 48 3 m
de.markt.arbeit.vermittler 140 3 m
de.markt.arbeit.biete.it-berufe 32 3 m
be.comp.networking 22 3 y
.
```

Reading Articles

Once you have selected a group, you can fetch any article that belongs to that group. There are four commands you can use: **STAT**, **HEAD**, **BODY**, and **ARTICLE**. All of the commands have similar responses and identical arguments.

You can use three different forms of the article-retrieval commands:

1. You can pass the article number to get a specific article.

2. You can send the article's unique ID (enclosed in angle brackets) to get an article using a specific ID. Note that you don't have to select a group if you use this method, although you typically will.

3. You can use no arguments, in which case the server will use the current article.

The **STAT** command only replies with a status message. The **HEAD** and **BODY** commands return the headers and the main text of the message, respectively. The **ARTICLE** command gets everything.

For the **ARTICLE** command, the server will send a reply line, the headers, a blank line, and the body text. The last line from **HEAD**, **BODY**, or **ARTICLE** will be a line with a single period.

```
ARTICLE 24145
220 24145 <961n$1@news.coriolis.com> article retrieved
From: alw@al-williams.com
Newsgroups: alt.test
Subject: A test
```

```
Date: Fri, 9 Feb 2001 16:31:47 +0530
Message-ID: <961n$l @news.coriolis.com>
This is a test!
.
```

Changing the Current Article

When you select a group, the server sets an internal current article pointer to the first article in that group. This is the article that you'll work with if you issue a **STAT**, **HEAD**, **BODY**, or **ARTICLE** command with no argument.

There are three ways you can change the current article:

1. First, you can use the **NEXT** and **LAST** commands, which are useful because article numbers are not necessarily contiguous.

2. You can also issue one of the article access commands with an article number, which causes the current article to change.

3. If you provide an article ID (such as **<961n$l@news.coriolis.com>**), the current article number does not change.

Finding New Articles

If you are only interested in articles posted after a certain date, you can issue a **NEWNEWS** command. This command requires a newsgroup name (you can use the * character as a wildcard) and the date and time (using the same format as **NEWGROUPS**).

WARNING! This command may generate a lot of data. In fact, some sites disable this command beause it generates so much data, so you should not depend on it.

Posting Articles

You can post articles to the server by using the **POST** command. This will elicit a 340 response (unless there is an error, of course). You send the message as a series of header lines, a blank line, and the text message. The last line is a single period. If an ordinary line begins with a period, you should double the period to prevent the server from accidentally treating it as an end of message. Because the article will have a "Newsgroups" header, you do not have to select a group before posting.

The only headers you must supply are the following:

- *From*—This is your email address. This can be anything, but many servers will also add an **X-Authenticated-User** header marking your real user ID, which may not be your complete email address. For example, I'm **alw@al-williams.com**, so the **X-Authenticated-User** (when posting from my server) might be "alw".

- *Newsgroups*—This header specifies which newsgroups you want to receive the message. You can send to multiple groups at once by separating the group names with a comma.

- *Subject*—This is how newsreaders will display your message.

Here is a simple posting transcript (the server responses are highlighted):

```
POST
340 Ok, recommended ID <3b2514bd_2@newsa.coriolis.com>
From:bogus@al-williams.com
Newsgroups: alt.test
Subject: testing

This is our test…
.
240 article posted ok, wait 3 minutes for it to appear
```

Using the **NewsClient** Class

The **NewsClient** class in Listing 9.1 can simplify many NNTP tasks. The typical order of operations is as follows:

1. Instantiate a **NewsClient** object.

2. Call **connect** on the object, providing a hostname, user ID, password, and a port number (or 0 to use the default).

3. Call **setGroup** if you wish to browse messages.

4. Issue **readMessage**, **nextPost**, **lastPost**, and other calls to manipulate messages.

The class uses the **MailMessage** object from Chapter 7 to hold messages. You can also post a message by sending a **MailMessage** object to the **postMessage** method.

Related solution	Found on page:
Using the **MailMessage** Object	234

Showing Articles on the Web

It is possible to use the class in Listing 9.1 to display and read articles via Web browser. By using the **NewsClient** object in a JSP, any Web browser can access the news server. Listing 9.2 shows a simple page that allows you to select a group from a predefined list. It sends the group name to the page in Listing 9.3 (news.jsp).

Listing 9.2   This JSP selects a group and forwards it to the news.jsp script.

```
<HTML><HEAD><TITLE>Select a NewsGroup</TITLE></HEAD>
<BODY BGCOLOR=cornsilk>
<H1>Select a news group</H1>
<FORM ACTION=news.jsp METHOD=POST>
<SELECT NAME=group>
<OPTION VALUE=comp.lang.java>comp.lang.java
<OPTION VALUE=comp.lang.java.api>comp.lang.java.api
<OPTION VALUE=comp.lang.java.beans>comp.lang.java.beans
<OPTION VALUE=comp.lang.java.gui>comp.lang.java.gui
<OPTION VALUE=comp.lang.java.programmer>comp.lang.java.programmer
</SELECT>
<INPUT TYPE=SUBMIT VALUE='View Group'>
</BODY>
</HTML>
```

The news.jsp script does the following:

1. Instantiates a **NewsClient** object

2. Calls **connect** on the object

3. Calls **setGroup** (which, incidentally sets the **count**, **first**, and **last** fields)

4. Reads the headers for a small number of messages

5. From the headers, displays the message subjects as links to a newsreader script

Here is an excerpt from the program (with some output for illustration):

```
MailMessage msg=news.readMessage(current--,"HEAD");
if (msg==null) break; // whoops?
if (++counter>pagesize) break; // only read some messages
// you could write just the subject here like this:
out.println(msg.subject);
```

9. NNTP

Listing 9.3   You can view the articles in a group with this script.

```
<%@ page import="java.util.*" %>
<%@ include file="newscfg.jsp" %>
<%
  int counter=0;
  NewsClient news = new NewsClient();
  if (!news.connect(server,user,pw,0)) {
     out.println("<H1>Can't connect to news server</H1>");
   }
  else {
   int current;
   int first;
   String firstStr=request.getParameter("first");
   int pagesize=25;
   String nxtfirstStr="-1";
   int nxtfirst;
   String group=request.getParameter("group");
   if (group==null || group.equals("")) group="alt.test";
   out.println("<H1>Welcome to WNews (" + group + ")</H1>");
   news.setGroup(group);
   if (firstStr!=null && !firstStr.equals(""))
     first=Integer.parseInt(firstStr);
   else
     first=news.last;
   current=first;
%>
<TABLE WIDTH=100% BORDER=1 BGCOLOR=cornsilk>
<TR><TD WIDTH=50%><B>Message</B></TD><TD WIDTH=25%><B>From</B></TD>
<TD WIDTH=25%><B>Sent</B></TD></TR></TABLE>
<%
   do {
     MailMessage msg=news.readMessage(current--,"HEAD");
     if (msg==null) break; // whoops?
     if (++counter>pagesize) break; // only read some messages
     String contenttype=(String)msg.headers.get("content-type");
     nxtfirstStr=(String)msg.headers.get("X-server-number");
     if (contenttype==null ||
        contenttype.substring(0,10).equals("text/plain")) {
  String sender=HtmlEncoder.encode(msg.sender.trim());
  if (sender==null || sender.equals("")) sender=" ";
  if (sender.length()>20) sender=sender.substring(0,17) + "...";
%>
<TABLE BGCOLOR=cornsilk WIDTH=100% BORDER=1>
<TR><TD WIDTH=50%><A HREF=newsread.jsp?group=<%= group %>&art=<%=
nxtfirstStr %>&first=<%=Integer.toString(first)%>><%=
HtmlEncoder.encode(msg.subject) %></A></TD>
```

```
<TD WIDTH=25%><FONT SIZE=2><%= sender %></FONT></TD><TD WIDTH=25%>
<FONT SIZE=2><%=(String)msg.headers.get("date")%></FONT></TD></TR></TABLE>
<%
        out.flush(); // won't really work with a single table
        }
    } while (counter<=pagesize);
%>
  </TABLE><HR>
<%
    nxtfirst=Integer.parseInt(nxtfirstStr);
    if (nxtfirst!=-1 && ++nxtfirst>news.first)
      out.println("<A HREF=news.jsp?group=" + group +
      "&first="+Integer.toString(nxtfirst)+
      ">View earlier messages</A><BR>");
    if (first!=news.last) {
      int nxt=first+pagesize;   // guess next number
      if (nxt>news.last) nxt=news.last;
      out.println("<A HREF=news.jsp?group=" + group +
        "&first="+Integer.toString(nxt)+
        ">View newer messages</A><BR>");
    }
}
%>
<A HREF=newsfront.jsp>Pick a new group</A>
```

Reading Articles on the Web

Listing 9.4 shows a script (newsread.jsp) that reads three parameters:

- **group**—The group name
- **art**—The article number to read
- **first**—The first article number displayed in the preceding list

Listing 9.4   When the user selects an article, this script displays it.

```
<%@ page import="java.util.*" %>
<%@ include file="newscfg.jsp" %>
<%
  String group=request.getParameter("group");
  String first=request.getParameter("first");
  if (group==null || group.equals("")) group="alt.test";
  NewsClient news=new NewsClient();
  if (!news.connect(server,user,pw,0)) {
    out.print("<H1>Can't connect to news server</h1>");
  }
```

9. NNTP

```
    else {
     news.setGroup(group);
     int n=Integer.parseInt(request.getParameter("art"));
     MailMessage msg=news.readMessage(n);
     out.print("<H1>"+HtmlEncoder.encode(msg.subject)+"</H1>");
     out.print("<h3>From:" + HtmlEncoder.encode(msg.sender)+"</H3>");
     out.print("<h4>Sent:" + (String)msg.headers.get("date") + "</h4>");
     out.print("<PRE>"+HtmlEncoder.encode(msg.body)+"</PRE>");
    }

%>
<A HREF=news.jsp?group=<%= group %>&first=<%= first %>>Back to main News
page</A>
```

The **first** parameter is only necessary when you want the list to start in the same place when the user links back to the list page (Listing 9.3). The other two parameters identify which message to read.

Once connected to the news server, the code is simple:

```
MailMessage msg=news.readMessage(n);
out.print("<H1>"+HtmlEncoder.encode(msg.subject)+"</H1>");
out.print("<h3>From:" + HtmlEncoder.encode(msg.sender)+"</H3>");
out.print("<h4>Sent:" + (String)msg.headers.get("date") + "</h4>");
out.print("<PRE>"+HtmlEncoder.encode(msg.body)+"</PRE>");
```

The Web browser will not correctly interpret special characters in the message, subject, and address lines, so the **HtmlEncoder.encode** method converts special characters to their HTML equivalent (for example, the < character is **<**). You can find this class in Listing 9.5.

Listing 9.5   HtmlEncoder is a general-purpose utility class that can convert special characters for display in a Web browser.

```
// HTMLEncoder
// only 1 static class that converts things like:
// 3<10 & 4>1 into:
// 3&lt;10 &amp; 4&gt;1

public class HtmlEncoder {
    public static String encode(String intext) {
        if (intext == null) return "";
        StringBuffer out = null;
        char[] orig = null;
        int start = 0, len = intext.length();
```

```
    for (int i = 0; i < len; i++){
        char c = intext.charAt(i);
        if (c==0||c=='&'||c=='<'||c=='>'||c=='"') {
            if (out == null){
                orig = intext.toCharArray();
                out = new StringBuffer(len+10);
            }
            if (i > start)
                out.append(orig, start, i-start);
            start = i + 1;
            switch (c){
            default: // case 0:
                continue;
            case '&':
                out.append("&amp;");
                break;
            case '<':
                out.append("&lt;");
                break;
            case '>':
                out.append("&gt;");
                break;
            case '"':
                out.append("&quot;");
                break;
            }
            break;
        }
    }
    if (out == null)
        return intext;
    out.append(orig, start, len-start);
    return out.toString();
    }
}
```

Both the news.jsp script (Listing 9.3) and newsread.jsp (Listing 9.4) require the server name, user ID, and password. To keep this information in one place, I put it in newscfg.jsp (Listing 9.6). Both files include a reference to the configuration data by using the **include** directive:

```
<%@ include file="newscfg.jsp" %>
```

Listing 9.6.   This script configures the other pages that require the NNTP server.

```
<%
  String server="news.al-williams.com";
  String user="alwill";
  String pw="bagworm";
%>
```

Posting Articles via the Web

Posting a message via the Web interface is simply a matter of collecting enough information to fill in a **MailMessage** object and sending it to the server via the **NewsClient.postMessage** method.

You can find an example in Listing 9.7. Notice that the form posts the data back to itself. When the script detects form data, it attempts to post to the server and then displays a status message along with the form, ready for another posting. The newscfg.jsp file contains the configuration parameters, just as it does for the news.jsp and newsread.jsp files shown earlier in Listings 9.3 and 9.4.

Listing 9.7   Posting articles with a JSP.

```
<%@ page import="java.util.*" %>
<%@ include file="newscfg.jsp" %>

<%  String status="";
    if (request.getParameter("group")!=null &&
      !request.getParameter("group").equals("")) {
      NewsClient news = new NewsClient();
      if (!news.connect(server,user,pw,0)) {
        status="<H1>Can't connect to news server</H1>";
      } else {
        MailMessage msg=new MailMessage(request.getParameter("from"),
          request.getParameter("group"),
          request.getParameter("subject"),
          request.getParameter("msg"));
        news.postMessage(msg);
        status=news.response;
        news.quit();
      }
    }
%>

<HTML>
<HEAD><TITLE>Post to Usenet</TITLE></HEAD>
```

9. NNTP

```
<BODY BGCOLOR=cornsilk>
<H1>Post to Usenet</H1>
<%= status %><BR>
<FORM ACTION=newspost.jsp METHOD=POST>
<TABLE BORDER=0 WIDTH=50%><TR><TD>
Group:</TD><TD><SELECT NAME=group>
<OPTION VALUE=alt.test>alt.test
<OPTION VALUE=comp.lang.java>comp.lang.java
<OPTION VALUE=comp.lang.java.api>comp.lang.java.api
<OPTION VALUE=comp.lang.java.beans>comp.lang.java.beans
<OPTION VALUE=comp.lang.java.gui>comp.lang.java.gui
<OPTION VALUE=comp.lang.java.programmer>comp.lang.java.programmer
</SELECT>
</TD></TR>
<TR><TD>
From:</TD><TD><INPUT NAME=from>
<FONT SIZE=1>Your email address</FONT>
</TD></TR>
<TR><TD>
Subject:</TD><TD><INPUT NAME=subject><BR>
</TR></TD>
<TR><TD VALIGN=top>
Article:</TD><TD>
<TEXTAREA NAME=msg COLS=80 ROWS=25>
</TEXTAREA>
</TR></TD>
<TR><TD> </TD><TD>
<INPUT TYPE=SUBMIT VALUE=Post>
</TD></TR></TABLE>
</FORM>
</BODY>
</HTML>
```

Chapter 10

HTTP Clients

In Depth

If you stop and think, it will shock you to realize that many people alive today have probably never played an ordinary, old-fashioned record. (On the other hand, you may be one of those people!) It is a good bet that half of the people reading this book have never physically touched an 8-track tape.

To a young person, it is hard to imagine music that doesn't play on a CD, just as it is probably difficult for baby boomers like me to imagine going to a silent movie or flying on a zeppelin.

Before the personal computer craze—and the Internet explosion—being a computer professional was a bit arcane. Normal people really didn't know what a computer did, much less want one in their home. Now many homes have computers, and they are primarily access terminals to the Web.

Although most people think of the Web when they think of the Internet, technical-minded people know that the Internet predates the Web by a wide margin. Before the Web, you could still extract information from computers all around the Internet, but it required a little more knowledge and skill. Although professionals know about File Transfer Protocol (FTP), Telnet, and other ways to access the network, many home users think these are as much an oddity as an 8-track tape player.

What the Web brought to the table was a simple way to retrieve and decode information from remote computers. You don't need to understand the difference between binary and text files, nor do you need to know how to decode files or join multiple files together. You simply point and click.

Two pieces make this work. First, the Hypertext Transfer Protocol (HTTP) allows servers to dispense files to clients. Second, Hypertext Markup Language (HTML) describes the data the server is sending to the client. Using HTML, you can create links to other documents, presumably also transferred by HTTP.

HTTP Protocol

The HTTP protocol has several different versions. Although you should strive to adhere to the latest standard, you'll find that many simple programs use the 1.0 standard defined in RFC1945; some even use a simple request from version 0.9. That's not a real problem because servers strive to be backward compatible with previous versions.

HTTP is quite similar to email with a real-time twist. Consider a Web browser trying to read a page on a Web site. A simple sequence of events takes place:

1. The browser opens a TCP (Transmission Control Protocol) port (usually port 80) to the server machine.

2. The browser sends a simple request. For example, "GET /index.htm".

3. The server responds with the actual HTML document.

For example, Listing 10.1 shows a transcript of a Telnet session with my Web server, which runs the Apache server.

Listing 10.1 Manually fetching a Web page with Telnet.

```
$ telnet www.al-williams.com 80
GET /

<html>

<head>
<title>Welcome to AWC</title>
<meta name="GENERATOR" content="Microsoft FrontPage 3.0">
</head>

<body bgcolor="#C0C0C0" background="new/_themes/capsules/captext.gif">

<h1>Welcome to AWC</h1>

<p>AWC operates three different Web sites,
please select the one you are interested in:

<ul>
  <li><a href="http://www.al-williams.com/new">AWC</a> - If you are
interested in Windows and Web development, consulting, training, books, and
Al Williams' regular Java@Work columns, this is the page for you. (Our new
look -- under construction)</li>
</ul>

<ul>
  <li><a href="http://www.al-williams.com/awce">AWCE</a> - Looking for
microcontroller development, consulting, our solderless breadboard products,
PAK coprocessors, and our famous Stamp Project of the Month? Here's the
place</li>
</ul>

<ul>
  <li><a href="http://www.al-williams.com/wd5gnr">WD5GNR</a> - Interested in
ham radio or hobby electronics? You'll find a wealth of projects, tips, and
```

```
more at Al's Ham Radio site. Check out the Basic Stamp Tip of the Day!</li>
</ul>

<hr>

<p align="right"><small>AWC<br>
310 Ivy Glen Ct.<br>
League City, TX 77573-5953<br>
             USA</small></p>

<p align="right"><small>(281) 334-4341  fax (281) 754-4462<br>
<a href="mailto:alw@al-williams.com">alw@al-williams.com</a></small></p>

<p> </p>
</body>
</html>
Connection closed by foreign host.
```

Here are a few things to notice about Listing 10.1:

- *The only line sent by the client is "GET /".*—The remaining lines are all from the server.

- *There is no additional information about the document.*—The return data does not contain headers. It only contains the HTML document.

- *The server closes the socket.*

This type of request is known as a simple request. However, it is so out of date that some servers do not recognize it and will always return the document in a newer format. For example, Listing 10.2 shows an excerpt of the same request made against the Coriolis Web server, which employs Microsoft's IIS Web server and uses Active Server Pages (ASP). Notice that this server returns headers similar to what you'd expect in an email message. These headers provide status information, the server name, and several other details about the message itself. These headers don't replace the HTML header (delimited by the **<HEAD>** tag) but instead offer network-related information about the document.

Listing 10.2   Microsoft ASP always returns headers to the browser.

```
$ telnet www.coriolis.com 80
GET /
HTTP/1.1 200 OK
Server: Microsoft-IIS/5.0
Date: Fri, 15 Jun 2001 18:57:44 GMT
Connection: Keep-Alive
Content-Length: 1713
```

```
Content-Type: text/html
Set-Cookie: ASPSESSIONIDGQGGGOZQ=OLIJPBCCPFOHEHFJIKLLHJAD; path=/
Cache-control: private


<!DOCTYPE HTML PUBLIC "-//W3C//DTD HTML 4.0 Transitional//EN">

<HTML>
<HEAD><TITLE>The Coriolis Group, LLC.</TITLE>
```

The addition of headers started with version 1.0 of HTTP, and to avoid this ambiguous situation, you should always use at least version 1.0 so you know how the server will reply.

Two major differences exist between a version 0.9 request and a newer request. First, the request line adds a special keyword to identify the version the browser understands. So, the **GET** request in the previous examples could be rewritten as follows:

```
GET / HTTP/1.1
```

The second difference is that the request can have headers to provide additional information. For version 1.0, the headers are completely optional, so you can just send a blank line if you don't need any headers. With version 1.1 (defined in RFC2616), however, you must at least include a **host** header. This identifies the server computer and may be used to provide virtual hosting (where one computer serves multiple Web sites). Also, unless you are prepared to handle some special version 1.1 protocols, you should include the **Connection: close** header. Therefore, a proper version 1.1 request would be as follows:

```
GET / HTTP/1.1
Host: www.al-williams.com
Connection: close
```

After the last header (**Connection**, in this case), you send a blank line, and the server begins its reply. Without the **Connection: close** header, the server may try to hold the socket open and transfer data differently—something that is allowed in version 1.1 but not version 1.0. For that reason, unless you need 1.1 features, you might consider falling back to the 1.0 version as a lingua franca that you can expect all modern Web servers to support consistently.

Of course, **GET** is only one type of request you can make. The standard defines several request types, many of which are not especially popular. Here are the ones you are likely to encounter:

- **GET**—Fetches a document. Data can be included as a query string.

- **HEAD**—Fetches just the headers for a document.

- **POST**—Sends data with the request (from a form) as the request's body.

In addition, HTTP 1.1 allows the **OPTIONS**, **TRACE**, **DELETE**, and **PUT** requests, but you won't encounter these very often.

Status Codes

When you make a request (except a simple request), the first line is a status return. It reports the HTTP version the server is using, which should be less than or the same as your request's version. It also includes a status return code and message. For example, in Listing 10.2 you'll see this line:

```
HTTP/1.1 200 OK
```

That's a normal return code indicating that the server found the document and is sending it to the browser. Like other Internet response codes, you can identify the approximate meaning of the three-digit codes by examining the first digit.

Numbers that start with a 1 are informational in nature. The 200-series numbers indicate a successful transaction, whereas codes 300 through 399 cause the browser to redirect to another page. Codes that range between 400 and 599 indicate errors (for example, the infamous 404 error when a page is not found).

Most of the headers in Table 10.1 (see Immediate Solution titled "Reading a Status Code") make sense at first glance. Obviously, 200 is the code you want to see. You frequently see 404 errors if you hit a broken link. You might wonder about the difference between codes 401 and 403. With a 401 response, you've requested a protected resource and need to provide authorization credentials, usually a user ID and password. On the other hand, a 403 response means you simply can't have that resource no matter what you try.

The 301 and 302 codes are often used to redirect existing links to a new document—or even a different Web site. This is often useful when you change domain names or redesign your Web site, but you don't want to break existing links.

The 100 response code is only useful when using HTTP 1.1. Before version 1.1, each Web request required a separate connection. This isn't great for performance, and it also makes it difficult to do things such as maintain a secure connection.

If you don't specify **Connection: close** in the request headers, the server will try to keep the connection open for a while, in case you might make further requests. For this to work, the server has to send data in a special format because otherwise you can't tell when the document has ended. If you are using this mode anyway, you can also ask the server if it will accept a certain request. If it will, it will return a status code 100, and you can proceed with sending the data. If the server would reject the request, you can terminate the transaction without sending the data unnecessarily.

Common Headers

The server can return any number of headers to provide information about a document to the client. In addition to the client, some intermediary computers, such as proxy servers and caches, may also read and handle these headers. In fact, some of the headers are only useful to proxy servers.

The standard headers defined in HTTP 1.1 include the following:

- **Accept**—Indicates what kind of data the sender can accept.
- **Accept-Charset**—Indicates what character set the sender would prefer to receive.
- **Accept-Encoding**—Indicates what encodings the sender can process.
- **Accept-Language**—Communicates which languages the sender would prefer to receive.
- **Accept-Ranges**—Tells the receiver that it may make requests for a portion of a document by specifying a range.
- **Age**—Provides an estimate of the age of a cached document.
- **Allow**—Indicates what methods (for example, **GET**) the server will accept for this resource.
- **Authorization**—Provides user credentials for documents not available to anonymous users.
- **Cache-Control**—Informs caches whether they are allowed to keep copies of the document.
- **Connection**—Determines if the server will attempt to hold the socket open after the request is completed.
- **Content-Encoding**—Allows the server to indicate that the document is being encoded using any of several methods. This can be used to send data in a compressed format, for example. (For an interesting use of this header, see **http://webwarper.net/ww.pl**.)
- **Content-Language**—Indicates the language the document uses.
- **Content-Length**—Indicates total size of the body in bytes.
- **Content-Location**—Specifies an alternate location for a document.
- **Content-MD5**—Provides an MD5 signature of the document (useful for checking for errors).

- **Content-Range**—Defines the portion of the document returned in the response.

- **Content-Type**—Indicates the type of the document (for example, text/html or image/gif).

- **Date**—Indicates the date and time the server sent the document.

- **Etag**—Used to differentiate different variations of a single document. The actual value is implementation-specific and allows a Web server to identify two documents as identical using its own rules. Each request that returns the same exact data should have the same **Etag**.

- **Expect**—Allows the sender to inform the recipient that it expects a particular response.

- **Expires**—Indicates the date and time of document expiration for caching purposes.

- **From**—Allows the browser to identify the user making the request.

- **Host**—Indicates the hostname of a request.

- **If-Match**—Allows the sender to match the request to a previous **Etag**.

- **If-Modified-Since**—Provides a date and time that usually corresponds to the **Date** header of a previous request. If the server determines the document has not changed since this date, it returns a status code 304 instead of the document.

- **If-None-Match**—Allows the sender to match negatively to a previous **Etag**.

- **If-Range**—Allows the sender to match against a particular range of bytes in the document.

- **If-Unmodified-Since**—Indicates the opposite condition of **If-Modified-Since**.

- **Last-Modified**—Provides the date and time the document was last modified.

- **Location**—Provides an alternate location for the document (used with redirection).

- **Max-Forwards**—Used with the **TRACE** command to limit the number of proxy servers that will forward the command.

- **Pragma**—Allows you to include custom headers.

- **Proxy-Authenticate**—Issued with a challenge by a proxy, if it requires authentication.

- **Proxy-Authorization**—Indicates the client response to proxy authentication requests.

- **Range**—Identifies the portion of the document sent.

- **Referer**—Although misspelled, identifies the document that contained the link to the document being requested.

- **Retry-After**—Allows the server to specify when it might be able to satisfy a request (for example, if a server is down for maintenance).

- **Server**—Indicates the type of server handling this request.

- **TE**—Specifies what transfer encodings the requestor will accept.

- **Trailer**—Specifies headers the server will provide after sending the response.

- **Transfer-Encoding**—Identifies what encoding the document uses.

- **Upgrade**—Specifies protocols the sender would prefer to use.

- **User-Agent**—Indicates information about the user's browser, as well as the operating system and other details.

- **Vary**—Specifies what headers can change without causing a new document to load.

- **Via**—Informs the receiver of proxy or gateway computers in the path.

- **Warning**—Provides informational messages in addition to the status code.

- **WWW-Authenticate**—Provides the browser with the server's authentication challenge.

Forms

When you want to send data from an HTML page to a server, you have to use forms. The form accepts data from the user and sends it to the server as an HTTP request. Of course, a normal HTML page can't process data, so you'd expect the request to be for a CGI (Common Gateway Interface) program or a script of some sort.

Following is a simple HTML form:

```
<FORM ACTION=http://www.al-williams.com/doForm.jsp METHOD=GET>
Your name: <INPUT TYPE=TEXT NAME=urName><BR>
<INPUT TYPE=HIDDEN NAME=sourceID VALUE=101>
<INPUT TYPE=SUBMIT VALUE=Go>
</FORM>
```

Each form has a number of **INPUT** fields that the user can fill in. Form authors can also use the **SELECT** tag to provide a list of possible entries. Some **INPUT** fields are hidden, such as the **sourceID** field in the above example. This is common when you want to pass some information to the server, but you don't want the user to control that data.

Each form has a submit button (the **INPUT** field with the type **SUBMIT**). When the user presses the **SUBMIT** button, the browser gathers the data together and sends it to the Web page named in the **ACTION** attribute of the **FORM** tag.

How does the browser send the data? That depends on the value of the **METHOD** attribute in the **FORM** tag. In the previous example, the **METHOD** attribute is **GET**. This causes the browser to attach the form data in the URL as a query string. So, for example, if the user typed the name "Boris", the browser would request the following URL:

```
http://www.al-williams.com/doForm.jsp?urName=Boris&sourceID=101
```

Of course, the hidden field is now visible in the URL. In addition, some servers limit the amount of data you can pass on the command line. The browser has to encode data that contains special characters—including spaces.

To sidestep these problems, most forms use the **POST** method instead. When using **POST**, the browser sends the form data as the request's body. Therefore, if you changed the **METHOD** attribute to **POST** in the above example, the request sent to the server might look like this:

```
POST /doForm.jsp HTTP/1.0
Content-Length: 24
Content-Type: application/x-www-form-urlencoded

urName=Boris&sourceID=101
```

In reality, very few people will ever need to directly decode incoming form data, although it is often useful to know how to form the requests. On the server, you'd typically use a servlet or Java Server Pages (JSP) to handle incoming form data, and in that case, the supporting objects predigest the incoming data for you.

However, it is useful to encode data to submit to servers. Listing 10.3 shows a Java-based interface to the U.S. Postal Service tracking system. You can enter a tracking number on the command line, and the program dumps out the Web page returned as HTML.

Listing 10.3   This Java program submits data to the Postal Service Web site.

```java
import java.net.*;
import java.io.*;
import java.util.*;

public class MailFind {
    public static void main(String args[]) throws Exception {
        System.out.println("Searching for " + args[0]);
        Socket sock=new Socket("new.usps.com",80);
        OutputStream str = sock.getOutputStream();
        InputStream istr=sock.getInputStream();
        String request;
```

```
    String data;
    // request data
    data="tracknbr="+args[0]+"\r\n";
    // Set up request
    request="POST /cgi-bin/cttgate/ontrack.cgi HTTP/1.0\r\n";
    request+="Content-Type: application/x-www-form-urlencoded\r\n";
    request+="Content-Length: " + (data.length())+"\r\n\r\n";
    request+=data;
    // Write it out
    str.write(request.getBytes());
    // For this example, just dump results
    int c;
    do {
        c=istr.read();
        if (c!=-1) System.out.print((char)c);
    } while (c!=-1);
    sock.close();
  }
}
```

Posting data to a Web page is a common operation that is easily wrapped into a class. You can find an example class in the "Automating Form Submission" section of this chapter (see Listing 10.12).

Forms are one way that the browser can pass data to the server. However, browsers can also communicate—in a way—with servers by using the HTTP cookie mechanism.

Cookies

One hallmark of a great restaurant is that the staff knows your name and remembers you when you visit. How many movies have you seen where someone orders "the usual" and the waiter or bartender knows what to do? Personally, I've only been to a few places that offer that level of service—maybe times have changed, or maybe it's just me.

The best Web sites do the same thing—they remember you. Maybe they know what background color you like, or what sports teams you follow. Some e-commerce sites remember your basic information, so you don't have to retype it for each order.

Unfortunately, remembering data about users isn't one of those things that comes easily on the Web. Each Internet transaction is typically an anonymous one-time affair. This has resulted in the emergence of a variety of techniques that let you identify and store data that pertains to a user.

10. HTTP Clients

Sessions

The HTTP protocol supports cookies—small bits of data that the server can deposit and retrieve from the user's browser. If the server assigns each browser a unique identifier, the server can identify repeated requests from the same browser. (Other ways exist to make this association, but cookies are the cleanest and the most common.) Browsers don't have to accept cookies, but because so many sites require them, most users don't completely shut them off.

When the server wants the browser to remember something, it sends a cookie in the headers, for example:

```
Set-Cookie: ASPSESSIONIDQQQQGJMO=CHNHAFMDHAOKPENB; path=/
```

When the client makes a request of the specific server that set the cookie, it will include the data in the cookie header:

```
Cookie: ASPSESSIONIDQQQQGJMO= CHNHAFMDHAOKPENB
```

Exactly where the cookie resides depends on the browser. Cookies can have expiration dates, in which case the browser will probably store them in a file (or files). Cookies with no expiration only last as long as the browser is open, so they probably are somewhere in memory.

JSP, like many similar systems, artificially creates the notion of a session. The first time a browser requests a page, the server assigns the browser a unique ID and stores it in a client-side cookie. Subsequent requests contain this cookie, so the server knows they originated from the same browser.

Session management is important in many cases. For example, when a customer fills a shopping cart, the retailer wants to remember the contents of that cart the entire time the customer visits the site. However, session management goes only so far. A browser can arbitrarily erase cookies whenever it wants, and cookies eventually expire. Typically, a session cookie will last around 30 minutes (each page view restarts the clock). It would be unusual to find a session that lasts for days or even hours. Also, cookies belong to a particular browser on a particular computer. Your session at work won't apply to your session at home.

The solution is to store session data in a persistent form, like in a database. Coupled with a way to let users identify themselves, you can recall preferences and other data on a per-user basis, instead of only for the session.

Beans and JSP

JSP has all the pieces you need to handle this situation easily. However, the logic is a bit complex—maybe too confusing to code completely in JSP. Instead, I decided to make a user-property database, JavaBean, that you could easily use from within JSP. The core bean is abstract—specific implementations could store data in a flat file, a property file, an XML (Extensible Markup Language) file, a database, or any place you want to store the data. The bean lets you easily associate a password-protected username with a set of properties.

JSP is a simplified way to create servlets. Most people would agree that creating a JSP script is simpler than writing a servlet from scratch. However, writing too much Java code in a JSP is often bad form. One of JSP's strengths is that it lets HTML authors and designers focus on the page structure and simply sprinkle in Java code where it's required. However, when the code overwhelms the HTML markup, much of this benefit evaporates.

Fortunately, there's a middle ground. You can write a custom JavaBean that you can easily incorporate into the JSP page. Don't worry about the complexity of JavaBeans. You'll find it's easy enough to create beans—they're little more than ordinary Java objects that follow a few naming conventions. In fact, you don't really have to create a JavaBean at all. However, JSP is especially adept at including beans, and the extra trouble to create one is minimal.

What makes a JavaBean? For the purposes of this discussion, a bean is any public Java class that doesn't expose public fields. That doesn't mean the object can't have fields, or even that the object can't share fields with outside programs—in a way. Instead of fields, beans have properties. A property appears to be similar to a field. However, when you change or read a property, you're really calling special functions within the bean to do the work. If you want a property named **xyz**, you'd provide **getXyz** and **setXyz** methods. Many bean-aware programs automatically generate these method calls when you request access to a property. Bean-aware programs understand that this is really a property.

Of course, the **get** and **set** methods might simply provide access to a nonpublic field. On the other hand, some properties don't directly correspond to a variable. For example, you might have a field called **isServerUp** that indicates if another machine is available on the network. The **getIsServerUp** method might not reflect a variable at all. Instead, it would poll to see if the server was running using a socket. A **setIsServerUp** method might not exist because that wouldn't make much sense. In that case, the property is read-only.

Is that all there is to JavaBeans? No. However, for adding functions to JSPs, it's all you really need to know.

Design

The base class for the property database is **UserDB** (see Listing 10.4). The class provides abstract methods that handle the actual transfer of data, particularly the following:

- **getProperty**—Fetches a property for the current user from the database
- **writeProperty**—Writes a property for the current user (not necessarily saving it)
- **save**—Saves the property database to persistent storage
- **load**—Loads the database for a specific user (validating the password)
- **create**—Creates a new user

Listing 10.4.   This base class allows you to remember user properties between sessions.

```
// UserDB object
import java.io.IOException;
import javax.servlet.http.*;

abstract public class UserDB implements HttpSessionBindingListener {
    protected String user;
    protected String dir;
    protected boolean autosave = false;
    protected boolean dirty=false;
    public boolean getAutosave() { return autosave; }
    public void setAutoSave(boolean b) { autosave=b; }
    public String getUser() { return user; }
    public void setUser(String user) { this.user=user; }
    public String getDir() { return dir; }
    public void setDir(String dir) { this.dir=dir; }
    abstract public String getProperty(String key,String deflt);
    abstract public void writeProperty(String key,String value);
    abstract public void save() throws IOException;
    abstract public boolean create(String password) throws IOException;
    abstract public boolean load(String password);
// methods to manage sessions
    public void valueBound(HttpSessionBindingEvent event) {
        // no action
    }
    public void valueUnbound(HttpSessionBindingEvent event) {
        if (autosave && dirty) {
            try {
                save();
                dirty=false;
            }
            catch (IOException e) { }
        }
    }
}
```

Although the abstract base class doesn't provide any of these functions, it does provide support for them. In particular, the base class maintains the user name, a directory prefix to identify the location of the data (this isn't necessarily an actual directory name—it could be, for example, a dataset name), an **autosave** flag, and a dirty flag. If you set the **autosave** flag, and the database is dirty (that is, changed), the base class code will automatically save data when the session expires.

To detect session expiration, the base class has to implement the simple two-method **HttpSessionBindingListener** interface. This interface lets you detect when a session begins and ends.

In general, a session begins when the user first views a page. It expires after a certain amount of time elapses with no activity from the user, or when your script explicitly invalidates the session. You can release an active session with the following code:

```
request.getSession(). invalidate();
```

Because the abstract base class fully implements **HttpSessionBindingListener**, there's no need for the derived classes to know anything about session management. All the work occurs behind the scenes.

Implementation

One possible database for user information is a collection of ordinary Java property files. I like to use property files as easy-to-understand, simplified databases for Java programs. Of course, for industrial-strength Web sites, you'd want to use a better database, but property files are easy to use for a modest site, and they keep the example code simple. The base class has no prejudice—you can easily derive a new class to use the database of your choice.

The property file implementation appears in Listing 10.5. You'll see that the only methods of substance are **create**, **load**, **save**, **getProperty**, and **writeProperty**. As you'd expect, these map to various methods of a protected instance of the **Properties** object. Each user has his or her own property file stored in the directory specified. The password appears unencrypted in the property file, so the directory shouldn't be accessible via the Web server.

Listing 10.5   This class uses a property file to store information about users.

```
// UserDB that uses Property files

import java.util.*;
import java.io.*;

public class UserDBProp extends UserDB {
    protected Properties prop;
```

```java
public boolean create(String password) throws IOException {
    FileInputStream istream;
    try {
        istream  = new FileInputStream(
          dir + "/" + user + ".properties");
          istream.close();
    }
    catch (FileNotFoundException e) {
        // ok to create
        prop=new Properties();
        prop.put("password",password);
        save();
        return true;
    }
    catch (IOException e) {
        return false;  // some error?
    }
    return false; // can't create -- already exists
}
public boolean load(String password) {
    FileInputStream istream;
            prop=new Properties();
    try {
        istream  = new FileInputStream(
          dir + "/" + user + ".properties");
        prop.load(istream);
        istream.close();
    }
    catch (IOException e) {
        prop=null;
        return false;
    }
    // check password
    if (!password.equals(prop.getProperty("password"))) {
        prop=null;
        return false;
    }
    return true;
}

public void save() throws IOException {
    FileOutputStream os=new FileOutputStream(
      dir + "/" + user + ".properties");
    // use save if JDK<1.2
    prop.store(os,"WebProperties");
    os.close();
}
```

```
public String getProperty(String key, String deflt) {
    if (prop==null) return deflt;
    String rv=prop.getProperty(key);
    if (rv==null || rv.equals("")) rv=deflt;
    return rv;
}
public void writeProperty(String key, String val) {
     if (prop==null) return;
    dirty=true;
    prop.put(key,val);
}
}
```

By default, the **autosave** feature is off, so you'll have to explicitly call **save** when you want to update the underlying property file. You can also turn on automatic saving so that the file updates when the session ends.

The hardest part of building the bean is making the JSP container recognize it. You want to put your beans in a directory along the server's class path. Exactly where to put your class files depends on what container you're using—and your particular setup. Typically, the bean's class file must reside in the WEB-INF/classes subdirectory of the JSP application directory.

Using the beans requires a few pages, no matter what. First, you need a login page that accepts the user's ID and password. Next, you probably want a page that lets you create a new ID. It's also handy to have a page that forces an end to the user's session. This effectively logs the user out of the system.

The key to making this system viable is to create the database bean with session scope. When you include a bean in a JSP page, you can specify the scope and name that you want it to have. Each time you include the bean, the JSP container first checks to see if the bean already exists in that scope. If it does, you simply get that instance of the bean. If it doesn't, the container creates a new bean for you.

Beans with session scope persist until the session is over, which means that if you create a database bean with session scope, every page the user visits will use the same bean. This lets you initialize the bean on the login page without having to reinitialize it on every successive page. Because each user has a separate session, you don't have any privacy problems with one user accessing a different user's settings. Of course, this simple system is far from secure. You'll want to avoid storing sensitive information—such as credit card numbers, for example—in a plain-text property file.

The JSP tag that creates or finds the bean follows:

```
<jsp:useBean id="upd" class="UserDBProp" scope="session"/>
```

The bean's name in this case is **upd**. In a way, this is similar to writing:

```
UserDBProp upd = new UserDBProp();
```

The big difference, however, is that if **upd** already exists with session scope, you'll simply retrieve the existing instance of the class.

You can also use special tags to access the properties of the bean (although you can refer to them in ordinary JSP scriptlets, as well). For example, here's a tag that sets the **dir** property:

```
<jsp:setProperty name="upd" property="dir" value="c:/tmp"/>
```

Don't forget that this results in the actual bean receiving a call to **setDir**. This tag doesn't directly attempt to access a field named **dir**, even though that seems to be the case.

You can find an example login script in Listing 10.6. The form submits data back to itself. If it detects data entry, it attempts to load the user's properties. If this fails (that is, the load returns false), then the same form will appear with an additional error message in red. If the load is successful, the script redirects to the home page automatically (see Listing 10.7).

Listing 10.6   This script asks the user to log in.

```
<jsp:useBean id="upd" class="UserDBProp" scope="session"/>
<jsp:setProperty name="upd" property="dir" value="c:/tmp"/>
<%
  boolean err=false;
  if (request.getParameter("uid")!=null) {
  upd.setUser(request.getParameter("uid"));
  if (upd.load(request.getParameter("pw"))) {
    response.sendRedirect("updhome.jsp");
  } else {
    err=true;
  }
  }
%>

<HTML>
<HEAD><TITLE>Please log in</TITLE>
</HEAD>
<BODY BGCOLOR="cornsilk">

<% if (err)
    out.print("<FONT COLOR=RED>Invalid ID or password. Please try again</
FONT><BR>");
```

```
%>
<TABLE>
<FORM METHOD=POST ACTION=updlogin.jsp>
<C<TR><TD>
UserID: </TD><TD><INPUT NAME=uid></TD></TR>
<TR><TD>
Password:</TD><TD> <INPUT NAME=pw TYPE=PASSWORD></TD></TR>
<TR><TD> </TD><TD>
<INPUT TYPE=SUBMIT VALUE="Login"></TD></TR>
</FORM>
</TABLE>
<BR><A HREF=updcreate.jsp>Need a user ID?</A>
</BODY></HTML>
```

Listing 10.7   This simple home page greets the user by name.

```
<jsp:useBean id="upd" class="UserDBProp" scope="session"/>
<jsp:setProperty name="upd" property="dir" value="c:/tmp"/>
<HTML>
<HEAD><TITLE>Home Page</TITLE>
</HEAD>
<BODY BGCOLOR=cornsilk>
<P>Welcome!
<% if (upd.getProperty("name","@").equals("@")) {
%>
unregistered user.
<% } else { %>
<%= upd.getProperty("name","") %>
<BR>
<A HREF=updlogout.jsp>Log out</A>
<% } %>
</BODY>
</HTML>
```

Creating a new user is practically the same operation (see Listing 10.8). The only difference is that in this case, the user must not already exist, and, upon success, the script creates the property file and redirects the user back to the login page.

Listing 10.8   This JSP creates a new user ID.

```
<jsp:useBean id="upd" class="UserDBProp" scope="session"/>
<jsp:setProperty name="upd" property="dir" value="c:/tmp"/>
<%
 String errormessage="";
 boolean err=false;
 if (request.getParameter("uid")!=null)  {
```

```
        if (!request.getParameter("pw").equals(request.getParameter("pw2"))) {
          errormessage="Passwords did not match";
          err=true;
        }
        if (request.getParameter("pw")==null ||
            request.getParameter("pw").equals("")) {
              errormessage="Password must not be blank";
              err=true;
         }
        if (!err) {
          upd.setUser(request.getParameter("uid"));
          if (upd.create(request.getParameter("pw"))) {
              upd.writeProperty("name",request.getParameter("uname"));
              upd.save();
              response.sendRedirect("updlogin.jsp");
              }
          errormessage="User ID in use.";
          err=true;
          }
      }


%>
<HTML>
<HEAD><TITLE>Creating new ID</TITLE>
</HEAD>
<BODY BGCOLOR="cornsilk">

<TABLE>
<% if (err) { %>
<BR>
  <FONT COLOR=RED SIZE=3><%= errormessage %></FONT>
<BR>
<% } %>
<FORM METHOD=POST ACTION=updcreate.jsp>
<TR><TD>
Name: </TD><TD><INPUT Name=uname></TD></TR>
<TR><TD>
UserID: </TD><TD><INPUT NAME=uid></TD></TR>
<TR><TD>
Password:</TD><TD> <INPUT NAME=pw TYPE=PASSWORD></TD></TR>
<TR><TD>
Verify password:</TD><TD><INPUT NAME=pw2 TYPE=PASSWORD></TD></TR>
<TR><TD> </TD><TD>
<INPUT TYPE=SUBMIT VALUE="Create"></TD></TR>
```

```
    </FORM>
    </TABLE>

    </BODY>
    </HTML>
```

Enhancements

Of course, one obvious enhancement you could make to this system is to use a true database, such as MySQL or Access, to store the data. Improved data security would also be nice. Another useful feature would be to remember the user's ID and password in a cookie for future logins or to offer a way for the user to retrieve a lost password via email.

You could even use this system to implement a rudimentary security system. Each page could include a JSP file that checks to see if the user's login was accepted. If not, it could redirect the user to the login page. This would make it nearly impossible to view a page without entering your password. A variation on this theme is to assign users a security clearance that controls what they can see. Certain pages might not be accessible unless your clearance is over, say, 100.

Applets

One reason that Java is so popular on the Web is security. Because applets run in the context of the browser, the browser can strictly control what the applet can and can't do. Although this is a benefit for users, for developers, it's somewhat restrictive.

Of course, you can digitally sign your applets and hope that users will elect to relax security restrictions against them, but this isn't an ideal solution. The best answer is to find a way to work within the existing security structure.

For example, suppose you want to write an applet that needs to store data. You have very few choices. You can't write to a file on the client computer. However, you can open a network connection back to the server and write the file on the server. This requires a program on the server that listens for the applet and handles its requests.

Here's another problem: You can open network connections only back to your own server. This prevents a malicious applet from sending email from your machine, for example. But it poses a problem if you want two applets on different machines to communicate. A multiplayer game, for example, can't simply connect two applets. The server has to act like a telephone switchboard, brokering data from one applet to the other.

10. HTTP Clients

I'll show you how to build a simple server that lets two applets communicate with each other. The example applet lets two players play tic-tac-toe (or naughts and crosses for my friends in the U.K.) over the Web. You can see a game in progress in Figure 10.1.

Many examples of applications that use this same sort of technology exist on the Web. Have a look at **play.yahoo.com** for some interesting multiplayer games. You'll also find Jeopardy, Wheel of Fortune, and more at **station.sony.com** (these use signed applets, the last time I checked).

Of course, there's more to server communications than just playing games. Server communications include many serious applications for custom servers, ranging from reading newsgroups to chat applets. You'll find real-time chat with a Java applet at **chat.yahoo.com**. If you want to cruise the newsgroups using a Java applet, companies have been known to offer that service (I don't know any that survived the .COM shakeout of 2000). It's easy to imagine a Java-based email client or a collaborative white board applet using these same principles.

The Server Protocol

The goal of this project is to have two identical applets running on different machines that ostensibly communicate well enough so that the users can play tic-tac-toe against one another. In reality, both applets communicate with the server, not with each other. A specific protocol must be present that defines the transactions the applets can use with the server.

To keep things simple, I decided to limit the data sent between the client and the server to one-byte commands. When the first player connects, the server sends a *W* character to inform the player's applet that the game is not ready to begin.

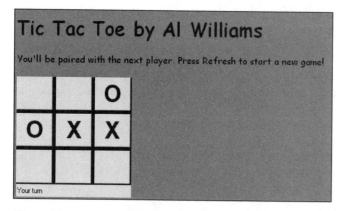

Figure 10.1   Browser-to-browser communications allows two people to play through a Web server.

Once a second player connects, the server sends the first player an *X* and the second player an *O*. This assigns a player to *X* and a player to *O*.

The simplest possible command is an ASCII digit from 0 to 8. When the *X* client receives this command, it indicates that the *O* client has moved to the indicated square on the game board. When the *X* client sends this command, it informs the server that the *X* player made a move. Neither client can send this command until the server sends an **M** command inviting a move.

During a game, either player may quit or disconnect. When this occurs, the server sends a **Q** to both clients. Either can also send a **Q** to initiate a disconnect. Other commands that may arrive include **W** (win), **L** (lose), and **G** (game over).

Unlike most servers, which use one thread per socket, the tic-tac-toe server uses one thread per pair of sockets. One thread handles both players, which is possible because the protocol is so simple. The applet clients can send data only when the server permits it, so the single thread is adequate for each pair of players.

Inside the Server

The server is surprisingly simple (see Listing 10.9). The main function creates a new server socket on port 9001. Then, in a loop, it accepts two connections on the socket and creates a new thread, passing the two sockets to the thread object via the constructor.

Listing 10.9   This server allows two applets to communicate with each other.

```
// tic-tac-toe server

import java.net.*;
import java.io.*;

public class TicServ {
    // write and flush to a socket
    public static void swrite(Socket sock,int s) throws IOException {
        OutputStream str=sock.getOutputStream();
        str.write(s);
        str.flush();
    }

    public static void main(String args[]) throws Exception {
        System.out.println("Tic Tac Toe Server by Al Williams");
        ServerSocket server = new ServerSocket(9001);
        // wait for connection pair and spin off thread
        while (true) {
            Socket sockx = server.accept();  // accept new connection
            swrite(sockx,'W');  // wait      // tell player 1 to wait
```

```
                        Socket socko = server.accept();  // accept player 2
                        new BackgroundTask(sockx,socko).start();  // start new thread
                }
        }
}

class BackgroundTask extends Thread {
        private Socket sockx;
        private Socket socko;
        private OutputStream strx;
        private OutputStream stro;
        private InputStream istrx;
        private InputStream istro;
        private int [] game = new int[9];
        BackgroundTask(Socket sockx,Socket socko) throws IOException
        {
                // cache away sockets and create I/O streams
                this.sockx = sockx;
                this.socko=socko;
                strx=sockx.getOutputStream();
                istrx=sockx.getInputStream();
                stro=socko.getOutputStream();
                istro=socko.getInputStream();
        }

        // write to stream
        private void wflush(OutputStream os,int s) throws IOException {
                os.write(s);
                os.flush();
        }

        public void run() {
                int ct=0;
                int i;
                for (i=0;i<9;i++) game[i]=0;
                try {
                        // set up both sides
                        wflush(strx,'X');  // X or 0
                        wflush(stro,'0');
                        while (true) {
                                int cmd;
                                ct++;   // next turn
                                // if ct==10 then draw game
                                if (ct==10) {
                                        wflush(strx,'G');
                                        wflush(stro,'G');
                                        break;
```

```
        }
        wflush(ct%2==0?stro:strx,'M');   // ask player for move
        cmd= (ct%2==0?istro:istrx).read();  // wait for it
        if (cmd=='Q') break;    // quit!
        wflush(ct%2==0?strx:stro,cmd);   // pass to peer
        // store move so we can check for wins
        game[cmd-'0']=ct%2==0?'0':'X';
        // check for wins
        // X win?
        if ((game[0]=='X' && game[1]=='X' && game[2]=='X') ||
            (game[3]=='X' && game[4]=='X' && game[5]=='X') ||
            (game[6]=='X' && game[7]=='X' && game[8]=='X') ||
            (game[0]=='X' && game[3]=='X' && game[6]=='X') ||
            (game[1]=='X' && game[4]=='X' && game[7]=='X') ||
            (game[2]=='X' && game[5]=='X' && game[8]=='X') ||
            (game[0]=='X' && game[4]=='X' && game[8]=='X') ||
            (game[6]=='X' && game[4]=='X' && game[2]=='X')) {
            // X wins
                wflush(strx,'W');
                wflush(stro,'L');
                break;
        }
        // 0 win?
        if ((game[0]=='0' && game[1]=='0' && game[2]=='0') ||
            (game[3]=='0' && game[4]=='0' && game[5]=='0') ||
            (game[6]=='0' && game[7]=='0' && game[8]=='0') ||
            (game[0]=='0' && game[3]=='0' && game[6]=='0') ||
            (game[1]=='0' && game[4]=='0' && game[7]=='0') ||
            (game[2]=='0' && game[5]=='0' && game[8]=='0') ||
            (game[0]=='0' && game[4]=='0' && game[8]=='0') ||
            (game[6]=='0' && game[4]=='0' && game[2]=='0')) {
                // 0 wins
                wflush(stro,'W');
                wflush(strx,'L');
                break;
        }
    }
} catch (Exception e) {
    e.printStackTrace();  // this shows up on server console
}
// somebody quit, tell everyone
// Each is in its own exception block so that if one throws an
// exception, the other statements still execute
try {
    wflush(strx,'Q');
} catch (Exception e) { };
```

```
        try {
            wflush(stro,'Q');
        } catch (Exception e) { };
        // close sockets
        try {
            sockx.close();
        } catch (Exception e) { };
        try {
            socko.close();
        } catch (Exception e) {}
    }
}
```

All the real work takes place in the thread object (**BackgroundTask**). The task constructor sets up input and output streams for both sockets. The **run** method takes care of the game logic.

The **run** method keeps track of the number of moves for several reasons. First, odd moves are for the *O* player, whereas even moves are for the *X* player. Also, after nine moves, the game is over (unless someone wins earlier).

The most complicated part of the server is the brute-force logic that checks for the winning player. The remaining code simply handles the command protocol between the two clients.

Inside the Applet

The applet code is somewhat more complex than the server code (see Listing 10.10). The bulk of the code, as always, deals with the user interface. To keep things simple, I used nine buttons in a grid layout to form the tic-tac-toe board. Instead of drawing lines between the buttons, I simply set the panel beneath the buttons to black. I also told the grid layout object to use a large gap between the buttons. This produces the tic-tac-toe board effect with minimal effort.

Listing 10.10   This applet serves as the user interface to the tic-tac-toe server.

```
/// This is the tic-tac-toe applet
import java.applet.*;
import java.awt.*;
import java.awt.event.*;
import java.net.*;
import java.io.*;


// Just a simple button with an integer tag
// could have used the ActionCommand, but that's a string
class TagBtn extends Button {
```

```java
    public int tag;
    TagBtn(String label, int tag)  {
        super(label);
        this.tag=tag;
    }
}


// The applet
public class TicTacToe extends Applet implements ActionListener {
    // arrays for buttons
    public TagBtn [][] btns = new TagBtn[3][3];
    // status message
    public Label lbl;
    // X or 0
    public String player;
    // no moves allowed unless this is true
    public volatile boolean mymove=false;
    // my move
    volatile int move;
    int xosize=20;  // size of X and 0
    String server;  // remote game host

    public void init() {
        int x;
        int y;
        String tmp;
        // Set X or 0 size
        tmp=getParameter("XOSize");
        try {
            xosize=Integer.parseInt(tmp);
            if (xosize==0) xosize=20;
        } catch (Exception e) { xosize=20; }
        // Get host name
        server=getParameter("Server");
        // set up GUI
        // The GUI has a border layout that contains a grid layout
        // The status window is south and the grid is north
        BorderLayout main = new BorderLayout();
        setLayout(main);
        Panel tictac = new Panel();
        tictac.setBackground(new Color(0,0,0));
        lbl = new Label("Tic Tac Toe by Al Williams");
        add(tictac,BorderLayout.CENTER);
        // gap of 5 makes the grid show up nicely
        GridLayout ly = new GridLayout(3,3,5,5);
```

```
            tictac.setLayout(ly);
            // Init buttons
            for (x=0;x<3;x++) {
                for (y=0;y<3;y++) {
                    btns[x][y]=new TagBtn(" ",y*3+x+'0');
                    btns[x][y].addActionListener(this);
                    btns[x][y].setFont(new Font("Helvtica",Font.BOLD,xosize));
                    tictac.add(btns[x][y]);
                }
            }
            add(lbl,BorderLayout.SOUTH);
            // start a thread to do all the network stuff
            new PlayThread(this).start();
        }


        // button press?
        public synchronized void actionPerformed(ActionEvent e) {
            TagBtn b = (TagBtn)e.getSource();
            // no move if not your turn or button has X or 0 in it already
            if (!mymove || !b.getLabel().equals(" ")) return;
            move=b.tag; // tell the thread
            notify();
            b.setLabel(player);
        }


        // This routine gets the next move... it won't return
        // until the actionPerformed function calls notify
        public synchronized int getMove() throws InterruptedException {
            wait();
            return move;
        }
    }


// This is the network thread
class PlayThread extends Thread {
    private TicTacToe host;

    PlayThread(TicTacToe host) { this.host = host; }
    public void run() {
        int c;
        // connect to host
        Socket sock;
        InputStream in;
        OutputStream out;
```

```
try {
    sock=new Socket(host.server,9001);   // port # could be a param
    in = sock.getInputStream();
    out=sock.getOutputStream();
    // this loop waits for our partner to connect
    while (true) {
        c=in.read();
        if (c=='Q') {
            host.lbl.setText(
                "Other player quit. Press Refresh for a new game.");
            return;
        }
        if (c=='X' || c=='O') {
            host.player=c=='X'?"X":"O";
            // small flaw... player X hardly gets a
            // chance to see this message
            host.lbl.setText("You are " + host.player);
            break;
        }
        if (c=='W') host.lbl.setText("Waiting....");
    }
    // both players ready to go!
    while (true) {
        c=in.read();
        if (c==-1) continue;  // no input
        if (c=='G') {
            host.lbl.setText("Game over! Press Refresh.");
            return;
        }
        if (c=='W') {
            host.lbl.setText("You win! Press Refresh.");
            return;
        }
        if (c=='L') {
            host.lbl.setText("You lose! Press Refresh.");
            return;
        }
        if (c=='Q') {
            host.lbl.setText("Other player quit. Press Refresh.");
            return;
        }
        // My turn?
        if (c=='M') {
            host.mymove=true;  // enable UI
            host.lbl.setText("Your turn");
            int m=host.getMove();  // wait for user to respond
```

```
                        host.lbl.setText("");  // disable UI
                        host.mymove=false;
                        // send it
                        out.write(m);
                        continue;
                }
                // hmmm must be a move for opposite player
                c=c-'0';
                host.btns[c%3][c/3].setLabel(
                        host.player.equals("X")?"O":"X");
                } // end while(true);

        } catch (Exception e) { e.printStackTrace(); }
    }
}
```

Once the applet initializes, it starts a thread that handles the communications back to the server. The thread is mostly straightforward code. It spends most of its time waiting for commands from the server and updating the user interface accordingly.

The code becomes somewhat complex in one spot. When the thread receives an **M** command from the server, it sets the **mymove** variable in the applet to **true**. The user interface code ignores all moves until this variable is set.

Once the thread sets this variable, it must wait until the user makes a move before continuing. One way to initiate the move would be to simply query the applet for a move in a loop. That's not very efficient, however, because the server's thread continues execution while waiting.

A better way to initiate the move is to use Java's built-in synchronization for threads. The **getMove** method in the applet calls **wait**. This call to wait causes any thread to halt until another piece of code in the applet object calls **notify**. When the player moves, the applet stores the square number in the move variable and calls **notify**. For this to work, both methods must have the synchronized keyword in their declarations.

Putting it Together

Because the clients are applets, you need an HTML page to launch them (see Listing 10.11). The applet lets you specify the size of the playing pieces, using the **xosize** parameter. You must also name the computer that's running the game server, using the **server** parameter. Remember, the server name must match the original location of the applet. You'll also have to run the server on the Web host before players load the HTML page.

Listing 10.11   This HTML page loads the tic-tac-toe applet.

```
<HTML>
<HEAD>
<TITLE>Tic Tac Toe!</TITLE>
</HEAD>
<BODY BGCOLOR=GRAY>
<H1>Tic-Tac-Toe by Al Williams</H1>
<P>You'll be paired with the next player. Press Refresh to start a new
game!</P>
<APPLET code=TicTacToe.class HEIGHT=200 WIDTH=200>
<PARAM name="server" value="www.al-williams.com">
<PARAM name="xosize" value="40">
</APPLET>
</BODY>
</HTML>
```

The simplest way to try out the system is to keep everything on one computer. Start running the server. Then you can load the HTML file using appletviewer. Set the server parameter on the Web page to **localhost**. Under Windows 98, for example, you might start an MS-DOS prompt or command window and enter:

```
start java TicServ
start appletviewer tictac.html
start appletviewer tictac.html
```

If you want to deploy this game on an externally hosted Web server, you'll need the kind of access that allows deploying of programs and not just data. Many Web-hosting providers don't allow this kind of access, at least at the basic level of service. Be sure to check with your provider before you try to run this program from your Web site. If your server is behind a firewall or a Network Address Translation switch (as many DSL connections are) you'll have to open port 9001 to allow the public to open that port on your PC.

Other Ideas

You could improve the tic-tac-toe game in many other ways. Some form of interactive chat would be nice, so you could taunt your opponent. It would also be nice if the user could pick a nickname. None of this would be very difficult to do, but it would complicate the protocol somewhat.

Immediate Solutions

Finding the HTTP Protocol Specification

Two versions of the HTTP protocol are in common use today. Version 1.0 is defined in RFC1945. For many purposes, this version is useful because it is somewhat simpler than version 1.1, which adds many features related to virtual hosting, proxy servers, and caching. You can find the version 1.1 specification in RFC2616.

Making a Simple Request

A simple request involves opening a TCP port to the Web server (usually on port 80) and sending a single-line request for a document:

```
GET /index.html
```

A properly operating version 0.9 server will simply return the document you request. However, some servers will always return headers and the document as though you made a newer-style request.

TIP: *Because servers don't reliably process this type of request, you should not use simple requests unless necessary. Generating a 1.0 request is only slightly more difficult and will generate a consistent response.*

Making a Version 1.0 Request

A version 1.0 request is superficially similar to a version 0.9 request, except that you can include headers that define information about the request. Like an email message, the headers end with a single blank line.

In addition, **GET** is not the only command verb you can use with a 1.0 request. The RFC defines several verbs, but the most common ones you'll use are **GET** and **POST** (use **POST** to send form data to the server).

To make a request, do the following:

1. Send a request line formed of the verb, the document, and the HTTP version you are using.

2. Send any headers you need to transmit to the server.

3. Send a blank line.

4. If you are performing a **POST**, you can send more data.

Here is an example of a request with no headers:

```
GET /test.htm HTTP/1.0
    note that this line is blank
```

Suppose you wanted to include a **User-Agent** header to identify the client program in use. Then the request would be as follows:

```
GET /test.htm HTTP/1.0
User-Agent: java Program by Al Williams
    note that this line is blank
```

Making a Version 1.1 Request

A version 1.1 request is nearly the same as a version 1.0 request (except, of course, for the version number). However, all version 1.1 requests must have at least one header. This header is the **host** header and allows servers that support multiple hosts to respond properly. Of course, you can add other headers as well.

Version 1.1 allows you to maintain a constant connection to a server using the **Connection** header. However, if you keep the socket open to the server, you can't be sure when the document is complete. Therefore, version 1.1 servers will often respond using a chunked encoding. If you don't want to hold the socket open, send the **Connection: close** header. However, you still may have to handle chunked encoding (indicated by a returned **Transfer-Encoding** header). Most servers only send chunked data when using a persistent connection.

Chunked responses appear as follows:

1. The first element in a chunked response is an ASCII string of hex digits that indicates the number of bytes in this chunk. The next bytes are part of the response text.

2. After one chunk is complete, another chunk may follow.

3. The last chunk has a length of zero and no text.

4. Immediately following the last chunk, there is a trailer, which may contain more headers (subject to the headers listed in the **Trailer** header). The end of the trailer is a blank line.

Here is a typical response from a server replying with chunked data:

```
HTTP/1.1 200 OK
Server: Microsoft-IIS/5.0
Date: Tue, 19 Jun 2001 20:32:28 GMT
Content-Type: text/html
Cache-control: private
Transfer-Encoding: chunked


14
6/19/2001 3:32:28 PM
0
Note: this line is blank
```

Reading a Status Code

If you make a simple request, the server simply returns the document you requested (or an error document). There is no simple way to determine if the request caused an error. However, other types of requests return a response code,
such as the following:

```
HTTP/1.1 200 OK
```

Here, the 200 indicates success. You can find a list of common status codes in
Table 10.1.

Table 10.1   Common HTTP status codes.

Status Code	Definition
100	Server will accept request (HTTP 1.1 only)
200	Success
204	No response
301	Moved permanently
302	Moved temporarily
304	Not modified
400	Bad syntax
401	Unauthorized
403	Forbidden
404	Not found

(continued)

Table 10.1   Common HTTP status codes *(continued)*.

Status Code	Definition
500	Internal error
501	Not implemented
502	Server too busy
503	Gateway time-out

Sending Form Data to a Server via HTML

The **POST** HTTP verb allows a client to send data to the server. The following is a simple HTML form:

```
<FORM ACTION=http://www.al-williams.com/aForm.jsp METHOD=POST>
Your name: <INPUT TYPE=TEXT NAME=myName><BR>
<INPUT TYPE=SUBMIT VALUE=Go>
</FORM>
```

When the user presses the submit button, an HTTP request is generated that looks like this:

```
POST /aForm.jsp HTTP/1.0
Content-Length: 24
Content-Type: application/x-www-form-urlencoded

myName=Al
```

The **METHOD** attribute has two possible values. **POST**, the one used in the example, sends the data as part of the request body. You may use the **GET** method, which places the data in the URL, so a **GET** request might look like this:

```
GET /aForm.jsp?myName=Al HTTP/1.0
```

Sending Form Data to a Server with Java

Mimicking form submission from within a Java program is not very difficult. With the **GET** method, you simply create a URL. Posting is a bit more difficult; simply follow these steps:

1. Build the request body in a string.
2. Build the headers in a separate string.

3. Use the length of the body string to determine the value of the **Content-Type** header in the header string.

4. Append the header and body strings.

5. Write the data to the server.

Here is an excerpt of some code that performs these steps:

```
String request;
String data;
// request data
data="tracknbr="+args[0]+"\r\n";
// Set up request
request="POST /cgi-bin/cttgate/ontrack.cgi HTTP/1.0\r\n";
request+="Content-Type: application/x-www-form-urlencoded\r\n";
request+="Content-Length: " + (data.length())+"\r\n\r\n";
request+=data;
// Write it out
str.write(request.getBytes());  // str is the socket's output stream
```

Encoding URL Data

When you send data to a Web server, you must encode it to hide special characters, such as spaces. The rule is to convert spaces into plus signs and any other character that could be misinterpreted into a hex equivalent with a percent-sign prefix. You could encode the entire string using this notation, so the string PAT could be %50%41%54. However, because this triples the size of the string, you'll usually only encode characters that have special meaning in URLs (for example, %, ?, and #).

The **java.net** package has a class named **URLEncoder** that can do this job for you:

```
public class URLEncode {
    public static void main(String args[]) {
        System.out.println(java.net.URLEncoder.encode(args[0]));
    }
}
```

Here, the static **encode** method (the only method in the class) converts the first argument to the correct format. So if you entered:

```
java URLEncode "A man & a plan = 100%"
```

You'd see the following output:

```
A+man+%26+a+plan+%3D+100%25
```

The & character becomes %26, the equal sign is %3D, and the percent sign is %25. Although you could encode spaces as %20, it is more efficient to use the plus sign notation (which, of course, means plus signs become %2B).

There is a corresponding class to decode these strings to their original format. The class is **java.net.URLDecoder**, and the static method is **decode**.

Automating Form Submission

Because posting data to a form is a common task, it is easy to wrap it into a class that does most of the work. Listing 10.12 shows such a class. The object derives from **java.util.Properties**. The code has an example **main** function that mimics the work done by Listing 10.3—namely, it sends a **tracknbr** field to the U.S. Postal Service's Web site to track a package.

The **main** program shows how easy it is to post the data. For each field you wish to send, you make an entry (with the same name) in the extended **Properties** object. For example:

```
post.put("tracknbr","03006000000373212757");
```

Once you have all the fields set, you simply call **send**, providing the page name and an **OutputStream** that corresponds to the socket's output.

Listing 10.12   This class simplifies posting data to a Web page.

```java
import java.net.*;
import java.util.*;
import java.io.*;

// Make an HTTP 1.0 post
public class HTTPForm extends Properties {
    public boolean send(String page, OutputStream outstr)
        throws IOException {
        StringBuffer data=new StringBuffer();
        String headers;
        Enumeration i=keys();
        while (i.hasMoreElements()) {
            String key=(String)i.nextElement();
```

```
                    data.append(URLEncoder.encode(key)
                         + "=" +
                         URLEncoder.encode((String)get(key))+
                         "&");
              }
              data.deleteCharAt(data.length()-1);  // remove last &
              headers="POST " + page + " HTTP/1.0\r\n"+
                  "Content-Type: application/x-www-form-urlencoded\r\n" +
                  "Content-Length: " + data.length() + "\r\n\r\n";
               outstr.write(headers.getBytes());
              outstr.write(data.toString().getBytes());
              return true;
          }


          // Test main -- duplicates MailFind
          public static void main(String args[]) throws Exception {
              HTTPForm test=new HTTPForm();
              Socket sock=new Socket("new.usps.com",80);
              OutputStream output=sock.getOutputStream();
              InputStream input=sock.getInputStream();
              test.put("tracknbr",args[0]);
              test.send("/cgi-bin/cttgate/ontrack.cgi",output);
    // For this example, just dump results
              int c;
              do {
                  c=input.read();
                  if (c!=-1) System.out.print((char)c);
              } while (c!=-1);
              sock.close();
          }
      }
```

Sending and Receiving Cookies

Cookies are small bits of data defined by RFC2965. The idea is simple: Each server can ask the browser to store data that the browser will then return on future requests. Not all browsers support cookies, and there are often differences in how browsers support cookies.

Also, a browser (or the user) may elect to delete or block cookies at any time, so you can't use cookies to store very important things. One of the best uses for cookies is to maintain state.

Normally, HTTP transactions have no state. When you request two pages from the same server, you make two completely separate transactions. The server has no way to know that the two pages are going to the same client (except, perhaps, by examining the client's address, which is not reliable because many users are behind firewalls, gateways, or Network Address Translation routers).

A common scheme is for the server to examine each request using the following rules:

1. Check for a cookie that contains an arbitrary session ID.

2. If the session ID exists, look it up in a local database of sessions.

3. If the cookie is empty, or doesn't contain the session ID, the server generates a new ID and sends it to the browser.

The client sends cookies to the server using the **Cookie** header, whereas the server responds with **Set-Cookie** if it wants the browser to store a cookie.

If you use advanced server tools, such as JSP, they will generally handle the cookie logic for you. However, if you are writing your own Java client, you may need to store cookies and send them back to the server to ensure proper operation. You can find a JSP example that uses cookies in the "In Depth" section (see Listings 10.4 through 10.8).

Opening Browser-to-Browser Communications

One way Web servers influence the Web browser is by loading and executing Java applets. These Java programs run inside the browser. However, most browsers will not let unknown applets do things that might compromise system security. This includes opening most network connections.

One exception to this security restriction is that the applet can open a network connection back to its originating server. By creating a custom Java server on your Web server machine, it is possible for the applet to tunnel through the server to another Web computer (for example, another Web browser).

For example, the "In Depth" section shows a series of programs that allow you to play tic-tac-toe with another user connected to the same server. This requires that you create a server program that runs on the same machine as the Web server.

In general, a tunneling server performs the following tasks:

1. Listens for incoming connections from applets on incoming ports.

2. Allows the applet to connect to another port on another machine.

3. Forwards everything sent by the applet to the remote machine and, conversely, forwards everything sent by the remote machine back to the applet.

The tic-tac-toe server in Listing 10.9 is a bit different. Its job is to pair up players, so it does not actually let the applet specify its own connection. Instead, the server assigns players in pairs. However, the idea is the same.

Checking for Valid Links

A Java program that scans a Web page for valid hyperlinks shows many of the concepts covered in this chapter. The program appears in Listing 10.13. The program takes the following steps:

1. The program makes an HTTP 1.0 request for the entire page named on the command line.

2. The program then picks the text of the page apart, looking for **HREF** attributes. The program doesn't attempt to exclude links that are inside comments or scripts, so it is possible to get some bad links, which is mainly harmless.

3. The **check** subroutine picks the URL apart and resolves relative links. It then issues an HTTP 1.1 **HEAD** request. There is no need to retrieve the entire body because the only point of interest is the response code.

4. If the server returns a 200 response, the program indicates the link is valid. Otherwise, it reports the link as invalid (even a redirect is considered invalid because you should probably be linking directly to the new location).

Listing 10.13   This program checks a page for valid hyperlinks.

```
// Link Checker
import java.net.*;
import java.io.*;
import java.util.*;

public class LinkCk {

    static int lastStatus=0;

    public static boolean check(String URL,String host,String root)
      throws IOException {
        String theHost=host;
        String dir="";
        int n,n1,port=80;
        // interpret URL
```

```
n=root.lastIndexOf('/');
if (n>0) dir=root.substring(0,n+1);
if (dir.length()!=0 && dir.charAt(0)!='/') dir="/"+dir;
// check for protocol string other than http:, forget it
n=URL.indexOf(':');
n1=URL.indexOf('/');
if (n!=-1 && (n1>n || n1==-1)) {
    if (URL.substring(0,5).compareToIgnoreCase("http:")!=0)
        return true;
    n=URL.indexOf('/',7);
    if (n==-1) {
        theHost=URL;
        URL="/";
    } else {
        theHost=URL.substring(0,n);
        URL=URL.substring(n);
    }
    theHost=theHost.substring(7); // remove http://
}
else {
    if (URL.charAt(0)!='/') URL=dir+URL;
}

n=theHost.indexOf('@');  // userid/password?
if (n!=-1) theHost=theHost.substring(n+1);
n=theHost.lastIndexOf(':');
try {
    if (n!=-1) {
        port=Integer.parseInt(theHost.substring(n+1));
        theHost=theHost.substring(0,n);
    }

    // try to guess if this is a directory
    // this is an imperfect guess
    if (URL.indexOf('.')==-1&&URL.charAt(URL.length()-1)!='/')
        URL=URL+"/";
    // make the request and see if it works
    String cmd="HEAD " + URL + " HTTP/1.1\r\n",line;
    Socket sock = request(theHost,port,cmd);
    BufferedReader rdr=new BufferedReader(
                new InputStreamReader(sock.getInputStream()));
    line=rdr.readLine();
    if (line==null) return false;
    return getStatus(line)==200;
}
```

```
            catch (Exception e) {
               System.out.println(e);
               return false;
            }
      }



      // Pick out the status
      public static int getStatus(String response) {
         StringTokenizer token = new StringTokenizer(response);
         token.nextToken();
         lastStatus=Integer.parseInt(token.nextToken());
         return lastStatus;
      }


      // Make a Version 1.1. request
      public static Socket request(String host,int port,String cmd)
         throws UnknownHostException, IOException {
         Socket skt = new Socket(host,port);
         cmd+="host: " + host +"\r\nconnection: close\r\n\r\n";
         skt.getOutputStream().write(cmd.getBytes());
         return skt;
      }



      public static void main(String[] args) throws Exception {
         String line;
         // make a 1.0 request here so we avoid the chunked response encoding
         String cmd="GET /" + args[1]+" HTTP/1.0\r\n";
         Socket skt = request(args[0],80,cmd);



         BufferedReader rdr=new BufferedReader(
                           new InputStreamReader(skt.getInputStream()));
         boolean headers=true;
         try {
            // check status code
            line=rdr.readLine();
            if (getStatus(line)!=200) {
               System.out.println(line);
               System.exit(0);
            }
            do {
               line=rdr.readLine();
               if (line!=null) {
```

```
                    if (line.equals("")) {
                        headers=false;
                        continue;
                    }
                    // skip headers
                    if (headers) continue;
                    String Uline = line.toUpperCase();
                    int n=0,n1;
                    // pick out hyperlinks
                    // don't try to exclude those commented out
                    do {
                        n=Uline.indexOf("HREF=",n);
                        if (n!=-1) {
                            n+=5;
                            if (line.charAt(n)=='"') {
                                n1=line.indexOf('"',++n);
                            }
                            else if (line.charAt(n)=='\'') {
                                n1=line.indexOf('\'',++n);
                            }
                            else {
                                int n2;
                                n1=line.indexOf(' ',n);
                                n2=line.indexOf('>',n);
                                if (n1==-1||n2<n1) n1=n2;
                            }
                            // detect empty tags (why do people do this?)
                            if (n==n1) continue;
                            String link=line.substring(n,n1);
                            if (link.charAt(0)=='#') continue; // local
                            System.out.print(link + "... ");
                            System.out.println(
                                    check(link,
                                    args[0],args[1])?"OK":("*BAD* " +
lastStatus));
                            n=n1;
                        }
                    } while (n!=-1); // try another line
                }

            } while (line!=null);
        }
        catch (IOException e) {        }
    }

}
```

Chapter 11

Protocol Handlers

In Depth

Learning math isn't what it used to be. I imagine this is mainly because of calculators. When I was a kid, there were not many calculators, and they were relatively expensive. Now, you can get free calculators with ads on them and pick up a great scientific calculator for a couple of bucks.

Before calculators, you had to really understand how math works to be able to do practically anything. Sure, we had slide rules, but reading a slide rule requires you to have some ideas about logarithms. Today, you'd be hard-pressed to find many people who can use logarithms or find a square root by hand, for example.

No one wants to laboriously do computations—that's what computers are for, after all. However, what many people don't realize is that for scientists and engineers, math is as much a way to develop intuition about how things work as to provide numerical answers. For example, consider the ideal gas law from physics. Even if you can't remember the exact formula, the useful part is to understand the relationship between gas volume, temperature, and pressure (for example, as volume increases at a constant temperature, pressure decreases).

Mathematical modeling can help you understand many processes, and that is often more valuable than the absolute numerical result. However, calculators have made intuitive math a lost art. Networking is similar. Every time you use a tool to abstract the network, you get further away from the details, which may help you understand what is happening.

The first 10 chapters of this book cover Java networking at a relatively low level. Even then, the techniques did not require you to know about arcane details like Internet Protocol (IP) headers and source routes. However, Java provides an even higher-level interface to networking that you can often—but not always—use to get quick results.

This higher-level interface works great for Web pages. However, for other protocols it isn't very programmer friendly, so you may want to continue using the **Socket** object as you have in the earlier chapters.

Inside URL

The **URL** class represents a resource in Uniform Resource Locator format, such as **http://www.coriolis.com**. Usually, you'll construct the object with the URL, although there are a variety of constructors that allow you to specify the URL in pieces instead of one string, if you prefer.

Once you have a **URL** object you can retrieve the contents of the URL in several different ways. For example, you can call **openStream** to fetch an **InputStream** that corresponds to the document. You can also call **getContent**, which returns an object dependent on the document's Multipurpose Internet Mail Extensions (MIME) type.

That means you can retrieve a Web page with just a few lines of code (see Listing 11.1). However, you don't get access to the headers, nor can you send data to the server. For that you need a **URLConnection** object (discussed shortly).

Listing 11.1   A simple way to read a Web page.

```
import java.net.*;
import java.io.*;

public class EZUrl {
    public static void main(String[] args) throws Exception {
      URL url = new URL(args[0]);
      InputStream html = url.openStream();
      int c;
      do {
        c=html.read();
        if (c!=-1) System.out.print((char)c);
        } while (c!=-1);
    }
}
```

Another problem with using **URL** (and more specifically, **getContent**): The classes that represent data are Sun-specific classes, unless you provide your own. They are not documented, and you can't be sure they will continue to exist. To see what I mean, try using the code in Listing 11.7 (in the "Immediate Solutions" section) to fetch some graphics interchange format (GIF) and Joint Photographic Experts Group (JPG) files from the Web. You'll see that GIF and JPG files are **sun.awt.image.URLImageSource** objects. A text file retrieved via a File Transfer Protocol (FTP) URL shows up as a **sun.net.www.content.text.PlainText-InputStream** class.

Inside URLConnection

Reading a URL with the **URL** object is very easy. However, what if you want more control over the Hyptertext Transport Protocol (HTTP) transaction? Perhaps you want to pass data to a server-side script or read headers. Then you probably want to use the URL object's **openConnection** member. This function returns a

URLConnection object. If the URL actually uses the HTTP protocol (in the case of a Web page, as opposed to, say, an FTP download), the object returns a subclass of **URLConnection** known as an **HttpURLConnection**. This connection object lets you set headers and requests before submitting the URL request.

For example, suppose you want to submit a request to a form on a Web server. You might use code like that in Listing 11.2 to do the job. The code creates the **URL** object as usual (in this case, it opens InterNIC's WHOIS form). The program casts the **URLConnection** object into a specialized subclass (the **HttpURL-Connection** object, covered shortly).

Before the program establishes a connection, it calls **setDoInput** and **setDoOutput** to signify that it wants to read from and write to the URL. The **setRequestMethod** tells the URL to use the HTTP Post method to submit form data. Finally, the **setRequestProperty** sets the request headers to indicate that the server can expect form data.

Once the program attends to these details, it connects, using the **connect** method. At this point, the program asks the URL for an **OutputStream** using **getOutputStream**. Writing to this stream causes data to flow from the program to the Web server. Data going to the server should be encoded, and that's the purpose of the **URLEncoder** object's static **encode** method. It replaces blanks with plus signs, and special characters with hexadecimal escape sequences, just the way the Web server wants it.

Listing 11.2   Submitting data with URLConnection.

```
//Sample Code to Submit a Form
import java.net.*;
import java.io.*;


class insearch
  {
  static public void main(String [] argv) throws Exception
    {
    URL url=new URL("http://www.internic.net/cgi-bin/whois");
    HttpURLConnection conn=(HttpURLConnection)url.openConnection();
    int c;
    conn.setDoInput(true);
    conn.setDoOutput(true);
    conn.setRequestMethod("POST");
    conn.setRequestProperty("Content-type",
        "application/x-www-form-urlencoded");
    conn.connect();
```

```
PrintWriter pout = new
    PrintWriter( new
    OutputStreamWriter(conn.getOutputStream(),
    "8859_1"), true );
pout.print("whois_nic=" + URLEncoder.encode(argv[0]) +
    "&submit=Search&type=domain");
pout.flush();
  // read results
System.out.println(conn.getResponseMessage());
InputStream is=conn.getInputStream();
do
  {
  char x;
  c=is.read();
  x=(char)c;
  if (c!=-1) System.out.print(x);
  } while (c!=-1);
  }
}
```

The **URLConnection** class has many methods, some of which are not very useful. Here are the most important ones:

- **getDefaultAllowUserInteraction**—This static method returns **true** or **false** depending on the system's default value for the internal flag that determines if objects can prompt the user for data like passwords. The default value applies to subsequently created instances.

- **setDefaultAllowUserInteraction**—This static method sets the interaction flag for all new instances.

- **getAllowUserInteraction**—Returns the value of the interaction flag for this object.

- **setAllowUserInteraction**—Sets the interaction flag for this instance of the object.

- **getFileNameMap**—You can use this method to retrieve a **FileNameMap** reference. You can use this to guess a MIME type from a file name (for example, a file ending in .txt will be text/plain).

- **setFileNameMap**—If you want to set your own **FileNameMap** object, you can use this method.

- **guessContentTypeFromName**—This method guesses a MIME type from a file name. It actually calls the default **FileNameMap** object, or the one set by **setFileNameMap** to do the work.

- **guessContentTypeFromInputStream**—Instead of using the MIME type, you can ask this method to examine a few bytes of the input stream to try to determine the type of data.

- **getContent**—This method has two variations. The first one returns an object that varies depending on the document's MIME type. For example, the function returns images as **sun.awt.image.URLImageSource** objects and text as a type of **InputStream**. This is similar to the **URL.getContent** method mentioned earlier in the chapter. The second version requires an array of **Class** objects. The method will then attempt to return one of those types, if possible.

- **getContentLength**, **getContentEncoding**, **getContentType**, **getDate**, **getExpiration**, **getLastModified**—These methods all return values from the corresponding headers of the document, if applicable.

- **setIfModifiedSince**—This method sets the **IfModifiedSince** header.

- **getHeaderField**, **getHeaderFieldDate**, **getHeaderFieldInt**, **getHeaderFieldKey**—You can use these methods to retrieve arbitrary headers, either as a **String** or as a specific data type (for example, **Date** or **int**).

- **setRequestProperty**—You can use this call to set an arbitrary header.

- **setDoInput**, **setDoOutput**, **getDoInput**, **getDoOutput**—By default, the object will only handle incoming data from the server. However, you can control the data directions using these methods.

- **connect**—This method actually contacts the server. Before calling **connect**, you must have any options and headers set.

- **getInputStream**, **getOutputStream**—These methods return streams you can use to communicate with the server. Keep in mind that these streams are subject to the state of the **setDoInput** and **setDoOutput** methods.

As you can see, although **URLConnection** is supposed to be general purpose, it is content handlers that do the actual work, and you can even create your own, if you like.

URLConnection Subclasses

You can use a subclass of **URLConnection**—**HttpURLConnection**—which is abstract. This is the actual class used by Listing 11.2. The only way to get one is to create a **URL** object with an http:// URL and call **openConnection** on the object. You can then cast the returned **URLConnection** to an **HttpURLConnection**.

This special subclass allows you to set the request type (for example, **GET** or **POST**) using **setRequestMethod**, get the response code with **getResponseCode**, and perform other HTTP-specific tasks.

In addition to the HTTP-specific subclass, you can use a special subclass for Java Archive (JAR) files, which are the same JAR files you use to package Java classes.

You can retrieve JAR files from a local file or via HTTP. To create a JAR connection for a file named inside.htm in the nettest.jar file, you again create a **URL** object. However, in this case, you provide a pseudo-URL, like these three:

```
jar:file://c%3A/lib/nettest.jar!/inside.htm
jar:http://www.coriolis.com/jars/nettest.jar!/inside.htm
jar:ftp://ftp.coriolis.com/jars/nettest.jar!/inside.htm
```

In the first example, the JAR file is a local file named nettest.jar in the c:\lib directory. Note that the colon requires encoding, but the slashes do not. In the second and third examples, the JAR file resides on a server at the indicated URL. In all cases, you want the inside.htm file from within the JAR. The exclamation mark simply ends the pseudo-URL and is not part of the JAR file name. The portion after the exclamation mark is the file name within the JAR file you want to extract.

Once you have the **URL** constructed with the special URL, you can read data from the file just as you would any other **URL**. That means you can call **openStream** or extract a **URLConnection** object and cast it to a **JarURLConnection**.

Protocol and Content Handlers

The **URL** and **URLConnection** objects rely on **URLStreamHandler** and **URLConnection** classes to perform protocol-specific processing. In addition, a **ContentHandler** class understands how to convert incoming data into a Java type. However, the official Java library doesn't have implementations for any of these classes. The classes you use when you use common protocols like HTTP or FTP are actually classes in the **sun** package and not part of the Java baseline.

Custom Protocols

Under the hood, the **URL** object examines the protocol portion of its URL and calls an object that implements **URLStreamHandlerFactory** (you set this object with the static **URL.setURLStreamHandlerFactory** method). This object is responsible for creating a **URLStreamHandler** subclass that corresponds to the specified protocol. However, you can only install one **URLStreamHandlerFactory**—once it is set, you can't change it again.

The object that subclasses **URLStreamHandler** creates a corresponding **URLConnection** object (or subclass of **URLConnection**). It also parses the URL, so you can define custom URL formats (like the jar: protocol that **JarURLConnection** object uses). The **URLConnection** object actually communicates with the server.

Ordinarily, you don't care about any of this because it just works transparently. However, if you want to add to a custom handler, you can by creating your own objects. Why would you want to create a handler? You might want to extend Java's **URL** object so that it understands, for example, the Finger protocol. You could define custom URLs that point to database tables or other custom resources. You'll have to do a bit of work at first, but after you have the classes available, it will be easy for you (or anyone else) to access your custom content. You can even load new handlers at runtime.

Listing 11.3 shows a subclass of **URLConnection** that knows how to open a time server on port 13. The **connect** method is where most of the work occurs. This method opens a socket on the correct port and sets the connected flag (part of **URLConnection**). Because this connection directly wraps a socket, the **getInputStream** method is trivial.

Listing 11.3   This specialized URLConnection class knows how to query a time server.

```
import java.net.*;
import java.io.*;

public class TimeURLConnection extends URLConnection {
    private Socket conn;
    public final static int DEFPORT=13;

    public TimeURLConnection(URL url) { super(url); }

    public synchronized void connect() throws IOException {
      if (!connected) {
          int port=url.getPort();
          if (port<=0) port=DEFPORT;
          conn=new Socket(url.getHost(),port);
          connected=true;
          }
    }

    public String getContentType() {
      return "text/plain";
      }

    public synchronized InputStream getInputStream() throws IOException {
        connect();
        return conn.getInputStream();
        }
}
```

How does the **URL** object know to use this particular connection object? The first part required is a **URLStreamHandler** subclass. This object knows how to create the correct **URLConnection** object and is quite simple (see Listing 11.4).

Listing 11.4   This simple class creates the correct **URLConnection** subclass on behalf of the **URL** class.

```
import java.net.*;
import java.io.*;

public class TimeHandler extends URLStreamHandler {
    public int getDefaultPort() {
        return TimeURLConnection.DEFPORT;
    }

    protected URLConnection openConnection(URL url) throws IOException {
        return new TimeURLConnection(url);
    }
}
```

You still have to inform the system to use this **URLStreamHandler** object. When you create a **URL** object, Java first looks to see if you've installed a **URLStream-HandlerFactory** class. If you have, it calls the **createURLStreamHandler** method of this class. If you didn't provide this class (or the method returns **null**), the system then looks in the system property named **java.protocol.handler.pkgs**. This property may contain a list of package names, separated by the vertical bar character (|).

If this property has a value, Java looks for a class that matches the protocol you are trying to use. For example, suppose the **java.protocol.handler.pkgs** property equals "**com.al_williams.proto|com.coriolis.java.phandlers**" and you are trying to load a **mailto** URL. Java will look for these classes along the **CLASSPATH**:

```
com.al_williams.proto.mailto.Handler
com.coriolis.java.phandlers.mailto.Handler
```

This class, if it exists, is a subclass of **URLStreamHandler** (like Listing 11.4). If you don't have a class that fits this description, Java finally looks for a class named **sun.net.www.protocol.mailto.Handler** (for the **mailto** protocol).

Of course, the custom **URLStreamHandlerFactory** offers the most control over the process, and it is simple to write (see Listing 11.5). Just remember that you can only install one **factory** class. Subsequent attempts to set the **factory** class will throw an exception.

Listing 11.5   The URLStreamHandlerFactory class selects a custom handler for a protocol.

```
import java.net.*;

public class MyStreamHandlerFactory implements URLStreamHandlerFactory {
    public URLStreamHandler createURLStreamHandler(String protocol) {
        if (protocol.equalsIgnoreCase("time"))
            return new TimeHandler();
        return null; // huh?
    }
}
```

If you are using a custom factory class, you should set it using the static **URL.setURLStreamHandlerFactory** method, as the program in Listing 11.6 does.

Listing 11.6   This simple program uses the custom protocol handler.

```
import java.net.*;
import java.io.*;

public class TimeURLTest {
    public static void main(String [] args) throws Exception {
        URL.setURLStreamHandlerFactory(new MyStreamHandlerFactory());
        URL url=new URL("time://tock.usno.navy.mil");
        InputStream is=url.openStream();
        int c;
        do {
            c=is.read();
            if (c!=-1) System.out.print((char)c);
        } while (c!=-1);
        is.close();
    }
}
```

Custom Content Handlers

The protocol handler and connection objects are purely concerned with the transmission of data. However, the **URL** object also converts data into a Java object when you call the **getContent** method. How can Java know what type of object to use? That is the province of a content handler derived from **ContentHandler**.

The class itself implements the **getContent** method that returns the appropriate type. Alternately, the calling program can specify a list of classes and **getContent** will return a type from this list, if possible.

The process that Java uses to find appropriate content handlers is similar to the one it uses for protocol handlers. First, the **URL** object calls the **URLConnection** object's **getContent** call. If you are writing a custom **URLConnection** object, you could handle everything at this point.

The default processing for **getContent**, however, looks to see if you have installed a **ContentHandlerFactory** class using the static **setContentHandlerFactory** method of **URLConnection**. If you have, Java calls the **createContentHandler** method to find a content handler. If this class has not been installed or the method returns **null**, Java examines package names in the system property **java.content.handler.pkgs**.

The **java.content.handler.pkgs** property contains a list of package names (separated by the vertical bar character). Java uses the MIME type as a class name and searches the packages listed for that class. For example, to locate a handler for the type application/x-video, Java would examine the packages for a class named **application.x_video** (you convert the dashes to underscores because dashes are not legal in class names).

If all else fails, Java will look for the default handler. For the example MIME type, the default handler would be at **sun.net.www.content.application.x_video**. You'll find an example content handler in the Immediate Solutions section of this chapter.

Immediate Solutions

Retrieving a URL's Data

If you want an **InputStream** that corresponds to a **URL**, you can easily obtain it by using the **URL** object. Here are the steps you'll use:

1. Create a **URL** object, passing a string representation of the URL to the constructor.

2. Call the **URL** object's **openStream** method to retrieve the **InputStream**.

Here's an example of the code (see Listing 11.1 for the complete listing):

```
URL url = new URL(args[0]);
InputStream html = url.openStream();
```

Retrieving a URL's Contents

For many MIME types, you can have the **URL** object directly return an object that corresponds to the document's data type. For an HTML document, that object is just a type of **InputStream**. However, other types—like images—can return ready-to-use image objects, for example.

The key is to call the **URL.getContent** method. This method retrieves the data, examines the MIME type of the document, and creates an appropriate object. Try entering URLs for different document types on the command line of the program in Listing 11.7. You'll see the object types returned by **getContent**.

Listing 11.7   This program shows the object types returned by getContent.

```
import java.net.*;
import java.io.*;

public class EZUrl2 {
    public static void main(String[] args) throws Exception {
      URL url = new URL(args[0]);
      Object doc = url.getContent();
      System.out.println(doc.getClass().getName());
      }
}
```

Setting Request Headers

If you want to set request headers, you won't be able to use the **URL** object's simple methods. Instead, you'll use the **openConnection** method to retrieve a **URLConnection** object.

This object provides—at least potentially—a two-way communication channel with the server. The **URLConnection** object has several methods that allow you to set request headers:

- **setIfModifiedSince**—Allows you to set the **setIfModifiedSince** header
- **setRequestProperty**—Sets an arbitrary request header
- **setDefaultRequestProperty**—Sets default headers (this method is static)

By default, the **URLConnection** class only allows incoming data. However, you can also write data to the server if you call **setDoOutput(true)**. You can use **getInputStream** and **getOutputStream** to find the actual streams you'll use to perform input and output.

Note that all of the methods mentioned (except for **getInputStream** and **getOutputStream** must be called before the **URLConnection** connects to the server (using **connect**).

Reading Response Headers

The **URLConnection** object also allows you to read response headers. You can read arbitrary headers as a **String** using **getHeaderField**. If the header has a particular format, you can use **getHeaderFieldDate** or **getHeaderFieldInt** to format the data as a **Date** object or an **int**, respectively.

In addition to these general-purpose methods, the object also provides handy methods to fetch specific headers, such as **getContentEncoding**, **getContentType**, **getDate**, **getExpiration**, and **getLastModified**. These retrieve the headers indicated in the method name.

Working with HTTP-Specific Connections

If the URL you pass to the **URL** object begins with **http**, the **openConnection** method will return a subclass of **URLConnection**. In particular, you'll receive an **HttpURLConnection**. This class has all the methods in an ordinary **URLConnection** plus additional methods that are specific to HTTP connections. Some of the methods you'll find in this class include the following:

- **setFollowRedirects**—Allows you to specify that the object should transparently handle redirections
- **setRequestMethod**—Sets the HTTP method (for example, **GET** or **POST**)
- **getResponseCode**—Returns the numeric response code from the server
- **getResponseMessage**—Returns the response message as a **String**

Of course, **openConnection** always returns a **URLConnection**. To take advantage of the special classes in **HttpURLConnection**, you have to cast the return value to the correct type:

```
HttpURLConnection conn=(HttpURLConnection)url.openConnection();
```

Posting Data to a Server

Using a **URLConnection** object, you can easily post data to a Web server. To do this, you must follow these steps:

1. Call **setDoOutput** passing a **true** argument.
2. Set the request method to **POST** using **setRequestMethod**.
3. Set any request headers required.
4. Call **connect** to initiate communications with the server.
5. Obtain the input and output streams from the **URLConnection** object.
6. Use the **URLEncoder.encode** method to encode the data you wish to post.
7. Write the data to the output stream.
8. Read the results from the input stream.

You can find the code that implements these steps in Listing 11.2.

Opening a JAR File as a URL

Java defines a custom URL type that allows you to manipulate JAR files on the local file system or over the network. The protocol for this type of URL begins with the **jar:** specifier. This custom URL actually contains another URL that determines where the JAR file resides. This nested URL ends with an exclamation point. Following the exclamation point, you can place the file name inside the JAR that you want to access.

For example, suppose you have a JAR file available on an FTP site named nettest.jar. You want to access a file within the JAR named jbb.txt. The pseudo-URL you'd use would be:

```
jar:ftp://ftp.coriolis.com/jars/nettest.jar!/jbb.txt
```

WARNING! *If you want to use a local file, you can use the file protocol. However, under Windows or MS-DOS, you'll have to be careful to encode the colon in the pathname to %3A. However, do not encode slashes or backslashes because those are legitimate parts of the URL. An example URL for c:\binks.jar would be: jar:file://c:%3A/binks.jar!script.txt.*

Once you have the special URL formed, you simply pass it to the constructor of a **URL** object, and you can treat it as though it were any other URL resource. If you need more control, you can call **URL.openConnection** and cast the returned **URLConnection** object into a **JarURLConnection** object. This object allows you to obtain manifest and security information about the JAR file.

Listing 11.8 shows a program that reads a JAR file using a **URL** object. The program takes two arguments: the name of the JAR file and the file name within the JAR file.

Listing 11.8   This program reads a file from a JAR file.

```java
import java.net.*;
import java.io.*;

public class JarPrinter {
    static public void main(String [] args) throws Exception {
        String jarfile;
        // MSDOS/Windows names have colons in them that need to convert to
        // %3A, but can't convert / or \ to their URL equivalents
        int n=args[0].indexOf(':');
        if (n==-1)
            jarfile=args[0];
        else
            jarfile=args[0].substring(0,n)+"%3A"+args[0].substring(n+1);
        String urlstring  = "jar:file://"+ jarfile + "!/"+args[1];
        System.out.println("Opening: " + urlstring);
        URL url = new URL(urlstring);
        InputStream is=url.openStream();
        int c;
        do {
            c=is.read();
            if (c!=-1) System.out.print((char)c);
        } while (c!=-1);
        is.close();
    }
}
```

Creating a Custom Protocol Handler

Java understands a few protocols, such as http, ftp, and the pseudo protocol for JAR files. However, you can extend the system to understand your own custom protocols. You must create two classes to control how the **URL** object loads data:

1. Most of the work will occur in a class derived from **URLConnection**. This class manages the physical connection (typically through a **Socket**) to the **URL**'s document.

2. You'll also create a class derived from **URLStreamHandler**. This class simply defines the correspondence between a particular protocol and your custom **URLConnection** class.

Listing 11.9 shows a **URLConnection** class that handles a special protocol known as the **string** protocol. The goal is to use this protocol in place of the HTTP protocol to retrieve a Web page as a Java **String**.

This custom class simply cuts the protocol identifier from the string passed into the **URL** constructor. Then the code adds the http:// protocol identifier. Later, you'll see that this will handle URLs like this:

```
string://www.coriolis.com
```

However, this class doesn't handle the conversion of the content into a **String**. For a simple case like this, you could simply override **getContent** in this class and do whatever processing is necessary there. However, for more complicated systems, you'll want to handle the content generation in a separate **ContentHandler** object (covered shortly).

Listing 11.9   This URLConnection class loads a page using the HTTP protocol.

```java
import java.net.*;
import java.io.*;

public class StringURLConnection extends URLConnection {
    private URL base;
    public final static int DEFPORT=80;
    public StringURLConnection(URL url) { super(url); }

    public String getContentType() { return "application/x-jstring"; }

    public synchronized void connect() throws IOException {
      if (!connected) {
// remove old protocol and substitute http://
        String newurl="http://" + url.toExternalForm().substring(9);
        base=new URL(newurl);
        }
    }
```

11. Protocol Handlers

```
    public synchronized InputStream getInputStream() throws IOException {
        connect();
        return base.openStream();
    }
}
```

You'd think that this class would be all you really need, but Java requires you to also define a class derived from **URLStreamHandler**. This object's sole purpose is to create an instance of the custom **URLConnection** object when required. Listing 11.10 does the job for the custom handler that appears in Listing 11.9.

Listing 11.10   This simple class creates an instance of the custom **URLConnection** object when required.

```
import java.net.*;
import java.io.*;

public class StringURLHandler extends URLStreamHandler {
    public int getDefaultPort() { return StringURLConnection.DEFPORT; }
    protected URLConnection openConnection(URL url) throws IOException {
      return new StringURLConnection(url);
      }

}
```

Installing a Custom Protocol Handler

Once you've written a custom protocol handler, you have to tell Java to use it when it sees the appropriate protocol string in a **URL** object. There are two ways you can accomplish this:

1. Create a **URLStreamHandlerFactory** class and register it using **URL.setURLStreamHandlerFactory**. The custom class creates **URLStreamHandler** objects based on a protocol string.

2. Create the **URLStreamHandler** object in a separate package. To use this method, you must properly set a special system property.

When using the first method, you have complete control over the creation of stream handlers. If you return **null** from the **createURLStreamHandler** method, Java searches for any handlers that use the second method. If that fails, Java looks for its default handlers.

***WARNING!** Once you call **setURLStreamHandlerFactory** once in a program, you can't call it again without generating an error.*

If you elect to use the second method, you have to place your **URLStreamHandler** class in a package. The protocol name will serve as a subpackage name, and the class name must be **Handler**. So to handle FTP, for example, you might write a class named **com.coriolis.protohandlers.ftp.Handler**. In addition, the system property **java.protocol.handler.pkgs** must contain the name of the package (**com.coriolis.protohandlers**, in this case). The property can contain multiple package names; you separate multiple names with a vertical bar character.

To install the handlers for the string URL (see the last section) you could use a **URLStreamHandlerFactory** like the one in Listing 11.11.

Listing 11.11   This URLStreamHandlerFactory class creates a custom stream handler.

```
import java.net.*;

public class StringSHFactory implements URLStreamHandlerFactory {
    public URLStreamHandler createURLStreamHandler(String proto) {
      if (proto.equalsIgnoreCase("string"))
         return new StringURLHandler();
      return null;
    }
}
```

Creating a Custom Content Handler

If you are reading a custom protocol, you'll not only want to customize the **URLConnection** class, but you'll also want to provide a special content handler to decode your data into an appropriate Java object.

The easiest way to do this is to simply override both versions of **getContent** in your subclass of **URLConnection**. However, this is not very flexible because one **URLConnection** might service different types of data (for example, an HTTP connection might receive text or graphics).

For cases like this, you'll need to write a custom content handler based on the **ContentHandler** class. This class will provide the brains behind the two **getContent** methods in **URLConnection**. The first version of **getContent** simply returns the default data type. The second version accepts an array of **Class** references. This array is a list of objects the caller would like to receive in order of preference. The **getContent** method will return the first object type it recognizes.

Of course, it is easy to write the first **getContent** in terms of the second version, so there isn't much work to do to write that first version. Listing 11.12 shows an implementation for the string URL developed in the previous sections. This content handler will satisfy requests for an **InputStream** (like a normal HTTP request) or as a **String**.

The first version of **getContent** simply calls the second version with a default data type array (in this case, it contains **String**). For efficiency, when the class returns a string, it reads data in blocks and uses a **StringBuffer** as an intermediate workspace.

Notice that the class in Listing 11.12 is in a package (**com.al_williams.content-handlers.application**). That's because the next session will install this handler so that Java automatically finds it. As you'll find in that section, the name of the class, in this case, is important.

Listing 11.12   This handler reads an entire Web page into a string and returns it.

```
package com.al_williams.contenthandlers.application;

import java.io.*;
import java.net.*;

public class x_jstring extends ContentHandler {
    public Object getContent(URLConnection urlc) throws IOException {
      Class [] clist=new Class[1];
      clist[0]=String.class;
      return getContent(urlc,clist);
    }
    public Object getContent(URLConnection urlc, Class [] clist)
      throws IOException {
      for (int i=0;i<clist.length;i++) {
          if (clist[i]==InputStream.class)
            return urlc.getInputStream();
          if (clist[i]==String.class) {
            StringBuffer rv=new StringBuffer();
            InputStream is=urlc.getInputStream();
            byte [] buffer=new byte[256];
            int len;
            do {
                len=is.read(buffer,0,buffer.length);
                if (len!=0)
                  rv.append(new String(buffer));
            } while (len==buffer.length);
            return rv.toString();
          }
      }
      return null;
    }
}
```

Installing a Custom Content Handler

Once you have a custom content handler, you have to inform Java that it should use it. This is similar to the way you install a protocol handler. Again, you have two choices:

1. Create a **ContentHandlerFactory** class and register it using **URLConnection.setContentHandlerFactory**. The custom class creates **ContentHandler** objects based on the data's MIME type.

2. Create the **ContentHandler** object in a separate package. To use this method, you must properly set a special system property.

If you use the first method, you'll write a **createContentHandler** method that creates the correct **ContentHandler**. If you don't want to handle a particular type, return **null** and Java will continue searching for another handler.

Using the second method requires that you put your content handling class in a package. If the MIME type is application/x-example, you'd name your class **application.x_example** (notice the dash becomes an underscore). You also have to set the **java.content.handler.pkgs** system property to point to the package. This list can have more than one item. You separate multiple items with vertical bar characters.

Notice in Listing 11.13 that the program reads the existing property and adds its custom package to the list. This prevents the program from wiping out any custom handlers the end user may have installed. The package name is **com.al_williams.contenthandlers** and the specific class is **com.al_williams. contenthandlers.application.x_jstring**, which corresponds to Listing 11.12.

Listing 11.13   This main program uses a system property to install a content handler and installs a custom connection handler factory.

```
import java.net.*;
import java.io.*;

public class URLStringTest {
    public static void main(String[] args) throws Exception {
// Custom Stream Handler Factory
        URL.setURLStreamHandlerFactory(new StringSHFactory());
        // Add our custom handler
        String path=System.getProperty("java.content.handler.pkgs","");
        if (!path.equals("")) path+="|";
        path+="com.al_williams.contenthandlers";
        System.setProperty("java.content.handler.pkgs",path);

        URL url=new URL("string://www.coriolis.com");
```

```
        Class [] clist = new Class[1];
        clist[0]=String.class;
        String s=(String)url.getContent(clist);
        System.out.println(s);
    }
}
```

Chapter 12

Interpreting HTML

In Depth

Like many authors, I lecture and teach classes on occasion. One thing I've learned is that when dealing with interpreters, it is extremely rude to talk to the interpreter. This is true for foreign language interpreters and sign language interpreters. You talk to the student, not the interpreter.

In previous chapters, the programs mostly dealt with reading or writing data across the network. However, an important component of many programs is to actually understand the data they obtain. Because most of the data you might want to process is in Hypertext Markup Language (HTML), it makes sense to study the actual structure and format of HTML along with techniques for parsing it.

Of course, interpreting HTML means different things to different people. At the simplest end, you may just want to display the HTML as a browser would. Programs that are slightly more ambitious may want to extract the underlying text. Smarter programs may want to develop a complete understanding of the document to validate syntax, check links, or transform the document in some way.

Display

Very few people will ever need to write a full-blown HTML rendering program. That's a good thing because the HTML specification is quite complex (and becoming more complex with each revision). Tables, style sheets, and frames would not be simple to implement.

Luckily, you don't have to write the code to display HTML because Java's Swing library already does a credible job of rendering HTML. Most Swing components will accept some HTML as long as you start their text with the **<HTML>** tag. For example:

```
JLabel lbl = new JLabel("<HTML>I'm feeling <B>Bold</B></HTML>");
```

You don't need to end with an **</HTML>** tag, although it is good practice to do so. Some older versions of Java didn't like uppercase tag names in this context, but recent versions handle it with no problems.

However, if you want full rendering of HTML you'll need to use **JEditorPane**. This is a standard Swing component, and you can set it to disallow editing (because you don't want users performing ordinary text editing on Web pages).

Listing 12.1 shows a very simple program that loads some HTML into a **JEditor-Pane** component. Here, the text is hard-coded into the program, but you could just as easily load it from the Web using any of the methods outlined in the last two chapters.

Even if you aren't familiar with Swing, you can still puzzle out the last portion of the program. The **JScrollPane** component adds scrollbars to the HTML display and the **JFrame** object holds everything in a single top-level window.

Listing 12.1   The JEditorPane component can display HTML.

```
import javax.swing.*;


public class ShowHTML {
    public static void main(String [] args) throws Exception {
        JEditorPane editor = new JEditorPane("text/html",
          "<H1>Wow!</H1><P><FONT COLOR=blue>That was easy</FONT></P>");
        editor.setEditable(false);
        JScrollPane pane = new JScrollPane(editor);
        JFrame f = new JFrame("HTML Demo");
        f.setDefaultCloseOperation(JFrame.EXIT_ON_CLOSE);
        f.getContentPane().add(pane);
        f.setSize(800,600);
        f.show();
    }
}
```

Although you could load HTML using any technique and place it in the **JEditor-Pane**, the component can actually do it for you. One of **JEditorPane**'s constructors accepts a URL in the form of a **String** (another version accepts a **URL** object). You can see an example in Listing 12.2.

Listing 12.2   The JEditorPane can directly load a URL.

```
import javax.swing.*;

public class ShowWeb {
    public static void main(String [] args) throws Exception {
    String url="http://www.yahoo.com";
    if (args.length>0) url=args[0];
    JEditorPane editor = new JEditorPane(url);
    editor.setEditable(false);
    JScrollPane pane = new JScrollPane(editor);
    JFrame f = new JFrame("HTML Demo");
    f.setDefaultCloseOperation(JFrame.EXIT_ON_CLOSE);
    f.getContentPane().add(pane);
```

```
      f.setSize(800,600);
      f.show();
   }
}
```

If you experiment with the minibrowser in Listing 12.2, you'll see that hyperlinks don't do anything. In addition, special features such as scripting and animation won't work the way they do on a full-blown browser.

Adding support for hyperlinks is relatively easy. Every time the user's pointer moves over a hyperlink, leaves the area of a hyperlink, or clicks on a hyperlink, the **JEditorPane** can fire an event.

To process this event you have to implement the **HyperlinkListener** interface in one of your classes. You'll pass a reference to an instance of that class to the **JScrollPane**'s **addHyperlinkListener** method. Listing 12.3 shows one possible implementation. I simply added the single method **hyperlinkUpdate** to the existing class. When the method detects hyperlink activation, it calls **setPage** to move to the new page. Because the call to **addHyperLinkListener** requires an object instance, I moved the program's logic from **main** to the **go** method, and then I called **go** from within **main**. Otherwise, this program is very similar to the previous one.

Listing 12.3 You can process hyperlinks with JEditorPane.

```
import javax.swing.*;
import javax.swing.event.*;


public class ShowWeb1 implements HyperlinkListener {
    JEditorPane editor;
    public void hyperlinkUpdate(HyperlinkEvent ev) {
    if (ev.getEventType()==HyperlinkEvent.EventType.ACTIVATED) {
       try {
         editor.setPage(ev.getURL());
       }
       catch (Exception e) {} // what to do?
   }

  }

   public void go(String [] args) throws Exception {
      String url="http://www.yahoo.com";
      if (args.length>0) url=args[0];
      editor = new JEditorPane();
      editor.addHyperlinkListener(this);
```

```
        editor.setEditable(false);
        editor.setPage(url);
        JScrollPane pane = new JScrollPane(editor);
        JFrame f = new JFrame("HTML Demo");
        f.setDefaultCloseOperation(JFrame.EXIT_ON_CLOSE);
        f.getContentPane().add(pane);
        f.setSize(800,600);
        f.show();
    }

    public static void main(String [] args) throws Exception {
        new ShowWeb1().go(args);
    }
}
```

The **JEditorPane** class also contains a **read** method that allows you to read HTML from an **InputStream**. This might be useful in cases where the input is from the network but not directly from a URL.

Processing HTML

Sometimes you'd like to actually read HTML and process individual tags instead of displaying the text. There are several approaches you might take. Of course, you could write a full-blown parser. In fact, the JavaCC tool (a free tool for creating parsers) has several example HTML grammars available. However, using these tools typically requires some knowledge of how parsers work and how to write formal grammars.

As an example, suppose you want to strip fancy formatting from arbitrary Web pages to make them more usable from a personal digital assistant (PDA) or other network appliance with limited display capabilities. You really don't care much about the exact structure of the document—you only need to pick out a few key tags, ignore comments, and extract the text.

Although you could write a full-blown formal grammar and parser, this seems to be overkill in this case. A better solution is to write a simple ad hoc parser that can read the HTML in the same way you might do it by hand. This technique is simpler to understand. The downside is that it can be difficult to get precise results, and making complex changes can be very difficult.

Implementing Ad Hoc

I decided to make the parser accept an **InputStream**. That way, you could parse a file, a Web site, or anything you can convert into an **InputStream**. Just because I wanted an easier way to do things doesn't mean I didn't want to reuse my finished code, so I wrote a general-purpose class that contains all the parsing logic (see Listing 12.4).

Listing 12.4   This class serves as a base class for parsing Web pages in an ad hoc fashion.

```java
import java.io.*;
import java.net.*;
import java.util.*;

public class AHParse {
    int lastchar=-2;
    StringBuffer current;

 public String parse(InputStream is) throws IOException {
    int c;
    int ender='<';
    int endoffset=0;
    boolean intag=false;
    boolean multicomment=false;
    int dashct=0;
    c=lastchar;
    current=new StringBuffer();
    if (c==-2) c=is.read();
    if (c<0) return null;
    if (c=='<') {
        intag=true;
        endoffset=1;
        ender='>';
        current.append((char)c);
        c=is.read();
        if (c=='!') {
        current.append((char)c);
        c=is.read();
        if (c=='-') {
            current.append((char)c);
            c=is.read();
            if (c=='-') multicomment=true;
        }
      }
    }
    // read to end
    while ((c!=ender && !multicomment)||
            (multicomment && c==ender && dashct!=2) ||
            (multicomment && c!=ender)) {
        current.append((char)c);
        c=is.read();
        if (c==-1) {
```

```
        endoffset=0;
        lastchar=-1;
        break;
        }
    if (lastchar=='-') dashct++; else dashct=0;
    lastchar=c;
  }
  while (endoffset--!=0) {
        current.append((char)c);
        lastchar=c=is.read();
  }
  return current.toString();
    }


    public void processURL(String urlstring) throws
       MalformedURLException,IOException {
  URL url=new URL(urlstring);
  InputStream is=url.openStream();
  String token;
  do {
        token=parse(is);
        // pass null to doElement to indicate EOF
        if (!doElement(token)) break;
  } while (token!=null);
  is.close();
    }


    // Override in subclass
  public boolean doElement(String token) {
   if (token==null) return true;
   System.out.println(token);
   System.out.println("###");
   return true; // keep going
    }

 public static void main(String args[]) throws Exception {
   AHParse parser = new AHParse();
   parser.processURL(args[0]);
    }


}
```

When you want to pick apart a Web page, you only need to extend this general-purpose class. You can pass the base class a URL, and it will repeatedly call **doElement** for each tag or text item in the Web page. Of course, that means you'll override **doElement** to perform whatever processing you require. Each call to **doElement** receives a tag or a nontag item (you can tell the difference because the tags start with an angle bracket). At the end, **doElement** receives a **null**, in case you'd like to write any closing information.

So, what are my ad hoc rules for parsing HTML? First, the program examines the first input character to see if it is an angle bracket or not. If it is, the next input token is an HTML tag. If it isn't, then it must be some text. The ender variable changes to signify what character will end this token. In the case of tags, ender is a closing bracket. For anything else, the end character is the open brace (which would signify a tag's beginning).

One problem with writing this sort of parser is that you usually examine one character too many. In other words, the stop character should be the start of the next token. Java has a **PushbackReader** class just for this purpose, but I decided to keep my own score of the last character in the imaginatively named **lastchar** variable.

Ordinary text is easy to read, but tags take a bit more work to identify comments. HTML supports old-style comments that look like this:

```
<! I am an old comment >
```

It also supports newer comments that start with **<!--** and end with **-->**, like this:

```
<!-- I am a newer comment -->
```

The old-style comments are just like any other tag. However, the new-style comments require special handling. The parser reads ahead enough to know what kind of comment it is dealing with and sets **multicomment** accordingly.

Ad Hoc Details

With the preliminary reading done, the parser simply loops until it finds an ending condition. Because of the new-style comments, the **while** loop is a bit more complicated than you would guess:

```
while ((c!=ender && !multicomment)||
       (multicomment && c==ender && dashct!=2) ||
       (multicomment && c!=ender)) {
```

In plain English, the loop continues when **multicomment** is **false** and the end character hasn't been read, or when **multicomment** is true and the end character is not present, or it is present, but the last two characters were not dashes.

Obviously, the code has to count consecutive dashes. It also keeps track of the **endoffset** variable, which indicates if the last character read is part of the token (as is the case with a tag) or the start of the next token. In addition, you'll notice that **lastchar** begins with a value of –2 indicating there was no last character. I'd have used –1, but because that indicates an end of file, I wanted a different value.

To make things more efficient, the code uses a **StringBuffer** to build the token. This is more efficient than a **String** because the code can directly modify the object instead of creating multiple **String** objects.

The **parse** method is all you really need to call from your main program. You can repeatedly call it until it returns **null**. However, I wanted to wrap the entire logic in the base class to avoid rewriting the same code repeatedly for different programs.

The **processURL** method requires a **String** containing the URL you want to parse. It uses the **URL** object's **openStream** method to retrieve an **InputStream** that corresponds to the URL's document. Then it calls **parse** and passes each token— including the final **null**—to the **doElement** routine. By default, this method only prints the token, but you can derive a new class to do anything you'd like. The class also has an example **main** routine, so you can test it from the command line:

```
java AHParse http://www.coriolis.com
```

Using AHParse

My original goal was to strip down complex Web pages into a format more suitable for appliance-style devices. With the HTML parser working, that's a relatively easy job. My plan was to process the page like this:

1. Emit a standard Web page header.
2. Strip JavaScript links.
3. Convert **<TABLE>** and **<TR>** tags to **
** tags.
4. Convert **<TD>** tags to spaces.
5. Translate **<IMG>** tags to special hyperlinks.
6. Ignore everything in **<SCRIPT>** tags.
7. Pass only **<B>**, **<PRE>**, **<P>**, **
, and **<A> tags (and the corresponding close tags).
8. Allow a list of images to block, for example, 1-pixel GIFs (graphics interchange format) used for formatting.

The completed code appears in Listing 12.5. The code is relatively straightforward, with only a few twists. One problem is that HTML is not case sensitive, but some items inside the HTML, such as URLs, are case sensitive. The **doElement** method makes an uppercase copy of the token and uses it when matching text. However, when it extracts a portion of the text, it uses the original string.

If the program passes a particular tag, it should also pass the corresponding closing tag. That's why before checking for a pass-through tag, the program executes the following line:

```
if (tag.charAt(0)=='/') tag=tag.substring(1);
```

That way, the rest of the code can check only for the base tag. In other words, after this line executes, both **A** and **/A** tags will match a test for **A**.

Listing 12.5 The WebParse program converts pages to their bare essence.

```java
import java.util.*;

public class WebParse extends AHParse {
    boolean first=true;
    boolean inscript=false;
    boolean inanchor=false;
    static String page;
    static Properties imageIgnore = new Properties();


    public void doHead() {
      System.out.println("<HTML><HEAD><TITLE>Clip from " + page+"</TITLE>");
      System.out.println("<BASE HREF=\"" + page + "\">");
      System.out.println("</HEAD><BODY>");
    }

    public void doEnd() {
      System.out.println("</BODY></HTML>");
    }


    // Assumes string is upper
    private String extractAttribute(String token,String tag,String defval) {
      String utoken=token.toUpperCase();
      int n=utoken.indexOf(tag),n1,n2;
      if (n==-1) {
        return defval;
      }
      char match = ' ';
      n+=tag.length();
```

```
    if (utoken.charAt(n)=='"') {
      match='"';
      n++;
    } else if (utoken.charAt(n)=='\'') {
      match='\'';
      n++;
  }
      if (match==' ') {
        n1=utoken.indexOf(' ',n);
        n2=utoken.indexOf('>',n);
        if (n1==-1 || (n2!=-1 && n2<n1)) n1=n2;
        }
      else
         n1=utoken.indexOf(match,n);
    if (n1==-1) return token.substring(n);   // technically an error!
    return token.substring(n,n1);
  }

public boolean doElement(String token) {
 if (token==null) {
     doEnd();
     return true;
 }
 if (first) doHead();
 first=false;
 if (token.charAt(0)=='<') {
     // tag
     boolean pass=false;
     String utoken=token.toUpperCase();
     String tag = new StringTokenizer(utoken.substring(1),
                " \t>").nextToken();
     if (tag.equals("A")) {
     String hrefurl=extractAttribute(token,"HREF=","");
     if (!hrefurl.equals("")) {
        if (hrefurl.length()>10 &&
        hrefurl.substring(0,10).compareToIgnoreCase("JAVASCRIPT")==0)
        return true; // ignore javascript links
        }
     inanchor=true;
     }
   if (tag.equals("/A")) inanchor=false;
   if (tag.equals("TABLE")) System.out.println("<BR>");
   if (tag.equals("/TD")) System.out.println("  ");
   if (tag.equals("/TR")) System.out.println("<BR>");
   if (tag.equals("IMG")) {
   int n;
```

```
        String src=extractAttribute(token,"SRC=","");
        if (src.equals("")) return true; // ???
        n=src.lastIndexOf('/');
        String srcbase = n==-1?src:src.substring(n+1);
        if (imageIgnore.get(srcbase)!=null) return true;
        String alt=
              extractAttribute(token,
                     "ALT=",srcbase);
        if (alt.equals("")) alt=srcbase; // real ALT=""
        if (!inanchor) {
            System.out.println("<A HREF=\"" +
                    src + "\">&lt;&lt;&lt;Image: "
                    + alt + "&gt;&gt;&gt;</A>");
        }
        else {
            System.out.println("&lt;&lt;&lt;Image: " + alt +
                    "&gt;&gt;&gt;");
        }
        return true;
        }
        if (tag.equals("SCRIPT")) inscript=true;
        if (tag.equals("/SCRIPT")) inscript=false;
        if (tag.charAt(0)=='/') tag=tag.substring(1);
        if (tag.equals("B")||tag.equals("I")||tag.equals("U")) pass=true;
        if (tag.equals("PRE")) pass=true;
        if (tag.equals("P")) pass=true;
        if (tag.equals("BR")) pass=true;
        if (tag.equals("A")) pass=true;
        if (pass) System.out.println(token);
    }
    else {
        // text
        if (!inscript) System.out.println(token);
    }
    return true;
    }

    public static void main(String [] args) throws Exception {
        page=args[0];
        for (int n=1;n<args.length;n++)
        imageIgnore.put(args[n],"y");
        new WebParse().processURL(page);
    }
}
```

Handling Images

I didn't want images cluttering up the page, but I still wanted users to be able to view an image if they wanted to do so. The solution was to convert **<IMG>** tags to hyperlinks. The program makes the text of the hyperlink equal to the **ALT** attribute of the image, or if there is no **ALT** text, the base name of the image file appears.

One thing I noticed very early was that many sites use spacer graphics that are everywhere on the page but have no meaning in this text-only view. Therefore, I added an ignore list that searches for the base name of the image. If the image name is on the list, the program drops that image from the final output. The program reads the list from any additional command-line arguments.

Another problem with linking to an image is when the image appears in a hyperlink itself. I modified the program to detect when it was in a hyperlink (the **inanchor** flag). When this flag is true, the program doesn't emit a hyperlink for the image, just the image's text. This prevents nested hyperlinks, which can be confusing.

Attribute Parsing

Although **AHParse** does most of the work, one parsing job belongs to the derived class. To properly transform the hyperlinks and images, the program needs to extract attribute values, such as **HREF** and **SRC**. That's the purpose of the **extractAttribute** method. This method requires three arguments: a string, an uppercase attribute name to extract, and a default value used if there is no attribute. So you might write:

```
String hrefurl=extractAttribute(token,"HREF=","NoLink.htm");
```

Notice that the HTML author can provide an empty attribute (such as **HREF=""**), and this will not return the default string because the attribute is not missing—it is simply empty.

Parsing the attribute value is tricky because there are three cases to handle:

- An attribute value with no spaces does not require quotation marks (**HREF=x.htm**).
- The value may be enclosed in single quotes (**HREF='x.htm'**).
- The value may be enclosed in double quotes (**HREF="x.htm"**).

The code assumes that an unquoted attribute will end with a space or a closing bracket. Any quoted attribute should end with a matching quote.

Improving Usability

After experimenting with the **WebParse** class for a while, I started to think about how it could be more useful. Clearly, the logic regarding the hyperlinks and the images can't be easily changed. However, it would be nice if there were an easier way to set what tags the program passes through.

The result was **WebParse2** (see Listing 12.6). This version requires two command-line arguments—the Web site and the name of a property file that contains the tags to pass through. Additional command-line arguments make up the image exclusion list as before.

Listing 12.6   This version of the Web parser is more flexible because it allows you to dynamically select what tags you'd like to pass to the output.

```java
import java.util.*;
import java.io.*;


public class WebParse2 extends AHParse {
    boolean first=true;
    boolean inscript=false;
    boolean inanchor=false;
    static String page;
    static Properties imageIgnore = new Properties();
    static Properties passtag = new Properties();


  public void doHead() {
    System.out.println("<HTML><HEAD><TITLE>Clip from " + page+"</TITLE>");
    System.out.println("<BASE HREF=\"" + page + "\">");
    System.out.println("</HEAD><BODY>");
    }

    public void doEnd() {
      System.out.println("</BODY></HTML>");
    }


    // Assumes string is upper
   private String extractAttribute(String token,String tag,String defval) {
    String utoken=token.toUpperCase();
    int n=utoken.indexOf(tag),n1,n2;
    if (n==-1) {
        return defval;
    }
    char match = ' ';
    n+=tag.length();
```

```
if (utoken.charAt(n)=='"') {
    match='"';
    n++;
} else if (utoken.charAt(n)=='\'') {
    match='\'';
    n++;
}
if (match==' ') {
    n1=utoken.indexOf(' ',n);
    n2=utoken.indexOf('>',n);
    if (n1==-1 || (n2!=-1 && n2<n1)) n1=n2;
    }
else
    n1=utoken.indexOf(match,n);
if (n1==-1) return token.substring(n);   // technically an error!
return token.substring(n,n1);
}

 public boolean doElement(String token) {
if (token==null) {
    doEnd();
    return true;
}
if (first) doHead();
first=false;
if (token.charAt(0)=='<') {
    // tag
    boolean pass=false;
    String utoken=token.toUpperCase();
    String tag = new StringTokenizer(utoken.substring(1),
            " \t>").nextToken();
    if (tag.equals("A")) {
    String hrefurl=extractAttribute(token,"HREF=","");
    if (!hrefurl.equals("")) {
       if (hrefurl.length()>10 &&
           hrefurl.substring(0,10).compareToIgnoreCase("JAVASCRIPT")==0)
         return true; // ignore javascript links
     }
     inanchor=true;
    }
    if (tag.equals("/A")) inanchor=false;
    if (tag.equals("TABLE")) System.out.println("<BR>");
    if (tag.equals("/TD")) System.out.println("  ");
    if (tag.equals("/TR")) System.out.println("<BR>");
    if (tag.equals("IMG")) {
    int n;
```

```
            String src=extractAttribute(token,"SRC=","");
            if (src.equals("")) return true; // ???
            n=src.lastIndexOf('/');
            String srcbase = n==-1?src:src.substring(n+1);
            if (imageIgnore.get(srcbase)!=null) return true;
            String alt=
                extractAttribute(token,
                    "ALT=",srcbase);
            if (alt.equals("")) alt=srcbase; // real ALT=""
            if (!inanchor) {
                System.out.println("<A HREF=\"" +
                    src + "\">&lt;&lt;&lt;Image: "
                    + alt + "&gt;&gt;&gt;</A>");
            }
            else {
                System.out.println("&lt;&lt;&lt;Image: " + alt +
                    "&gt;&gt;&gt;");
            }
            return true;
            }
            if (tag.equals("SCRIPT")) inscript=true;
            if (tag.equals("/SCRIPT")) inscript=false;
            if (tag.charAt(0)=='/') tag=tag.substring(1);
            if (passtag.get(tag)!=null) pass=true;
            if (pass) System.out.println(token);
        }
        else {
            // text
            if (!inscript) System.out.println(token);
        }
        return true;
    }

    public static void main(String [] args) throws Exception {
        page=args[0];
        for (int n=2;n<args.length;n++)
            imageIgnore.put(args[n],"y");
        FileInputStream file=new FileInputStream(args[1]);
        passtag.load(file);
        new WebParse2().processURL(page);
    }
}
```

Swing Revisited

Earlier in this chapter, you saw how to use Swing components to display HTML. It stands to reason that Swing has some method for parsing HTML. If you can figure out how to use the Swing parser, you won't have to write your own.

The **JEditorPane** class uses the **javax.swing.html.HTMLEditorKit.Parser** class to break apart HTML. This class is actually abstract, but the library provides an implementation in the **javax.swing.text.html.parser.ParserDelegator** class.

This class accepts input from a **Reader** stream and searches for any of the following:

- Start tags
- End tags
- Simple tags
- Text
- Comments

These are the portions of an HTML file most likely to be of interest to your program. When the parser locates one of these items, it calls a callback method you provide, so you can take whatever action you'd like.

Tags that the parser doesn't recognize still generate a call as any simple tag. In addition, you can ask the parser for the value of any attributes the tag has (for example, an **HREF** attribute for an **<A>** tag).

Listing 12.7 shows a simple program that uses the Swing parser to generate a Web page containing the links on a specified Web page.

Listing 12.7   This program uses Swing to parse HTML.

```
import javax.swing.text.*;
import javax.swing.text.html.*;
import javax.swing.text.html.parser.*;
import java.net.*;
import java.io.*;



public class LinkPage extends HTMLEditorKit.ParserCallback {

    public void handleStartTag(HTML.Tag t,
             MutableAttributeSet a,
             int pos) {
        if (t== HTML.Tag.A) {
```

```
        System.out.println(
                "<A HREF=\"" +
                a.getAttribute(HTML.Attribute.HREF)+
                "\">" +
                a.getAttribute(HTML.Attribute.HREF) +
                "</A><BR>");
  }
}


  public static void main(String args[]) throws Exception {
    URL url=new URL(args[0]);
    Reader reader = new InputStreamReader((InputStream)url.getContent());
    System.out.println("<HTML><HEAD><TITLE>Links for " + args[0]+
            "</TITLE>");
    System.out.println("<BASE HREF=\"" + args[0] + "\"></HEAD>");
    System.out.println("<BODY>");
    new ParserDelegator().parse(reader, new LinkPage(), false);
    System.out.println("</BODY></HTML>");
  }
}
```

The object extends **HTMLEditorKit.ParserCallback**. Because it only needs to process the **<A>** tag, the subclass only overrides **handleStartTag**. Further, the program only cares about **<A>** tags, so it compares the **HTML.Tag** argument with **HTML.Tag.A**. If there is a match, it examines the provided **MutableAttribute-Set** object to learn the value of the **HREF** attribute.

The **main** routine simply opens a stream to the desired URL, converts it to a **Reader**, and passes it to the **ParserDelegator.parse** method. Aside from some boilerplate text at the start and end of the output, the program creates the output from within the callback routine.

Immediate Solutions

Using HTML with Swing

The Swing library is typically used for programs that require advanced user interfaces. Most Swing components, such as labels, will accept some HTML to change their textual display. For example:

```
JLabel lbl = new JLabel("<HTML><I>Italics are easy</I></HTML>");
```

However, as you'll see in the next section, you can use Swing's **JEditorPane** component to fully display HTML pages.

Displaying HTML with **JEditorPane**

The **JEditorPane** can display complex HTML directly from a URL. You can initialize the component in several ways:

- Create the **JEditorPane** object using a two-argument constructor. The first argument is the MIME type (text/html) and the second argument is the HTML to display.

- Create the **JEditorPane** object using a **URL** object or a **String** that represents the URL.

- Call **setPage** to load a particular URL.

- Call **setContentType** (passing text/html) and then call **setText**.

- Use the **read** method to pass the **JEditorPane** an **InputStream**.

You can find example code in Listings 12.1 and 12.2. The construction of the **JEditorPane** component is straightforward:

```
JEditorPane editor = new JEditorPane(url);
editor.setEditable(false);
```

The **setEditable** call prevents users from changing the contents of the editor.

Displaying HTML with Hyperlinks

If you use a **JEditorPane** to display HTML, you may want to react to hyperlinks—something the standard component does not do. You can provide an object that implements **HyperlinkListener** to perform actions when the user's pointer moves into a hyperlink area, moves out of the area, or activates the hyperlink.

This interface only has a single method, **hyperlinkUpdate**. This method receives a single argument, a **HyperlinkEvent** object. Using this object, you can learn the URL of the hyperlink and what event the editor is reporting. Here is an example of this method:

```
    public void hyperlinkUpdate(HyperlinkEvent ev) {
       if (ev.getEventType()==HyperlinkEvent.EventType.ACTIVATED) {
// perform the action you want when the user clicks the hyperlink
       }
    }
```

The full implementation in Listing 12.3 uses **setPage** to move the display to the new URL.

Using **AHParse**

If you want to garner meaning from an HTML file, you can pick it apart the same way you would if you were reading it yourself. This type of parsing—often called ad hoc parsing—is simple to understand and implement. Listing 12.4 shows one possible implementation.

In the following manner, the **AHParse** class takes HTML files apart, correctly accounting for quoted strings and comments:

- Each HTML element the parser encounters causes a call to **doElement**.
- The code in this method can distinguish between tags and ordinary text because tags begin with an angle bracket.
- When the file is complete, the parser calls **doElement** with a **null**.

To create a program that parses an HTML file, you'll only have to extend the **AHParse** class:

```
public class myParser extends AHParse {  . . .
```

In the subclass, you'll implement a **doElement** method that performs whatever tasks you need. Listings 12.5 and 12.6 show an example that strips complex pages into simpler, yet equivalent, pages.

12. Interpreting HTML

Parsing Tags with Swing

The Swing library provides an HTML parser that Swing components use internally. However, you can also use this parser if you know how to make it work. The class that Swing uses as a parser is **javax.swing.text.html.parser. ParserDelegator**. It accepts input from a **Reader** stream and searches for various portions of the HTML document. When it finds an element it calls a corresponding method in a class you provide:

- *Start tags*—**handleStartTag**
- *End tags*—**handleEndTag**
- *Simple tags*—**handleSimpleTag**
- *Text*—**handleText**
- *Comments*—**handleComment**
- *Errors*—**handleError**

Listing 12.8 shows an example that reports on the various elements in a Web page. You'll notice that the Swing parser treats unknown tags as simple tags, even if they really have a closing tag. Another oddity is that the parser adds tags to form a correct document. For example, if the document does not have **<HTML>** or **<BODY>** tags, the parser will generate these tags and report them even though they don't actually appear in the document.

Listing 12.8   This program prints a report about various elements in a Web page.

```
import javax.swing.text.*;
import javax.swing.text.html.*;
import javax.swing.text.html.parser.*;
import java.net.*;
import java.io.*;



public class HTMLParse extends HTMLEditorKit.ParserCallback {
    public void handleText(char[] data, int pos) {
      System.out.println(data);
    }

    public void handleStartTag(HTML.Tag t,
            MutableAttributeSet a,
            int pos) {
      System.out.println("+" + t.toString());
    }
```

```
    public void handleSimpleTag(HTML.Tag t,
          MutableAttributeSet a,
          int pos) {
      System.out.println("*" + t.toString());
    }


    public void handleEndTag(HTML.Tag t, int pos) {
        System.out.println("-" + t.toString());
    }


    public static void main(String args[]) throws Exception {
    URL url=new URL(args[0]);
    Reader reader = new InputStreamReader((InputStream)url.getContent());
    new ParserDelegator().parse(reader, new HTMLParse(), false);
    }
}
```

Parsing Attributes with Swing

Some tags, of course, have attributes. For example, the **<IMG>** tag has a **SRC** attribute that names the file that contains the image. The **handleStartTag** and **handleSimpleTag** methods both receive a **MutableAttributeSet** object that you can use to find the value of the attributes. For example:

```
    public void handleStartTag(HTML.Tag t,
             MutableAttributeSet a,
             int pos) {
    if (t== HTML.Tag.IMG) {
      System.out.println(
             "Source = " +
             a.getAttribute(HTML.Attribute.SRC));
      }
    }
```

In addition to the normal HTML attributes, the parser adds additional attributes to impart information about the parse process you may need to know. For example, when the parser generates artificial tags to stand in for missing tags, it sets the **ParserCallback.IMPLIED** attribute. An unknown ending tag will have the **HTML.Attribute.ENDTAG** attribute.

Parsing Text with Swing

Although you often think of using the Swing parser to decode tags, the Swing parser will also retrieve the text an HTML document contains. You simply provide an implementation of **handleText** in your **ParserCallback**-derived class. Listing 12.9 shows a simple example.

Listing 12.9   Extracting the text from an HTML document.

```
import javax.swing.text.*;
import javax.swing.text.html.*;
import javax.swing.text.html.parser.*;
import java.net.*;
import java.io.*;



public class TextOnly extends HTMLEditorKit.ParserCallback {
    public void handleText(char[] data, int pos) {
        System.out.println(data);
    }

    public static void main(String args[]) throws Exception {
        URL url=new URL(args[0]);
        Reader reader = new InputStreamReader((InputStream)url.getContent());
        new ParserDelegator().parse(reader, new TextOnly(), false);
    }
}
```

Chapter 13

Serving HTML

In Depth

Reese's Peanut Butter Cups—a long-time product of the Hershey company—has a famous ad campaign where a chocolate lover and a peanut butter lover collide and make history. I doubt that collision really happened, but it might have happened for the World Wide Web. The Web is the conjunction of two old technologies: networking and hypertext.

Talk to your nontechnical neighbor or relative and you may find they think the Web *is* the Internet. Of course, the Internet predates the Web by many years. Vannevar Bush first envisioned hypertext in 1945. These ideas are not new. Sure, more people are on the Internet now than in, say, 1976, and therefore more information is available online. However, the Web did not enable people to share new information. It only allowed them to share information very easily.

There is no doubt that the Web made the Internet accessible and did a lot to fuel its explosive growth. What's interesting, though, is that most of the complexity is really on the client side of the equation. Clients (that is, Web browsers) have to handle display formatting, hyperlinks, style sheets, and a myriad of other issues. The simplest server just accepts requests and sends files with a few basic headers.

Of course, a modern server might have to do much more than that. Today's servers can incorporate scripting languages, security features, and interfaces to complex transaction management systems. In addition, for high-volume Web servers, performance can be critical.

It is unlikely you'll have to write a large, full-featured Web server. Plenty of them are available from major vendors, and several popular ones are free. However, knowing how to write small Web servers can be useful. Specialized servers can fulfill many roles and even help you debug large systems.

If you think you want to write a Web server, your first question should be: "Do I have to?" Many Web servers now support Java Server Pages (JSP) and servlets. With JSP and servlets, you can write small Java programs that run as part of the existing Web server. Often this will let you do what you want without having to duplicate the server's core logic.

Still, there are times you'll want to write a server or use an open source server for a special task. Luckily, a simple Web server isn't that complex, as you'll see in this chapter.

About JSP

One of Java's biggest strengths is also its primary weakness: It runs everywhere. Sure, Java's cross-platform agility makes it attractive, but it also requires that every user have a properly installed Java virtual machine (JVM) that operates the way you expect it to work. Sometimes this can be a tall order. Does the user have Swing or the latest version of JVM? I recently worked through the process of signing a Java applet and found that every Web browser requires a different procedure—and some don't allow signing at all.

You can control these platform problems by running all your Java code yourself—that is, by using Java to generate HTML pages and serve them to the clients. Such server-side programming, whether with Java or other technologies, has become the technique of choice for many Web sites. Because you don't have to concern yourself with compatibility issues in each individual browser, you can control the environment and ensure that your programs will run correctly.

One way to incorporate Java into your Web server is to use servlets. However, servlets are specialized Java programs (similar to an applet on the client side), and that makes them somewhat complex to write.

That's where JSP enters the picture. JSP lets you write scripts that interweave Java code and HTML. The server—or a special extension to the server—compiles the JSP file into a servlet as needed. This is the easy way to use servlets—almost anyone can create JSPs. The JSP system compiles the page into a servlet.

Suppose you want to create a simple template system that converts formatted text documents into Web pages so that they have a consistent appearance. The system would let content developers focus on the information on the page, while a central authority determines the overall layout and design.

If you run a Web site for a club, school, or even a business in which people want to create their own content, but you want to enforce a particular style on the site, this would be ideal. By combining JSP with a system to let users upload their own files, you can easily make a club membership roster, or other similar sites.

With a few modifications, you also can make this into an online catalog, driven by files or a database. Of course, you'd need a little extra data. The first few lines of the file can specify the item's picture file, the price, and other catalog-related data. You can even arrange to parse Extensible Markup Language (XML) to generate the catalog pages.

What You Need

If you want to get started with server-side Java, you need a Web host that supports JSP. Luckily, nearly all servers have some way to incorporate JSP. However, you may be nervous about trying it on your production server. If this is the case, get a copy of Microsoft's Personal Web Server (free with Windows 98) and add Allaire's demo version of JRun (also free). This will be a good start for testing JSP, but you won't want to run a real Web site with these tools because there are limits on the number of simultaneous connections you can serve. However, this is perfectly adequate for development—and you can't beat the price.

A number of JSP add-ons are available for other servers—many of them free. You can find a comprehensive list at **www.serverpages.com**. Even the famous GNU project has a JSP package that works with many popular servlet add-ons (such as **JServe** for Apache). Tomcat, from the Apache project, is also very popular.

Ready, Set, . . .

Once you have your server ready to handle JSP, you can try writing a simple JSP script. Keep in mind that JSP pages go through the regular Java compiler. (And don't get confused: This isn't JavaScript—it's the real deal.) Create a file name test0.jsp that includes all of the following code:

```
<%
   java.util.Date dt = new java.util.Date();
   out.println(dt.toString());
%>
```

If you think this looks suspiciously like Microsoft's Active Server Pages (ASP), you're right. JSP and ASP have striking similarities (read about them at **http://java.sun.com/products/jsp/jsp-asp.html**). But although ASP interprets JavaScript, VBScript, or PerlScript, JSP compiles real Java code.

You can guess what the test0.jsp file does. Creating a new **Date** object with the default constructor lets you access the current time and date. Using **toString** converts that time and date into a human-readable string. The **out** object is one of several built-in objects that you can use when writing JSP scripts. As the name suggests, the **out** object lets you output Hypertext Markup Language (HTML) code from your script.

Notice that the JSP file contains both Java and HTML. By the time the browser sees the file, however, there's nothing but HTML left. You can even mix Java and HTML, like this:

```
<%
  java.util.Date dt = new java.util.Date();
  out.println(dt.toString());
  int n=dt.getDay();
%>
<BR>
<%

  if (n==0) {
%>
    The <b>weekend</b> is almost over!
<%
    }

  else if (n==6) {
%>
    The <b>weekend<b> is here!
<%
      }

  else if (n==5) {
%>
  TGIF
<%
      }
  else
      {
%>
  Another weekday
<%
    }

%>
```

This JSP script greets the user with a time-specific message (of course, that's the time on the server, not the machine that's running the browser).

A Useful Project

Armed with JSP, it's fairly simple to serve content from ordinary files. The heart of the system is index.jsp (see Listing 13.1). This page is practically a microserver by itself. It examines the **doc** query string to determine which document to display (or uses index.txt by default). It opens the document and displays it in a predetermined format.

Listing 13.1   This JSP serves pages using text files and a predefined layout.

```
<%@ page import="java.io.*" %>
<%@ page import="java.util.*" %>
<%
  FileReader r;
  String s;
  String errm = ""; // error message?
// find file name
  String doc= request.getParameter("doc");
// if no doc use index.txt
  if (doc==null) doc="index.txt";
  try {
      r = new FileReader(application.getRealPath(doc));
    }
  catch (IOException e) {
// whoops set error message and open error.txt instead.
    errm = e.getMessage();
    r = new FileReader(application.getRealPath("error.txt"));
    }
  BufferedReader br=new BufferedReader(r);
  s=br.readLine();  // get title
%>
<html>
<head>
<title><%= s %></title>
</head>
<body bgcolor=#FFFFF0>
<H1><%= s %></H1>
<%
 if (errm!="") {
   out.println(errm);
   out.println("<BR>");
   }
 boolean ul=false;
 do {
   s=br.readLine();
   if (s!=null && s.length()!=0) {
     if (s.charAt(0)=='*') {
       if (!ul) out.println("<UL>");
       ul=true;
       out.println("<LI>");
       s=s.substring(1);
       }
     else if (ul==true) {
       ul=false;
```

```
        out.println("</UL>");
        }
    }
   if (s!=null) out.println(s);
   } while (s!=null);
 r.close();
// produce footer
%>
<hr>
<%= new Date().toString() %><BR>

</body>
</html>
```

The document files are plain text files that hold your content. The first line is parsed by the JSP script and used as the title of the resulting Web page. The remainder of the document file is just ordinary HTML, with the exception that you can't use major tags such as **<HTML>**, **<HEAD>**, or **<BODY>**. These tags all help define the structure of a document, but because the JSP script will do that for us, we don't need or want them in the document file. Other than that, you can use tags such as **<P>** and **
** for basic document formatting. The script itself does not respect line breaks in the document file—which is no different from the way browsers treat HTML files—but it would be easy to modify index.jsp to do so, if you wanted it to work that way.

The only out-of-the-ordinary processing the JSP file performs on the file itself is when it detects a line that starts with an asterisk. It treats any such line as part of a bulleted list and emits the proper HTML. You can make any number of changes to the index.jsp file to change the appearance of the page or the way the script processes the file.

If you're accustomed to dealing with applets, you might be surprised to find that the JSP script can read files. Remember, the JSP script turns into a regular Java program that runs on your server—not an applet that runs in the browser. That means all the usual security restrictions that apply to applets aren't enforced for JSP scripts (or servlets, for that matter).

Inside index.jsp

Initially, index.jsp attempts to open the document file. To do this, it first needs to read the query string at the end of the requested Uniform Resource Locator (URL). JSP provides an object called **request** that lets you read the query string, form variables, and other things you typically consider as input. The expression **request.getParameter("doc")** returns the document name (which may be empty). In the case of a **null** return, which usually means that the visitor has navigated to a URL that doesn't exist on your site, the code sets the **doc** variable to index.txt, the default document (see Listing 13.2).

Listing 13.2   An example text template.

```
An example page
This page is an example of the JSP presentation framework.
You can <i>still</i> use HTML tags, and in fact you must use
them to create line breaks and other special elements.
<BR>
Features:<BR>
* Central administration of page look and feel
* Addition of standardized headers, footers, or table elements
* Automatic lists (like this one)
<BR>
Have fun! -- Al Williams
<BR>
<A HREF=?doc=test2.txt>Another automatic page</A>
```

If there's data in the **doc** variable, the code constructs a path to the document using **application.getRealPath**. This function takes a document's virtual path (like /test.txt) and returns the physical path (like c:\inetpub\wwwroot\test.txt). The script uses this full path name to construct a **FileReader** object. This call might throw an exception if there are any errors in the file name or in accessing the file. In a normal program or applet, you must write extra code that handles the exception (or at least declare that your function might pass on the error by throwing the exception itself). However, the JSP script runs in a wrapper that catches all exceptions. So if your code throws an exception, the JSP system will report it to the user.

Of course, you can still write code to catch the exception if you don't want the user to see a raw error message, or if for some reason you want to act on the error before continuing. In the case of my script, I've decided to handle exceptions so that I can return the error.txt file—a standard error-handling page—instead of the specified page that the user was trying to find. You can, of course, put anything you want in error.txt to inform the user that an error occurred.

Once the **FileReader** object has been constructed, it points to a file: either the requested file, the default index.txt file, or the error.txt file. The script uses this object to construct a **BufferedReader** object. **BufferedReader** has a **readLine** method that picks up lines from the file one at a time.

The first line that the script reads is considered the title for the resulting HTML page. The script writes this line inside the **<TITLE>** tag and also in the body of the page, using an **<H1>** tag. For both of these tasks, my script makes use of a special JSP tag, **<%= %>**. Using this tag in a JSP script is similar to using **out.println**.

Whatever lies between the **<%=** and the closing **%>** tags will be evaluated and will appear in the resulting HTML. Note that you don't have to use semicolons at the end of the expression, and there can only be one expression within the tag.

After the script outputs the title, it outputs any error messages that might have been produced when opening the **FileReader** object. Once this preamble is complete, the script walks through the file line by line. If a line begins with an asterisk, the script begins a new list with the **<UL>** tag (unless there's already a list in progress—then it just continues the current list). The script also emits a **<LI>** tag for each line that begins with an asterisk. If the script comes across a line that doesn't start with an asterisk, it assumes that the list is finished and prints a closing **</UL>** tag.

Once the script processes all the lines, it writes out a footer consisting of a horizontal rule (**<HR>**) and the current date and time. Of course, you could change this, which is the entire point of the script—to let you easily customize the appearance of the template that's applied to each page.

Custom Servers in Tandem

In Chapter 10 we looked at how to write custom servers in Java that can handle specialized tasks on behalf of a Java applet. The example program, a tic-tac-toe game, used a custom server to connect applets on different machines.

This works well for applets, but sometimes an applet isn't the best answer to a problem. In client/server programming today, it's clear that the Web browser is the ultimate client. Not only does everyone have a Web browser these days but also big companies like Microsoft are pouring tremendous sums of money into their development. It's unlikely that on my budget I'm going to come up with a piece of client software to rival Microsoft's or Netscape's.

Consider a very simple case. Suppose your sales force wants to enter orders on a personal computer for input into an order-entry system on a mainframe. Of course, there are various ways to do this, but to keep things simple, further suppose that you want to save the input to some comma-delimited files on the server. Perhaps the mainframe will read them as a batch.

This isn't very hard. You could do it with Perl, of course, or any Common Gateway Interface (CGI)-scripting language. Active Server Pages (ASP) would work and so would Java servlets. However, all of these methods presuppose one thing: that you can connect to a server. In other words, as long as the salespeople are in the office (and the network is up), no problem. But what happens if they're in the field and don't have a connection to the server?

In this case, the client software should write to a local file on the user's hard disk. Sounds good, but how? A normal Web page—including normal applets—can't write to a user's hard disk. You can sign the applet, but then it needs to perform two separate functions: write to the server using a network connection (and a custom server) and write to the hard disk. That also assumes that the user allows signed applets to write to the disk, which is not always true.

ActiveX would work but, for the most part, only with Internet Explorer. How can you design a simple way to store files on the server or the local disk?

One possible answer is to write a custom Web server on the client computer. This isn't nearly as far out as it sounds at first. Java does most of the work in managing a network connection. What's more, plenty of example servers are floating around on the Web. Your only task would be to make the server do whatever specialized processing you require. When you run with the network, you use the regular server, but when you run without the network, you can use the local server.

Why not use a regular Web server locally? First, a complete server is usually more software than a laptop user wants to install. Then there are the maintenance and licensing headaches. If it's easy enough to roll your own, why not?

Don't get the wrong idea. You probably won't take the time to write a Web server that rivals Apache or WebSphere, but then again, do you really need to do that? Probably not.

The Plan

To keep things simple, I drew up a few ground rules for the server. First, it didn't need to support scripting, CGI, or the **POST** method, just the good old-fashioned Hypertext Transport Protocol (HTTP) 1.0 **GET** method. Second, I wanted the server to recognize requests for CGI scripts and do the processing in Java instead. Obviously, if you can add general-purpose functions to the server easily, that's even better.

My pseudo-CGI script simply looks for a form entry named **Filename** (case is important). If the script finds this entry, it assumes that it should write out all the other entries in a comma-delimited format, appending it to the file named in **Filename**. Usually, **Filename** will be a hidden field on a form and set to some appropriate value by JavaScript running on the browser.

Step 1: Stand on Someone's Shoulders

One great thing about the Internet is that someone has probably already written everything you can imagine. If you can "beg, borrow, steal," or even buy it from them, that makes sense. A quick search on AltaVista turned up dozens of candidates. The Sun Java Server exists, of course, but it's too complicated and more than we need.

However, I found a plethora of examples written for books, college classes, and the like. After examining a few, I decided I liked the one at **richard5.net/projects/ webster.php3**. The server's name is Webster. It didn't do everything I wanted it to do, but it was a good start. Besides, the author lets you copy it under the GNU public license, so you can reuse it with no trouble.

The server's code is remarkably short—fewer than 150 lines (even fewer if you take out blank lines and comments). However, the server doesn't correctly handle URL encoding (the process that browsers use to transform certain characters into their hex equivalents). This is not hard to fix.

Configuring the server depends on two files: server.properties and mimetypes. properties. The server.properties file sets the root directory for the server, the port number, and the default server file. The mimetypes.properties file sets the relationship between file extensions and document types (for example, .txt is text/plain and .htm is text/html).

The server.properties file can contain any of the following keys:

- **portnumber**—The port number for the server

- **root**—The document directory

- **defaultfile**—The file to use when the browser requests a directory

Here's a simple example of mimetypes.properties file:

```
htm=text/html
html=text/html
jpg=image/jpeg
jpeg=image/jpeg
gif=image/gif
```

Of course, you can add more types as you need them.

Step 2: Make Changes

To press the Webster code into service, I wanted to add four things:

- Correct handling of URL encoded strings

- Parsing of the query string passed to the server (for example, as part of a **FORM** with a **GET** action)

- A function you could override to perform work after parsing the file name and query string, but before sending the file to the client

- Handling of simple HTTP requests

The first change was easy enough. Although the **URL** object has a method for encoding strings, it doesn't do the reverse decoding. It's simple enough, however, to scan through the string to replace plus signs with spaces and hex sequences (that is, hex numbers preceded by percent signs) with the correct equivalent. You can find the **URLDecode** method (along with the rest of the server code) in Listing 13.3, the **HttpServer** class.

Listing 13.3   A base class for HTTP servers.

```
// Small HTTP Server by Al Williams
// This code is based on the Webster server at
// http://richard5.net/projects/webster.php3
// which is covered by the GNU General Public License
// detailed at http://www.gnu.org/copyleft/gpl.html

import java.net.*;
import java.io.*;
import java.util.*;

public class HttpServer implements Runnable {

    private ServerSocket ss;
    boolean simple;  // simple request?
    private Thread runner=null;

    // The server's configuration information is stored in these properties
    protected static Properties props = new Properties();

    // The mime types information is stored in this properties list
    protected static Properties MimeTypes = new Properties();


    HttpServer() {    // main constructor
        runner = new Thread(this);
        runner.start();
    }

    public static void main(String[] args) {
        new HttpServer();
    }

    // override this to provide an action
    public String action(String filename, Hashtable vars) {
        System.out.println("Serving: "+filename + " " + vars);
        return filename;
    }

  // override this if you want to provide a raw file
```

13. Serving HTML

```java
public DataInputStream openFile(String filename, Hashtable vars)
   throws IOException {
      return new DataInputStream(
        new BufferedInputStream (new
        FileInputStream(fullFileName(filename))));
      }

public String fullFileName(String filename) {
  return HttpServer.props.getProperty("root") +
    filename;
  }

  public void run() {
      try{
          loadProps();
          loadMimes();
          System.out.println("HttpServer listening on port:" +
                      props.getProperty("portnumber"));
          // setup serversocket
          ss = new ServerSocket( (new Integer(props.getProperty
                              ("portnumber"))).intValue() );
          while(true) {
              Socket s = ss.accept(); // accept incoming requests
              new Thread(new SendFile(this,s)).start();
          }
      } catch(Exception e) {
          System.out.println("Main Serve thread " + e );
      }
  }

  // load the properties file
  static void loadProps() throws IOException {
      File f = new File("server.properties");
      if (f.exists()) {
          InputStream is =
              new BufferedInputStream(new FileInputStream(f));
          props.load(is);
          is.close();
      }
  } // end of loadProps

  // load the properties file
  static void loadMimes() throws IOException {
      File f = new File("mimetypes.properties");
```

13. Serving HTML

```
              if (f.exists()) {
                  InputStream is =
                        new BufferedInputStream(new FileInputStream(f));
                  MimeTypes.load(is);
                  is.close();
              }
         }   // end of loadMimes

    }   // end of Serve class

class SendFile implements Runnable{
    private Socket client;
    private String fileName,header;
    private String query;
    private DataInputStream requestedFile;
    private int fileLength;
    private HttpServer svr;


    SendFile(HttpServer svr,Socket s) {   // constructor
        client = s;
        this.svr=svr;
    }

    public void run() {
        String line;
        try {
            BufferedReader dis =
                  new BufferedReader(new InputStreamReader
                                              (client.getInputStream()));
            // read request from browser and parse
            while((line=dis.readLine())!=null) {
                StringTokenizer tokenizer = new StringTokenizer(line," ");
                if (!tokenizer.hasMoreTokens()) break;
                if (tokenizer.nextToken().equals("GET")) {
                    fileName = tokenizer.nextToken();
                    if (fileName.endsWith("/")) {
                        fileName = fileName +
                              HttpServer.props.getProperty("defaultfile");
                    } else {
                        fileName = fileName.substring(1);
                    }
                  String type;
                try {
                    type=tokenizer.nextToken();
                    }
```

```
        catch (NoSuchElementException nsee)
          {
          type=null;
          }
        svr.simple=type==null;
        if (svr.simple) break;
        }
}
if (fileName.charAt(0)!='/') fileName = "/" + fileName;
int n=fileName.indexOf('?');
if (n!=-1) {
    query=fileName.substring(n+1);
    fileName=fileName.substring(0,n);
}
else
    query="";
fileName=URLDecode(fileName);
// decode query string
Hashtable qvars = new Hashtable(64);
int n0,n1;
do {
    String val,key;
    n0=query.indexOf('&');
    if (n0==-1) n0=query.length();
    if (n0<=0) break;
    String vpart = query.substring(0,n0);
    if (n0==query.length()) query="";
    else query=query.substring(n0+1);
    n1=vpart.indexOf('=');
    if (n1==-1) {
        val="";
        key=vpart;
    } else {
        val = vpart.substring(n1+1);
        key = vpart.substring(0,n1);
    }
    qvars.put(URLDecode(key),URLDecode(val));
} while (!query.equals(""));
fileName=svr.action(fileName,qvars);
try {
    requestedFile=svr.openFile(fileName,qvars);
    fileLength = requestedFile.available();
    constructHeader();
} catch(IOException e) { // file not found send 404.
    header = "HTTP/1.0 404 File not found\n" +
             "Allow: GET\n" +
```

```
                              "MIME-Version: 1.0\n"+
                              "Server : HttpServer: a Java Local HTTP Server\n"+
                              "\n\n <H1>404 File not Found</H1>\n";
                fileName = null;
            }
            int i;
            DataOutputStream clientStream =
                new DataOutputStream(new BufferedOutputStream(client.
                                        getOutputStream()));
            if (!svr.simple) clientStream.writeBytes(header);
            if (fileName != null) {
                while((i = requestedFile.read()) != -1) {
                    clientStream.writeByte(i);
                }
            }
            clientStream.flush();
            clientStream.close();
            dis.close();
            client.close();
            if (requestedFile!=null) requestedFile.close();
        } catch(Exception e) {
            System.out.print("Error closing Socket\n"+e);
        }
    }


    public String URLDecode(String in)
    {
        StringBuffer out = new StringBuffer(in.length());
        int i = 0;
        int j = 0;
        while (i < in.length())
        {
            char ch = in.charAt(i);    i++;
            if (ch == '+') ch = ' ';
            else if (ch == '%')
            {
                ch = (char) Integer.parseInt(
                                in.substring(i,i+2), 16);
                i+=2;
            }
            out.append(ch);
            j++;
        }
        return new String(out);
    }
```

```
    private void constructHeader() {
        String fileType;
        fileType = fileName.substring(fileName.
                    lastIndexOf(".")+1,fileName.length());
        fileType = HttpServer.MimeTypes.getProperty(fileType);
        header = "HTTP/1.0 200 OK\n" +
                "Allow: GET\nMIME-Version: 1.0\n"+
                "Server : HttpServer : a Java Local HTTP Server\n"+
                "Content-Type: " + fileType + "\n"+
                "Content-Length: " + fileLength +
                "\n\n";
    }
}
```

Parsing the query string seemed a natural place to use a hash table. A **Hashtable** object is—for practical purposes—an associative array. So, given a **Hashtable** name **vars** and a URL of

```
http://host/somefile.htm?Name=Al&Member=Y
```

you'd like to be able to write code like this:

```
if (vars.get("Member").equals("Y")) memberpage();
```

This is a simple matter of working through the string searching for ampersands and equal signs. The URL decoding occurs after parsing so that any equal signs or ampersands in the data remain encoded and don't confuse the parsing code.

Once the program populates the **Hashtable**, it calls the **action** method. The **action** method requires two arguments: the file name, and a **Hashtable** with the query string variables in it. The function returns the file name that the server should deliver to the client. This file name will determine the document's MIME type (from the mimetypes.properties file).

The action function in Listing 13.3 simply prints the contents of both arguments to the Java console and returns the same file name that the server passed to it. However, classes that extend the server class will provide more meaningful implementations of action.

In addition to the **action** method, the new code supplies another method you can override, **openFile**. This method takes the same arguments as **action** but returns a **DataInputStream**. The server uses a **Stream** instead of a **Reader** because the Web server only returns bytes anyway.

The final change uses the new **simple** variable. If there is any third identifier on the request line, the server assumes it is some HTTP version number (such as

HTTP/1.0) and sets **simple** to **false**. If there is no third identifier, the server sets **simple** to **true** and doesn't wait for any headers. Also, if **simple** is **true**, the server does not return any headers.

With these changes made, the class becomes a useful base class that you can extend to make customized servers with very little work.

Step 3: The Solution

As you'll recall, the original problem was to save forms into comma-delimited files. Armed with the **HttpServer** class from Listing 13.3, this becomes a trivial task. In Listing 13.4, you'll find the code for **LocalServer**, which does the job.

Listing 13.4   This local server allows a Web page to store files.

```
import HttpServer;
import java.util.*;
import java.io.*;

public class LocalServer extends HttpServer {
    public static void main(String[] args) {
        new LocalServer();
    }


    public String action(String filename, Hashtable vars) {
        String realfile=filename;
        // here we see if there is file name query
        // variable--if there is, we assume
        // this is really the "CGI" file
        if (vars.containsKey("Filename")) {
            try {
                int items=0;
                FileWriter fw =
                    new FileWriter((String)vars.get("Filename"),true);
                vars.remove("Filename");
                Enumeration e=vars.keys();
                while (e.hasMoreElements()) {
                    if (items++!=0) fw.write(",");
                    Object k=e.nextElement();
                    fw.write("\""+k+"\"=\"" + vars.get(k) + "\"");
                }
                fw.write('\n');
                fw.close();
            } catch (IOException e) {
                realfile="error.htm";
            }
        }
```

```
        else
            realfile="/response.htm";
        return realfile;
    }
}
```

The **LocalServer** class contains a **main** routine (so it can execute) and an over-ride of **action**. That's all it needs to perform this simple task. The **action** routine assumes that any page with a **Filename** variable is a pseudoscript. It checks for this using the following line of code:

```
if (vars.containsKey("Filename")) {
```

The keyword **Filename** is case sensitive. Once the program detects this variable it uses it as a file name to open for appending. It also removes the variable from the **Hashtable**, so the program doesn't write this internal variable out to the file.

Opening the file is simple with the **FileWriter** class. This class has a two-argument constructor that takes a file name and a Boolean append flag. Once the object is ready, simple calls to **write** will emit whatever data we want. A call to **close** will close the file.

Because my goal was to support a single user with this server, I took no special care to prevent multiple users from trying to write into the same file at the same time. This wouldn't be hard to add, though. Synchronizing the action method would do the trick (although at the expense of performance).

Once the program opens the file, it enumerates through each key in the **Hashtable** (remember, the **Filename** key is gone). It then writes out a single line for the variables. If the URL was:

```
http://localhost/anything.cgi?Name=Al&Extension=32
```

the program would write:

```
"Name"="Al","Extension"="32"
```

I made no provisions for having quotes inside the data, but it would be simple to replace quotes with \" or "" or whatever syntax you need to accommodate the programs reading the files.

Beyond LocalServer

This simplistic example has a lot of potential for expansion. Using **LocalServer**, you can make any number of derived classes that have their own **action** methods. Of course, you can run only one server on one port at a time, but you can also set a different port in the server.properties file. So, if the port number is 88, you might use the URL **http://localhost:88/foo.txt**.

Here are a few ideas on how you might use the **HttpServer** class:

When a request arrives for a particular file, you could read data from another source (for example, the network or serial port) and deliver that data instead. This would let you show realtime network status, data from sensors, and so on.

You could build on this idea and have **action** call Perl or the shell (using the **exec** method of the **Runtime** object). Then you could write real Perl CGI scripts. This would make the server more like a complete Web server, but at some point you might as well use a complete Web server.

It would be possible to have the server check for the presence of a real network server. If it found the real server, the Java program could issue an HTTP redirect to force the browser to the real page.

A nice feature would be to require the **action** routine to open a byte stream that would be sent to the local server. Because this byte stream would not have to be a file, it would let the **action** routine emit customized data without an intermediate file.

Once you make a simple Web server, you'll find yourself thinking of the Web browser as more of a front end for Java programs. By combining HTML and Java, you'll have a new way to field programs that run over the Web or locally and in a portable manner.

If you know how Web servers work, it isn't very hard to write one. However, one thing that made this project much easier is that I was able to find free, available source code on the Web. Don't forget to survey the Web before you start any project—you might save yourself some work. Even if you don't use the code you find directly, studying it will often be helpful when writing your own code.

Small servers have many uses, and Java makes it very simple to write them. The class I've presented here makes it even easier through Java's object orientation. You simply extend the **HttpServer** class and provide the specifics that you need.

Web by Proxy

Today's workplace is a lot more litigious than it used to be. If you snoop on employees, you might be sued. Then again, you also might be sued if one employee exposes another to offensive material. Beyond the legal issues, monitoring employees raises a number of controversial moral issues. It seems like it's a no-win situation.

Although you can't control everything employees see, you can use a proxy server to control what they access on the Internet while they're at work. For example, proxy servers can block access to certain types of Web site content or even to specific Web sites.

But legal monitoring is just the tip of the iceberg. Essentially, a proxy server acts as an intermediary between a browser and a Web server to process requests the way you want it to. Proxy servers let you perform all kinds of processing on browser requests—processing that's both benign and a bit Orwellian. It can filter out things like advertisements, referrer strings, and cookies, or prefetch and cache Web pages to make dial-up connections faster. Proxy servers can also regulate throughput and track Web access.

Foundations

Regardless of how you decide to use them, proxy servers monitor HTTP traffic like this:

1. An internal Web browser sends a request to the proxy server, which resides on a firewall or gateway computer. The first line of the request contains the desired URL.

2. The proxy server reads, then retrieves the URL and forwards the request to the appropriate destination.

3. The proxy server receives a response from the Internet destination and routes it to the appropriate, internal Web browser.

For example, say an employee attempts to access the application Web site. Without a proxy server, the employee's browser opens a socket to the Web server that hosts that Web site, and data from that Web server travels directly back to the employee's browser. However, if the browser is set to use a proxy server, the request travels to the proxy server. Then, the proxy server retrieves the URL from the first line of the request and opens a socket to the **WebTechniques.com** Web server. When data returns from that Web server, the proxy routes it to the employee's browser.

Some HTTP proxies read header files to control things like caching. For example, the proxy might save (cache) pages so that it can satisfy future requests without accessing the remote server. In this case, the proxy must respect headers that control cache expiration and cache control. Simple proxies don't need to respond to any headers.

Not Just for the Company

Of course, proxy servers aren't just for corporate use. As a developer, I have found that having my own proxy server is useful because it lets me examine the traffic between my browser and a Web server. This can be critical when I'm troubleshooting problems with a Web application. You can even use multiple proxy servers (most proxies let you chain more than one together). For example, one might be the corporate proxy server, and another might be a Java-based proxy server that lets you gather debugging information. Bear in mind, though, that each proxy in the chain costs a little more in terms of performance.

Just a Server

As its name implies, a proxy server is really just a specialized server. Like most servers, if you want it to handle multiple requests, you'll need to use threads. Here's the basic plan:

1. Wait for a connection from a client (a Web browser).

2. Start a new thread to handle the connection.

3. Read the first line of the browser request (the line containing the destination URL).

4. Parse the name and port number of the destination's Web host from the first line of the request.

5. Open a socket to the destination's Web host—or the upstream proxy server, if applicable.

6. Send the first line of the request to the outbound socket.

7. Send the rest of the request to the outbound socket.

8. Send data that returns from the destination's Web host (through the socket) to the requesting browser.

Of course, the details are a bit more complicated. Essentially, there are two major hurdles to overcome: First, it's preferable to read data line by line from the sockets, but that can create a performance bottleneck. Second, you need an efficient way to connect the two sockets. Several ways exist to achieve both goals, each with their own trade-offs. For example, if you filter data (or respond to headers) as it comes in, reading that data line by line may be the best option. Most of the time, however, you'd be better off sending data as soon as it arrives at the proxy server. Also, you could use separate threads for sending and receiving, but creating and destroying lots of threads can cause performance problems. Therefore, I decided to use one thread to handle both sending and receiving for each request and to try to send the data as soon as it arrives at the proxy.

The Example

It's a good idea to make a Java-based, object-oriented proxy server reusable. That way, you can use it for other projects in which you want to process browser requests differently. Of course, you want to balance flexibility with efficiency. To build my proxy server, I created the **HttpProxy** class to extend the **Thread** base class. (See Listing 13.5 for the source code.) My class includes properties that let me customize some of the proxy server's behaviors (see Table 13.1 in "Writing a Proxy Server" later in this chapter).

Listing 13.5 This class can act as a proxy server or can provide a base class for custom proxies.

```
/**************************************
 * Proxy Server Base Class - Williams
 **************************************
*/
import java.net.*;
import java.io.*;

public class HttpProxy extends Thread {
    static public int CONNECT_RETRIES=5;
    static public int CONNECT_PAUSE=5;
    static public int TIMEOUT=50;
    static public int BUFSIZ=1024;
    static public boolean logging = false;
    static public OutputStream log=null;
    // inbound
    protected Socket socket;
    // optional parent proxy
    static private String parent=null;
    static private int parentPort=-1;
    static public void setParentProxy(String name, int pport) {
     parent=name;
     parentPort=pport;
     }

    // Create a proxy thread on a given socket
    public HttpProxy(Socket s) { socket=s; start(); }

    public void writeLog(int c, boolean browser) throws IOException {
      log.write(c);
    }

    public void writeLog(byte[] bytes,int offset, int len,
      boolean browser) throws IOException {
     for (int i=0;i<len;i++) writeLog((int)bytes[offset+i],browser);
    }


    // Subclasses may override
    // By default, just log to stdout
```

```
public String processHostName(String url, String host, int port,
  Socket sock) {
    java.text.DateFormat cal=
      java.text.DateFormat.getDateTimeInstance();
    System.out.println(cal.format(new java.util.Date()) + " - " +
      url + " " + sock.getInetAddress()+"<BR>");
    return host;
}


// Here is the thread that does the work
public void run() {
  String line;
  String host;
  int port=80;
  Socket outbound=null;
  try {
      socket.setSoTimeout(TIMEOUT);
      InputStream is=socket.getInputStream();
      OutputStream os=null;
      try {
        // get request line
        line="";
        host="";
        int state=0;
        boolean space;
        while (true) {
            int c=is.read();
            if (c==-1) break;
            if (logging) writeLog(c,true);
            space=Character.isWhitespace((char)c);
            switch (state) {
            case 0:
              if (space) continue;
                state=1;
            case 1:
              if (space) {
                  state=2;
                  continue;
              }
              line=line+(char)c;
              break;
            case 2:
              if (space) continue; // skip multiple spaces
                  state=3;
```

```
      case 3:
        if (space) {
            state=4; // doesn't really matter
            // isolate just host name
            String host0=host;
            int n;
            n=host.indexOf("//");
            if (n!=-1) host=host.substring(n+2);
            n=host.indexOf('/');
            if (n!=-1) host=host.substring(0,n);
            // need to parse possible port from host
            n=host.indexOf(":");
            if (n!=-1) {
              port=Integer.parseInt(host.substring(n+1));
              host=host.substring(0,n);
            }
            host=processHostName(host0,host,port,socket);
            if (parent!=null) {
              host=parent;
              port=parentPort;
            }
            int retry=CONNECT_RETRIES;
            while (retry--!=0) {
              try {
                  outbound=new Socket(host,port);
                  break;
              } catch (Exception e) { }
              // wait
              Thread.sleep(CONNECT_PAUSE);
            }
            if (outbound==null) break;
            outbound.setSoTimeout(TIMEOUT);
            os=outbound.getOutputStream();
            os.write(line.getBytes());
            os.write(' ');
            os.write(host0.getBytes());
            os.write(' ');
      pipe(is,outbound.getInputStream(),os,socket.getOutputStream());
            break;
        }
        host=host+(char)c;
        break;
      }
  }
}
catch (IOException e) { }
```

```
          } catch (Exception e) { }
          finally {
                  try { socket.close();} catch (Exception e1) {}
                  try { outbound.close();} catch (Exception e2) {}
             }
          }


          void pipe(InputStream is0, InputStream is1,
              OutputStream os0,  OutputStream os1) throws IOException {
            try {
                int ir;
                byte bytes[]=new byte[BUFSIZ];
                while (true) {
                  try {
                      if ((ir=is0.read(bytes))>0) {
                        os0.write(bytes,0,ir);
                        if (logging) writeLog(bytes,0,ir,true);
                      }
                      else if (ir<0)
                        break;
                  } catch (InterruptedIOException e) { }
                  try {
                      if ((ir=is1.read(bytes))>0) {
                        os1.write(bytes,0,ir);
                        if (logging) writeLog(bytes,0,ir,false);
                      }
                      else if (ir<0)
                        break;
                  } catch (InterruptedIOException e) { }
                }
            } catch (Exception e0) {
                System.out.println("Pipe Exception: " + e0);
            }
          }


          static public void startProxy(int port,Class clobj) {
            ServerSocket ssock;
            Socket sock;
              try {
                ssock=new ServerSocket(port);
                while (true) {
                  Class [] sarg = new Class[1];
                  Object [] arg= new Object[1];
                  sarg[0]=Socket.class;
```

```
        try {
            java.lang.reflect.Constructor cons =
              clobj.getDeclaredConstructor(sarg);
            arg[0]=ssock.accept();
// create new HttpProxy or subclass
            cons.newInstance(arg);
            } catch (Exception e) {
          Socket esock = (Socket)arg[0];
          try { esock.close(); } catch (Exception ec) {}
        }
      }
    } catch (IOException e) {
    }
    // if we return something is wrong!
  }


// Very simple test main
    static public void main(String args[]) {
      System.out.println("Starting proxy on port 808<BR>");
      HttpProxy.log=System.out;
      HttpProxy.logging=true;
      HttpProxy.startProxy(808,HttpProxy.class);
      }
    }
```

After the proxy server connects to the Web host, I use a simple loop to relay data between the sockets. A potential problem is that calls to the **read** method can cause your program to block if no data is available, hanging the program. To prevent this from happening, I use the **setSoTimeout** method to set a time-out on the sockets (see Listing 13.5). That way, if one socket isn't active, the other still has a chance to process, and I don't have to create a new thread. For large amounts of data, it might be more efficient to create another thread. But, for smaller amounts, the overhead cost of creating a new thread could negate potential savings.

Listing 13.5 also shows a very simple **main** method you can use to try out the **HttpProxy** class. The bulk of the work occurs in a static method called **start-Proxy**. This method uses an unusual technique to allow its one static member to create an instance of the **HttpProxy** class (or a subclass of it). The idea is to pass a **Class** object into the **startProxy** method. Then, the **startProxy** method uses reflection (a facility in recent versions of Java) and a **getDeclaredConstructor** method to determine which constructor for that **Class** object accepts a **Socket** as an argument. Finally, the **startProxy** method calls the **newInstance** method to create an instance of the object.

This technique lets you extend the **HttpProxy** class without creating a custom version of the **startProxy** method. To find a **Class** object for a particular class type, simply append **.class** to the ordinary name. (If you have an instance of an object, call the **getClass** method instead.) Because you pass the **Class** object to the **startProxy** method, you don't have to make special changes when creating a subclass of **HttpProxy**. (Listing 13.14, in "Writing a Proxy Server" later in this chapter, shows a simple subclassed proxy server.)

The Thread

Like all thread objects, the **HttpProxy** class does its primary work inside the **run** method. The **run** method implements a simple state machine that reads characters one at a time from the Web browser. It continues until it gathers enough information to find the target Web server. Then, **run** opens a socket to this Web server. (If there are multiple proxies chained together, the **run** method opens a socket to the next proxy server in the chain).

After the socket is open, **run** sends the partial request to the socket and calls the **pipe** method. The **pipe** method simply reads and writes between the two sockets with minimal interference.

Customization

There are two ways to use a subclass to customize or leverage a proxy server's behavior—by changing the hostname or by capturing all the data that flows through the proxy. The **processHostName** method lets the proxy examine, and potentially change, the hostname. If logging is enabled, the proxy server calls the **writeLog** method for each character that passes through the proxy.

What you do with that information is up to you—the code can write the data to a log file, send it to the console, or do whatever suits your purposes. A Boolean flag in the **writeLog** output indicates whether it's from a Web browser or a Web host.

What's Next?

Like most tools, proxy servers aren't inherently good or bad. It depends on how you use them. A proxy can invade privacy, but it can also protect your network from snoopers and you from lawsuits.

I like to think of a proxy server as a way to extend a Web browser, even if it's not on the same computer. For example, you could use a proxy to compress data before you send it to the browser. A very sophisticated proxy could even translate from one language to another, manipulating the **accept** headers as it goes.

13. Serving HTML

Auction Servers

Like many people, I've been known to buy and sell things on eBay. Recently, my mother, a relative newcomer to the Web, wanted to buy a few items from the auction site, so I tried to explain the ins and outs of online bidding to her. One of the hardest things to explain to a novice is how people "snipe" auctions—they wait until the last minute to place their bid so that no one has a chance to outbid them. In traditional auctions, of course, this isn't possible—the auction won't close until everyone has had a chance to bid.

Some other auction sites get around this by automatically extending the end of the auction until bidding ceases. However, as my son Patrick points out, it still doesn't quite catch the flavor of a real auction. That got me thinking about implementing a better realtime auction. To solve the problem, I decided to create a live auction environment in which the buyers bid against each other in realtime and where the auction doesn't close until everyone is finished bidding.

Because data is constantly changing in a realtime auction, the system requires a constant connection between the bidding applets and the auction server. To make this possible, I created a custom Java server that interacts with applets running in each buyer's Web browser. Each auction requires a separate server to create a socket and listen for connections. That means that each auction process will have to use a separate port number.

Most of the information about an auction is static (the description, the image, the starting bid), so I decided to use a JSP script to show this content. A simple, static HTML page wouldn't be enough because the page is different for each auction. And having the applet display this information would be more work than it's worth because you'd have to format and lay out all the data. So the system has several parts:

- A custom server
- An applet
- A JSP page on a standard Web server
- A database with the auction data in it

Poor Man's Database

Although the system uses three distinct parts—a Java server, an applet, and a JSP page—they all work in concert. That means the system will require some way to keep the three parts in sync. Ideally, the auction data would reside in a database that's accessible to all three components. However, I wanted to keep things simple, so I opted to use a Java property file. For this purpose, it is all the database you need. Of course, the applet can't read a property file on the Web server, but because it has to communicate with the custom server anyway, I've designed the program so that it gets the data it needs through this second channel.

One advantage to property files is that they're easy to create with an ordinary text editor. It is straightforward to access them from a servlet, which is what JSP files become, or from an ordinary Java application, which I've used for the server. With both techniques, you can write a property file back out to the server if you want to mark the results of the auction.

To access a property file, you create an **InputStream** object (using, for example, **FileInputStream**) and pass it to a **Properties** object's load method. Keep in mind that within a JSP file, you want to open the file relative to the server's root. The trick is to use the **getServletContext** method to retrieve a **ServletContext** object. You can then call the **getResourceAsStream** method to convert a server-relative URL into an input stream.

Listing 13.6 shows an auction property file. The octothorpe (#) character indicates a comment, so the text following it is not really part of the database. The **Description** property can be either text or a relative URL containing the description. If the property begins with a slash, the server assumes it's a URL; otherwise, it treats the property as text.

Listing 13.6   This property file defines a single auction.

```
IMG=http\://www.al-williams.com/wd5gnr/tivo.jpg   # Item image
port=7542                                          # Server port
Description=/auction/tivo.htm                       # Description
StartBid=11.00                                      # Start bid
EndAt=30                                            # Duration (minutes)
title=Phillips\ TiVo\ Digital\ Recorder            # Title
Short=Phillips\ TiVo                                       # Short description
```

A Java Auction Server

The code for the entire server appears in Listing 13.7. Because you'll start the server from the command line, I've implemented the static **main** function. Most of the code in this function initializes variables.

Listing 13.7   The auction server works in conjunction with a JSP and a custom applet.

```
// Auction Server

import java.io.*;
import java.util.*;
import java.net.*;
```

```
public class AuctServer extends Thread
  {
  static String ulist;

  Socket csock;              // the socket
  static Calendar endtime;   // end time of auction
  static float highbid=0.0f; // high bid
  static String bidder;      // high bidder
  static boolean done=false; // finished?
  static String pfn;         // property file name
  static Properties p;       // property database

  public AuctServer(Socket skt) { csock=skt; }

// handle a bid
  synchronized private void bid(String bidid, float bidamt)
  // synchronized
    {
      Calendar cal=Calendar.getInstance();
      long diff;
      System.out.println(bidid + " bids " + bidamt);
    // check for time
      if (cal.after(endtime)) return;   // too late
    // check for bid amount
      if (highbid>=bidamt) return;
    // if all OK set high bid
      System.out.println("High bid: " + bidid + " = " + bidamt);
      highbid=bidamt;
      bidder=bidid;
    //    and adjust time if <60 seconds left
      diff=(endtime.getTime().getTime()-cal.getTime().getTime())/1000;
      if (diff<60) endtime.add(Calendar.SECOND,60);
      // add 1 more minute
    }

// generate status
  synchronized private void status(PrintWriter pw)
    {
      Calendar cal=Calendar.getInstance();
      long diff;
    // check time
      diff=(endtime.getTime().getTime()-cal.getTime().getTime())/1000;
      if (diff<=0 && !done)
        {  // if first time we've noticed we are done, complete auction
        done=true;
```

13. Serving HTML

```
            p.put("HighBid",Float.toString(highbid));
            p.put("HighBidder",bidder);
                System.out.println("Auction complete "+ bidder
                    + " " + highbid);
            try
             {
              p.store(new FileOutputStream(pfn),"");
               // p.save is deprecated!
             } catch (Exception e)
               {
               System.out.println("Error ending auction");
               System.out.println(e.getMessage());
               e.printStackTrace(System.out);
               }
         }
         if (diff<0) diff=0;    // don't return negative time
         pw.print(diff);
         pw.print(":");
         pw.print(highbid);
         pw.print(":");
         pw.print(bidder);
         pw.print("\n");
         pw.flush();
      }


// each client thread runs this code
  public void run()
     {
     String cmd;
     try
       {
       InputStream istream = csock.getInputStream();
       PrintWriter pw = new PrintWriter(csock.getOutputStream());

       OutputStream ostream = csock.getOutputStream();
       BufferedReader br = new
           BufferedReader(new InputStreamReader(istream));
// read commands
       while (true) {
         cmd=br.readLine();
         if (cmd==null) break;    // connection dropped?
         if (cmd.charAt(0)=='S')  // status command
           {
           status(pw);
           }
```

```
        if (cmd.charAt(0)=='B')  // bid
          {
          String id;
          float amt;
          int n;
          n=cmd.indexOf(':');
          id=cmd.substring(1,n);
          amt=Float.valueOf(cmd.substring(n+1)).floatValue();
          bid(id,amt); // parse these out
           status(pw);
           }
         }
      } catch (Exception e) { }
   }

// This is the server's main entry point
  public static void main(String args[]) throws Exception
    {
    ServerSocket sock;
    p=new Properties();
    pfn="auction" + args[0] + ".properties";
    p.load(new FileInputStream(pfn));    // read database

  // compute end time
    endtime=Calendar.getInstance();
    endtime.add(Calendar.MINUTE,
        Integer.parseInt(p.getProperty("EndAt")));

  // create server socket
    sock=new ServerSocket(Integer.parseInt(p.getProperty("port")));

  // accept connections from clients
    while (true) {
      new AuctServer(sock.accept()).start();
      }
    }
  }
```

The **AuctServer** class extends **Thread**, so when this static function creates a new instance, it actually begins a new thread of execution. Static member variables allow all the instances to communicate.

The client (the applet) can send two commands. All commands end with a newline character. The **S** command requires no parameters and causes the server to send back a status string. The **B** command places a bid. Immediately following the **B** is the user's ID, a colon, and the bid amount. This command also sends back the current auction status.

The auction status is a string that the client can use to display the state of the auction. The string has the number of seconds remaining in the auction, a colon, the high bid amount, a colon, and the ID of the high bidder. The status string also ends with a newline character.

Because the **bid** and **status** methods alter shared variables, they require the synchronized attribute. This prevents multiple threads from accessing them at one time and confusing the auction's state.

The server doesn't accept bids after the end of the auction, or if the bid is lower than (or the same as) the current price. However, if there is less than a minute left in an auction and someone bids successfully, the end time increases by a minute. This is equivalent to the "going once, going twice . . ." call in a real auction. It ensures that everyone gets a chance to bid.

The **status** command will not report a negative duration. When the status reads 0 seconds left, the auction is over. The first status request when the auction is over will cause the server to print the results of the auction and save them in the property file.

The server requires you to specify a string on the command line that it uses to find the correct property file. For example, if you put a "1" on the command line, the server uses the auction1.properties file. Because the server's port number is stored in the property file, this lets you run multiple auctions at the same time.

Testing the Server

One of the problems with writing a system with separate pieces is that you need all the pieces to do any real testing. If you're like me, however, the chances of writing each piece correctly on the first try are pretty small.

To help work out those early bugs, I often write small test programs to exercise a part of the program. Because these test programs are quick and simple to write, you can use them to debug the bigger program before going to the next major module. I wrote two very simple programs that serve this purpose: t.java (Listing 13.8) simulates a bid, and ts.java (Listing 13.9) requests status from the server. These programs, along with some temporary **System.out.println** statements in the server, allowed me to get the **AuctServer** object up and running.

Listing 13.8   This program sends test bids to the server.

```
import java.io.*;
import java.util.Properties;
import java.net.*;
```

```
public class t
  {
  static public void main(String args[]) throws Exception
    {
    Socket sock = new Socket("127.0.0.1",7542);
    PrintWriter pw=new PrintWriter(sock.getOutputStream());
    InputStream istream = sock.getInputStream();
    BufferedReader br = new BufferedReader(new InputStreamReader(istream));
    String response;
    pw.print("S\n");
    pw.flush();
    response=br.readLine();
    if (response==null) response="Connection terminated";
    System.out.println(response);
    br.close ();


    }
  }
```

Listing 13.9   This test program queries the server for status.

```
import java.io.*;
import java.util.Properties;
import java.net.*;


public class ts
  {
  static public void main(String args[]) throws Exception
    {
    Socket sock = new Socket("127.0.0.1",7542);
    PrintWriter pw=new PrintWriter(sock.getOutputStream());
    InputStream istream = sock.getInputStream();
    BufferedReader br = new BufferedReader(new InputStreamReader(istream));
    String response;

    pw.print("S\n");
    pw.flush();

    response=br.readLine();
    if (response==null) response="Connection terminated";
    System.out.println(response);
    pw.close();
    br.close();
    }
  }
```

Creating the Applet

Given the specification for the server, the applet almost writes itself. The applet, called client.java (see Listing 13.10), uses several parameters:

- **id**—The user's email
- **port**—The server port to use
- **bgcolor**—The hex color code for the applet background

The applet also uses threads because it polls the server every second that the auction is active. When the auction's duration is zero, the applet stops making status requests. This helps reduce overall server loading.

Listing 13.10   The auction system also uses this applet in addition to the JSP and custom server.

```
// Auction Applet

import java.applet.*;
import java.awt.*;
import java.awt.event.*;
import java.io.*;
import java.net.*;

// parameters
// id = user's email or other id
// port = auction socket
// bgcolor = background color (hex)

public class AuctionApplet extends
    Applet implements Runnable, ActionListener
  {
// User interface elements
  Label hb= new Label("High Bid: ");
  Label hbval = new Label("00.00");
  Label hbidder = new Label("by:");
  Label hbidderval = new Label("                          ");
  Label bidlbl = new Label("Your bid: $");
  TextField bid = new TextField(" 1.00");
  Button bidnow=new Button("Bid");
  Label tleft = new Label("Time Left:");
  Label tleftval = new Label("?????");

// Sockets and streams
  Socket sock;
  PrintWriter pw;
  BufferedReader br;
  String response;
```

```
   boolean auctionactive=true;

// helper: get parameter with default value
  private String getDefParam(String name,String def)
    {
    String rv=getParameter(name);
    if (rv==null) rv=def;
    return rv;
    }

// helper: get integer parameter (with default value)
  private int getIntParam(String name,int radix,int defv)
    {
    int rv=defv;
    String p=getParameter(name);
    if (p!=null)
       try {
       rv=Integer.parseInt(p,radix);
       }
    catch (Exception e)  { }
    return rv;
    }

// parse status response
  private synchronized void status()
    {
     try {
        response=br.readLine();
        }
     catch (Exception e) {  response=null; }
     if (response==null)  {
       tleftval.setText("Error");
       }
     else {
       int seconds;
       String timer;
       float highbid;
       String highbidder;
       String sep;
       int n,n1;
       java.text.NumberFormat fmt=
          java.text.NumberFormat.getCurrencyInstance();
       n=response.indexOf(':');
       seconds=Integer.parseInt(response.substring(0,n));
       if (seconds==0) auctionactive=false;
       n1=response.indexOf(':',n+1);
```

```
            highbid=Float.valueOf(response.substring(n+1,n1)).floatValue();
            highbidder=response.substring(n1+1);
            sep=":";
            if (seconds%60<10) sep=sep+"0";
            timer = Integer.toString(seconds/60)
               +sep+Integer.toString(seconds%60);
            tleftval.setText(timer);
            hbval.setText(fmt.format(highbid));
            hbidderval.setText(highbidder);
            }
        }

// get started
  public void init()
    {
    setLayout(new FlowLayout(FlowLayout.LEFT));
    setBackground(new Color(getIntParam("bgcolor",16,0xFFFFFF)));
// add elements
    add(hb);
    add(hbval);
    add(hbidder);
    add(hbidderval);
    add(bidlbl);
    add(bid);
    add(bidnow);
    add(tleft);
    add(tleftval);
    bidnow.addActionListener(this);
    bid.setText(getDefParam("StartBid","1.00"));
// open up socket
    try
       {
// Important: you must run this via
//    http://somehost to get the following to work
// if you are running from a file, you should
//    hard-code your machine name here!
        sock = new Socket(getDocumentBase().getHost(),
            getIntParam("port",10,0));
        pw=new PrintWriter(sock.getOutputStream());
        br=new BufferedReader(new
            InputStreamReader(sock.getInputStream()));
        new Thread(this).start();  // start status update thread
        }
    catch (Exception e)
       {
       tleftval.setText("Net Error");
```

```
        }
      }

// button pushed?
  public void actionPerformed(ActionEvent e)
    {
    if (auctionactive)
      {
// make bid!
      pw.print("B"+getParameter("ID")+":"+bid.getText()+"\n");
      status();
      }
    }

// thread to wait for 1 second and ask for status
  public void run()
    {
    while (auctionactive)
      {
      pw.print("S\n");
      pw.flush();
      status();
      try {
        Thread.sleep(1000);
        } catch (Exception e) { }
      }
    try
      {
      sock.close();
      }
    catch (Exception e) { }
    }


  public void destroy()
    {
    try
      {
      sock.close();
      }
    catch (Exception e) { }
    }
}
```

The server implements threads by extending the **Thread** class. That's not an option for the applet because it has to extend the **Applet** class. Therefore, the applet implements the **Runnable** class (in other words, it has a **run** method) and creates a new **Thread** object that refers to the applet.

The applet's thread primarily sleeps for a period of one second and then issues a status request. If the user pushes the Bid button, the applet issues a **bid** command to the server.

I deliberately made the applet look like a bar so that it would fit at the bottom of the auction Web page. Of course, you could make the entire page an applet, but that would create problems. For example, it's difficult to show HTML-formatted text in an applet. In a JSP page, it's the simplest thing you can do.

Scripting with JSP

In a real-life system, you'd want to have a mechanism to let your bidders create usernames and validate them in some way. For this example, I simply collect the bidder's name and email address (in index.jsp; Listing 13.11) and assume they are correct. It would also be useful to show a list of current auctions, but for this example, the login always uses an auction ID of 1.

Listing 13.11   Users use this main JSP to access the auction system.

```
<%@ page import="java.io.*" %>
<%@ page import="java.util.Properties" %>


<%!
  String propfile;

  String name;
  String email;
  Properties p;
  InputStream str;
  ServletContext ctx;
%>

<%
  propfile="/auction/auction";
  p=new Properties();
  ctx=getServletContext();
  name=request.getParameter("UName");
  email=request.getParameter("Email");

  if (name==null || name.equals("") || email==null || email.equals("")) {
%>
    <jsp:forward page="index.jsp" >
```

13. Serving HTML

```
        <jsp:param name="err" value="Please enter a valid name and e-mail
address."/>
    </jsp:forward>

<%
    }
  propfile=propfile + request.getParameter("ANO") + ".properties";
  str=ctx.getResourceAsStream(propfile);
  if (str==null)
    out.println("Internal server error:" + propfile );
  else
    {
    p.load(str);
    str.close();
    }


%>
<HTML>
<HEAD><TITLE>Live auction</TITLE></HEAD>
<BODY BGCOLOR=WHITE>
<H1>
 <%= p.getProperty("Short") %>
</H1>
<P ALIGN=CENTER><IMG SRC=<%= p.getProperty("IMG") %>></P>
<P><FONT SIZE=+1>
<%
    String desc;
    desc=p.getProperty("Description");
    if (desc.charAt(0)=='/')
      {
      int c;
      InputStream is=ctx.getResourceAsStream(desc);
      try
       {
       while ((c=is.read())!=-1) {
         out.print((char)c);
         }
       }
      catch (Exception e) { }
      }
    else
      out.println(desc);
%>
<HR>
<P>Starting bid: $<%= p.getProperty("StartBid"); %>
```

```
</P>
<!-- start bidding applet -->
<APPLET code=AuctionApplet.class Width=640 Height=50>
<PARAM name=port Value=<%= p.getProperty("port") %>>
<PARAM name=bgcolor value=FFFFFF>
<PARAM name=ID value='<%= email %>'>
<PARAM name=StartBid value='<%= p.getProperty("StartBid"); %>'>
</APPLET>
</BODY>
</HTML>
```

The main auction page requires a parameter (the **ANO** variable) to tell it which auction to display. The page validates that there is a name and email address present. Next, it opens the property file and reads the information about the auction.

The remainder of the page is simply formatting the information. The only tricky part is when the description property begins with a slash. This indicates it is a URL, not a text string. Once again, the **getResourceAsStream** method converts the URL into an **InputStream** object. From there, it's simple to copy the characters from the stream to the Web browser.

Putting It All Together

Of course, the applet does the real work in the Web page. Note that in the page resulting from the JSP script, the **<APPLET>** tag, causes the browser to load the applet. The script writes several of the applet's properties dynamically into the resulting HTML page.

To test the system yourself, you'll need to follow a few steps:

1. Build a properties file named auctionXX.properties.

2. Start the server with a command line similar to java AuctServer XX. You must start the auction server on the same machine as your Web server because, for security reasons, the applet can connect only to that machine.

3. Change the **ANO=1** parameter to **ANO=XX** in index.jsp.

4. Use a Web browser to view the index.jsp file once it's on your Web server. (I used Allaire's JRun 3.0 and IIS 5.0.)

5. Log in. You may want to log in from several browsers, either from the same machine or from different ones, to simulate a number of bidders at once.

6. Bid away.

The Best Tool

This example illustrates something I've mentioned before: One tool is not always the best way to do everything. This auction application would be difficult to

13. Serving HTML

implement using only JSP scripts. Using applets alone would not work at all (unless they were signed, and even then it would be difficult). And a custom client/server system might work, but it would be much harder to create.

However, combining all three techniques—a Java server, applets, and JSP—results in a nice system that wasn't too hard to develop. Don't be slavish to one tool or technology—it can often make your life harder or even limit what you can do.

13. Serving HTML

Immediate Solutions

Using JSP for Server-Side Processing

When you need to process Web browser requests, your first impulse might be to write a custom server. Although this is one option, it is often more effective to use a commercial server that supports JSP.

A JSP server allows you to extend the Web server using small Java programs called servlets. These are specialized Java programs that can interact with the user's browser. However, because servlets are somewhat complex to write, you can use JSP instead. JSP lets you add bits of Java code into an HTML file. The server compiles the JSP into a servlet and then compiles the servlet into ordinary Java class files. The server can then execute the servlet to handle user requests.

Some JSP servers stand alone. Others are meant to attach to other Web servers. Several popular choices are available to developers:

- *Tomcat*—The Apache project's JSP server
- *JRun*—A JSP server from Allaire that can integrate with most popular servers

Reading Input from a JSP

Like any Web page, a JSP receives input from the browser as either a query string or form data from an HTTP **POST** operation. A query string is one or more variable assignments that appear in a URL following a question mark. For example, consider this URL:

```
http://www.coriolis.com/test.jsp?fname=Nick&lastname=Rivers
```

The entire query string in this case is **fname=Nick&lastname=Rivers**. There are two query string parameters: **fname** and **lastname**. Keep in mind that you must encode any characters that have special meaning within a URL. For example, if you wanted to set a variable named **fullname** to "Nick Rivers," you'd have to encode it as:

```
Fullname=Nick+Rivers
```

The static function **URLEncoder.encode** can perform this style of encoding.

The other way a browser can pass information to a Web page is to use a form and the **POST** method. If you use the **GET** method with a form, the data winds up in the query string of the request.

When using **POST**, the data—still encoded—resides in the content portion of the HTTP request. When using JSP, you can easily read parameters from either a query string or a post. The JSP calls you'll use split the data into separate variables and decode any special encoding.

Here is a snippet of JSP code that reads the **fname** parameter. The JSP searches the form data and the query string. It will return **null** if it can't locate a parameter named **fname**.

```
String usersName = request.getParameter("fname");
```

Writing to the Browser from JSP

When you want to send data back to the browser, you have two options:

- *You can use the **out** object.* The out object refers to a special type of **PrintWriter** that allows you to write to the HTML output stream.

- *You can use a special pair of tags.* You can use the **<%=** and **%>** tags to enclose a single expression that you want to send to the browser.

Which form should you use? It depends. If you are inside a complex portion of code and need to generate output, you'll probably use the **out** object. For example, consider this piece of code from a JSP:

```
<HR>
<%
    int x=func1();
    int y=func2();
    out.println("Result=" + x + " and " + y + "<BR>");
    int z=func3();
    out.println("Z=<B>" + z + "</B><BR>");
%>
```

On the other hand, if the main flow of your page focuses on HTML, you'd probably use the bracket syntax. For example:

```
<% Date today = new Date(); %>
Hello, today is <%= today.toString() %>
```

Using JSP Page Directives

Another special tag is the **<%@** tag. This is useful for introducing **import** statements. For example:

```
<%@ page import="java.io.*" %>
<%@ page import="java.util.*" %>
```

Writing a Simple Web Server

A Web server is no more complex than other servers you've examined in other chapters. The Web server has to perform three basic steps:

1. Receive requests (typically on port 80).

2. Send response headers to the requestor.

3. Send the requested document to the requestor.

For a simple HTTP request, you don't even send headers.

The code in Listing 13.3 is the **HttpServer** class. It performs these steps, and you may use it as a base class for custom servers.

The server only recognizes **GET** requests. It assumes each request will contain two or three parts:

• *Part one*—the word **GET**

• *Part two*—the document the browser is requesting

• *Part three (optional)*—an HTTP version number

The server doesn't actually interpret the third argument. If it is present, then the server assumes the HTTP request version is 1.0 or greater. In this case, the server replies with a 1.0 response (the highest version it supports). If there is no version token, the server assumes the request is a simple HTTP (also known as an HTTP 0.9 request). In this case, the server doesn't accept headers, nor does it produce headers.

Configuring **HttpServer**

The **HttpServer** class can serve as a basis for your own Web server classes. The server relies on two property files to control its operation. The first file, server.properties, can contain three parameters:

13. Serving HTML

- **portnumber**—The port the server listens to for requests

- **root**—The root directory for documents

- **defaultdocument**—The document name used when the browser requests a directory

The second file is mimetypes.properties. This contains keys that show the **Content-Type** header that corresponds to file extensions. For example:

```
htm=text/html
html=text/html
jpg=image/jpeg
jpeg=image/jpeg
gif=image/gif
```

Customizing **HttpServer**

You can easily subclass **HttpServer** to provide custom actions. To simplify reuse, the object provides an **action** routine. A subclass can override this method to provide custom processing.

When the server recognizes a valid request, it calls **action**, passing it two arguments: the file name in the request and a **Hashtable** that contains any query string passed with the request.

Your custom **action** method returns a file name that the server will use as the file to return to the browser. The simplest **action** method returns the file name passed in as an argument. However, the method can also recognize special file names and perform any sort of processing required. Then, if necessary, you can change the file name the server will provide.

For example, consider Listing 13.12. This program recognizes the special document name **time**. The **action** routine writes the current time and day to the time.htm file and serves it instead of the requested file. Here's the code that does the work:

```
if (fn.equals("/time")) {
  PrintWriter tout=
    new PrintWriter(
    new FileWriter(props.getProperty("root")+"/time.htm"));
  Date d=new Date();
  tout.println(d);
  tout.close();
  return "/time.htm";
```

Of course, if many users were asking for the time at once, you might be writing to the time.htm file while someone else is reading from it, and that might cause problems.

Listing 13.12   This server uses a custom action method to handle a time request.

```
// Time Server
// Each request to the special file
// "time" will cause time.htm to
// get the current time and
// then serve that file name
// probably not safe for multiple accesses!
import java.util.*;
import java.io.*;

public class TimeHttp extends HttpServer {
  public String action(String fn, Hashtable vars) {
    try {
      if (fn.equals("/time")) {
        PrintWriter tout=
          new PrintWriter(
          new FileWriter(props.getProperty("root")+"/time.htm"));
        Date d=new Date();
        tout.println(d);
        tout.close();
        return "/time.htm";
        }
      }
    catch (Exception e) {
     System.out.println("Except: " + e);
     return "err.htm"; }
     return fn;
   }

  public static void main(String[] args) {
      new TimeHttp();
  }

 }
```

A better way to supply the time would be to provide a **String** for the server to send. Even then you need to transform the **time** keyword into a .htm file name so the server can correctly guess the MIME type. However, in this case, the server will not actually open the file.

The key to writing this type of server is to use the **openFile** method to provide a **String** for the server to read. Listing 13.13 shows a simple implementation. This program still provides a custom **action** method and marks the process flag **true** if the **openFile** method should provide custom processing.

The real work occurs in **openFile**. When the process flag is **true**, the code builds a **String** with the current time and date and returns a **DataInputStream** that reflects the contents of the **String**. The compiler will complain that **StringBufferInputStream** is deprecated, but because the original server code uses a **DataInputStream**, you can use the newer **StringReader** object without major surgery on the original server code.

If the **process** variable is **false**, the program simply calls the **base class** method. This allows ordinary requests to proceed as before.

Listing 13.13   This server uses a **String** to provide the current time.

```
// This server subclass uses a string to send the browser
// dynamic content
import java.util.*;
import java.io.*;

public class Time1Http extends HttpServer {
  private boolean process=false;  // special request?
  public String action(String fn, Hashtable vars) {
      if (fn.equals("/time")) {
        process=true;
        return "/time.htm"; // fake name
        }
      process=false;
      return fn;
      }


   public DataInputStream openFile(String fn, Hashtable vars)
     throws IOException {
     if (process) {
        String res = new Date().toString();
// StringBufferInputStream is deprecated, but can't use StringReader
// without changing base class
        return new DataInputStream(new StringBufferInputStream(res));
        }
     else
// do original code
        return super.openFile(fn,vars);
     }
```

```
public static void main(String[] args) {
    new Time1Http();
}


}
```

Writing a Proxy Server

The simplest form of proxy server acts as both a Web server and a Web client. When the user instructs the browser to use a proxy, it sends all HTTP requests to the proxy instead of sending it to port 80 of the Web server. The proxy's job is to forward the request to the correct server (unless it won't allow the request). Then, the proxy must also forward the return data from the server back to the client.

This is useful for the following tasks:

- Caching Web server content
- Disallowing access to certain Web sites
- Filtering words from a Web site
- Translating or formatting Web content
- Logging Web accesses

Listing 13.5 shows a base class for a proxy server. You can use this class directly, or you can derive a new class to customize the server's operation. Table 13.1 summarizes the method available.

Table 13.1   The proxy base class provides several useful methods and variables.

Variable/Method	Description
BUFSIZ	Size of the socket input buffer
CONNECT_PAUSE	Amount of time to pause between connection attempts
CONNECT_RETRIES	Number of tries to connect to the remote host before giving up
log	An **OutputStream** object to which the default log routines write logging information
logging	Whether you want the proxy to log all transferred data (**true** indicates yes)
setParentProxy	Lets you chain this proxy server to another (you specify the name and port number of the other proxy server)
TIME-OUT	Amount of time to wait for socket input

13. Serving HTML

To create a customized version of the server, follow these steps:

1. Create a subclass of **HttpProxy**.

2. Provide an override of the **writeLog**, if you wish to log characters. The method receives two arguments: **c** is the character being sent, and the browser flag (a boolean) is **true** if the character is from the browser.

3. Provide an override of **processHostName**. This function receives data about the HTTP request and must return the hostname that should satisfy the request. This method can change the host (although this is unusual) and it can also log the URL the browser is requesting.

4. Write a suitable **main** that calls **startProxy** with the proxy's port number and the derived class object that corresponds to the custom proxy's code.

5. Provide a constructor that properly initializes the base class. Usually, this will be a constructor that takes a **Socket** and simply passes it to the base class constructor via **super**.

You can find an example of a simple custom proxy in Listing 13.14. This proxy doesn't do anything with the hostname, but it does write out characters that it processes.

Listing 13.14 This proxy writes a simple log file.

```java
// Trivial subclass of HttpProxy
// Does not log hostnames and
// puts a * in front of each line of log output

import java.io.*;
import java.net.*;

public class SubHttpProxy extends HttpProxy {
    static private boolean first=true;
    public SubHttpProxy(Socket s) {
      super(s);
      }
    public void writeLog(int c, boolean browser) throws IOException {
      if (first) log.write('*');
      first=false;
      log.write(c);
      if (c=='\n') log.write('*');
    }
    public String processHostName(String url, String host, int port, Socket
sock) {
// do nothing
    return host;
    }
```

```
// Very simple test main
    static public void main(String args[]) {
        System.out.println("Starting Subproxy on port 808<BR>");
        HttpProxy.log=System.out;
        HttpProxy.logging=true;
        HttpProxy.startProxy(808,SubHttpProxy.class);
    }


}
```

Debugging with a Proxy Server

Another use for a proxy server is for debugging Web applications. You can build a simple proxy that echoes all traffic to the console or a file. This allows you to view a complete transcript of the data flowing to and from the server. That data includes cookies and other headers.

As an example, imagine you are troubleshooting an application that uses cookies. It is often difficult to see exactly which cookies the server is setting and those that the browser is receiving. See Chapter 10 for more information about Cookies.

You can write a proxy server that prints out cookies as the server sends them (the **Set-Cookie** header) or as the client returns them to the server (the **Cookie** header). The proxy server appears in Listing 13.15. It builds up two lines (in the **line** array): one line for the data to the browser and another for data from the browser. When the server detects an end-of-line character, it examines the line to see if it might be a cookie-related header.

Listing 13.15   This proxy server displays cookie transactions.

```
// Show cookie headers
import java.io.*;
import java.net.*;

public class CookieProxy extends HttpProxy {
    static private StringBuffer line[];
    public CookieProxy(Socket s) {
        super(s);
        line=new StringBuffer[2];
        line[0]=line[1]=null;
    }
```

13. Serving HTML

```
    public void writeLog(int c, boolean browser) throws IOException {
        int index=browser?1:0;
        if (line[index]==null) line[index]=new StringBuffer();
        if (c=='\r' || c=='\n') {
            // Heuristic guesses when it sees a cookie header
            // not perfect, but good enough
            if (line[index]==null) return; // nothing
            if (line[index].length()<(browser?7:11)) return;

            if (line[index].substring(0,browser?6:10).
              compareToIgnoreCase(browser?"cookie":"set-cookie")==0) {
                System.out.print(browser?"Sent ":"Received ");
                System.out.println(line[index]);
            }
            line[index]=null;
            return;

        }
        line[index].append((char)c);
    }
    public String processHostName(String url, String host, int port,
      Socket sock) {
// do nothing
        return host;
    }
// Very simple test main
    static public void main(String args[]) {
        System.out.println("Starting Cookieproxy on port 808<BR>");
        HttpProxy.log=System.out;
        HttpProxy.logging=true;
        HttpProxy.startProxy(808,CookieProxy.class);
    }


}
```

Because the server is just for debugging, I decided not to overthink the design. The heuristic the server uses for identifying cookie headers could possibly show a few false positives (for example, if the word "Cookie" appeared at the start of a line within the document). In practice, this isn't a problem because you'll rarely get false hits, and it will be obvious to you when you do get one.

WARNING! *A proxy server like this is not especially efficient because it builds up lines one character at a time. For debugging, this isn't a problem. However, you wouldn't want to leave the proxy enabled all the time, unless you enjoy slow Web surfing. Also, the more debugging output you generate, the slower the proxy will operate.*

13. Serving HTML

Of course, the proxy won't work until you follow these steps:

1. Run the proxy server as you would any Java program.

2. Set your browser to use a proxy server and point it at the port the server is using. For recent versions of Internet Explorer, you can use the Tools | Internet Options menu and select the Connections tab. From there, you can enter the proxy's IP address (127.0.0.1 if you are using a single computer) and the port number (808, by default).

With the proxy running, you'll see output on the Java output console that shows you what cookies are sent. For example, here is one from the USA Today Web site:

```
Sent Cookie: RMID=cfdaf5063a37e340
```

Most sites don't set cookies any more often they have to, so you may have to change a customized page or make other changes to a site to see the site send you a cookie. For example, **www.alltheweb.com** sent this cookie when I changed my preferences:

```
Received Set-Cookie: PREF=cs=iso-8859-1:cwo=lang:l=any:no=off;
    expires=Tue, 30 Jul 02 14:29:58 GMT; path=/
```

13. Serving HTML

Chapter 14

XML

In Depth

You can learn a lot by reading science fiction novels. When I was a kid, I read a lot. One of my favorite authors was Harry Harrison. Some of his books are humorous (like the Stainless Steel Rat series). His Eden stories are more serious. The Deathworld trilogy is somewhere in between.

One thing that features prominently in several of Harrison's stories is Esperanto. Esperanto was a language developed by a Dr. Ludwig L. Zamenhof (an eye doctor, if I recall) around 1877. The doctor felt like the world needed a universal language that was easy to learn, easy to spell, and easy to pronounce. The result was Esperanto. For a while, it looked like Esperanto might catch on as a universal second language. Today you don't hear much about Esperanto, but there is a small community of people all around the world who speak it (estimates show it is as common as Hebrew or Lithuanian). There are Esperanto magazines and newspapers and even conferences.

A universal language is bound to draw comparisons to the Web and the Internet. The Internet makes it easy for people all around the world to communicate. However, it doesn't really address making those people understand each other. Hypertext Transport Protocol (HTTP), for example, ensures that you can sit in your living room and load a Web page from Burkina Faso (which, you surely know, is a country in Africa about the size of Colorodo). However, if that page is in a Sudanic dialect (the likely language of a page from Burkina Faso), you probably won't be able to read it.

Although there are some machine translation options (for example, **http://babelfish.altavista.com**), they are less than perfect. For human languages, this is probably the best you can expect for the near future—imperfect translations of major languages (I doubt Babel Fish can translate Sudanic).

For machines, however, it shouldn't be this difficult. Why is it so hard for an IBM mainframe using Database 2 (DB2) to share data with a PC that uses Access? To combat this problem, many applications are turning to Extensible Markup Language (XML). Superficially, XML looks like Hypertext Markup Language (HTML), but there are subtle differences in their syntax.

The big difference, however, is that XML and HTML are not solving the same problem. Many people make the mistake of thinking that because HTML looks similar to XML, the two are closely related. In fact, HTML and XML are completely different things.

HTML, of course, allows you to model a page you'd like to display or print, usually from within a Web browser. For human consumption, this works well because HTML allows you to define headers, hyperlinks, and inline images.

Consider this Web page:

```
<html>
<body>
<h1>Java Network Programming Black Book</h1>
<P>We have 10 of these paperback books by Al Williams.</P>
<h2>Shelving</h2>
<ul>
<li>Computer
<li>Java
<li>Programming
</ul>
</body>
</html>
```

It is obvious—to a human, at least—what this page means. You can easily tell the author's name, that the vendor has 10 books in stock, and that the book is in paperback. What's more, you can see where the vendor thinks the books are shelved.

From a machine's point of view, this page is less than ideal. The **<H1>** tag, for example, obviously introduces the book's title, but—of course—it could represent anything. The data in the main text is free form, and though you could pick apart the meaning by applying some heuristics, any change in the page's contents would confuse most programs.

The problem is that the tags don't convey meaning about the content; they identify parts of the document. The browser wants to know about headings, but programs that interpret data want to know about the content, not the presentation.

Another problem with HTML is that the content and the presentation are intermixed. Suppose you have a series of Web pages that contain many books, with one file corresponding to one book. What if you want to generate a list of those books? Or perhaps you want to strip information from the file to play over a telephone using text-to-speech technology?

Enter XML

XML attempts to solve these problems by focusing on representing data. If you want to display the data, you need something that tells the browser (or the server) how to format that data. The formatting is not important to XML.

XML does use a tag structure similar to HTML. However, it has practically no pre-defined tags. You (and the recipient of the data) define your own tags. Listing 14.1 shows a simple XML document:

Listing 14.1   This simple XML file describes this book.

```
<?xml version='1.0' encoding='UTF-8'?>
<book title="Java Network Programming Black Book" author="Al Williams">
    <quantity>10</quantity>
    <paperback/>
    <shelving>
      <shelve>Computer</shelve>
      <shelve>Java</shelve>
      <shelve>Programming</shelve>
    </shelving>
</book>
```

This document contains all the same information as the HTML example. However, it is in an unambiguous format. Assuming the program reading this file is aware of the tags employed, it can easily cull the data about this book.

If you try to view the XML file in an XML-aware Web browser, you'll see a display of the source code with color-coded elements and level indentations—not something a user will want to view. There are ways to use special style sheets to display the XML file in different ways, but most people use a special formatting language known as Extensible Style Language (XSL) to do that task.

XML Syntax

Listing 14.1 almost looks like an HTML file with unusual tags. However, there are a few key points about the syntax that may not be apparent from a quick glance:

- *The first line is a <?xml> tag.* This tag identifies the file as an XML document and the version of XML that it uses.

- *The first tag is the root tag of the document.* This is similar to an **<HTML>** tag because it is the tag that contains all of the other tags. In XML, this tag is not optional, although you can name it anything you want (in Listing 14.1 it is the **<book>** tag).

- *All tags must have a closing tag.* If there is nothing between an opening and closing tag, you can abbreviate it. For example, the **<paperback/>** tag is both a starting and ending tag. It is equivalent to **<paperback></paperback>**.

- *Tags are case sensitive.*

- *XML tags must nest properly.* If the file contains an **<A>** tag followed by a **<B>** tag, then the **</B>** tag must appear before the **</A>** tag.

14. XML

- *XML documents preserve spaces.* The exception to this rule is that carriage return and line feed pairs become single line feeds.

- *Attributes must be quoted with single or double quotes.* You must do this even if they don't contain blanks.

The quotes are especially hard to remember if you are used to writing HTML by hand. In HTML, it is legal to write:

```
<IMG SRC=mylogo.gif>
```

If the file name has a space in it, you'd have to use quotes:

```
<IMG SRC="my new logo.gif">
```

With XML, you must always use the quotes—even if the value has no spaces or other special characters.

Because of these strict rules, a program can easily parse an XML file, even if it doesn't understand the tags in use. Writing an HTML parser is much more difficult because most browsers will accept tags that don't nest properly, and they even accept tags that should have closing tags, but don't. It is very difficult to decide what to do with this bit of HTML, for example:

```
<P><B><I>Hello</B><P>There</I>
```

Even for an XML document with **<P>**, **<B>**, and **<I>** tags, that bit of code is illegal. Of course, it is also technically illegal in HTML, but most browsers won't mind. XML programs won't be so forgiving. You'd have to change it like this (ignoring the root tag):

```
<P><B><I>Hello</I></B></P><P><I>There</I></P>
```

Although you can make up names, there are a few rules:

- Names can't start with a number or punctuation character, for example.

- Names also can't contain spaces and must not start with the letters XML (this is case insensitive, so your names can't start with xml, XmL, or any other combination that spells XML).

- You should also avoid using the colon in names.

TIP: *Although XML and HTML are different, it is possible to define XML versions of HTML tags. To do this you have to eliminate tags that don't have ending tags (like **
**) and require quoting and correct tag nesting. The resulting XML-friendly version of HTML is known as XHTML. XHTML requires tag names to be lowercase because XML is case sensitive.*

Valid XML

If you can make up your own tags, how do you know when you've made a legal XML file? Obviously, if you are the program that is trying to read the data, you simply look to see if you are missing any required tags or if there are any tags you don't understand. However, what about programs that just need to test that the XML file is valid? For example, an editor that knew how to import XML needs to know the file is correct but doesn't really care what is in the file.

The structure of an XML document can be defined in several ways. One way is the DTD or Document Type Definition. This is another document that defines the structure of any XML document.

Listing 14.2 shows the same book document with a DTD embedded in it. You can also refer to the DTD in a separate file. Consider Listing 14.3. This is the same XML file, but instead of using an internal DTD, it uses the DTD in Listing 14.4.

Listing 14.2   An XML document with an embedded DTD.

```
<?xml version='1.0' encoding='UTF-8'?>
<!DOCTYPE book [
  <!ELEMENT book (quantity,(paperback|hardback),shelving)>
  <!ATTLIST book title CDATA #REQUIRED >
  <!ATTLIST book author CDATA #REQUIRED >
  <!ELEMENT quantity (#PCDATA)>
  <!ELEMENT shelving (shelve+)>
  <!ELEMENT shelve (#PCDATA)>
  <!ELEMENT paperback EMPTY>
  <!ELEMENT hardback EMPTY>
  ]>

<book title="Java Network Programming Black Book" author="Al Williams">
    <quantity>10</quantity>
    <paperback/>
    <shelving>
      <shelve>Computer</shelve>
      <shelve>Java</shelve>
      <shelve>Programming</shelve>
    </shelving>
</book>
```

The **!DOCTYPE** tag identifies the embedded definition. Each **!ELEMENT** tag defines a single XML tag and includes information about what may appear within the tag. The special token **#PCDATA** indicates normal text that XML will parse for tags and special characters (as opposed to **#CDATA**, which is not parsed). Notice that the **paperback** and **hardback** tags use **EMPTY** because they contain no data at all.

The **!ELEMENT** tag for **book** defines a choice. There can be one **paperback** tag or one **hardback** tag, but not both. Similarly, the **shelving** tag can have one or more **shelve** tags (indicated by the plus sign). Instead of a plus sign, you can use an asterisk to indicate 0 or more, or a question mark to indicate one or 0 occurrences of a tag.

Listing 14.3   An XML document with an external DTD.

```
<?xml version='1.0' encoding='UTF-8'?>
<!DOCTYPE book SYSTEM "book.dtd">
<book title="Java Network Programming Black Book" author="Al Williams">
    <quantity>10</quantity>
    <paperback/>
    <shelving>
      <shelve>Computer</shelve>
      <shelve>Java</shelve>
      <shelve>Programming</shelve>
    </shelving>
```

Listing 14.4   This file is an external DTD.

```
<!ELEMENT book (quantity,(paperback|hardback),shelving)>
<!ELEMENT quantity (#PCDATA)>
<!ELEMENT shelving (shelve+)>
<!ELEMENT shelve (#PCDATA)>
<!ELEMENT paperback EMPTY>
<!ELEMENT hardback EMPTY>
<!ATTLIST book title CDATA #REQUIRED >
<!ATTLIST book author CDATA #REQUIRED >
```

In addition to the **!ELEMENT** tags, the DTD also defines which tags may have attributes. In Listing 14.4, there are two attributes, both of which belong to the **book** tag. Both attributes, **title** and **author**, consist of character data, and neither attribute has a default value. They are both required, as indicated by the **#REQUIRED** keyword.

One thing you might notice about DTDs is that they are not XML. It is possible to describe an XML file using another XML file. This is known as XSchema—or sometimes just Schema. An XSchema file serves the same purpose as a DTD, but it is written as an XML file. That means you can use the same tools and techniques with an XSchema file that you use with any other XML file. By convention, these schemas appear in files with an .xsd extension.

You can read entire books about XML. However, these basics will allow you to get started with XML and Java. There are two main tasks you may want your Java program to perform with XML. One is to create XML files, and the other is to read (and interpret) them.

14. XML

The Document Object Model

It might not be obvious from looking at an XML file as text, but XML data naturally organizes in a tree structure. Every XML file has a root tag. This tag could be the root of a tree. That root tag has certain predefined child tags. Those child tags may also have their own children.

A common way of expressing this idea is the DOM or Document Object Model. So the example in Listing 14.3, for example, has seven nodes: **book**, **quantity**, **paperback**, **shelving**, and three **shelve** nodes. The **book** node is the root and has three children (**quantity**, **paperback**, and **shelving**). The **shelving** node has three **shelve** nodes as children.

Obviously, you could model these nodes as Java objects. Later in this chapter, you'll see how special Java libraries can create a DOM from an XML file. Conversely, you can create a DOM and use it to correctly output an XML file.

Namespaces

One other important idea in XML is the namespace. Because you can make up your own tag names, mixing two or more XML documents can be a problem. Suppose you want to create a document that contains elements from two different XML DTDs. This is a common occurrence, for example, when creating style sheets or complex composite documents.

Consider the case where you have a DTD that defines a tag named **address**. The **address** tag might appear in a file like this:

```
<address>
<street>14455 North Hayden Road</street>
<suite>220</suite>
<city>Scottsdale</city>
<state>AZ</state>
<zip>85260</zip>
</address>
```

However, suppose there is another DTD that defines an Internet Protocol (IP) address and it also uses the **address** tag:

```
<address>
<ip>38.187.128.45</ip>
<host>coriolis.com</host>
</address>
```

If you don't mix these tags, you don't have a problem. But suppose you want to incorporate both of these elements into a single file (perhaps you want to associ-

ate Web addresses with physical addresses). How can arbitrary programs understand which **address** tag you want to use without scanning ahead?

The answer is to use namespaces. A namespace is a URL-like string—technically,
a Uniform Resource Identifier (URI)—that uniquely identifies a set of tags. The
URI doesn't really point to a Web resource—you could use http://x-y-z as a URL—
it is simply a unique identifier. Because it should be globally unique, you should
use a domain name you own to avoid collisions with other people's URLs.

Consider this document:

```
<address xmlns="http://www.al-williams.com/xml/address">
<street>14455 North Hayden Road</street>
<suite>220</suite>
<city>Scottsdale</city>
<state>AZ</state>
<zip>85260</zip>
</address>
```

This made-up URL (part of the **xmlns** attribute) identifies this set of tags uniquely.
You might then write an IP address as follows:

```
<address xmlns="http://www.coriolis.com/xmlns/ipaddress">
<ip>38.187.128.45</ip>
<host>coriolis.com</host>
</address>
```

Now it is clear which tag is which. In this case, the namespace specified by the
xmlns attribute applies to all the tags contained by the **address** tag. It is also
possible to assign a local name to a namespace, like this:

```
<staddress:address xmlns:staddress="http://www.al-williams.com/xml/address">
<staddress:street>14455 North Hayden Road</staddress:street>
<staddress:suite>220</staddress:suite>
<staddress:city>Scottsdale</staddress:city>
<staddress:state>AZ</staddress:state>
<staddress:zip>85260</staddress:zip>
</staddress:address>
```

This is mostly useful when you are blending two items into one document:

```
<webhost xmlns:staddress="http://www.al-williams.com/xml/address"
             xmlns:ipaddress="http://www.coriolis.com/xmlns/ipaddress">
<staddress:address> . . . </staddress:address>
<ipaddress:address> . . . </ipaddress:address>
```

Even if you don't plan on intermixing XML documents, you'll probably encounter namespaces when using other XML-based documents, like JSPs.

Java Support for XML

There are many ways to use XML from a Java program or Java Server Pages (JSP) script. Of course, you can just manually create XML, but that doesn't take advantage of the many Java features, nor does it ensure a correctly formed document. However, as a starting point, consider the JSP in Listing 14.5. This is the same XML document as before, except this time, most of the critical values are Java variables. In this example, I simply set the variables to constants. In real life, you'd load the variables from a database or otherwise generate them dynamically.

Listing 14.5   A dynamic XML document using JSP.

```
<?xml version="1.0" ?>
<%@ page contentType="text/xml" %>
<%
// fake database read
  String title="Java Network Programming Black Book";
  String author="Al Williams";
  int quan=33;
  boolean paper=true;
%>


<!DOCTYPE book [
  <!ELEMENT book (quantity,(paperback|hardback),shelving)>
  <!ELEMENT quantity (#PCDATA)>
  <!ELEMENT shelving (shelve+)>
  <!ELEMENT shelve (#PCDATA)>
  <!ELEMENT paperback EMPTY>
  <!ELEMENT hardback EMPTY>
  <!ATTLIST book title CDATA #REQUIRED >
  <!ATTLIST book author CDATA #REQUIRED >
  ]>

<book title="<%= title %>" author="<%= author %>">
    <quantity><%= quan %></quantity>
<% if (paper) { %>
    <paperback/>
<% } else { %>
    <hardback/>
<% } %>
    <shelving>
      <shelve>Computer</shelve>
```

```
      <shelve>Java</shelve>
      <shelve>Programming</shelve>
   </shelving>
</book>
```

It is important to realize that even though this is an XML file, it has a .jsp extension so that the server will process it as a JSP. It is very important that the **page** directive specifies a **contentType** of **text/xml**. Without this statement, the JSP would generate an HTML file.

The four variables involved in this document are **title**, **author**, **quan**, and **paper**. All of these simply appear in the script except for **paper**. The **paper** variable is a **boolean**, and it controls if the document contains a **<paperback/>** tag or a **<hardback/>** tag.

Creating a JSP file to write out XML is one way to create XML documents. You can view XML in most modern browsers, but to actually format it, you'll need a style sheet or XSL document to transform the XML into a Web page. Although this is simple, Java has many more powerful ways to handle XML.

XML Libraries

You can use several Java technologies to handle XML:

- *JAXP*—The Java API for XML Parsing allows you to read XML files and interpret them in various ways.

- *JAXB*—The Java Architecture for XML Binding allows you to write a Java object as an XML file and reconstitute it later from the same XML file.

- *JDOM*—The Java Document Object Model converts an XML file into a tree of Java objects.

- *JAXM*—Java API for XML Messaging allows programs to exchange XML-based messages.

- *JAXR*—Java API for XML Registries allows you to publish the existence of XML services for other programs to find.

Sun knows that many developers will want to download all the XML APIs and libraries. That's why it built the JAX Pack (**http://java.sun.com/xml/jaxpack.html**). From this page you can do one download and get practically everything.

The JAXP allows you to work with Simple API for XML parsers (SAX parsers) or you can use a **DocumentBuilder** object to create a DOM from XML input. One important note: JAXP is an interface to XML parsers, but it is not actually an XML parser (although several parsers ship with JAXP). The reason this is important is that you are free to substitute other parsers at will. As long as they work with

JAXP, your code will not change. You can control which parsers you use by setting system properties. The **javax.xml.parsers.SAXParserFactory** property controls parser use, whereas the **javax.xml.parsers.DocumentBuilderFactory** property handles **DocumentBuilder** objects.

There are several libraries that make up the key components for JAXP:

- *javax.xml.parsers*—The main JAXP interface
- *org.w3c.dom*—Document Object Model classes
- *org.xml.sax*—The SAX interface
- *javax.xml.transform*—Allows you to transform XML to other formats

What's the difference between the SAX interface and the DOM interface? As I mentioned earlier, working with XML as a DOM presents you with a complete tree of objects, where one object corresponds to one tag. The problem with this approach is you have to read the entire XML document before you can do any processing.

On the other hand, the SAX interface processes XML files element by element. The SAX parser will call special methods you provide to inform you when it finds different kinds of elements. You can start processing an XML file via SAX immediately, even if you don't have the entire file yet.

JAXP requires you to use several Java Archive (JAR) files. Table 14.1 shows which files you need and what they contain.

Using SAX

If you want to read through an XML file and examine all the different parts, you'll probably want a SAX-based parser, such as the one that appears in Listing 14.6. The program uses **import** to include the major XML libraries it uses. In addition, you'll need to make sure your **CLASSPATH** contains jaxp.jar and crimson.jar to run the program.

The **XMLEcho** class extends **DefaultHandler**—a helper class that has placeholders for the methods the parser will call. Each time the parser detects an ele-

Table 14.1   JAXP uses three different JAR files and many different packages.

Jar File	Packages	Contents
jaxp.jar	**javax.xml.parsers**, **javax.xml.transform**	Interfaces
crimson.jar	**org.xml.sax**, **org.w3c.dom**	Interfaces and helper classes
xalan.jar	**javax.xml.parsers**, **javax.xml.transform**, **org.xml.sax**, **org.w3c.dom**	Implementation classes

ment in the XML input, it calls the corresponding method in the callback object (**XMLEcho**, in this case).

First, you need to get an instance of the SAX parser factory, which you can do by calling **SAXParserFactory.newInstance**. Armed with this object, you can call **newSAXParser** to create an actual parser object. Then, you'll call **parse** to start the parsing process. The **parse** method requires a **File** object and a callback object reference.

Table 14.2 shows the callback methods the SAX parser may call. Because **DefaultHandler** provides implementations for these methods, **XMLEcho** only supplies the ones it wants to use.

The example program in Listing 14.6 re-creates a copy of the XML file on the standard output (using the **emit** method). It also reports information about the file on the standard error stream. So you can run the program like this:

```
java XMLEcho test.xml >testout.xml
```

This will allow you to see the report on the screen, while saving the new copy of the XML file to another file.

In addition to the content handler methods in Table 14.2, the **DefaultHandler** also provides methods for the **DTDHandler**, **EntityResolver**, and **ErrorHandler** interfaces. You can use these methods to capture information about DTDs, provide custom entity values, and handle errors.

14. XML

Table 14.2   Parser callback methods.

Method	Called
characters	When parsing character data
endDocument	End of document detected
endElement	End of element detected
endPrefixMapping	Found end of prefix scope
ignorableWhitespace	Detected unimportant white space
processingInstruction	Found a processing instruction (**<? ?>** tags)
setDocumentLocator	Optionally called to inform callback current location in document (useful for error reporting)
skippedEntity	Skipped an entity (for example, external entities)
startDocument	Found start of document
startElement	Found start of element
startPrefixMapping	Beginning of namespace prefix scope

Listing 14.6   A SAX-based XML parser.

```java
// XML parser (uses SAX)
// usage java XMLEcho file.xml >outputfile.xml
// Sends report to console

import java.io.*;
import org.xml.sax.*;
import org.xml.sax.helpers.DefaultHandler;
import javax.xml.parsers.SAXParserFactory;
import javax.xml.parsers.ParserConfigurationException;
import javax.xml.parsers.SAXParser;

public class XMLEcho extends DefaultHandler {
    static private Writer out;
    public static void main(String args[]) throws Exception {
        // Use an instance of ourselves as the SAX event handler
        DefaultHandler handler = new XMLEcho();

        // Use the default (non-validating) parser
        SAXParserFactory factory = SAXParserFactory.newInstance();

        // Set up output stream
        out = new OutputStreamWriter(System.out, "UTF8");

        // Parse the input
        SAXParser saxParser = factory.newSAXParser();
        File ifile = new File(args[0]);
        saxParser.parse( ifile, handler );

    }

    private void emit(String s)  // write output
        throws SAXException     {
        try {
            out.write(s);
            out.flush();
        } catch (IOException e) {
            throw new SAXException("I/O error", e);
        }
    }


    private void nl()
        throws SAXException     {
        String lineEnd =  System.getProperty("line.separator");
```

```
    try {
        out.write(lineEnd);

    } catch (IOException e) {
        throw new SAXException("I/O error", e);
    }
}

public void startDocument()
throws SAXException     {
    emit("<?xml version='1.0' encoding='UTF-8'?>");
    System.err.println("Start document");
    nl();
}

public void endDocument()
throws SAXException     {
    try {
        System.err.println("End document");
        nl();
        out.flush();
    } catch (IOException e) {
        throw new SAXException("I/O error", e);
    }
}




public void startElement(String namespaceURI,
                         String sName, // simple name (localName)
                         String qName, // qualified name
                         Attributes attrs)
throws SAXException     {
    String eName = sName; // element name
    if ("".equals(eName)) eName = qName; // namespaceAware = false
    emit("<"+eName);
    System.err.println("TAG: " + eName);
    if (attrs != null) {
        for (int i = 0; i < attrs.getLength(); i++) {
            String aName = attrs.getLocalName(i); // Attr name
            if ("".equals(aName)) aName = attrs.getQName(i);
            emit(" ");
            emit(aName+"=\""+attrs.getValue(i)+"\"");
        }
    }
    emit(">");
}
```

```
        public void endElement(String namespaceURI,
                               String sName, // simple name
                               String qName  // qualified name
                              )
    throws SAXException     {
        String eName = sName; // element name
        if ("".equals(eName)) eName = qName; // namespaceAware = false
        emit("</"+eName+">");
        System.err.println("End tag: " + eName);
    }


        public void characters(char buf[], int offset, int len)
        throws SAXException     {
            String s = new String(buf, offset, len);
            if (len!=0&&(len!=1||buf[offset]!='\n'))
                System.err.println("Content: [" + s + "]");
            emit(s);
        }

    }
```

Of course, you'll usually want to do something more interesting than just print the same XML file. You might want to transform the XML into another format or make entries into a database based on the XML data. However, if you can pick apart the individual tags and recognize them, you can easily implement whatever logic you want.

WARNING! *The XMLEcho class will not properly create XML files that contain certain entities. For example, when the parser encounters the > entity, it automatically converts it to the correct character ('>') for your Java program. However, when you write that character out to the new file, it should transform back to the entity form. If you fail to do this, other XML parsers will not be able to understand the resulting file. You can see this if you process a file with < and > through XMLEcho. The resulting output will have a pair of angle brackets, which is not correct.*

However, CDATA sections don't use entities, so to properly handle this substitution you'd need to know when you were processing ordinary characters or CDATA characters. Unfortunately, this requires the LexicalHandler interface, which SAX parsers are not required to support.

Another place where the parser falls short is in processing comments. When you process an input file that contains comments, the comments will not appear in the output file. That's because the SAX parser digests them at the lexical analysis stage before proper parsing begins. Again, the answer is to use the optional **LexicalHandler** interface.

The **DefaultHandler** base class does not implement **LexicalHandler**, so you'll have to do that yourself. The interface consists of the following methods:

- **comment**—The parser detected a comment.
- **startCDATA**—The parser is starting to process unparsed character data.
- **endCDATA**—The parser reached the end of the unparsed characters it was processing.
- **startEntity**—The parser found the start of an entity.
- **endEntity**—The parser encountered the end of an entity.
- **startDTD**—The parser found a DTD in the document.
- **endDTD**—The parser reached the end of the DTD.

The **startCDATA** and **endCDATA** methods are useful for setting a flag so that other methods, such as the **characters** method, can know if the data is in a **CDATA** section or not. If you want to process comments, you can provide code in the **comment** section. Keep in mind that because there is no base implementation of this interface in **DefaultHandler**, you'll have to provide at least empty bodies for all of these methods.

Once you have the **LexicalHandler** interface built, you have to inform the parser that you want to use this interface. The **LexicalHandler** callbacks are not part of the parser per se, but are actually a part of the **XMLReader** class the parser uses to read input. To set a callback, you need to write:

```
saxParser.getXMLReader().setProperty(
        "http://xml.org/sax/properties/lexical-handler",
        self);
```

Listing 14.7 shows a modified parser that implements the **LexicalHandler** interface. When the parser encounters a comment, it writes a warning message to the console. You could easily extend the program to pass the comments to the output if you wanted to do so.

Listing 14.7   This parser warns if comments appear in the original source.

```
// XML parser (uses SAX)
// usage java XMLEcho1 file.xml >outputfile.xml
// Sends report to console
// This version uses a Lexical Handler

import java.io.*;
import org.xml.sax.*;
import org.xml.sax.helpers.DefaultHandler;
import javax.xml.parsers.SAXParserFactory;
```

```
import javax.xml.parsers.ParserConfigurationException;
import javax.xml.parsers.SAXParser;
// Import for lex handling
import org.xml.sax.ext.LexicalHandler;


public class XMLEcho1 extends DefaultHandler
   implements LexicalHandler {
     static private Writer out;
     public static void main(String args[]) throws Exception {
         // Use an instance of ourselves as the SAX event handler
         XMLEcho1 self = new XMLEcho1();
         DefaultHandler handler = self;

         // Use the default (non-validating) parser
         SAXParserFactory factory = SAXParserFactory.newInstance();

         // Set up output stream
         out = new OutputStreamWriter(System.out, "UTF8");

         // Parse the input
         SAXParser saxParser = factory.newSAXParser();
         File ifile = new File(args[0]);
// Set Lex callback
         saxParser.getXMLReader().setProperty(
                 "http://xml.org/sax/properties/lexical-handler",
                  self);

         saxParser.parse( ifile, handler );
     }

    private void emit(String s)
        throws SAXException      {
        try {
           out.write(s);
           out.flush();
        } catch (IOException e) {
           throw new SAXException("I/O error", e);
        }
    }


    private void nl()
    throws SAXException      {
        String lineEnd =  System.getProperty("line.separator");
```

14. XML

```java
    try {
        out.write(lineEnd);

    } catch (IOException e) {
        throw new SAXException("I/O error", e);
    }
}

public void startDocument()
throws SAXException      {
    emit("<?xml version='1.0' encoding='UTF-8'?>");
    System.err.println("Start document");
    nl();
}

public void endDocument()
throws SAXException      {
    try {
        System.err.println("End document");
        nl();
        out.flush();
    } catch (IOException e) {
        throw new SAXException("I/O error", e);
    }
}


public void startElement(String namespaceURI,
                         String sName, // simple name (localName)
                         String qName, // qualified name
                         Attributes attrs)
throws SAXException      {
    String eName = sName; // element name
    if ("".equals(eName)) eName = qName; // namespaceAware = false
    emit("<"+eName);
    System.err.println("TAG: " + eName);
    if (attrs != null) {
        for (int i = 0; i < attrs.getLength(); i++) {
            String aName = attrs.getLocalName(i); // Attr name
            if ("".equals(aName)) aName = attrs.getQName(i);
            emit(" ");
            emit(aName+"=\""+attrs.getValue(i)+"\"");
        }
    }
    emit(">");
}
```

```
        public void endElement(String namespaceURI,
                               String sName, // simple name
                               String qName  // qualified name
                              )
        throws SAXException    {
            String eName = sName; // element name
            if ("".equals(eName)) eName = qName; // namespaceAware = false
            emit("</"+eName+">");
            System.err.println("End tag: " + eName);
        }


        public void characters(char buf[], int offset, int len)
        throws SAXException    {
            String s = new String(buf, offset, len);
            if (len!=0&&(len!=1||buf[offset]!='\n'))
                System.err.println("Content: [" + s + "]");
            emit(s);
        }


    // The Lex interface

    public void comment(char[] ch, int start, int length)
    throws SAXException    {
      System.err.println("Warning: Comment discarded");
        }

    public void startCDATA()  throws SAXException    {
    }

    public void endCDATA() throws SAXException    {
    }

    public void startEntity(String name) throws SAXException    {
    }

    public void endEntity(String name)  throws SAXException    {
    }

    public void startDTD(String name, String publicId, String systemId)
    throws SAXException  {
    }

    public void endDTD()    throws SAXException    {
    }
}
```

The parsers in Listings 14.6 and 14.7 do not attempt to validate the text with the document's DTD (if the input document even has a DTD). If you want to have validation occur, you need to set the factory object to return a validating parser. So instead of

```
SAXParserFactory factory = SAXParserFactory.newInstance();
```

you would write the following:

```
SAXParserFactory factory = SAXParserFactory.newInstance();
factory.setValidating(true);
```

You can also use **setNamespaceAware** to make the factory return a parser that understands namespaces. Of course, you can also make both calls to get a namespace-aware, validating parser if you wish.

When you make a validating parser, the document you are parsing must contain a DTD, or else you will receive a warning and then an error. Also, the parsers will use any DTD to consume unimportant white space. That means the output may not have the same spacing as the input—unless you modify the code to pass unimportant white space.

Listing 14.8 shows a variation of the basic SAX parser that uses validation. Notice that a parse error results in a call to one of the **ErrorHandler** interface methods. Because **DefaultHandler** already implements this interface, all you have to do is provide override methods. Often, these methods will do little more than throw the exception they receive as an argument.

Listing 14.8   This parser validates the XML file against its DTD.

```
// XML parser (uses SAX)
// usage java XMLValid file.xml >outputfile.xml
// Sends report to console

import java.io.*;
import org.xml.sax.*;
import org.xml.sax.helpers.DefaultHandler;
import javax.xml.parsers.SAXParserFactory;
import javax.xml.parsers.ParserConfigurationException;
import javax.xml.parsers.SAXParser;

public class XMLValid extends DefaultHandler {
    static private Writer out;
    public static void main(String args[]) throws Exception {
        // Use an instance of ourselves as the SAX event handler
        try{
            DefaultHandler handler = new XMLValid();
```

```
                SAXParserFactory factory = SAXParserFactory.newInstance();
                factory.setValidating(true);

                // Set up output stream
                out = new OutputStreamWriter(System.out, "UTF8");

                // Parse the input
                SAXParser saxParser = factory.newSAXParser();
                File ifile = new File(args[0]);
                saxParser.parse( ifile, handler );
        } catch (SAXParseException ex) {
            System.out.println("\n** Parsing error"
                + ", line " + ex.getLineNumber()
                + ", uri " + ex.getSystemId());
            System.out.println("   " + ex.getMessage() );

            // Use the contained exception, if any
            Exception  x = ex;
            if (ex.getException() != null)
                x = ex.getException();
            x.printStackTrace();

        } catch (SAXException sxe) {
            // Error generated by this application
            // (or a parser-initialization error)
            Exception  x = sxe;
            if (sxe.getException() != null)
                x = sxe.getException();
            x.printStackTrace();

        } catch (ParserConfigurationException pce) {
            // Parser with specified options can't be built
            pce.printStackTrace();

        } catch (IOException ioe) {
            // I/O error
            ioe.printStackTrace();
        }

    }

    private void emit(String s)  throws SAXException     {
        try {
            out.write(s);
            out.flush();
```

```java
        } catch (IOException e) {
            throw new SAXException("I/O error", e);
        }
    }


    private void nl()    throws SAXException    {
        String lineEnd =  System.getProperty("line.separator");
        try {
            out.write(lineEnd);

        } catch (IOException e) {
            throw new SAXException("I/O error", e);
        }
    }

    public void startDocument() throws SAXException     {
        emit("<?xml version='1.0' encoding='UTF-8'?>");
        nl();
    }

    public void endDocument()   throws SAXException     {
        try {
            nl();
            out.flush();
        } catch (IOException e) {
            throw new SAXException("I/O error", e);
        }
    }



    public void startElement(String namespaceURI,
                             String sName, // simple name (localName)
                             String qName, // qualified name
                             Attributes attrs)
      throws SAXException     {
        String eName = sName; // element name
        if ("".equals(eName)) eName = qName; // namespaceAware = false
        emit("<"+eName);
        if (attrs != null) {
            for (int i = 0; i < attrs.getLength(); i++) {
                String aName = attrs.getLocalName(i); // Attr name
                if ("".equals(aName)) aName = attrs.getQName(i);
                emit(" ");
                emit(aName+"=\""+attrs.getValue(i)+"\"");
            }
        }
```

```
                                emit(">");
                }

                public void endElement(String namespaceURI,
                                        String sName, // simple name
                                        String qName  // qualified name
                                      )  throws SAXException    {
                    String eName = sName; // element name
                    if ("".equals(eName)) eName = qName; // namespaceAware = false
                    emit("</"+eName+">");
                }


                public void characters(char buf[], int offset, int len)
                throws SAXException     {
                    String s = new String(buf, offset, len);
                    emit(s);
                }

        // ErrorHandler Interface

                // watch for errors
                public void error(SAXParseException e)
                    throws SAXParseException {
                    throw e;
                }

                // and warnings
                public void warning(SAXParseException e)
                    throws SAXParseException {
                    System.out.println("Warning at " + e.getLineNumber() + " " +
                                    e.getMessage());
                }

        }
```

Using DOM

The SAX parser strategy processes the XML file as it reads it. This is quite efficient. You can load large XML files without worrying about excessive memory consumption. However, some programs need to process information about the XML file in a nonsequential way.

Because every XML document consists of a root tag and a hierarchy of child tags, XML documents easily fit into a tree structure. You could build a tree from within the callback routines of a SAX parser. However, this is such a common operation, you don't need to do it yourself. JAXP will do it for you.

In fact, reading an XML file and creating a DOM is extremely simple. You must construct a **DocumentBuilder** object (the process is very similar to obtaining a SAX parser). Then you call one method:

```
document = builder.parse( new File("an_xml_file.xml") );
```

The only problem now is that there is no standard way to display a DOM. The Sun implementation of the DOM parser does have a method for dumping a DOM, but it may not work for every parser.

The code in Listing 14.9 shows a DOM parser. It also implements a method named **walk**. This method starts with the root **Node** object (the **Document** object returned by **parse** is a type of **Node**). The **walk** method displays a text representation of the node and then recursively calls itself to display child nodes. Here is an example of the output from the program:

```
Level 1 Document:#document
      Level 2 Element:book
              Level 3 Comment:#comment
              Level 3 Element:quantity
                      Level 4 Text:10
              Level 3 Element:paperback
              Level 3 Element:shelving
                      Level 4 Element:shelve
                              Level 5 Text:Computer
                      Level 4 Element:shelve
                              Level 5 Text:Java
                      Level 4 Element:shelve
                              Level 5 Text:Programming
```

The **walk** method offers several insights into the structure of the DOM. Each **Node** may have child nodes. Further, text information is always in **TEXT_NODE** nodes, so each element node may have a **TEXT_NODE** beneath it. Don't expect the element node itself to contain content data. For example, in the sample document, the **quantity** node does not contain the actual quantity (10). Instead, a **text** node under the **quantity** node has the value.

Listing 14.9   This program reads XML using a DOM.

```
// Read XML via a DOM
import javax.xml.parsers.DocumentBuilder;
import javax.xml.parsers.DocumentBuilderFactory;
import javax.xml.parsers.FactoryConfigurationError;
import javax.xml.parsers.ParserConfigurationException;
```

```java
        import org.xml.sax.SAXException;
        import org.xml.sax.SAXParseException;

        import java.io.File;
        import java.io.IOException;

        import org.w3c.dom.*;


        public class DomDemo{
            static Document document;
            static int level=0;

// convert a node type to a string
            public static String nodeType(Node node) {
                switch (node.getNodeType()) {
                case Node.ATTRIBUTE_NODE:
                    return "Attribute";
                case Node.CDATA_SECTION_NODE:
                    return "CDATA Section";
                case Node.COMMENT_NODE:
                    return "Comment";
                case Node.DOCUMENT_FRAGMENT_NODE:
                    return "Doc Fragment";
                case Node.DOCUMENT_NODE:
                    return "Document";
                case Node.DOCUMENT_TYPE_NODE:
                    return "Document Type";
                case Node.ELEMENT_NODE:
                    return "Element";
                case Node.ENTITY_NODE:
                    return "Entity";
                case Node.ENTITY_REFERENCE_NODE:
                    return "Entity Reference";
                case Node.NOTATION_NODE:
                    return "Notation";
                case Node.PROCESSING_INSTRUCTION_NODE:
                    return "Processing Instruction";
                case Node.TEXT_NODE:
                    return "Text";
                default:
                    return "Unknown";
                }
            }
```

14. XML

```
// recursively walk the nodes
    public static void walk(Node node) {
        NodeList nodes=node.getChildNodes();
        String val;
        if (node.getNodeType()==Node.TEXT_NODE) {
            val=node.getNodeValue().trim();
            if (val.length()==0) return; // don't print pure white space
        }
        else
            val=node.getNodeName();
        for (int j=0;j<level;j++) System.out.print("\t");
        System.out.print("Level " + ++level);
        System.out.println(" " + nodeType(node) + ":" + val);
        for (int i=0;i<nodes.getLength();i++)
            walk(nodes.item(i));
        level--;
    }

    public static void main(String argv[]) throws Exception
    {
        DocumentBuilderFactory factory =
            DocumentBuilderFactory.newInstance();
        try {
            DocumentBuilder builder = factory.newDocumentBuilder();
// This one line loads the whole document!
            document = builder.parse( new File(argv[0]) );
            walk(document);

        } catch (SAXException sxe) {
            // Error generated during parsing)
            Exception  x = sxe;
            if (sxe.getException() != null)
                x = sxe.getException();
            x.printStackTrace();

        } catch (ParserConfigurationException pce) {
            // Parser with specified options can't be built
            pce.printStackTrace();

        } catch (IOException ioe) {
            // I/O error
            ioe.printStackTrace();
        }
    } // main

}
```

You may notice, however, that the program in Listing 14.9 does not display attributes. Although there is an **ATTRIBUTE_NODE** node type, it doesn't appear in the normal tree structure.

If you want to process attributes, you have to call **getAttributes** on the element in question. The method returns a **NamedNodeMap** object. This is simply a collection of **Node** objects, each one corresponding to an attribute. These nodes will be **ATTRIBUTE_NODES**, and their values will be the attribute value. That is to say, there won't be a text node under the attribute as there is with element nodes.

Listing 14.10 shows a modified DOM program that emits the attribute values. The biggest change is that the code examines each element to see if it has attributes. If it does, the program calls **walk** again on those nodes after processing the element node, but before processing any children. Here is the output from Listing 14.10:

```
Level 1 Document:#document
        Level 2 Element:book
        Level 2 Attribute:Java Network Programming Black Book
        Level 2 Attribute:Al Williams
                Level 3 Comment:#comment
                Level 3 Element:quantity
                        Level 4 Text:10
                Level 3 Element:paperback
                Level 3 Element:shelving
                        Level 4 Element:shelve
                                Level 5 Text:Computer
                        Level 4 Element:shelve
                                Level 5 Text:Java
                        Level 4 Element:shelve
                                Level 5 Text:Programming
```

Listing 14.10   An attribute-aware DOM program.

```java
// Read XML via a DOM
import javax.xml.parsers.DocumentBuilder;
import javax.xml.parsers.DocumentBuilderFactory;
import javax.xml.parsers.FactoryConfigurationError;
import javax.xml.parsers.ParserConfigurationException;

import org.xml.sax.SAXException;
import org.xml.sax.SAXParseException;

import java.io.File;
import java.io.IOException;

import org.w3c.dom.*;
```

```
public class DomDemo{
    static Document document;
    static int level=0;

// convert a node type to a string
    public static String nodeType(Node node) {
        switch (node.getNodeType()) {
        case Node.ATTRIBUTE_NODE:
            return "Attribute";
        case Node.CDATA_SECTION_NODE:
            return "CDATA Section";
        case Node.COMMENT_NODE:
            return "Comment";
        case Node.DOCUMENT_FRAGMENT_NODE:
            return "Doc Fragment";
        case Node.DOCUMENT_NODE:
            return "Document";
        case Node.DOCUMENT_TYPE_NODE:
            return "Document Type";
        case Node.ELEMENT_NODE:
            return "Element";
        case Node.ENTITY_NODE:
            return "Entity";
        case Node.ENTITY_REFERENCE_NODE:
            return "Entity Reference";
        case Node.NOTATION_NODE:
            return "Notation";
        case Node.PROCESSING_INSTRUCTION_NODE:
            return "Processing Instruction";
        case Node.TEXT_NODE:
            return "Text";
        default:
            return "Unknown";
        }
    }

// recursively walk the nodes
    public static void walk(Node node) {
        NodeList nodes=node.getChildNodes();
        String val;
        NamedNodeMap attr=null;
        if (node.getNodeType()==Node.TEXT_NODE ||
            node.getNodeType()==Node.ATTRIBUTE_NODE) {
            val=node.getNodeValue().trim();
            if (val.length()==0) return; // don't print pure white space
        }
```

14. XML

```
                    else {
                        val=node.getNodeName();
                        attr=node.getAttributes();
                    }
                    for (int j=0;j<level;j++) System.out.print("\t");
                    System.out.print("Level " + level+1);
                    System.out.println(" " + nodeType(node) + ":" + val);
                    if (attr!=null){
                        for (int j=0;j<attr.getLength();j++)
                            walk(attr.item(j));
                    }
                    level++;
                    for (int i=0;i<nodes.getLength();i++)
                        walk(nodes.item(i));
                    level--;
            }


    public static void main(String argv[]) throws Exception
    {
        DocumentBuilderFactory factory =
            DocumentBuilderFactory.newInstance();
        try {
            DocumentBuilder builder = factory.newDocumentBuilder();
// This one line loads the whole document!
            document = builder.parse( new File(argv[0]) );
            walk(document);

        } catch (SAXException sxe) {
            // Error generated during parsing)
            Exception  x = sxe;
            if (sxe.getException() != null)
                x = sxe.getException();
            x.printStackTrace();

        } catch (ParserConfigurationException pce) {
            // Parser with specified options can't be built
            pce.printStackTrace();

        } catch (IOException ioe) {
            // I/O error
            ioe.printStackTrace();
        }
    } // main


}
```

Just as it is possible to read an XML file into a DOM, it is also easy to create a DOM and then use it to build an output file or otherwise process data that might not reside in an XML file as though it were an XML file.

You'll find an example of this in Listing 14.14 and Listing 14.15 in the Immediate Solutions section. You simply construct the DOM tree using the DOM's **createObject** method to form a root object. Then you use **appendChild** to append child nodes to their parent nodes.

You can also transform a DOM into an output document using a transformer. The steps are very similar to those you use when you create a parser. First, you get a **TransformerFactory**. Then you ask the factory for an instance of a **Transformer** object. You also must set the output stream you want to use for the output by creating a **StreamResult** object. Finally, you construct a **DOMSource** object that encapsulates the DOM (or a part of the DOM) that you want to transform into XML.

Armed with a **Transformer**, a **StreamResult**, and a **DOMSource**, you simply call **Transformer.transform** and pass it the **DOMSource** and **StreamResult** objects. The transformer will write out the appropriate XML to the stream you specified. If you'd like to view an example, see Listing 14.15 in the Immediate Solutions section.

14. XML

Immediate Solutions

Installing Java XML Extensions

Sun knows that many developers will want to download all the XML APIs and libraries. That's why they built the JAX Pack (**http://java.sun.com/xml/jaxpack.html**). From this page you can download one package that contains the following:

- *JAXP*—Read and interpret XML files using a standard interface to a variety of parsers

- *JAXB*—Allows you to write a Java object as an XML file and read XML files into an object

- *JDOM*—Converts an XML file into a tree of Java objects

- *JAXM*—Allows programs to exchange XML-based messages

- *JAXR*—Allows you to publish the existence of XML services for other programs to find

To use JAXP, you'll have to have the jaxp.jar and crimsom.jar files in your **CLASSPATH**. In addition, JAXP can interface with third-party parsers, or you can use the parsers Sun provides. If you use another parser, you'll need to follow the instructions for the parser you are using. Typically, you'll need to include more files in your **CLASSPATH** and modify the **javax.xml.parsers.SAXParserFactory** and **javax.xml.parsers.DocumentBuilderFactory** properties.

Creating XML from a JSP

You can easily write XML output from a JSP. The key is to use the **page** directive to set the **contentType** attribute to **text/xml**. Of course, you also need to observe the correct formatting for an XML document.

Follow these steps to build an XML-generating JSP:

1. Make the first line of your JSP an **<?xml ?>** tag. This is the first line of every XML file.

2. On the second line, use a **<%@ page %>** directive to set the **contentType** attribute to **text/xml**.

14. XML

3. Write the remaining XML file as usual. You can use standard JSP tags (**<% %>** or **<%=%>**) to output all or parts of XML tags.

Listing 14.11 shows a JSP that reads data from a properties file (see Listing 14.11) and emits an XML file.

Listing 14.11   This JSP writes out a property file as an XML document.

```
<?xml version="1.0" ?>
<%@ page contentType="text/xml" %>
<%@ page import="java.util.*" %>
<%@ page import="java.io.*" %>
<%
  Properties prop=new Properties();
  FileInputStream fis = new FileInputStream(
    getServletContext().getRealPath(request.getParameter("prop")));
  prop.load(fis);
  String title=prop.getProperty("title");
  String author=prop.getProperty("author");
  int quan=Integer.parseInt(prop.getProperty("quantity"));
  boolean paper=prop.getProperty("paperback").charAt(0)=='t';
%>


<!DOCTYPE book [
  <!ELEMENT book (quantity,(paperback|hardback))>
  <!ELEMENT quantity (#PCDATA)>
  <!ELEMENT paperback EMPTY>
  <!ELEMENT hardback EMPTY>
  <!ATTLIST book title CDATA #REQUIRED >
  <!ATTLIST book author CDATA #REQUIRED >
  ]>

<book title="<%= title %>" author="<%= author %>">
    <quantity><%= quan %></quantity>
<% if (paper) { %>
    <paperback/>
<% } else { %>
    <hardback/>
<% } %>
</book>
```

Listing 14.12   A sample properties file that will work with the program in Listing 14.11.

```
title=Java Network Programming Black Book
author=Al Williams
quantity=104
paperback=true
hardback=false
```

Creating a Parser

When you want to create a JAXP parser, you'll follow these basic steps:

1. Create a factory class by calling a static method **newInstance** of the factory class.

2. Use the methods from the factory to create a new instance of the parser.

3. Call the **parse** method of the parser.

You have two choices when creating a parser. A SAX parser will allow you to process an XML document serially. The parser calls methods that you specify when it detects different elements of the XML file. For this style of parser, you'll use the **SaxParserFactory** class as the factory. The **newSAXParser** method then creates the actual **SAXParser** object.

You can find a sample SAX parser program in Listing 14.6. Here's the code from that program that constructs the SAX parser:

```
// Use the default (non-validating) parser
SAXParserFactory factory = SAXParserFactory.newInstance();
// Parse the input
SAXParser saxParser = factory.newSAXParser();
```

Another way to parse XML data is to use a DOM parser. The process is similar. You'll use the **DocumentBuilderFactory** as a factory object. The factory's **newDocumentBuilder** method will create a **DocumentBuilder** object. This object will then create a DOM from XML input, resulting in a **Document** object. You can find an example DOM parser in Listing 14.9. Here's the relevant code that creates the parser from that program (without exception handling):

```
DocumentBuilderFactory factory =
    DocumentBuilderFactory.newInstance();
    DocumentBuilder builder = factory.newDocumentBuilder();
```

Creating a Validating Parser

You can cause a parser factory to generate a validating parser by calling **setValidating** on the factory object and passing it **true** as an argument. With a validating parser, the input document must have an associated DTD. The parser will call a specified error callback if it detects a syntax that does not match the DTD.

Creating a Namespace-aware Parser

If you want the XML parser to understand XML namespaces, you can call **set-NamespaceAware** on the factory object. You'll pass this method a **true** argument.

Using a SAX Parser

When using a SAX parser, you must provide one or more callback objects. These objects implement specific interfaces that the parser will call as it detects items in the XML file. Although you could write these methods yourself, it is easier to extend the **DefaultHandler** object. This object provides stubs for callbacks for the **ContentHandler**, **DTDHandler**, **EntityResolver**, and **ErrorHandler** interfaces.

Of these, the **ContentHandler** interface (see Table 14.2) is the most useful. You can simply override the methods in **DefaultHandler** that you wish to process. For example, here is the code that detects the start of a document (an excerpt from Listing 14.6):

```
public void startDocument()
throws SAXException    {
    emit("<?xml version='1.0' encoding='UTF-8'?>");
    System.err.println("Start document");
    nl();
}
```

Of course, you have to inform the parser of your callback object. You do this by calling **parse** and passing your object as the second argument. The first argument is the file you want to parse:

```
saxParser.parse( ifile, handler );
```

Validating with SAX

You'd think that creating a validating parser would be all that is required to validate an XML document against a DTD. However, this is not the case. The catch is that the parser uses another callback interface, **ErrorHandler**, to report errors. Because **DefaultHandler** implements **ErrorHandler**, it quietly consumes any validation errors that occur.

The answer, of course, is to override the methods that catch the errors you want to process. The interface is simple enough, with only three methods:

- **error**—The parser calls this method when it detects a recoverable error. For example, failing DTD validation will cause the parser to call **error**.

- **fatalError**—You receive a call to **fatalError** when the parser finds something severe, such as an improperly formed XML document. Notice that a document that fails DTD validation still may be well formed.

- **warning**—When the parser sees something suspicious, it reports it as a warning. For example, if you are working with a validating parser and the document does not contain a DTD, the parser will call **warning**. Of course, as soon as it parses an element, it will also call **error**, in this case.

The methods in the **ErrorHandler** interface receive **SAXParseException** objects. You could throw these so that normal exception handling would apply. The objects contain information about the location of the error you may use when reporting the error. For example, here is a simple pair of handlers for **error** and **warning**:

```
// ErrorHandler Interface

    // watch for errors
    public void error(SAXParseException e)
        throws SAXParseException {
        throw e;
    }

    // and warnings
    public void warning(SAXParseException e)
        throws SAXParseException {
        System.out.println("Warning at " + e.getLineNumber() + " " +
                            e.getMessage());
    }
```

Notice that the **error** method actually throws the error (presumably to be caught by the caller). The **warning** method, however, simply prints a message and resumes parsing.

Creating a DOM from an XML File

If you are working with a DOM, you simply call the **DocumentBuilder** object's **parse** method. This returns a **Document** object, which is a subclass of **Node**.

```
// This one line loads the whole document!
          document = builder.parse( new File(argv[0]) );
```

You can examine the entire document by walking through the nodes. Each **Node** object has methods that allow you to find the child nodes, if any. For example, you can call **getChildNodes**, which returns a **NodeList**.

Each node has a type (use **getNodeType** to find it). Element nodes that represent tags have children that are text nodes. These text nodes contain the data the tags hold (available with **getNodeValue**). For example, suppose the XML file contains:

```
<pages>40</pages>
```

The corresponding DOM will have an element node for the **pages** tag. That node will have a child text node that contains the enclosed string ("40").

Reading Attributes

One thing that does not appear in the structured DOM tree directly is attributes. Consider this tag:

```
<width units="in">33</width>
```

If you use **getChildNodes** and traverse the tree using the given **NodeList**, you won't see an entry for the **units** attribute. Instead, you must query each **Node** using **getAttribute**. This returns either **null** or a **NamedNodeMap**. If you receive a valid **NamedNodeMap**, it will contain one or more attribute nodes. You can use **getNodeValue** to find the value of the attribute (**getNodeName** will tell you the name of the attribute).

```
NamedNodeMap attr=node.getAttributes();
```

Listing 14.13 shows a **Node** walking method modified to read the attribute values and display them in the same way that it displays ordinary nodes. The **walk** method examines the node for attributes and then displays the current node. After the display, it calls **walk** recursively to display the attributes before calling **walk** again to process any child nodes.

Listing 14.13   This walk method handles attributes.

```
// recursively walk the nodes
    public static void walk(Node node) {
        NodeList nodes=node.getChildNodes();
        String val;
        NamedNodeMap attr=null;
        if (node.getNodeType()==Node.TEXT_NODE ||
            node.getNodeType()==Node.ATTRIBUTE_NODE) {
            val=node.getNodeValue().trim();
            if (val.length()==0) return; // don't print pure white space
        }
        else {
            val=node.getNodeName();
            attr=node.getAttributes();
        }
        for (int j=0;j<level;j++) System.out.print("\t");
        System.out.print("Level " + level+1);
        System.out.println(" " + nodeType(node) + ":" + val);
        if (attr!=null){
            for (int j=0;j<attr.getLength();j++)
                walk(attr.item(j));
        }
        level++;
        for (int i=0;i<nodes.getLength();i++)
            walk(nodes.item(i));
        level--;
    }
```

Constructing a DOM

Sometimes it is useful to build a DOM programmatically instead of reading an XML file. For example, you could load a DOM from an existing (non-XML) data source and then use the DOM to create the corresponding XML.

Consider the code fragment in Listing 14.14. The **makeDOM** method obtains a **DocumentBuilder** object as usual, but instead of loading an XML file, it calls **newDocument** to create an empty DOM.

Armed with this blank DOM, the method calls **createElement** and **appendChild** to populate the tree. The tree you create will be just like a tree you'd read from the corresponding XML. For example, notice the **title** element. It is an element node, and the actual text of the title is a child element (a text node).

Listing 14.14   This method creates a DOM from scratch.

```
public static void makeDOM() {
    DocumentBuilderFactory factory=
        DocumentBuilderFactory.newInstance ();
    try {
        DocumentBuilder builder=factory.newDocumentBuilder();
        document=builder.newDocument();
        Element root =
            (Element) document.createElement("book");
        document.appendChild(root);
        Element title = (Element) document.createElement("title");
        root.appendChild(title);
        title.appendChild( document.createTextNode("DeathWorld") );

    }
    catch (ParserConfigurationException e) {
        e.printStackTrace();
        System.exit(1);
    }

}
```

Writing a DOM

If you have a DOM you've read or built from some other source, you can convert it back to XML by using a **Transformer** object. Constructing a **Transformer** is similar to constructing a parser:

1. Call the static method **TransformerFactory.newInstance**.

2. Use the **TransformerFactory.newTransformer** method to return an actual instance of a **Transformer**.

3. Construct a **DOMSource** object that contains the DOM you wish to convert (this may be an entire DOM or a subtree of a larger DOM).

4. Construct a **StreamResult** object that reflects the output stream you wish to use.

5. Call **Transformer.transform** to write the DOM to the stream as an XML file.

Listing 14.15 shows the complete process from a DOM that is constructed programmatically. The **makeDOM** method builds the DOM, and the program simply writes out the XML to the system console.

---

*TIP: In addition to the jaxp.jar and crimson.jar files, you'll also need to add the xalan.jar file to your **CLASSPATH** before compiling and running Listing 14.15.*

Listing 14.15   You can write out a DOM to XML with this program.

```java
import javax.xml.parsers.DocumentBuilder;
import javax.xml.parsers.DocumentBuilderFactory;
import javax.xml.parsers.FactoryConfigurationError;
import javax.xml.parsers.ParserConfigurationException;
import javax.xml.transform.*;
import javax.xml.transform.dom.DOMSource;
import javax.xml.transform.stream.StreamResult;


import java.io.File;
import java.io.IOException;

import org.w3c.dom.*;



public class DomXform {
    static Document document;
    private static Element makeElementText(String element,String text) {
      Element e = (Element) document.createElement(element);
      e.appendChild(document.createTextNode(text));
      return e;
      }

    public static void makeDOM() {
        DocumentBuilderFactory factory=
          DocumentBuilderFactory.newInstance ();
        try {
            DocumentBuilder builder=factory.newDocumentBuilder();
            document=builder.newDocument();
            Element root =
                (Element) document.createElement("book");
            document.appendChild(root);
            root.appendChild(makeElementText("title","Deathworld"));
            root.appendChild(makeElementText("author","Harrison"));
            Element shelving =
                (Element) document.createElement("shelving");
            root.appendChild(shelving);
            shelving.appendChild(makeElementText("shelve","scifi"));
            shelving.appendChild(makeElementText("shelve","trilogies"));
            shelving.appendChild(makeElementText("shelve","Harrison"));
        }
        catch (ParserConfigurationException e) {
            e.printStackTrace();
            System.exit(1);
        }
```

```
    }
    static int level=0;

// convert a node type to a string
    public static String nodeType(Node node) {
        switch (node.getNodeType()) {
        case Node.ATTRIBUTE_NODE:
            return "Attribute";
        case Node.CDATA_SECTION_NODE:
            return "CDATA Section";
        case Node.COMMENT_NODE:
            return "Comment";
        case Node.DOCUMENT_FRAGMENT_NODE:
            return "Doc Fragment";
        case Node.DOCUMENT_NODE:
            return "Document";
        case Node.DOCUMENT_TYPE_NODE:
            return "Document Type";
        case Node.ELEMENT_NODE:
            return "Element";
        case Node.ENTITY_NODE:
            return "Entity";
        case Node.ENTITY_REFERENCE_NODE:
            return "Entity Reference";
        case Node.NOTATION_NODE:
            return "Notation";
        case Node.PROCESSING_INSTRUCTION_NODE:
            return "Processing Instruction";
        case Node.TEXT_NODE:
            return "Text";
        default:
            return "Unknown";
        }
    }

    public static void main(String argv[]) throws Exception
    {
        try {
// This one line loads the whole document!
            makeDOM();
            // Create a transformer
            TransformerFactory tFactory =
                TransformerFactory.newInstance();
            Transformer transformer = tFactory.newTransformer();

            DOMSource source = new DOMSource(document);
            StreamResult result = new StreamResult(System.out);
```

```
            // Write it out
            transformer.transform(source, result);



        } catch (Exception e) {
            e.printStackTrace();
        }
    } // main



}
```

Listing 14.16 shows the output from the program as an XML file. Notice that the transformer doesn't insert line breaks or indent tags the way a human might. Still, the XML is correct, if hard to read.

Listing 14.16   The XML output from the program in Listing 14.14.

```
<?xml version="1.0" encoding="UTF-8"?>
<book><title>Deathworld</title><author>Harrison</author><shelving>
<shelve>scifi</shelve><shelve>trilogies</shelve><shelve>Harrison</shelve>
</shelving></book>
```

Chapter 15

A Bit of Security

In Depth

Would you stand in the middle of a shopping mall and shout out your checkbook balance and the results of your last medical exam? Probably not. However, you might well discuss either of these things on the telephone. You are in your house, and you expect to have a certain level of privacy, right?

We had a baby monitor in the house when my youngest son was small. It also picked up one of our neighbor's cordless phone conversations. I won't go into detail, but I certainly found out more about that particular neighbor than I wanted to know—quite a bit more. Even if you don't use a cordless phone, long distance calls are sometimes transmitted by radio, to say nothing of cell phones. Perhaps you aren't using a wireless phone, but the person you are calling may be.

My point is that privacy isn't a problem when you know you have no privacy. However, when you have the illusion of privacy, you have to be extra careful. There have been several well-publicized cases where email—something many people think is private—came back to haunt the sender (or receiver). From Gene Wang to Oliver North, public exposure of private emails has caused several public figures grief.

But security isn't just for email. As you've seen in earlier chapters, every time you send a password to an FTP (File Transfer Protocol) or Telnet server, you are sending it through your Internet connection. How smart is that? Sure, baby monitors don't overhear IP (Internet Protocol) connections, but all it takes is someone on your network with a sniffer or a promiscuous network card to eavesdrop on your connection. Anyone who has access to the routers at your ISP (Internet Service Provider)—or at any network center between you and the server—can certainly watch your network traffic (and may even have a log of it to examine at their leisure). Finally, administrators of the server can probably find a way to listen in on your communications.

There are several ways to secure network communications, including the following:

- *Wrappers*—For programs such as email or FTP, you can encode your data before you send it. This assumes that the recipient knows how to decode it. Encoding doesn't really require any special server or client features, but some mail clients do provide easy ways for you to work with encryption and decryption tools.

- *Secure protocols*—Several protocols allow you to use alternate methods for sending passwords. For example, a server might encode some random string by combining it in a secret way with your password. Then, the server sends that string to the client. The client must decode the string, which isn't especially secret, and return it to the server. This proves the client knows the password without actually transmitting the password. Without knowing the algorithm and the random string, you'd have a tough time re-creating the password.

- *Encrypted sockets*—Because networking operates using layers, it is possible to insert an encryption layer between layers of network stack. For example, in theory, you could build network cards (for a private network) that encrypt data. This would lock your network from all but the most sophisticated hackers. It would also prevent you from interoperating with the rest of the Internet, of course. A more practical solution is to use a secure layer under the TCP (Transmission Control Protocol) layer. Secure Socket Layer (SSL) is a popular choice. Replacements for many insecure programs are available. For example, instead of Telnet, many sites now use SSH (Secure Shell), which encrypts all data, not just passwords.

- *Data hiding*—Steganography hides your sensitive data in something innocuous, such as a GIF (graphics interchange format) file or an MP3 file. To the naked eye (or ear) the file will appear normal, but if you know how the data is hidden you can recover it. This may not be very secure, but it has the advantage of not being an obvious secret message. If I send you a message that says "F$IDIF DIDFE 98DE#A," then anyone seeing it can guess that it means something. If I send you a picture of my two dogs, who would guess it really contains my secret shrimp sauce recipe? Often, steganography hides data that was encrypted using another method.

Security at the deepest level is best left to specialists. However, you can use security in your programs without having to know all the details involved.

Encryption Overview

I've always found it interesting that advanced specialized technology usually takes about 10 years to become commonplace. For example, when I started working with computers, the programmer was responsible for blocking and deblocking records to fit in hardware device sectors. Who has done that lately? The operating system takes care of it, and the idea that logical records don't have to fit into sectors is commonplace. Networking and graphical programming are two more examples—once the province of experts, now they are common techniques.

Security has a similar background. Only hardcore experts understand all the intricacies of security. However, security has crept into common use and is usable by the average programmer—without having to understand every bit of theory behind it.

Of course, for maximum security, there is one unbreakable code. Suppose I'm in Houston, and you are in San Francisco. My company is about to buy one of three companies, and I want to let you know which one we've decided on so you can buy up its stock (by the way, this is highly illegal, but just pretend for a minute that we are nefarious). On my last trip to the Moscone center, we met in a private place and agreed to assign each company a code word: baseball, pizza, and television. When I send you a message, it will only contain one of these words, and the word it contains tells you which stock to buy.

That's unbreakable. No matter how many messages someone intercepts from me telling you how I enjoyed the pizza you made when I was in town, he'll never figure out what that means unless he learns our secret.

This is very secure, but it has one major disadvantage. It is completely inflexible. What if my company decides not to buy anything? Or we decide to buy a new company? We don't have a code word for that. In real life, computer programs want to transmit arbitrary text, such as credit card numbers, addresses, and bank balances. Therefore, there has to be a more flexible way to encode and decode any string.

When you add the ability to encode or decode arbitrary strings, you also invite attack on the encryption. That means that someone who wants to know our secret can use mathematics or other methods to decode the messages. Alan Turing and his group successfully decoded German Enigma transmissions during World War II, and this gave the Allies a tremendous advantage (to be fair, the Japanese used a machine called Purple, which was also decoded by the Allies). The Enigma was a sophisticated machine and parts of it were classified for many years after the war. But if the machine can encode something, another machine can decode it, and that was what Turing did, building one of the first real computers to handle the decoding.

Think of encryption as a lock. Would you lock up your home with a cheap bicycle padlock? How about your bank's vault that holds your money? There is no reason to lock up a $100 bicycle with a $2,500 security system. Securing a data transmission is no different. Yes, several world governments probably have the computing power to break your browser's 128-bit encryption in a few days or weeks. But why would they? If you aren't Dr. Evil plotting world domination in your dark tower, you probably don't have to worry.

One method for encoding and decoding is the secret key method. In this strategy, a secret key is known to you and the data's recipient. For example, we might decide to replace all "A" characters with an "X", all "B" characters with an "F", and so on. The problem is, if I know how to encode a message, I also know how to decode it. Further, we have to have some secret way to exchange the key. If I send you a regular email with our private code in it, that isn't very secure.

To work around this, mathematicians developed public key cryptography. With public key cryptography, two keys exist. The first one is private, and you keep it to yourself. The second key is public, and you can broadcast it to anyone you like. Anyone can use the public key to encrypt a message that you can decrypt with the private key. The mathematics are such that you can't easily deduce the private key from the public key.

This has many advantages over a single secret key. First, you don't have to transmit your private key to anyone. Second, you can tell everyone your public key. An interloper with your public key still can't read encoded messages.

In theory, someone could encrypt a message with your key and then use the result to deduce your key, but it takes a tremendous amount of computing power. You can increase the difficulty by increasing the number of bits used in the key. For example, a recent group of networked computers cracked a 56-bit key in just over 22 hours. That sounds impressive until you find out that the network contained 100,000 PCs and was testing 245 billion keys per second. Honestly, my credit cards don't have a high enough limit to make it worthwhile for someone to use 100,000 PCs just to get my number.

Today, most browsers in the United States use 128-bit keys. Cracking a key of this length would be very difficult, unless someone develops a smarter algorithm to crack the code.

You can use a variation on the public key theme to authenticate a message as well. Suppose I encrypt a publicly known message using my private key and send it to you. You decrypt the message using my public key and determine that the message is correct. You now have a high-level of confidence that I sent the message because only someone with my secret key could encode the message. Of course, I could also encrypt using my private key and then encrypt with your public key so that only you can read the message (with your private key) and you can be sure I sent the message (by applying my public key).

Often the publicly known message is actually a digest (in effect, a lengthy checksum) of the message. When you recover the digest, you compute your own digest and compare the two. This tells you not only that I sent the message but also that the message wasn't changed in transit.

Of course, applying lengthy keys to large blocks of data can be very time-consuming. To ease the burden on the computer, some systems use public key encryption to encrypt a secret key. Then the secret key encrypts the rest of the message. In this way, you use the simpler encryption algorithm for the majority of the message.

Java Security

If you find all of the security permutations confusing, don't worry. As usual, a Java library takes most of the pain out of using secure sockets. In particular, the Java Secure Socket Extensions (JSSE) (available at **http://java.sun.com/ products/jsse**) makes it simple to create a secure socket. If you are using the Java Development Kit (JDK) 1.4 or later, you already have JSSE. Otherwise, you'll need to download it from the Sun Web site.

The extension has three packages:

• **javax.net.ssl**—Abstract class definitions

• **javax.net**—Factories used to create secure sockets

• **com.sun.net.ssl**—Sun's reference implementation of JSSE

In addition, you may need to use **java.security.cert**, which handles security certificates.

Unlike a regular socket, which has a constructor, you'll use a special factory class to build a secure socket. What's more, you'll use another method to find the factory class. This indirection is necessary because JSSE is really just a shell over a set of implementation classes. Although you'll typically use Sun's reference implementation in **com.sun.net.ssl**, you could—in theory—use objects from another source.

You can find an example in Listing 15.1. This program accepts a hostname on the command line and attempts to open a secure connection with a Web server on port 443 (the default port for the https protocol). Once connected, the program issues a standard HTTP 1.0 **GET** request and displays the result.

The static **SSLSocketFactory.getDefault** method returns the socket factory. You can call **createSocket** against the factory to create a new socket. After that, the program looks just like any other socket program.

Although the program looks very similar to a normal socket program, you'll notice that it takes much longer to execute than a similar socket program that uses a regular socket. That's because SSL sockets must complete a complicated handshake to exchange keys and other information before the program can begin transferring data.

Listing 15.1   This program requests the default page from a secure Web server.

```
import java.net.*;
import javax.net.ssl.*;
import java.security.*;
import java.io.*;
```

```
public class SSLGet {
    public static void main(String[] args) throws Exception {
        int port=443; // HTTPS uses 443 by default
        String server=args[0];
        SSLSocketFactory factory;
        factory=(SSLSocketFactory)SSLSocketFactory.getDefault();
        SSLSocket socket=(SSLSocket)factory.createSocket(server,port);
        Writer out=new OutputStreamWriter(socket.getOutputStream());
        out.write("GET https://" + server + "/ HTTP/1.0\r\n\r\n");
        out.flush();
        BufferedReader in = new BufferedReader(
                    new InputStreamReader(socket.getInputStream()));
        int c;
        while ((c=in.read())!=-1) System.out.print((char)c);
        out.close();
        in.close();
        socket.close();
    }
}
```

About Certificates

If you start working with security, you'll probably need a certificate sooner or later. The JDK contains a program named keytool that can help you create your own keys. This program allows you to build and maintain keystores. By default, a keystore is a file, but—in theory—it could be a database, a removable smart card, or any other storage medium.

Each keystore can contain two different items: key entries, which contain private keys, and trusted certificate entries, which are public keys that you (the owner of the keystore) trust. Keystore entries have aliases, which are case-sensitive names you can use to refer to the entry. Keytool can work with X.509 certificates (a standard type of certificate).

You can even create new certificates, but no one will really trust them. Web browsers and other secure programs will trust a handful of root certification authorities (CAs). For the browser to trust you, your certificate must be signed by a root CA. Keep in mind that signing may involve a chain of CAs. So the certificate might be signed by me, my certificate might be signed by Coriolis, and the Coriolis certificate might be signed by a root CA. The effect is the same as the root CA directly signing your certificate.

Table 15.1 shows the information that appears in a certificate. Typically, the CA will charge you a fee to sign your certificate. The CA will only validate information it knows to be true about you.

Table 15.1   Information that appears in an X.509 certificate (version 1).

Field	Description
Version	This X.509 version. The keytool program will read up to version 3, but only creates version 1 certificates.
Serial Number	This is a unique serial number.
Signature Algorithm Identifier	This identifies the algorithm used by the CA to sign the certificate.
Issuer Name	The X.500 Distinguished Name of the entity that signed the certificate (normally a CA).
Validity Period	The starting and ending time and date for this certificate.
Subject Name	The name of the entity whose public key the certificate identifies.
Subject Public Key Information	This is the public key of the entity being named and an algorithm identifier.

The biggest CA is VeriSign (**www.verisign.com**). At the time of this writing, this CA will give you a simple certificate (mostly for signing email) for $14.95. It bought another CA, Thawte, which offers free email-signing certificates (**www.thawte.com**). The CA will send you emails to verify that your email address is one you can read and will verify your email address. It won't, however, verify your name, your phone number, or any other information that the CA doesn't verify itself.

Table 15.2 (in the Immediate Solutions section) shows you the options you can use with keytool.

Hiding Data

I've been accused of having strange dreams, and I suppose that's true. One night I dreamt of sending secret data by causing a subtle frequency drift in airplane transponders. To outward appearances, the signal was ordinary, but if you knew where to look, there was a message. When I woke up, I thought that was an interesting idea, so I did some research.

Turns out I was 7,000 years too late to file a patent application. The Greek Histiaeus wrote secret messages on the shaved head of a slave and then dispatched the slave after his hair grew back. This is known as steganography, and it is alive and well to this day.

Computers have revolutionized steganography. Think of all the files that fly across the Internet every day. If you see a message that says BEGIN PGP, you know it was encrypted with the Pretty Good Privacy program. You may not know what it says, but you do know that the sender and the recipient are exchanging secret information. On the other hand, if the email is a picture of a car or a computer, you might not find that as suspicious. Steganography programs can hide data inside a picture so that the picture looks the same (or nearly the same) to the naked eye, but it contains data that you can see if you know where to look.

Imagine a hacker breaks into your server. You can tempt him with dummy credit card numbers, while he ignores the pictures of your hometown. Of course, the file hidden in those pictures can be further encrypted using PGP or any other method. But you have to find the files before you can actually try to crack them.

I decided I wanted to experiment with simple steganography that could be decoded by hand, if necessary. Several programs are available that can hide text inside other text by manipulating word or letter patterns. However, I wanted something that would integrate into Java I/O and would be suitable for use from a JSP or an applet. In fact, I wanted to integrate steganography with Java's I/O system.

Java's I/O System

Working with Java I/O reminds me of plumbing. You take two pipes, put them together, and then find an adapter that makes them fit. You can join lots of pipes together if you have enough different adapters.

Modern Java programs use classes derived from **Reader** and **Writer** for most of their I/O. These are better than the old-fashioned stream classes because they handle Unicode mapping. If you have a stream (like the console that looks like an **InputStream** and an **OutputStream**), you can wrap it in an **InputStreamReader** or **OutputStreamWriter** object to make it act like a reader or writer.

The idea in Java is to start with a basic I/O object and wrap it in other objects that add the functions you require. For example, suppose you start with a file (using **FileReader**). If all you want is to read characters from the file, that's fine. However, you might want to buffer your reading to improve performance. A buffer would also allow you to read an entire line of text at a time. In that case, you could wrap the **FileReader** object in a **BufferedReader** wrapper. If you also need to keep track of the line number you are on, you could use a subclass of **BufferedReader**, **LineNumberReader**. On the other hand, you might want the ability to push back one or more characters after you've read them. In that case, you could add a **PushbackReader**.

It is perfectly acceptable to mix more than one adapter to fit the plumbing pipes together. For example, suppose you are writing a network program that uses the **Socket** class. You can read or write to the socket using streams (from the **getInputStream** and **getOutputStream** methods). You might use an **InputStreamReader** to convert the stream to a reader object. Then you might pass the **InputStreamReader** to the constructor for a **LineNumberReader**, for example.

If you are a Unix user, this might remind you of how you perform many tasks in Unix: You use pipes. So, although cat foo | more shows you a file, cat foo | sort | more shows you the same file with its lines sorted. This is such a powerful idea, you'll probably want to write your own plug-in modules that can alter a stream of input or output. That's what my steganography object does—it attaches to an output stream. That allows you to hide or reveal a stream of data quite easily.

This isn't a new idea. For example, similar objects are in the **java.util.zip** package to perform zip file compression and decompression. It is a flexible technique, too. After all, you can make an ordinary string appear as a stream using **String-Reader** or **StringWriter**, so you can perform these filtering operations on strings, sockets, files, pipes—anything that can produce a stream. Other objects can convert arrays to streams, so you could apply filters to arrays as well.

Enter FilterWriter

These filtering modules are so commonplace that Java provides special prototype classes you can subclass to produce them. In particular, **FilterInputStream**, **FilterOutputStream**, **FilterReader**, and **FilterWriter** can allow you to preprocess data for an **InputStream**, **OutputStream**, **Reader**, or **Writer** object respectively.

You won't use these classes directly. Instead, you'll create a subclass of them to do whatever specialized processing you need. Although each class has quite a few functions, you'll mostly need to override the **read** or **write** methods. Your job is simple because you can usually write one function to handle single characters and then define the remaining functions in terms of the character-oriented function.

For example, consider the class in Listing 15.2 (**UCWriter**). This object forces all the output to a writer into uppercase. Notice that only the **write(int)** method contains actual code. The other two **write** functions call that function to perform the conversion. Of course, in this case, it might be more efficient at runtime to perform the conversion differently in each function. However, for more complex conversions, you'll probably be better off writing the code once and using it again from the other functions.

Listing 15.2   This filter forces a stream into uppercase.

```
// Force a stream to upper case
import java.io.*;

public class UCWriter extends FilterWriter {
    public UCWriter(Writer out) {
      super(out);
    }
```

15. A Bit of Security

```
public  void write(int c) throws IOException {
  super.write(Character.toUpperCase((char)c));
}
public void write(char[] cbuf,int off,int len) throws IOException {
  while (len--!=0) {
  write((int)cbuf[off++]);
  }
}
public void write(String str,int off,int len) throws IOException {
      while (len--!=0) {
          write((int)str.charAt(off++));
      }
}
public static void main(String args[]) {
  PrintWriter console = new PrintWriter(new
          UCWriter(new
            OutputStreamWriter(System.out)));
    console.println("hello there web techniques!");
    console.flush ();
}
}
```

When the filter class wants to write to the underlying writer, it uses the protected **out** field from **FilterWriter**. Nothing actually appears on the output until the class specifically writes to the **out** writer.

The class contains an example **main** function. This program converts **System.out** to an **OutputStreamWriter** and then attaches that writer to a **UCWriter**. Finally, it attaches the entire set of writers and streams to a **PrintWriter**, which does formatting. The end result is a stream that prints everything in uppercase to the system console.

Steganography

The **FilterWriter** class is what I wanted to use to implement a simple text-based steganography class, the idea being that I could attach my class to an existing **Writer** class and then either encode or decode hidden text.

My algorithm is very simple (see Listing 15.3). The encoder reads a template file of plain text. As it writes the text out, it uses the spaces between words to encode the bits of the file you want to hide. Two spaces indicate a distinct state, and a single space indicates a different state. The states alternate between 1 and 0, so if two consecutive words have two spaces after them, and the first one indicates a 1, the second set of two blanks encodes a 0.

Listing 15.3   This filter hides the data using steganography.

```
// steganography class -- Williams
import java.io.*;

public class Steg extends FilterWriter {
    protected Reader plainmessage;   // template
    protected String plainmsgfile;   // file name for template
    protected boolean newline;       // need a newline
    protected boolean encoding;      // true if hiding
    protected boolean decphase=false;  // decoding phase
    protected int decodech=0;        // decoding character
    protected int decodectr=1;       // current bit decoding
    // when phase is false, 1 space is a 0
    // and 2 spaces is a 1
    // otherwise, invert
    protected boolean phase=false;


    // This is the encoding constructor
    public Steg(String plainmsg,Writer out) throws IOException {
      super(out);
      plainmsgfile=plainmsg;
      plainmessage=new BufferedReader(new FileReader(plainmsgfile));
      encoding=true;
    }


    // This is the decoding constructor
    public Steg(Writer out) {
      super(out);
      encoding=false;
    }


    // Read a character
    // if EOF, return a space and rewind
    protected char readChar() throws IOException {
        int c;
        c=plainmessage.read();
        if (c==-1) {
           plainmessage.close();
           plainmessage=new FileReader(plainmsgfile);
           c=' ';
           }
        return (char)c;
    }
```

```
// Read a word. Skip leading blanks and set newline
// if you encounter a newline
protected String readWord() throws IOException {
  StringBuffer wordBuf = new StringBuffer();
  char c;
  newline=false;
  do {
     c=readChar();
     if (c=='\n') newline=true;
  } while (Character.isWhitespace(c));  // skip lead blanks
  do {
    wordBuf.append(c);
    c=readChar();
    if (c=='\n') newline=true;
    } while (!Character.isWhitespace(c)); // read to blank
   return wordBuf.toString();
}


// Encrypt or decrypt according to flag
public void write(int c) throws IOException {
 // do the "encryption"
   if (encoding) {
   String word,sep;
   boolean bit;
   for (int i=0;i<16;i++) { // unicode is 16 bits
     word=readWord();
     out.write(word);
     if ((c&(1<<i))==0) bit=false; else bit=true;
     if (phase)
        if (bit) sep=" "; else sep="  ";
     else
        if (bit) sep="  "; else sep=" ";
     phase=!phase;
     out.write(sep);
     if (newline) out.write('\n');
     }
  }
  else {
// decoding
     if (!decphase) {
       if (c==' ') decphase=true;
       }
     else {
       if (c=='\n'||c=='\r') return; // ignore eol
       decphase=false;
```

```
          if (c==' '&&!phase || c!=' ' && phase) {
              decodech|=decodectr;
          }
          decodectr<<=1;
          phase=!phase;
          if (decodectr==0x10000) {
              out.write(decodech);
              decodectr=1;
              decodech=0;
          }


    }
  }
}


// This write simply delagates to the first write
public void write(char[] cbuf,int off, int len) throws IOException {
  while (len--!=0) {
    write((int)cbuf[off++]);
  }
}


// This write simply delagates to the first write
public void write(String str,int off, int len) throws IOException {
    while (len--!=0) {
      write((int)str.charAt(off++));
      }
    }


// Support for the test main
static void encodetest(String encfile,String inpf) throws Exception {
 FileReader inp=new FileReader(inpf);
 OutputStreamWriter writer = new OutputStreamWriter(System.out);
 Steg stegout=new Steg(encfile,writer);
 do {
     int c=inp.read();
     if (c==-1) break;
     stegout.write(c);
 } while (true);
 stegout.flush();
}


// Support for the test main
static void decodetest(String fn) throws Exception  {
 OutputStreamWriter writer = new OutputStreamWriter(System.out);
 Steg stegin=new Steg(writer);
```

```
    FileReader fread=new FileReader(fn);
    do {
        int c=fread.read();
        if (c==-1) break;
        stegin.write(c);
    } while (true);
    stegin.flush();
    }


    // Test main -- if two arguments, encode
    // if 1 argument, decode
    // anything else prints help message
    public static void main(String args[]) throws Exception {
      if (args.length==2){
        encodetest(args[0],args[1]);
        System.exit(0);
        }
      if (args.length==1) {
        decodetest(args[0]);
        System.exit(0);
        }
      System.out.println("Usage: Steg template file " +
          "(to encode)\nSteg file (to decode)");
    }


}
```

This isn't a perfect scheme because Unicode characters have 16 bits, and the compression ratio is terrible (of course, you can always compress the resulting file). Also, if there is any text added to the beginning of the file, it will not decode correctly. You could resolve this by making the decoder search for a particular keyword to begin the decoding (and perhaps another to end decoding). The encoder could then frame the file with these particular words.

The object maintains a boolean (**encoding**) that tracks if it is hiding text or unhiding it. There are two different constructors, so the state of **encoding** depends on which constructor created the object. When encoding, the object needs a template file that contains the dummy text that will hide the hidden file.

Of course, the hidden file may require more text than the template contains, so I wanted to rewind the template file to the beginning after reaching the end. Unfortunately, **FileReader** does not support the **reset** method, so I had to improvise.

I could force a **FileReader** to support mark/reset by adding a **BufferedReader**, but then I would have to agree to buffer the entire file. That seemed wasteful to me. The encoding constructor accepts the file name of the template text. It then creates a **FileReader** that the rest of the code uses. The **readChar** method then closes this **FileReader** when it reaches the end of the file and re-creates it using the name of the file. Although this seems inefficient, I thought it was better than buffering the entire file in memory.

The **readChar** and **readWord** routines are used internally by the encoder to strip words from the template file. The methods also provide a way for the caller to determine if the end of the word was a new line character. The encoder preserves these to make the text look more realistic. On decoding, the routine ignores any new line characters in case any line wrapping has occurred (for example, when an email client tries to reformat a message).

Using the Class

You could easily use the **Steg** class from any Java program, including a servlet or a JSP page. I included a sample **main**, so you can test the class from the command line. Prepare a template file named template.txt (which should be quite long compared to your input text). Also create a text file that you wish to hide (I'll name mine input.txt). Then issue the following command:

```
java Steg template.txt input.txt >output.txt
```

To recover the hidden text, issue this command:

```
java Steg output.txt
```

Just to get a sense for how an encoded message looks, try decoding Listing 15.4. If you really want to know what it says, try running the **Steg** class against the file on the CD-ROM. If you found this message in someone's inbox, you wouldn't give it a second thought.

Listing 15.4   Can you decode this secret message?

```
This  is  not  SPAM!  You have  asked  to  be kept  informed of  important
information  about how  to secure  your  financial freedom.
Are you  tired  of working  for some  one else  and never
being better  off? Are  you tired of having  a little  extra
month  at the  end  of  the  money? If
this  sounds  like  you,  you  should send  away for  our special
opportunity. If  you  have  a computer and 30 free  minutes
a day,  you could  make a  handsome residual  income -- one
that you can build  to  a level  you are  comfortable with  and
then  retire. Sounds
too  good to be true?  That's  what I  used to  think. However,
using this  system  for  only 30 minutes a day  has  paid
```

off my house, my car, and allowed me to play golf 5 days a
week. It could happen to you. But it won't if you don't respond now. How
do you get started? It's easy. You've already taken the first step.
Now all you need to do is hit reply and put I WANT TO WIN in
the subject line. I WANT TO WIN. It's that simple. But
wait! How do you know this is a legitimate offer? What do you have
to lose? If you send me an e-mail, what did it cost? Nothing. If
I send you back a silly picture of a monkey, what does it cost you?
Nothing. But what if I really do have a endless fountain of money
and can show you how to duplicate it? Then not replying will
be what costs you. But
you won't get a silly picture of a monkey. In fact, what you will
get is information on a time tested way to put money in your pocket.
And not just spare change -- real big bucks. Let
chumps work for their pay. You and I know there is a better way. Get
started today. Thanks
for your

How Secure?

This method of encoding is probably not all that secure from attack. It doesn't have to be. Before you can crack an encoding method, you have to recognize that one is in use. For maximum security, however, you could also encrypt the file before hiding it. That way, an intruder would probably ignore the files. However, if for some reason they were able to reveal the actual files, they would still be encrypted.

You could improve the program's resistance to attack in many ways. For example, you could add the start and stop keywords that I mentioned earlier and then put dummy text before and after those keywords. This would make it more difficult to decode without knowing the keywords. You could also compress the data (using classes from the **java.util.zip** package) before hiding it. Compression, by definition, will tend to remove patterns from the data (that is, increase the average entropy) making statistical analysis more difficult. If you know how to use the Java cryptography libraries, you could easily use them to perform actual encryption of the data at the same time you are hiding it.

Beyond Hiding

Although this class might be useful, it also illustrates an interesting point about the Java I/O system. It is simple to write filter classes that can plug into existing stream classes to provide them with extra features. For example, you might write buffering classes that have special knowledge about the data your program uses to improve performance.

Because streams can be network sockets, strings, arrays, files, or pipes, the code you write as a filter will be useful in many situations. In fact, you can see that many of the predefined classes in the **java.io** package are just filters.

Immediate Solutions

Creating a Secure Socket Factory

If you want to create an SSL socket, you'll first call the static **getDefault** method of the **SSLSocketFactory** object. This factory can create secure socket instances. Here's some example code (refer to Listing 15.1 for a complete example):

```
SSLSocketFactory factory;
factory=(SSLSocketFactory)SSLSocketFactory.getDefault();
```

Creating a Secure Socket

Armed with an **SSLSocketFactory**, you can create socket instances using the **createSocket** method. This roundabout method is required because the **SSLSocketFactory** is really just a wrapper around a set of provider classes that you don't directly interface with. Here is the code you'll need (see Listing 15.1 for a complete example):

```
SSLSocket socket=(SSLSocket)factory.createSocket(server,port);
```

Connecting to a Secure Web Server

Perhaps the most common reason you'll want to use a secure socket is to connect to a secure Web server. By default, secure Web servers use port 443. Of course, many sites don't have a secure server, and most that do have a conventional server on port 80, as well.

Posting to a secure server is very similar to posting to a normal server, except for a few special considerations:

- You must use a secure socket.
- The request must specify the entire Uniform Resource Locator (URL).
- In most cases, you should use **POST**, so the variables sent to the server don't remain visible (for example, in the browser's URL line).

Listing 15.5 shows a simple program that posts a single field to the server. The program requires three command-line arguments:

- The name of the host (**www.al-williams.com**) that contains the secure server (the program assumes port 443).

- The name of the script (for example, ssl/calc.jsp).

- The data to post (for example, val=100). The program assumes you've already encoded it appropriately (in other words, you've converted spaces to plus signs and other URL encoding replacements).

The target file can be a JSP or other server-side program that does something simple. I used a simple JSP file with one line in it:

```
<%= 2*Integer.parseInt(request.getParameter("val")) %>
```

I put the script in a file named calc.jsp. Then, I could test the SSLPost program with the following command line (you'll need to adjust this to suit your specific server and details, of course):

```
java SSLPost www.al-williams.com ssl/calc.jsp val=150
```

The resulting Web page output will reflect the correct answer of 300.

Listing 15.5   Posting to a secure server.

```
import java.net.*;
import javax.net.ssl.*;
import java.security.*;
import java.io.*;

public class SSLPost {
    public static void main(String[] args) throws Exception {
        int port=443; // HTTPS uses 443 by default
        String server=args[0];
        SSLSocketFactory factory;
        factory=(SSLSocketFactory)SSLSocketFactory.getDefault();
        SSLSocket socket=(SSLSocket)factory.createSocket(server,port);
        Writer out=new OutputStreamWriter(socket.getOutputStream());
        out.write("POST  https://" + server + "/" + args[1] +
            " HTTP/1.0\r\n");
        out.write("Content-Type: application/x-www-form-urlencoded\r\n");
        out.write("Content-Length: " + args[2].length() + "\r\n");
        out.write("\r\n");
        out.write(args[2]);
        out.flush();
```

15. A Bit of Security

```
        BufferedReader in = new BufferedReader(
                    new InputStreamReader(socket.getInputStream()));
        int c;
        while ((c=in.read())!=-1) System.out.print((char)c);
        out.close();
        in.close();
        socket.close();
    }
}
```

Using Steganography

Listing 15.3 shows a class that performs steganography encoding and decoding by extending **FilterWriter**. Steganography is the process of hiding data in some other data format. For example, you might hide a file inside a GIF or JPEG (Joint Photographic Experts Group) file. The class in Listing 15.3 hides data in text. The class manipulates the spaces between words to encode 0 or 1 bits. The program requires a template file of text that it writes out with varying spaces between words to encode the target text. You can also reverse the process to transform a file with the peculiar spacing into plain text.

The **FilterWriter** class is very useful for encoders and decoders of any type. The **FilterWriter** constructor accepts a **Writer** and allows you to filter output destined for that **Writer** object.

Here's an example of writing characters to **System.out** and encoding them through the **Steg** class:

```
FileReader inp=new FileReader(inpf);  // source of characters
OutputStreamWriter writer = new OutputStreamWriter(System.out);
Steg stegout=new Steg(encfile,writer);  // attach Steg to out
do {
    int c=inp.read();   // get characters
    if (c==-1) break;
    stegout.write(c);   // filter them through to output
} while (true);
stegout.flush();
```

The **Steg** constructor, in this case, takes two arguments. The first argument specifies a file of template text. The filter uses the words in this file to construct the text that will hide the data. The second argument is the **Writer**. You can also reverse the process and decode a file by constructing the **Steg** object with a single argument. The argument to the constructor when decoding is simply the output

Writer. The object detects which constructor you call and modifies its behavior accordingly. Here's some sample code:

```
OutputStreamWriter writer = new OutputStreamWriter(System.out);
Steg stegin=new Steg(writer);
FileReader fread=new FileReader(fn);
do {
    int c=fread.read();
    if (c==-1) break;
    stegin.write(c);
} while (true);
stegin.flush();
```

Obtaining Certificates

You can build your own test certificate using the keytool program. The Sun documentation has complete information. You can use the **genkey** option to generate a new set of keys. The file you store them in is a *keystore* and the identifier you use to refer to the keys is the *alias*.

Here is a transcript of using the keytool program to create a keystore named awc.keys that contains a key named mykey:

```
$ keytool -genkey -alias mykey -keystore awc.keys
Enter keystore password:  pontoon
What is your first and last name?
  [Unknown]:  Al Williams
What is the name of your organizational unit?
  [Unknown]:  N/A
What is the name of your organization?
  [Unknown]:  AWC
What is the name of your City or Locality?
  [Unknown]:  League City
What is the name of your State or Province?
  [Unknown]:  Texas
What is the two-letter country code for this unit?
  [Unknown]:  TX
Is CN=Al Williams, OU=N/A, O=AWC, L=League City, ST=Texas, C=TX correct?
  [no]:  yes

Enter key password for <mykey>
        (RETURN if same as keystore password):
```

However, a certificate like this won't be trusted by anyone. You need a certificate signed by a root CA, such as VeriSign (**www.verisign.com**) or Thawte (**www.thawte.com**). Actually, VeriSign bought Thawte, but it still operates it as a separate company. It is possible to get free test certificates (and certain user-oriented certificates). But for a real certificate that you can do actual work with, expect to pay.

The CA should provide instructions on how to request a signed certificate. The keytool command has a **–certreq** command that you can use to generate a signing request. You'll usually send this request to the CA, who will return the proper certificate for you to import (see the "Importing Certificates" section later in this chapter).

You can also use command-line options to prevent keytool from prompting you for any extra information. For example, this one command line will do it all (even though the example appears on multiple lines, it is just a single command line):

```
keytool -genkey -dname "cn=Joe Jones, ou=NA, o=AWC, c=US" -alias Jones
 -keypass arg99a -keystore keys -storepass x99101 -validity 30
```

This generates the keys keystore with a password of **x99101**. The keystore will have a certificate named **Jones** with a password of **arg99a**. The certificate will have a common name (**cn**) of **Joe Jones**. The organizational unit (**ou**) is **NA** and the organization (**o**) is **AWC**. The country (**c**) is **US**. The key is valid for 30 days.

Displaying Certificates

You can display a keystore or certificate using the **–list** option of the keytool program. You can specify a keystore alone to list everything in the keystore. You can also specify an alias. For example:

```
keytool -list -keystore awc.keys
keytool -list -keystore awc.keys -alias mykey
```

You can also keytool to view a certificate stored in a file:

```
keytool -printcert -file alw.cer
```

Importing Certificates

You can import certificates into a keystore using the **–import** option to keytool. If you name an existing alias, keytool assumes you are signing an existing key with a CA certificate (see the discussion of **–certreq** in "Obtaining Certificates" section). If you name a new alias, keytool will treat the certificate file as a public key that you trust. Here's the command you'll use:

```
keytool -import -alias al_williams -file alw.cer
```

Exporting Certificates

You can export a certificate from a keystore to a file that you could then import into another keystore. Here's a sample command:

```
keytool -export -alias al_williams -file alw.cer
```

Appendix A

Active RFCs

If you need detailed information about anything on the Internet, the RFCs are the source to turn to. Unfortunately, with thousands of RFCs, it is difficult to know which one you need to read. To make matters worse, many RFCs are no longer active, which can be confusing.

Some RFCs (like RFC1000) are an index to the other RFCs. Also, online search engines such as the one at **www.faqs.org/rfcs** can be very helpful. You can also find a complete list at **www.ietf.org/iesg/1rfc_index.txt** and retrieve documents from **www.rfc-editor.org/rfc.html**.

RFCs can be received via email. The email address is RFC-INFO@ISI.EDU. You can obtain an index of RFCs by sending:

HELP: rfc_index

Complete help is available with this command:

HELP: help

To retrieve a specific RFC, send:

Retrieve: RFC
Doc-ID: RFC1000

Keep in mind that not all RFCs are standards. Some of them are even humorous (notice RFC 1149, for example). The true standard documents (and their corresponding RFCs) appear in Table A.1.

Table A.1   Internet Standard Documents.

Standard	Title	Authors	Date	Obsoletes	RFC(s)
STD0001	Internet Official Protocol Standards	J. Reynolds R. Braden, S. Ginoza	May 2001	RFC2700	RFC2800
STD0002	Assigned Numbers	J. Reynolds, J. Postel	October 1994	RFC1340	RFC1700
STD0003	Requirements for Internet Hosts	R. Braden, Ed.	October 1989		RFC1122, RFC1123
STD0004	Reserved for Router Requirements				
STD0005	Internet Protocol	J. Postel	September 1981		RFC0791, RFC0792, RFC0919, RFC0922, RFC0950, RFC1112
STD0006	User Datagram Protocol	J. Postel	August 1980		RFC0768
STD0007	Transmission Control Protocol	J. Postel	September 1981		RFC0793
STD0008	Telnet Protocol	J. Postel, J. Reynolds	May 1983		RFC0854, RFC0855
STD0009	File Transfer Protocol	J. Postel, J. Reynolds	October 1985		RFC0959, RFC2228, RFC2640
STD0010	Simple Mail Transfer Protocol	J. Postel	August 1982	RFC788, RFC780, RFC772	RFC0821, RFC2821
STD0011	Standard for the Format of ARPA Internet Text Messages	D. Crocker	August 1982	RFC733	FC0822, RRFC2822
STD0012	Reserved for Network Time Protocol (NTP)				
STD0013	Domain Name System	P. Mockapetris	November 1987		RFC1034, RFC1035

(continued)

Appendix A Active RFCs

Table A.1   Internet Standard Documents *(continued).*

Standard	Title	Authors	Date	Obsoletes	RFC(s)
STD0014	Obsolete: Was Mail Routing and the Domain System				
STD0015	Simple Network Management Protocol	J. Case, M. Fedor, M. Schoffstall, J. Davin	May 1990		RFC1157
STD0016	Structure of Management Information	M. Rose, K. McCloghrie	May 1990	RFC1065	RFC1155
STD0017	Management Information Base	K. McCloghrie, M. Rose	March 1991	RFC1158	RFC1213
STD0018	Obsolete: Was Exterior Gateway Protocol (RFC 904)				
STD0019	NetBIOS Service Protocols	NetBIOS Working Group	March 1987		RFC1001, RFC1002
STD0020	Echo Protocol	J. Postel	May 1983		RFC0862
STD0021	Discard Protocol	J. Postel	May 1983		RFC0863
STD0022	Character Generator Protocol	J. Postel	May 1983		RFC0864
STD0023	Quote of the Day Protocol	J. Postel	May 1983		RFC0865
STD0024	Active Users Protocol	J. Postel	May 1983		RFC0866
STD0025	Daytime Protocol	J. Postel	May 1983		RFC0867
STD0026	Time Server Protocol	J. Postel	May 1983		RFC0868
STD0027	Binary Transmission Telnet Option	J. Postel, J. Reynolds	May 1983		RFC0856
STD0028	Echo Telnet Option	J. Postel, J. Reynolds	May 1983		RFC0857
STD0029	Suppress Go Ahead Telnet Option	J. Postel, J. Reynolds	May 1983		RFC0858
STD0030	Status Telnet Option	J. Postel, J. Reynolds	May 1983		RFC0859
STD0031	Timing Mark Telnet Option	J. Postel, J. Reynolds	May 1983		RFC0860

(continued)

Table A.1   Internet Standard Documents *(continued).*

Standard	Title	Authors	Date	Obsoletes	RFC(s)
STD0032	Extended Options List Telnet Option	J. Postel, J. Reynolds	May 1983		RFC0861
STD0033	Trivial File Transfer Protocol	K. Sollins	July 1992		RFC1350
STD0034	Replaced by STD0056				
STD0035	ISO Transport Service on top of the TCP (Version: 3)	M. Rose, D. Cass	May 1978		RFC1006
STD0036	Transmission of IP and ARP over FDDI Networks	D. Katz	January 1993		RFC1390
STD0037	An Ethernet Address Resolution Protocol	D. C. Plummer	November 1982		RFC0826
STD0038	A Reverse Address Resolution Protocol	R. Finlayson, T. Mann, J. Mogul, M. Theimer	June 1984		RFC0903
STD0039	Obsolete: Was BBN Report 1822 (IMP/Host Interface)				
STD0040	Host Access Protocol Specification	Bolt, Beranek and Newman	August 1993		RFC0907
STD0041	Standard for the Transmission of IP Datagrams over Ethernet Networks	C. Hornig	April 1984		RFC0894
STD0042	Standard for the Transmission of IP Datagrams over Experimental Ethernet Networks	J. Postel	April 1984		RFC0895
STD0043	Standard for the Transmission of IP Datagrams over IEEE 802 Networks	J. Postel, J.K. Reynolds	August 1993	RFC0948	RFC1042
STD0044	DCN Local-Network Protocols	D.L. Mills	August 1993		RFC0891

(continued)

Appendix A   Active RFCs

Table A.1   Internet Standard Documents *(continued).*

Standard	Title	Authors	Date	Obsoletes	RFC(s)
STD0045	Internet Protocol on Network System's HYPER-channel: Protocol Specification	K. Hardwick, J. Lekashman	August 1993		RFC1044
STD0046	Transmitting IP Traffic over ARCNET Networks	D. Provan	August 1993	RFC1051	RFC1201
STD0047	Nonstandard for Transmission of IP Datagrams over Serial Lines: SLIP	J.L. Romkey	August 1993		RFC1055
STD0048	Standard for the Transmission of IP Datagrams over NetBIOS Networks	L.J. McLaughlin	August 1993		RFC1088
STD0049	Standard for the Transmission of 802.2 Packets over IPX Networks	L.J. McLaughlin	August 1993		RFC1132
STD0050	Definitions of Managed Objects for the Ethernet-like Interface Types	F. Kastenholz	July 1994	RFC1623, RFC1398	RFC1643
STD0051	The Point-to-Point Protocol (PPP)	W. Simpson, Editor	July 1994	RFC1549	RFC1661, RFC1662
STD0052	The Transmission of IP Datagrams over the SMDS Service	D. Piscitello, J. Lawrence	March 1991		RFC1209
STD0053	Post Office Protocol—Version 3	J. Myers, M. Rose	May 1996	RFC1725	RFC1939
STD0054	OSPF Version 2	J. Moy	April 1998		RFC2328
STD0055	Multiprotocol Interconnect over Frame Relay	C. Brown, A. Malis	September 1998	RFC1490, RFC1294	RFC2427
STD0056	RIP Version 2	G. Malkin	November 1998	RFC1723	RFC2453

(continued)

Appendix A

Appendix A Active RFCs

Table A.1   Internet Standard Documents *(continued)*.

Standard	Title	Authors	Date	Obsoletes	RFC(s)
STD0057	RIP Version 2 Protocol Applicability Statement	G. Malkin	November 1994		RFC1722
STD0058	Structure of Management Information Version 2 (SMIv2)	K. McCloghrie, D. Perkins, J. Schoenwaelder	April 1999	RFC1902	RFC2578, RFC2579
STD0059	Remote Network Monitoring Management Information Base	S. Waldbusser	May 2000	RFC1757	RFC2819
STD0060	SMTP Service Extension for Command Pipelining	N. Freed	September 2000	RFC2197	RFC2920
STD0061	A One-Time Password System	N. Haller, C. Metz, P. Nesser, M. Straw	February 1998	RFC1938	RFC2289

Often, it is easier to find the standard you need by referencing the common name of the protocol it defines. Table A.2 shows this relationship:

Table A.2   STD documents by protocol mnemonic.

Mnemonic	Title	STD	RFC
ARP	Ethernet Address Resolution Protocol; or, Converting Network Protocol Addresses to 48.bit Ethernet Address for Transmission on Ethernet Hardware	37	826
CHARGEN	Character Generator Protocol	22	864
Concise-MI	Concise MIB definitions	16	1212
CONF-MIB	Conformance Statements for SMIv2	58	2580
CONV-MIB	Textual Conventions for SMIv2	58	2579
DAYTIME	Daytime Protocol	25	867
DISCARD	Discard Protocol	21	863
DOMAIN	Domain names—Implementation and Specification	13	1035

(continued)

Appendix A   Active RFCs

Table A.2   STD documents by protocol mnemonic *(continued)*.

Mnemonic	Title	STD	RFC
DOMAIN	Domain names—Concepts and Facilities	13	1034
ECHO	Echo Protocol	20	862
ETHER-MIB	Definitions of Managed Objects for the Ethernet-like Interface Types	50	1643
FTP	File Transfer Protocol	9	959
ICMP	Internet Control Message Protocol	5	792
IGMP	Host Extensions for IP Multicasting	5	1112
IP	Internet Protocol	5	791
IP-ARC	Transmitting IP Traffic over ARCNET Networks	46	1201
IP-DC	DCN Local-Network Protocols	44	891
IP-E	Standard for the Transmission of IP Datagrams over Ethernet Networks	41	894
IP-EE	Standard for the Transmission of IP Datagrams over Experimental Ethernet Networks	42	895
IP-FDDI	Transmission of IP and ARP over FDDI Networks	36	1390
IP-FR	Multiprotocol Interconnect over Frame Relay	55	2427
IP-HC	Internet Protocol on Network System's HYPERchannel: Protocol specification	45	1044
IP-IEEE	Standard for the Transmission of IP Datagrams over IEEE 802 Networks	43	1042
IP-IPX	Standard for the Transmission of 802.2 Packets over IPX Networks	49	1132
IP-NETBIOS	Standard for the Transmission of IP Datagrams over NetBIOS Networks	48	1088
IP-SLIP	Nonstandard for Transmission of IP Datagrams over Serial Lines: SLIP	47	1055
IP-SMDS	Transmission of IP Datagrams over the SMDS Service	52	1209
IP-WB	Host Access Protocol specification	40	907
MAIL	Standard for the Format of ARPA Internet Text Messages	11	822
MIB-II	Management Information Base for Network Management of TCP/IP-based Internets:MIB-II	17	1213
NETBIOS	Protocol Standard for a NetBIOS Service on a TCP/UDP Transport: Detailed Specifications	19	1002
NETBIOS	Protocol Standard for a NetBIOS Service on a TCP/UDP Transport: Concepts and Methods	19	1001

(continued)

Table A.2   STD documents by protocol mnemonic *(continued)*.

Mnemonic	Title	STD	RFC
ONE-PASS	A One-Time Password System	61	2289
OSPF2	OSPF Version 2	54	2328
POP3	Post Office Protocol—Version 3	53	1939
PPP	The Point-to-Point Protocol (PPP)	51	1661
PPP-HDLC	PPP in HDLC-like Framing	51	1662
QUOTE	Quote of the Day Protocol	23	865
RARP	Reverse Address Resolution Protocol	38	903
RIP2	RIP Version 2	56	2453
RIP2-APP	RIP Version 2 Protocol Applicability Statement	57	1722
RMON-MIB	Remote Network Monitoring Management Information Base	59	2819
SMI	Structure and Identification of Management Information for TCP/IP-based Internets	16	1155
SMIv2	Structure of Management Information Version 2 (SMIv2)	58	2578
SMTP	Simple Mail Transfer Protocol	10	821
SMTP-Pipe	SMTP Service Extension for Command Pipelining	60	2920
SMTP-SIZE	SMTP Service Extension for Message Size Declaration	10	1870
SNMP	Simple Network Management Protocol (SNMP)	15	1157
TCP	Transmission Control Protocol	7	793
TELNET	Telnet Option Specifications	8	855
TELNET	Telnet Protocol Specification	8	854
TFTP	The TFTP Protocol (Revision 2)	33	1350
TIME	Time Protocol	26	868
TOPT-BIN	Telnet Binary Transmission	27	856
TOPT-ECHO	Telnet Echo Option	28	857
TOPT-EXTOP	Telnet Extended Options: List Option	32	861
TOPT-STAT	Telnet Status Option	30	859
TOPT-SUPP	Telnet Suppress Go Ahead Option	29	858
TOPT-TIM	Telnet Timing Mark Option	31	860
TP-TCP ISO	Transport Services on top of the TCP: Version 3	35	1006
UDP	User Datagram Protocol	6	768
USERS	Active Users	24	866

Below (in Table A.3) is a list of the most useful or interesting (and active) RFCs, as of the time this was written, along with information about the RFCs they update or obsolete. I've also made this information available on the CD-ROM so you can search it easily. The RFCs that are also standards are noted with their standard number in the Title column of the table. Notice that some standards have multiple RFCs, and these are not reflected in the table.

Table A.3   Useful RFCs.

RFC	Title	Author(s)	Date	Updates	Obsoletes
0001	Host Software	S. Crocker	Apr-07-1969		
0002	Host Software	B. Duvall	Apr-09-1969		
0008	Functional Specifications for the ARPA Network	G. Deloche	May-05-1969		
0009	Host Software	G. Deloche	May-01-1969		
0012	IMP-Host Interface Flow Diagrams	M. Wingfield	Aug-26-1969		
0013	Zero Text Length EOF Message	V. Cerf	Aug-20-1969		
0015	Network Subsystem for Time Sharing Hosts	C.S. Carr	Sep-25-1969		
0017	Some Questions Re: Host-IMP Protocol	J.E. Kreznar	Aug-27-1969		
0018	IMP-IMP and HOST-HOST Control Links	V. Cerf	Sep-01-1969		
0020	ASCII Format for Network Interchange	V.G. Cerf	Oct-16-1969		
0022	Host-host Control Message Formats	V.G. Cerf	Oct-17-1969		
0023	Transmission of Multiple Control Messages	G. Gregg	Oct-16-1969		
0024	Documentation Conventions	S.D. Crocker	Nov-21-1969	RFC0010, RFC0016	RFC0016
0027	Documentation Conventions	S.D. Crocker	Dec-09-1969	RFC0010, RFC0016, RFC0024	
0028	Time Standards	W.K. English	Jan-13-1970		
0029	Response to RFC 28	R.E. Kahn	Jan-19-1970		

(continued)

Table A.3   Useful RFCs *(continued)*.

RFC	Title	Author(s)	Date	Updates	Obsoletes
0030	Documentation Conventions	S.D. Crocker	Feb-04-1970	RFC0010, RFC0016, RFC0024, RFC0027	
0031	Binary Message Forms in Computer	D. Bobrow, W.R. Sutherland	Feb-01-1968		
0033	New Host-Host Protocol	S.D. Crocker	Feb-12-1970		RFC0011
0036	Protocol Notes	S.D. Crocker	Mar-16-1970	RFC0033	
0038	Comments on Network Protocol from NWG/RFC #36	S.M. Wolfe	Mar-20-1970		
0039	Comments on Protocol Re: NWG/RFC #36	E. Harslem, J.F. Heafner	Mar-25-1970	RFC0036	
0040	More Comments on the Forthcoming Protocol	E. Harslem, J.F. Heafner	Mar-27-1970		
0042	Message Data Types	E. Ancona	Mar-31-1970		
0046	ARPA Network Protocol Notes	E. Meyer	Apr-17-1970		
0089	Some Historic Moments in Networking	R.M. Metcalfe	Jan-19-1971		
0093	Initial Connection Protocol	A.M. McKenzie	Jan-27-1971	RFC0066, RFC0080	
0097	First Cut at a Proposed Telnet Protocol	J.T. Melvin, R.W. Watson	Feb-15-1971		
0103	Implementation of Interrupt Keys	R.B. Kalin	Feb-24-1971		
0114	File Transfer Protocol	A.K. Bhushan	Apr-10-1971		
0128	Bytes	J. Postel	Apr-21-1971		
0137	Telnet Protocol— a Proposed Document	T.C. O'Sullivan	Apr-30-1971		
0139	Discussion of Telnet Protocol	T.C. O'Sullivan	May-07-1971	RFC0137	
0141	Comments on RFC 114: A File Transfer Protocol	E. Harslem, J.F. Heafner	Apr-29-1971	RFC0114	
0147	Definition of a Socket	J.M. Winett	May-07-1971	RFC0129	
0163	Data Transfer Protocols	V.G. Cerf	May-19-1971		

(continued)

Appendix A Active RFCs

Table A.3 Useful RFCs *(continued)*.

RFC	Title	Author(s)	Date	Updates	Obsoletes
0183	EBCDIC Codes and their Mapping to ASCII	J.M. Winett	Jul-21-1971		
0204	Sockets in Use	J. Postel	Aug-05-1971		
0205	NETCRT—a Character Display Protocol	R.T. Braden	Aug-06-1971		
0206	User Telnet—Description of an Initial Implementation	J.E. White	Aug-09-1971		
0208	Address Tables	A.M. McKenzie	Aug-09-1971		
0210	Improvement of Flow Control	W. Conrad	Aug-16-1971		
0236	Standard Host Names	J. Postel	Sep-27-1971		RFC0229
0281	Suggested addition to File Transfer Protocol	A.M. McKenzie	Dec-08-1971	RFC0265	
0318	Telnet Protocols	J. Postel	Apr-03-1972	RFC0158	
0322	Well known Socket Numbers	V. Cerf, J. Postel	Mar-26-1972		
0328	Suggested Telnet Protocol Changes	J. Postel	Apr-29-1972		
0340	Proposed Telnet Changes	T.C. O'Sullivan	May-15-1972		
0347	Echo Process	J. Postel	May-30-1972		
0348	Discard Process	J. Postel	May-30-1972		
0385	Comments on the File Transfer Protocol	A.K. Bhushan	Aug-18-1972	RFC0354	
0412	User FTP Documentation	G. Hicks	Nov-27-1972		
0414	File Transfer Protocol (FTP) Status and Further Comments	A.K. Bhushan	Dec-29-1972	RFC0385	
0429	Character Generator Process	J. Postel	Dec-12-1972		
0435	Telnet Issues	B. Cosell, D.C. Walden	Jan-05-1973	RFC0318	
0448	Print Files in FTP	R.T. Braden	Feb-27-1973		
0461	Telnet Protocol Meeting Announcement	A.M. McKenzie	Feb-14-1973		
0468	FTP Data Compression	R.T. Braden	Mar-08-1973		

(continued)

Table A.3   Useful RFCs *(continued).*

RFC	Title	Author(s)	Date	Updates	Obsoletes
0480	Host-dependent FTP Parameters	J.E. White	Mar-08-1973		
0495	Telnet Protocol Specifications	A.M. McKenzie	May-01-1973		RFC0158
0559	Comments on The New Telnet Protocol and its Implementation	A.K. Bhushan	Aug-15-1973		
0560	Remote Controlled Transmission and Echoing Telnet Option	D. Crocker, J. Postel	Aug-18-1973		
0561	Standardizing Network Mail Headers	A.K. Bhushan, K.T. Pogran, R.S. Tomlinson, J.E. White	Sep-05-1973		
0562	Modifications to the Telnet Specification	A.M. McKenzie	Aug-28-1973		
0630	FTP Error Code Usage for more Reliable Mail Service	J. Sussmann	Apr-10-1974		
0640	Revised FTP Reply Codes	J. Postel	Jun-19-1974	RFC0542	
0652	Telnet Output Carriage-Return Disposition Option	D. Crocker	Oct-25-1974		
0653	Telnet Output Horizontal Tabstops Option	D. Crocker	Oct-25-1974		
0654	Telnet Output Horizontal Tab Disposition Option	D. Crocker	Oct-25-1974		
0655	Telnet Output Formfeed Disposition Option	D. Crocker	Oct-25-1974		
0656	Telnet Output Vertical Tabstops Option	D. Crocker	Oct-25-1974		
0657	Telnet Output Vertical Tab Disposition Option	D. Crocker	Oct-25-1974		
0658	Telnet Output Linefeed Disposition	D. Crocker	Oct-25-1974		
0659	Announcing Additional Telnet Options	J. Postel	Oct-18-1974		
0678	Standard File Formats	J. Postel	Dec-19-1974		

(continued)

Table A.3   Useful RFCs *(continued).*

RFC	Title	Author(s)	Date	Updates	Obsoletes
0679	February, 1975, Survey of New-Protocol Telnet servers	D.W. Dodds	Feb-21-1975		
0680	Message Transmission Protocol	T.H. Myer, D.A. Henderson	Apr-30-1975	RFC0561	
0681	Network UNIX	S. Holmgren	Mar-18-1975		
0697	CWD Command of FTP	J. Lieb	Jul-14-1975		
0698	Telnet Extended ASCII Option	T. Mock	Jul-23-1975		
0706	On the Junk Mail Problem	J. Postel	Nov-08-1975		
0717	Assigned Network Numbers	J. Postel	Jul-01-1976		
0726	Remote Controlled Transmission and Echoing Telnet Option	J. Postel, D. Crocker	Mar-08-1977		
0727	Telnet Logout Option	M.R. Crispin	Apr-27-1977		
0728	Minor Pitfall in the Telnet Protocol	J.D. Day	Apr-27-1977		
0730	Extensible Field Addressing	J. Postel	May-20-1977		
0732	Telnet Data Entry Terminal Option	J.D. Day	Sep-12-1977		RFC0731
0734	SUPDUP Protocol	M.R. Crispin	Oct-07-1977		
0735	Revised Telnet Byte Macro Option	D. Crocker, R.H. Gumpertz	Nov-03-1977		RFC0729
0736	Telnet SUPDUP Option	M.R. Crispin	Oct-31-1977		
0737	FTP Extension: XSEN	K. Harrenstien	Oct-31-1977		
0738	Time Server	K. Harrenstien	Oct-31-1977		
0743	FTP Extension: XRSQ/XRCP	K. Harrenstien	Dec-30-1977		
0748	Telnet Randomly-Lose Option	M.R. Crispin	Apr-01-1978		
0752	Universal Host Table	M.R. Crispin	Jan-02-1979		
0753	Internet Message Protocol	J. Postel	Mar-01-1979		
0756	NIC Name Server— A Datagram-Based Information Utility	J.R. Pickens, E.J. Feinler, J.E. Mathis	Jul-01-1979		
0759	Internet Message Protocol	J. Postel	Aug-01-1980		

(continued)

Appendix A   Active RFCs

Table A.3   Useful RFCs *(continued).*

RFC	Title	Author(s)	Date	Updates	Obsoletes
0761	DOD Standard Transmission Control Protocol	J. Postel	Jan-01-1980		
0767	Structured Format for Transmission of Multi-media Documents	J. Postel	Aug-01-1980		
0768	User Datagram Protocol (STD0006)	J. Postel	Aug-28-1980		
0774	Internet Protocol Handbook: Table of Contents	J. Postel	Oct-01-1980		RFC0766
0775	Directory Oriented FTP Commands	D. Mankins, D. Franklin, A.D. Owen	Dec-01-1980		
0779	Telnet Send-Location Option	E. Killian	Apr-01-1981		
0781	Specification of the Internet Protocol (IP) Timestamp Option	Z. Su	May-01-1981		
0791	Internet Protocol (STD0005)	J. Postel	Sep-01-1981		RFC0760
0792	Internet Control Message Protocol	J. Postel	Sep-01-1981		RFC0777
0793	Transmission Control Protocol (STD0007)	J. Postel	Sep-01-1981		
0794	Pre-emption	V.G. Cerf	Sep-01-1981	IEN 125	
0795	Service Mappings	J. Postel	Sep-01-1981		
0796	Address Mappings	J. Postel	Sep-01-1981		IEN 115
0797	Format for Bitmap Files	A.R. Katz	Sep-01-1981		
0799	Internet Name Domains	D.L. Mills	Sep-01-1981		
0813	Window and Acknowledgement Strategy in TCP	D.D. Clark	Jul-01-1982		
0814	Name, Addresses, Ports, and Routes	D.D. Clark	Jul-01-1982		
0815	IP Datagram Reassembly Algorithms	D.D. Clark	Jul-01-1982		

(continued)

Appendix A Active RFCs

Table A.3   Useful RFCs *(continued)*.

RFC	Title	Author(s)	Date	Updates	Obsoletes
0816	Fault Isolation and Recovery	D.D. Clark	Jul-01-1982		
0817	Modularity and Efficiency in Protocol Implementation	D.D. Clark	Jul-01-1982		
0818	Remote User Telnet Service	J. Postel	Nov-01-1982		
0826	Ethernet Address Resolution Protocol; or, Converting Network Protocol Addresses to 48.bit Ethernet address for Transmission on Ethernet Hardware (STD0037)	D.C. Plummer	Nov-01-1982		
0830	Distributed System for Internet Name Service	Z. Su	Oct-01-1982		
0854	Telnet Protocol Specification (STD0008)	J. Postel, J.K. Reynolds	May-01-1983		RFC0764
0855	Telnet Option Specifications	J. Postel, J.K. Reynolds	May-01-1983		NIC 18640
0856	Telnet Binary Transmission (STD0027)	J. Postel, J.K. Reynolds	May-01-1983		NIC 15389
0857	Telnet Echo Option (STD0028)	J. Postel, J.K. Reynolds	May-01-1983		NIC 15390
0858	Telnet Suppress Go Ahead Option (STD0029)	J. Postel, J.K. Reynolds	May-01-1983		NIC 15392
0859	Telnet Status Option (STD0030)	J. Postel, J.K. Reynolds	May-01-1983		RFC0651
0860	Telnet Timing Mark Option (STD0031)	J. Postel, J.K. Reynolds	May-01-1983		NIC 16238
0861	Telnet Extended Options: List Option (STD0032)	J. Postel, J.K. Reynolds	May-01-1983		NIC 16239
0862	Echo Protocol (STD0020)	J. Postel	May-01-1983		
0863	Discard Protocol (STD0021)	J. Postel	May-01-1983		
0864	Character Generator Protocol (STD0022)	J. Postel	May-01-1983		
0865	Quote of the Day Protocol (STD0023)	J. Postel	May-01-1983		

(continued)

Table A.3   Useful RFCs *(continued)*.

RFC	Title	Author(s)	Date	Updates	Obsoletes
0866	Active Users (STD0024)	J. Postel	May-01-1983		
0867	Daytime Protocol (STD0025)	J. Postel	May-01-1983		
0868	Time Protocol (STD0026)	J. Postel, K. Harrenstien	May-01-1983		
0869	Host Monitoring Protocol	R. Hinden	Dec-01-1983		
0872	TCP-on-a-LAN	M.A. Padlipsky	Sep-01-1982		
0876	Survey of SMTP Implementations	D. Smallberg	Sep-01-1983		
0879	TCP Maximum Segment Size and Related Topics	J. Postel	Nov-01-1983		
0885	Telnet End of Record Option	J. Postel	Dec-01-1983		
0886	Proposed Standard for Message Header Munging	M.T. Rose	Dec-15-1983		
0887	Resource Location Protocol	M. Accetta	Dec-01-1983		
0894	Standard for the Transmission of IP Datagrams over Ethernet Networks (STD0041)	C. Hornig	Apr-01-1984		
0895	Standard for the Transmission of IP Datagrams over Experimental Ethernet Networks (STD0042)	J. Postel	Apr-01-1984		
0896	Congestion Control in IP/TCP Internetworks	J. Nagle	Jan-06-1984		
0897	Domain Name System Implementation Schedule	J. Postel	Feb-01-1984	RFC0881	
0903	Reverse Address Resolution Protocol (STD0038)	R. Finlayson, T. Mann, J.C. Mogul, M. Theimer	Jun-01-1984		
0906	Bootstrap Loading Using TFTP	R. Finlayson	Jun-01-1984		
0907	Host Access Protocol Specification (STD0040)	Bolt, Beranek and Newman, Inc.	Jul-01-1984		

(continued)

Table A.3 Useful RFCs *(continued).*

RFC	Title	Author(s)	Date	Updates	Obsoletes
0908	Reliable Data Protocol	D. Velten, R.M. Hinden, J. Sax	Jul-01-1984		
0913	Simple File Transfer Protocol	M. Lottor	Sep-01-1984		
0917	Internet Subnets	J.C. Mogul	Oct-01-1984		
0919	Broadcasting Internet Datagrams	J.C. Mogul	Oct-01-1984		
0920	Domain Requirements	J. Postel, J.K. Reynolds	Oct-01-1984		
0927	TACACS User Identification Telnet Option	B.A. Anderson	Dec-01-1984		
0932	Subnetwork Addressing Scheme	D.D. Clark	Jan-01-1985		
0933	Output Marking Telnet Option	S. Silverman	Jan-01-1985		
0934	Proposed Standard for Message Encapsulation	M.T. Rose, E.A. Stefferud	Jan-01-1985		
0935	Reliable Link Layer Protocols	J.G. Robinson	Jan-01-1985		
0936	Another Internet Subnet Addressing Scheme	M.J. Karels	Feb-01-1985		
0937	Post Office Protocol: Version 2	M. Butler, J. Postel, D. Chase, J. Goldberger, J.K. Reynolds	Feb-01-1985		RFC0918
0946	Telnet Terminal Location Number Option	R. Nedved	May-01-1985		
0947	Multi-network Broadcasting within the Internet	K. Lebowitz, D. Mankins	Jun-01-1985		
0949	FTP Unique-Named Store Command	M.A. Padlipsky	Jul-01-1985		
0950	Internet Standard Subnetting Procedure	J.C. Mogul, J. Postel	Aug-01-1985	RFC0792	
0951	Bootstrap Protocol	W.J. Croft, J. Gilmore	Sep-01-1985		

(continued)

Appendix A Active RFCs

Table A.3   Useful RFCs *(continued).*

RFC	Title	Author(s)	Date	Updates	Obsoletes
0953	Hostname Server	K. Harrenstien, M.K. Stahl, E.J. Feinler	Oct-01-1985		RFC0811
0954	NICNAME/WHOIS	K. Harrenstien, M.K. Stahl, E.J. Feinler	Oct-01-1985		RFC0812
0956	Algorithms for Synchronizing Network Clocks	D.L. Mills	Sep-01-1985		
0959	File Transfer Protocol (STD0009)	J. Postel, J.K. Reynolds	Oct-01-1985		RFC0765
0972	Password Generator Protocol	F.J. Wancho	Jan-01-1986		
0977	Network News Transfer Protocol	B. Kantor, P. Lapsley	Feb-01-1986		
1000	Request for Comments Reference Guide	J.K. Reynolds, J. Postel	Aug-01-1987		RFC0999
1011	Official Internet Protocols	J.K. Reynolds, J. Postel	May-01-1987		RFC0991
1042	Standard for the Transmission of IP Datagrams over IEEE 802 Networks (STD0043)	J. Postel, J.K. Reynolds	Feb-01-1988		RFC0948
1047	Duplicate Messages and SMTP	C. Partridge	Feb-01-1988		
1049	Content-Type Header Field for Internet Messages	M.A. Sirbu	Mar-01-1988		
1055	Nonstandard for Transmission of IP Datagrams over Serial Lines: SLIP (STD0047)	J.L. Romkey	Jun-01-1988		
1057	RPC: Remote Procedure Call Protocol Specification: Version 2	Sun Microsystems	Jun-01-1988		RFC1050
1058	Routing Information Protocol	C.L. Hedrick	Jun-01-1988		
1071	Computing the Internet Checksum	R.T. Braden, D.A. Borman, C. Partridge	Sep-01-1988		

(continued)

Table A.3   Useful RFCs *(continued)*.

RFC	Title	Author(s)	Date	Updates	Obsoletes
1073	Telnet Window Size Option	D. Waitzman	Oct-01-1988		
1078	TCP Port Service Multiplexer (TCPMUX)	M. Lottor	Nov-01-1988		
1079	Telnet Terminal Speed Option	C.L. Hedrick	Dec-01-1988		
1082	Post Office Protocol— Version 3: Extended Service Offerings	M.T. Rose	Nov-01-1988		
1088	Standard for the Transmission of IP Datagrams over NetBIOS Networks (STD0048)	L.J. McLaughlin	Feb-01-1989		
1089	SNMP over Ethernet	M.L. Schoffstall, C. Davin, M. Fedor, J.D. Case	Feb-01-1989		
1090	SMTP on X.25	R. Ullmann	Feb-01-1989		
1091	Telnet Terminal-type Option	J. VanBokkelen	Feb-01-1989		RFC0930
1096	Telnet X Display Location Option	G.A. Marcy	Mar-01-1989		
1097	Telnet Subliminal-Message Option	B. Miller	Apr-01-1989		
1101	DNS Encoding of Network Names and Other Types	P.V. Mockapetris	Apr-01-1989	RFC1034, RFC1035	
1106	TCP Big Window and NAK Options	R. Fox	Jun-01-1989		
1110	Problem with the TCP Big Window Option	A.M. McKenzie	Aug-01-1989		
1112	Host Extensions for IP Multicasting	S.E. Deering	Aug-01-1989	RFC0988, RFC1054	
1118	Hitchhikers Guide to the Internet	E. Krol	Sep-01-1989		
1122	Requirements for Internet Hosts—Communication Layers (STD0003)	R. Braden, Ed.	October 1989		

(continued)

Table A.3   Useful RFCs *(continued).*

RFC	Title	Author(s)	Date	Updates	Obsoletes
1123	Requirements for Internet Hosts— Applicationand Support	R. Braden, Ed.	October 1989	RFC0822	
1129	Internet Time Synchronization: The Network Time Protocol	D.L. Mills	Oct-01-1989		
1141	Incremental Updating of the Internet Checksum	T. Mallory, A. Kullberg	Jan-01-1990	RFC1071	
1144	Compressing TCP/IP Headers for Low-Speed Serial Links	V. Jacobson	Feb-01-1990		
1146	TCP Alternate Checksum Options	J. Zweig, C. Partridge	Mar-01-1990		RFC1145
1149	Standard for the Transmission of IP Datagrams on Avian Carriers	D. Waitzman	Apr-01-1990		
1153	Digest Message Format	F.J. Wancho	Apr-01-1990		
1166	Internet Numbers	S. Kirkpatrick, M.K. Stahl, M. Recker	Jul-01-1990		RFC1117, RFC1062, RFC1020
1176	Interactive Mail Access Protocol—Version 2	M.R. Crispin	Aug-01-1990		RFC1064
1180	TCP/IP Tutorial	T.J. Socolofsky, C.J. Kale	Jan-01-1991		
1184	Telnet Linemode Option	D.A. Borman	Oct-01-1990		RFC1116
1191	Path MTU Discovery	J.C. Mogul, S.E. Deering	Nov-01-1990		RFC1063
1203	Interactive Mail Access Protocol—Version 3	J. Rice	Feb-01-1991		RFC1064
1256	ICMP Router Discovery Messages	S. Deering	Sep-01-1991		
1263	TCP Extensions Considered Harmful	S. O'Malley, L.L. Peterson	Oct-01-1991		
1288	The Finger User Information Protocol	D. Zimmerman	December 1991		RFC1196, RFC1194, RFC0742

(continued)

Table A.3 **Useful RFCs** *(continued).*

RFC	Title	Author(s)	Date	Updates	Obsoletes
1301	Multicast Transport Protocol	S. Armstrong, A. Freier, K. Marzullo	February 1992		
1305	Network Time Protocol (Version 3) Specification, Implementation	David L. Mills	March 1992		RFC0958, RFC1059, RFC1119
1332	The PPP Internet Protocol Control Protocol (IPCP)	G. McGregor	May 1992		RFC1172
1350	The TFTP Protocol (Revision 2) (STD0033)	K. Sollins	July 1992		RFC0783
1372	Telnet Remote Flow Control Option	C. Hedrick, D. Borman	October 1992		RFC1080
1393	Traceroute Using an IP Option	G. Malkin	January 1993		
1408	Telnet Environment Option	D. Borman, Editor	January 1993		
1411	Telnet Authentication: Kerberos Version 4	D. Borman, Editor	January 1993		
1412	Telnet Authentication: SPX	K. Alagappan	January 1993		
1421	Privacy Enhancement for Internet Electronic Mail: Part I: Message Encryption and Authentication Procedures	J. Linn	February 1993		RFC1113
1422	Privacy Enhancement for Internet Electronic Mail: Part II: Certificate-Based Key Management	S. Kent	February 1993		RFC1114
1423	Privacy Enhancement for Internet Electronic Mail: Part III: Algorithms, Modes, and Identifiers	D. Balenson	February 1993		RFC1115
1424	Privacy Enhancement for Internet Electronic Mail: Part IV: Key Certification and Related Services	B. Kaliski	February 1993		
1429	Listserv Distribute Protocol	E. Thomas	February 1993		

(continued)

Appendix A Active RFCs

Table A.3   Useful RFCs *(continued).*

RFC	Title	Author(s)	Date	Updates	Obsoletes
1436	The Internet Gopher Protocol (a distributed document search and retrieval protocol)	F. Anklesaria, M. McCahill, P. Lindner, D. Johnson, D. Torrey, B. Albert	March 1993		
1437	The Extension of MIME Content-Types to a New Medium	N. Borenstein, M. Linimon	Apr-01-1993		
1459	Internet Relay Chat Protocol	J. Oikarinen, D. Reed	May 1993		
1571	Telnet Environment Option Interoperability Issues	D. Borman	January 1994	RFC1408	
1572	Telnet Environment Option	S. Alexander	January 1994		
1579	Firewall-Friendly FTP	S. Bellovin	February 1994		
1630	Universal Resource Identifiers in WWW: A Unifying Syntax for the Expression of Names and Addresses of Objects on the Network as used in the World-Wide Web	T. Berners-Lee	June 1994		
1652	SMTP Service Extension for 8bit-MIMEtransport	J. Klensin, N. Freed, M. Rose, E. Stefferud, D. Crocker	July 1994		RFC1426
1661	The Point-to-Point Protocol (PPP) (STD0051)	W. Simpson, Editor	July 1994		RFC1548
1663	PPP Reliable Transmission	D. Rand	July 1994		
1681	On Many Addresses per Host	S. Bellovin	August 1994		
1700	Assigned Numbers (STD0002)	J. Reynolds, J. Postel	October 1994		RFC1340
1734	POP3 AUTHentication Command	J. Myers	December 1994		
1736	Functional Recommend-ations for Internet Resource Locators	J. Kunze	February 1995		

(continued)

Appendix A   Active RFCs

Table A.3   Useful RFCs *(continued).*

RFC	Title	Author(s)	Date	Updates	Obsoletes
1737	Functional Requirements for Uniform Resource Names	K. Sollins, L. Masinter	December 1994		
1738	Uniform Resource Locators (URL)	T. Berners-Lee, L. Masinter, M. McCahill	December 1994		
1751	A Convention for Human-Readable 128-bit Keys	D. McDonald	December 1994		
1777	Lightweight Directory Access Protocol	W. Yeong, T. Howes, S. Kille	March 1995		RFC1487
1785	TFTP Option Negotiation Analysis	G. Malkin, A. Harkin	March 1995	RFC1350	
1788	ICMP Domain Name Messages	W. Simpson	April 1995		
1796	Not All RFCs are Standards	C. Huitema, J. Postel, S. Crocker	April 1995		
1808	Relative Uniform Resource Locators	R. Fielding	June 1995	RFC1738	
1834	WHOIS and Network Information Lookup Service, WHOIS++	J. Gargano, K. Weiss	August 1995		
1844	Multimedia E-mail (MIME) User Agent Checklist	E. Huizer	August 1995		RFC1820
1845	SMTP Service Extension for Checkpoint/Restart	D. Crocker, N. Freed, A. Cargille	September 1995		
1846	SMTP 521 Reply Code	A. Durand, F. Dupont	September 1995		
1847	Security Multiparts for MIME: Multipart/Signed and Multipart/Encrypted	J. Galvin, S. Murphy, S. Crocker, N. Freed	October 1995		

(continued)

Appendix A   Active RFCs

Table A.3   Useful RFCs *(continued).*

RFC	Title	Author(s)	Date	Updates	Obsoletes
1848	MIME Object Security Services	S. Crocker, N. Freed, J. Galvin, S. Murphy	October 1995		
1864	The Content-MD5 Header Field	J. Myers, M. Rose	October 1995		RFC1544
1870	SMTP Service Extension for Message Size Declaration	J. Klensin, N. Freed, K. Moore	November 1995		RFC1653
1873	Message/External-Body Content-ID Access Type	E. Levinson	December 1995		
1896	The Text/Enriched MIME Content-Type	P. Resnick, A. Walker	February 1996		RFC1523, RFC1563
1928	SOCKS Protocol Version 5	M. Leech, M. Ganis, Y. Lee, R. Kuris, D. Koblas, L. Jones	March 1996		
1929	Username/Password Authentication for SOCKS V5	M. Leech	March 1996		
1939	Post Office Protocol— Version 3 (STD0053)	J. Myers, M. Rose	May 1996		RFC1725
1945	Hypertext Transfer Protocol—HTTP/1.0	T. Berners-Lee, R. Fielding, H. Frystyk	May 1996		
1957	Some Observations on Implementations of the Post Office Protocol (POP3)	R. Nelson	June 1996	RFC1939	
1990	The PPP Multilink Protocol (MP)	K. Sklower, B. Lloyd, G. McGregor, D. Carr, T. Coradetti	August 1996		RFC1717
1991	PGP Message Exchange Formats	D. Atkins, W. Stallings, P. Zimmermann	August 1996		

(continued)

Table A.3 Useful RFCs *(continued)*.

RFC	Title	Author(s)	Date	Updates	Obsoletes
2015	MIME Security with Pretty Good Privacy (PGP)	M. Elkins	October 1996		
2017	Definition of the URL MIME External-Body Access-Type	N. Freed, K. Moore, A. Cargille	October 1996		
2018	TCP Selective Acknowledgement Options	M. Mathis, J. Mahdavi, S. Floyd, A. Romanow	October 1996		RFC1072
2030	Simple Network Time Protocol (SNTP) Version 4 for IPv4, IPv6 and OSI	D. Mills	October 1996		RFC1769
2034	SMTP Service Extension for Returning Enhanced Error Codes	N. Freed	October 1996		
2045	Multipurpose Internet Mail Extensions (MIME) Part One: Format of Internet Message Bodies	N. Freed, N. Borenstein	November 1996		RFC1521, RFC1522, RFC1590
2046	Multipurpose Internet Mail Extensions (MIME) Part Two: Media Types	N. Freed, N. Borenstein	November 1996		RFC1521, RFC1522, RFC1590
2047	MIME (Multipurpose Internet Mail Extensions) Part Three: Message Header Extensions for Non-ASCII Text	K. Moore	November 1996		RFC1521, RFC1522, RFC1590
2048	Multipurpose Internet Mail Extensions (MIME) Part Four: Registration Procedures	N. Freed, J. Klensin, J. Postel	November 1996		RFC1521, RFC1522, RFC1590
2049	Multipurpose Internet Mail Extensions (MIME) Part Five Conformance Criteria and Examples	N. Freed, N. Borenstein	November 1996		RFC1521, RFC1522, RFC1590
2060	Internet Message Access Protocol—Version 4rev1	M. Crispin	December 1996		RFC1730

(continued)

Appendix A Active RFCs

Table A.3   Useful RFCs *(continued).*

RFC	Title	Author(s)	Date	Updates	Obsoletes
2061	IMAP4 Compatibility with IMAP2bis	M. Crispin	December 1996		RFC1730
2062	Internet Message Access Protocol—Obsolete Syntax	M. Crispin	December 1996		
2066	TELNET CHARSET Option	R. Gellens	January 1997		
2075	IP Echo Host Service	C. Partridge	January 1997		
2076	Common Internet Message Headers	J. Palme	February 1997		
2083	PNG (Portable Network Graphics) Specification Version 1.0	T. Boutell	March 1997		
2086	IMAP4 ACL Extension	J. Myers	January 1997		
2087	IMAP4 QUOTA Extension	J. Myers	January 1997		
2088	IMAP4 Non-synchronizing Literals	J. Myers	January 1997		
2090	TFTP Multicast Option	A. Emberson	February 1997		
2131	Dynamic Host Configuration Protocol	R. Droms	March 1997		RFC1541
2132	DHCP Options and BOOTP Vendor Extensions	S. Alexander, R. Droms	March 1997		RFC1533
2141	URN Syntax	R. Moats	May 1997		
2145	Use and Interpretation of HTTP Version Numbers	J. C. Mogul, R. Fielding, J. Gettys, H. Frystyk	May 1997		
2227	Simple Hit-Metering and Usage-Limiting for HTTP	J. Mogul, P. Leach	October 1997		
2228	FTP Security Extensions	M. Horowitz, S. Lunt	October 1997	RFC0959	
2311	S/MIME Version 2 Message Specification	S. Dusse, P. Hoffman, B. Ramsdell, L. Lundblade, L. Repka	March 1998		

(continued)

Table A.3 Useful RFCs *(continued).*

RFC	Title	Author(s)	Date	Updates	Obsoletes
2312	S/MIME Version 2 Certificate Handling	S. Dusse, P. Hoffman, B. Ramsdell, J. Weinstein	March 1998		
2315	PKCS #7: Cryptographic Message Syntax Version 1.5	B. Kaliski	March 1998		
2318	The text/css Media Type	H. Lie, B. Bos, C. Lilley	March 1998		
2347	TFTP Option Extension	G. Malkin, A. Harkin	May 1998	RFC1350	RFC1782
2348	TFTP Blocksize Option	G. Malkin, A. Harkin	May 1998	RFC1350	RFC1783
2349	TFTP Timeout Interval and Transfer Size Options	G. Malkin, A. Harkin	May 1998	RFC1350	RFC1784
2368	The Mailto URL Scheme	P. Hoffman, L. Masinter, J. Zawinski	July 1998	RFC1738, RFC1808	
2387	The MIME Multipart/Related Content-Type	E. Levinson	August 1998		RFC2112
2388	Returning Values from Forms: multipart/form-data	L. Masinter	August 1998		
2389	Feature Negotiation Mechanism for the File Transfer Protocol	P. Hethmon, R. Elz	August 1998		
2392	Content-ID and Message-ID Uniform Resource Locators	E. Levinson	August 1998		RFC2111
2414	Increasing TCP's Initial Window	M. Allman, S. Floyd, C. Partridge	September 1998		
2424	Content Duration MIME Header Definition	G. Vaudreuil, G. Parsons	September 1998		
2425	A MIME Content-Type for Directory Information	T. Howes, M. Smith, F. Dawson	September 1998		
2426	vCard MIME Directory Profile	F. Dawson, T. Howes	September 1998		

(continued)

Appendix A Active RFCs

Table A.3   Useful RFCs *(continued)*.

RFC	Title	Author(s)	Date	Updates	Obsoletes
2428	FTP Extensions for IPv6 and NATs	M. Allman, S. Ostermann, C. Metz	September 1998		
2433	Microsoft PPP CHAP Extensions	G. Zorn, S. Cobb	October 1998		
2437	PKCS #1: RSA Cryptography Specifications Version 2.0	B. Kaliski, J. Staddon	October 1998		RFC2313
2440	OpenPGP Message Format	J. Callas, L. Donnerhacke, H. Finney, R. Thayer	November 1998		
2449	POP3 Extension Mechanism	R. Gellens, C. Newman, L. Lundblade	November 1998	RFC1939	
2460	Internet Protocol, Version 6 (IPv6) Specification	S. Deering, R. Hinden	December 1998		RFC1883
2484	PPP LCP Internationalization Configuration Option	G. Zorn	January 1999	RFC2284, RFC1994, RFC1570	
2507	IP Header Compression	M. Degermark, B. Nordgren, S. Pink	February 1999		
2516	A Method for Transmitting PPP Over Ethernet (PPPoE)	L. Mamakos, K. Lidl, J. Evarts, D. Carrel, D. Simone, R. Wheeler	February 1999		
2525	Known TCP Implementation Problems	V. Paxson, M Allman, S. Dawson, W. Fenner, J. Griner, I. Heavens, K. Lahey, J. Semke, B. Volz	March 1999		
2554	SMTP Service Extension for Authentication	J. Myers	March 1999		

(continued)

Table A.3   Useful RFCs *(continued).*

RFC	Title	Author(s)	Date	Updates	Obsoletes
2557	MIME Encapsulation of Aggregate Documents, such as HTML (MHTML)	J. Palme, A. Hopmann, N. Shelness	March 1999		RFC2110
2577	FTP Security Considerations	M. Allman, S. Ostermann	May 1999		
2581	TCP Congestion Control	M. Allman, V. Paxson, W. Stevens	April 1999		RFC2001
2616	Hypertext Transfer Protocol—HTTP/1.1	R. Fielding, J. Gettys, J. Mogul, H. Frystyk, L. Masinter, P. Leach, T. Berners-Lee	June 1999		RFC2068
2617	HTTP Authentication: Basic Authentication	J. Franks, J. Hostetler, S. Lawrence, P. Leach, A. Luotonen, L. Stewart	June 1999		RFC2069
2632	S/MIME Version 3 Certificate Handling	B. Ramsdell, Ed.	June 1999		
2633	S/MIME Version 3 Message Specification	B. Ramsdell, Ed.	June 1999		
2634	Enhanced Security Services for S/MIME	P. Hoffman, Ed.	June 1999		
2637	Point-to-Point Tunneling Protocol	K. Hamzeh, G. Pall, W. Verthein, J. Taarud, W. Little, G. Zorn	July 1999		
2646	The Text/Plain Format Parameter	R. Gellens	August 1999	RFC2046	
2659	Security Extensions For HTML	E. Rescorla, A. Schiffman	August 1999		
2660	The Secure HyperText Transfer Protocol	E. Rescorla, A. Schiffman	August 1999		

(continued)

Appendix A Active RFCs

Table A.3   Useful RFCs *(continued).*

RFC	Title	Author(s)	Date	Updates	Obsoletes
2774	An HTTP Extension Framework	H. Nielsen, P. Leach, S. Lawrence	February 2000		
2779	Instant Messaging/ Presence Protocol Requirements	M. Day, S. Aggarwal, G. Mohr, J. Vincent	February 2000		
2800	Internet Official Protocol Standards (STD0001)	J. Reynolds, R. Braden, S. Ginoza	May 2001		RFC2700
2810	Internet Relay Chat: Architecture	C. Kalt	April 2000	RFC1459	
2811	Internet Relay Chat: Channel Management	C. Kalt	April 2000	RFC1459	
2812	Internet Relay Chat: Client Protocol	C. Kalt	April 2000	RFC1459	
2813	Internet Relay Chat: Server Protocol	C. Kalt	April 2000	RFC1459	
2821	Simple Mail Transfer Protocol (STD0010)	J. Klensin, Editor	April 2001		RFC0821, RFC0974, RFC1869
2822	Internet Message Format (STD0011)	P. Resnick, Editor	April 2001		RFC0822
2849	The LDAP Data Interchange Format (LDIF)—Technical Specification	G. Good	June 2000		
2854	The 'text/html' Media Type	D. Connolly, L. Masinter	June 2000		RFC2070, RFC1980, RFC1942, RFC1867, RFC1866
2898	PKCS #5: Password-Based Cryptography Specification Version 2.0	B. Kaliski	September 2000		
2912	Indicating Media Features for MIME Content	G. Klyne	September 2000		
2913	MIME Content Types in Media Feature Expressions	G. Klyne	September 2000		

(continued)

Appendix A Active RFCs

Table A.3   Useful RFCs *(continued)*.

RFC	Title	Author(s)	Date	Updates	Obsoletes
2941	Telnet Authentication Option	T. Ts'o, Editor, J. Altman	September 2000		RFC1416
2942	Telnet Authentication: Kerberos Version 5	T. Ts'o	September 2000		
2943	TELNET Authentication Using DSA	R. Housley, T. Horting, P. Yee	September 2000		
2944	Telnet Authentication: SRP	T. Wu	September 2000		
2945	The SRP Authentication and Key Exchange System	T. Wu	September 2000		
2946	Telnet Data Encryption Option	T. Ts'o	September 2000		
2947	Telnet Encryption: DES3 64 bit Cipher Feedback	J. Altman	September 2000		
2948	Telnet Encryption: DES3 64 bit Output Feedback	J. Altman	September 2000		
2949	Telnet Encryption: CAST-128 64 bit Output Feedback	J. Altman	September 2000		
2950	Telnet Encryption: CAST-128 64 bit Cipher Feedback	J. Altman	September 2000		
2951	Telnet Authentication Using KEA and SKIPJACK	R. Housley, T. Horting, P. Yee	September 2000		
2952	Telnet Encryption: DES 64 bit Cipher Feedback	T. Ts'o	September 2000		
2953	Telnet Encryption: DES 64 bit Output Feedback	T. Ts'o	September 2000		
2964	Use of HTTP State Management	K. Moore, N. Freed	October 2000		
2965	HTTP State Management Mechanism	D. Kristol, L. Montulli	October 2000		RFC2109
2980	Common NNTP Extensions	S. Barber	October 2000		
3023	XML Media Types	M. Murata, S. St.Laurent, D. Kohn	January 2001	RFC2048	RFC2376
3030	SMTP Service Extensions for Transmission of Large and Binary MIME Messages	G. Vaudreuil	December 2000		RFC1830

(continued)

Appendix A Active RFCs

Table A.3   Useful RFCs *(continued)*.

RFC	Title	Author(s)	Date	Updates	Obsoletes
3075	XML-Signature Syntax and Processing	D. Eastlake, J. Reagle, D. Solo	March 2001		
3076	Canonical XML Version 1.0	J. Boyer	March 2001		
3143	Known HTTP Proxy/ Caching Problems	I. Cooper, J. Dilley	June 2001		

Appendix B

Port Assignments

Port numbers can range from 0 to 65535. The ports from 0 to 1023 are known as the well-known ports. On Unix systems, you may need to have root access to use these ports. You shouldn't use these ports except for their intended purpose. The ports from 1024 to 49151 are registered ports. While you might be able to use these ports for your own programs, you can expect conflicts with the registered programs if you use your programs publicly. Finally the remaining ports, those at 49152 and above, are free for any use you like.

Table B.1 shows the most common well-known ports you'll encounter. For a complete and up-to-date list, refer to the IANA page at **www.iana.org/assignments/ port-numbers**.

Table B.1   Common well-known port assignments.

ID	Port/Type	Description
tcpmux	1/tcp	TCP Port Service Multiplexer
tcpmux	1/udp	TCP Port Service Multiplexer
rje	5/tcp	Remote Job Entry
rje	5/udp	Remote Job Entry
echo	7/tcp	Echo
echo	7/udp	Echo
discard	9/tcp	Discard
discard	9/udp	Discard
systat	11/tcp	Active Users
systat	11/udp	Active Users
daytime	13/tcp	Daytime (RFC 867)
daytime	13/udp	Daytime (RFC 867)
qotd	17/tcp	Quote of the Day

(continued)

Table B.1 Common well-known port assignments *(continued)*.

ID	Port/Type	Description
qotd	17/udp	Quote of the Day
msp	18/tcp	Message Send Protocol
msp	18/udp	Message Send Protocol
chargen	19/tcp	Character Generator
chargen	19/udp	Character Generator
ftp-data	20/tcp	File Transfer [Default Data]
ftp-data	20/udp	File Transfer [Default Data]
ftp	21/tcp	File Transfer [Control]
ftp	21/udp	File Transfer [Control]
ssh	22/tcp	SSH Remote Login Protocol
ssh	22/udp	SSH Remote Login Protocol
telnet	23/tcp	Telnet
telnet	23/udp	Telnet
	24/tcp	any private mail system
	24/udp	any private mail system
smtp	25/tcp	Simple Mail Transfer
smtp	25/udp	Simple Mail Transfer
msg-icp	29/tcp	MSG ICP
msg-icp	29/udp	MSG ICP
msg-auth	31/tcp	MSG Authentication
msg-auth	31/udp	MSG Authentication
	35/tcp	any private printer server
	35/udp	any private printer server
time	37/tcp	Time
time	37/udp	Time
rap	38/tcp	Route Access Protocol
rap	38/udp	Route Access Protocol
rlp	39/tcp	Resource Location Protocol
rlp	39/udp	Resource Location Protocol
nameserver	42/tcp	Host Name Server
nameserver	42/udp	Host Name Server
nicname	43/tcp	Who Is
nicname	43/udp	Who Is

(continued)

Appendix B Port Assignments

Table B.1   **Common well-known port assignments** *(continued).*

ID	Port/Type	Description
ni-ftp	47/tcp	NI FTP
ni-ftp	47/udp	NI FTP
tacacs	49/tcp	Login Host Protocol (TACACS)
tacacs	49/udp	Login Host Protocol (TACACS)
re-mail-ck	50/tcp	Remote Mail Checking Protocol
re-mail-ck	50/udp	Remote Mail Checking Protocol
la-maint	51/tcp	IMP Logical Address Maintenance
la-maint	51/udp	IMP Logical Address Maintenance
domain	53/tcp	Domain Name Server
domain	53/udp	Domain Name Server
	57/tcp	any private terminal access
	57/udp	any private terminal access
	59/tcp	any private file service
	59/udp	any private file service
whois++	63/tcp	whois++
whois++	63/udp	whois++
tacacs-ds	65/tcp	TACACS-Database Service
tacacs-ds	65/udp	TACACS-Database Service
sql*net	66/tcp	Oracle SQL*NET
sql*net	66/udp	Oracle SQL*NET
bootps	67/tcp	Bootstrap Protocol Server
bootps	67/udp	Bootstrap Protocol Server
bootpc	68/tcp	Bootstrap Protocol Client
bootpc	68/udp	Bootstrap Protocol Client
tftp	69/tcp	Trivial File Transfer
tftp	69/udp	Trivial File Transfer
gopher	70/tcp	Gopher
gopher	70/udp	Gopher
	75/tcp	any private dial out service
	75/udp	any private dial out service
	77/tcp	any private RJE service
	77/udp	any private RJE service
finger	79/tcp	Finger

(continued)

Table B.1   Common well-known port assignments (continued).

ID	Port/Type	Description
finger	79/udp	Finger
http	80/tcp	World Wide Web HTTP
http	80/udp	World Wide Web HTTP
hosts2-ns	81/tcp	HOSTS2 Name Server
hosts2-ns	81/udp	HOSTS2 Name Server
mfcobol	86/tcp	Micro Focus Cobol
mfcobol	86/udp	Micro Focus Cobol
	87/tcp	any private terminal link
	87/udp	any private terminal link
kerberos	88/tcp	Kerberos
kerberos	88/udp	Kerberos
npp	92/tcp	Network Printing Protocol
npp	92/udp	Network Printing Protocol
dcp	93/tcp	Device Control Protocol
dcp	93/udp	Device Control Protocol
hostname	101/tcp	NIC Host Name Server
hostname	101/udp	NIC Host Name Server
rtelnet	107/tcp	Remote Telnet Service
rtelnet	107/udp	Remote Telnet Service
pop2	109/tcp	Post Office Protocol—Version 2
pop2	109/udp	Post Office Protocol—Version 2
pop3	110/tcp	Post Office Protocol—Version 3
pop3	110/udp	Post Office Protocol—Version 3
sunrpc	111/tcp	SUN Remote Procedure Call
sunrpc	111/udp	SUN Remote Procedure Call
auth	113/tcp	Authentication Service
auth	113/udp	Authentication Service
sqlserv	118/tcp	SQL Services
sqlserv	118/udp	SQL Services
nntp	119/tcp	Network News Transfer Protocol
nntp	119/udp	Network News Transfer Protocol
ntp	123/tcp	Network Time Protocol
ntp	123/udp	Network Time Protocol

(continued)

Table B.1   Common well-known port assignments *(continued).*

ID	Port/Type	Description
pwdgen	129/tcp	Password Generator Protocol
pwdgen	129/udp	Password Generator Protocol
statsrv	133/tcp	Statistics Service
statsrv	133/udp	Statistics Service
epmap	135/tcp	DCE endpoint resolution
epmap	135/udp	DCE endpoint resolution
netbios-ns	137/tcp	NETBIOS Name Service
netbios-ns	137/udp	NETBIOS Name Service
netbios-dgm	138/tcp	NETBIOS Datagram Service
netbios-dgm	138/udp	NETBIOS Datagram Service
netbios-ssn	139/tcp	NETBIOS Session Service
netbios-ssn	139/udp	NETBIOS Session Service
imap	143/tcp	Internet Message Access Protocol
imap	143/udp	Internet Message Access Protocol
sql-net	150/tcp	SQL-NET
sql-net	150/udp	SQL-NET
sqlsrv	156/tcp	SQL Service
sqlsrv	156/udp	SQL Service
snmp	161/tcp	SNMP
snmp	161/udp	SNMP
snmptrap	162/tcp	SNMPTRAP
snmptrap	162/udp	SNMPTRAP
print-srv	170/tcp	Network PostScript
print-srv	170/udp	Network PostScript
irc	194/tcp	Internet Relay Chat Protocol
irc	194/udp	Internet Relay Chat Protocol
ipx	213/tcp	IPX
ipx	213/udp	IPX
imap3	220/tcp	Interactive Mail Access Protocol v3
imap3	220/udp	Interactive Mail Access Protocol v3
fln-spx	221/tcp	Berkeley rlogind with SPX auth
fln-spx	221/udp	Berkeley rlogind with SPX auth
rsh-spx	222/tcp	Berkeley rshd with SPX auth

(continued)

Table B.1   Common well-known port assignments *(continued).*

ID	Port/Type	Description
rsh-spx	222/udp	Berkeley rshd with SPX auth
set	257/tcp	Secure Electronic Transaction
set	257/udp	Secure Electronic Transaction
http-mgmt	280/tcp	http-mgmt
http-mgmt	280/udp	http-mgmt
ups	401/tcp	Uninterruptible Power Supply
ups	401/udp	Uninterruptible Power Supply
https	443/tcp	http protocol over TLS/SSL
https	443/udp	http protocol over TLS/SSL
biff	512/udp	used by mail system to notify users
login	513/tcp	remote login a la telnet;
who	513/udp	maintains data bases showing who's
shell	514/tcp	cmd
syslog	514/udp	
printer	515/tcp	spooler
printer	515/udp	spooler
talk	517/tcp	like tenex link, but across
talk	517/udp	like tenex link, but across
ntalk	518/tcp	
ntalk	518/udp	
utime	519/tcp	unixtime
utime	519/udp	unixtime
efs	520/tcp	extended file name server
router	520/udp	local routing process (on site);
ripng	521/tcp	ripng
ripng	521/udp	ripng
ulp	522/tcp	ULP
ulp	522/udp	ULP
ncp	524/tcp	NCP
ncp	524/udp	NCP
timed	525/tcp	timeserver
timed	525/udp	timeserver
tempo	526/tcp	newdate
irc-serv	529/tcp	IRC-SERV

(continued)

Table B.1   Common well-known port assignments *(continued)*.

ID	Port/Type	Description
irc-serv	529/udp	IRC-SERV
conference	531/tcp	chat
conference	531/udp	chat
netnews	532/tcp	readnews
netnews	532/udp	readnews
netwall	533/tcp	for emergency broadcasts
netwall	533/udp	for emergency broadcasts
uucp	540/tcp	uucpd
uucp	540/udp	uucpd
uucp-rlogin	541/tcp	uucp-rlogin
uucp-rlogin	541/udp	uucp-rlogin
new-rwho	550/tcp	new-who
new-rwho	550/udp	new-who
cybercash	551/tcp	cybercash
cybercash	551/udp	cybercash
nntps	563/tcp	nntp protocol over TLS/SSL (was snntp)
nntps	563/udp	nntp protocol over TLS/SSL (was snntp)
whoami	565/tcp	whoami
whoami	565/udp	whoami
sntp-heartbeat	580/tcp	SNTP HEARTBEAT
sntp-heartbeat	580/udp	SNTP HEARTBEAT
doom	666/tcp	doom Id Software
doom	666/udp	doom Id Software
corba-iiop	683/tcp	CORBA IIOP
corba-iiop	683/udp	CORBA IIOP
corba-iiop-ssl	684/tcp	CORBA IIOP SSL
corba-iiop-ssl	684/udp	CORBA IIOP SSL
uuidgen	697/tcp	UUIDGEN
uuidgen	697/udp	UUIDGEN
kerberos-adm	749/tcp	kerberos administration
kerberos-adm	749/udp	kerberos administration
kerberos-iv	750/udp	kerberos version iv

Appendix B Port Assignments

Index

N